"Well, for goodness' sake, aren't you going to say anything?

"Apologize or something? I mean, the very least you could do is get off your idle backside and let me in! I'm soaked to the skin, I'm freezing to death and you don't give a damn."

God, Lucie was beautiful, with her hair a wild tangle of damp curls and steam coming out of her ears! Her eyes were spitting green sparks, and her mouth, when she finally paused for breath was soft, lush and too wide for conventional beauty. But he could imagine it trailing over his poor wounded body and kissing it better. Will stifled a groan and met her furious eyes.

"You're late. Help me up," he said gruffly, and she stopped in her tracks, her soft, pretty mouth falling open in surprise.

"Excuse me?"

"The ladder slipped. I think my arms are broken. Could you please help me up?"

Her jaw flapped for a moment, and her eyes widened, tracking over him and filling with horror. "Well, why on earth didn't you *say* so, instead of just sitting there?"

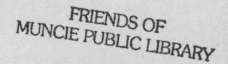

Dear Reader,

Some books tug at the heartstrings. Others are fun. Over the years and the many books I've written, there have been stories from both camps that needed to be told. This is one of the fun ones. Although it's mostly set in Suffolk, where I live, the book was actually inspired by a holiday my husband and I took to Hereford. We stayed in a little cottage, a converted barn by a farmhouse at the end of a long and extremely bumpy track.

And that track presented me with so many possibilities for tormenting my hero and heroine! By the time we arrived at the cottage I was getting that vacant look that my family have come to recognize. Their questions answered with "Mmm. Yes, dear," and so on.

I hope you enjoy the story, certainly more than Lucie and Will enjoyed each other at first. Still, love triumphs in the end, of course, which just demonstrates the huge capacity we have for forgiveness. I hope they remember that, if by some twist of fate my characters and I ever come face-to-face!

All the best,

Caroline

Rescuing Dr. Ryan

Caroline Anderson

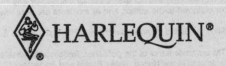

HARLEQUIN®

TORONTO • NEW YORK • LONDON
AMSTERDAM • PARIS • SYDNEY • HAMBURG
STOCKHOLM • ATHENS • TOKYO • MILAN • MADRID
PRAGUE • WARSAW • BUDAPEST • AUCKLAND

ISBN 0-373-06311-3

RESCUING DR. RYAN

First North American Publication 2001

Copyright © 2001 by Caroline Anderson

This edition published by arrangement with Harlequin Books S.A.

® and TM are trademarks of the publisher. Trademarks indicated with
® are registered in the United States Patent and Trademark Office, the
Canadian Trade Marks Office and in other countries.

Visit us at www.eHarlequin.com

Printed in U.S.A.

CHAPTER ONE

'AH, NO!'

Will rammed his hands through his hair and stared disbelievingly at the wide, wet stain on the mattress. Cocking his head a little, he looked up at the ceiling, and winced. Yup, there was a corresponding stain, right over the middle of the bed. The new bed.

Great. There must be a missing tile on the roof, just over the bedroom, and, of course, as luck would have it, it had been the wettest March on record.

He sniffed experimentally, and sighed. Mildew. Lovely. Probably soaked right through the bed and rotted the carpet underneath. He said something his grandmother wouldn't have understood, and stomped out, slamming the door behind him.

Before anyone could use the little cottage, it would need a new bed—another one—and a new carpet— and Lucie Compton, their new GP registrar, was due in two hours. He crossed the yard, turned and squinted up into the sun. Yes, there it was—or wasn't. A neat hole in the middle of the roof slope. Still, it could have been worse. The tile was sitting in the gutter and hadn't smashed on the ground— although if it had smashed at least he would have stood a chance of noticing it sooner.

He gave a hefty sigh and fetched the ladder and some tools from the barn. Within moments he'd put the tile back and secured it, and checked the others around it. All looked fine.

Good. He put the tools away and came back for the ladder, and as he carried it round the end of the little converted barn he noticed Minnie, the tiny little Siamese kitten, running across the roof and crying.

'Oh, Minnie, how did you get up there?' he asked, exasperated.

'Mreouw—rrr,' she replied.

'Did you? Well, that'll teach me to leave the ladder there for you, won't it?'

'Mreow.'

'OK, I'm coming,' he said. He glanced at his watch. One hour seventeen minutes and counting. Hell.

He stuck the ladder up against the side of the barn, checked that it was steady and gave the sloping ground a dubious look. Oh, dammit. He didn't have time to tie it. He rattled it again, just to make sure it was secure, and climbed carefully to the top.

'Come on, Minnie. Come here.'

The kitten came almost within reach, sat down and cried piteously.

'Well, come here, then!' he coaxed with the last shred of his patience. He held out his fingers and she brushed against them. If he could just reach out...

The ladder jolted, lurching slightly to the side, and he grabbed the rungs and hung on, freezing for a moment.

Hmm. Now what? Minnie came to the top, within reach, and rubbed herself against the top rung. 'Damn cat,' he said with affection, and reached for her cautiously.

There was another lurch, and he felt the ladder sliding out from under him. He grabbed the top rung and prayed, but God was either elsewhere or had decided it was time Will was taught a lesson.

It was, he thought with strange detachment, almost like watching something in slow motion. The ladder skidded, dropped below the guttering and then slid down the side of the barn, gathering speed as it neared the ground.

Oh, hell, he thought. I really don't need this.

Then he hit the deck.

Everything hurt. His head hurt, his legs hurt, his ribs felt crushed, but it was his arms that were really, really giving him stick.

He rested his forehead on the rung in front of him and instantly regretted it. He shifted, finding a bit that wasn't bruised, and lay still for a moment, waiting for his chest to reinflate and his heart to slow down.

He was also waiting for the pain to recede, but he was a realist. Five minutes later his breathing and heart rate were back to normal, and he decided that two out of three weren't bad. Given a choice, he would have gone for a different two, of course.

The kitten rubbed herself against his head, and he cracked open an eye and glared at her balefully.

'I am going to kill you,' he said slowly and clearly. 'Just as soon as I work out how to get out of here.'

Unabashed, she sat down just inches away and washed herself.

Will ignored her. He had other problems more immediate than a bit of cathartic blood-letting. He shifted experimentally, and gasped. OK. Not a good idea to press down on his right arm. What about the left?

Nope.

Knees? Better. And shoulders were OK. Now, if he could just roll over...

He bit back a string of choice epithets, and rolled onto his back, falling with a sickening jolt to the ground beside the ladder.

Phase one completed. Now all he had to do was get to his feet, go inside and call for help.

Hah!

He lifted his head a fraction, and stifled a groan. Damn. Headache. He persisted, peering at his arms which lay awkwardly across his chest.

No doubt about the right one, he thought in disgust. He'd be lucky to get away without pinning and plating. And the left?

His wrist was swelling before his eyes, and if it got much bigger his watch was going to cut off the circulation to his hand. Wonderful. He closed his eyes with a sigh and laid his head back down carefully on the ground. He'd just have to wait for Lucie Compton to arrive and rescue him.

There was a lump of something hard sticking into his spine, but it was beyond him to shift himself away from it. It was just one more small pain amongst many. If he were a philosopher, he'd welcome the pain as proof that he was alive. However, he wasn't, and at that particular moment he wouldn't have minded being dead.

And then, just as if survival itself wasn't a big enough bundle of laughs, he felt the first heavy splash of rain hit his face....

Lucie was late. Lucie was usually late, but she really, really hadn't needed Fergus giving her the third degree on the way out.

He *knew* she had to do this, *knew* that spending time in a general practice was part of her GP training, *knew* that it was only temporary.

Well, not any more. Not the separation, at any rate, although her sojourn into the countryside would be as brief as she could get away with. Six months tops. That, on top of the six months she'd already spent in her inner-city practice, would see her qualified to practise as a GP, and then she'd be back in the city like a rat out of a trap.

Of course, she didn't *have* to spend the time in the country. She could quite easily have found another London practice but, to be honest, Fergus was one of the reasons she'd wanted to get away, at least just for a while, to put some distance between them and see if what they had was a forever thing or just a temporary habit that needed breaking.

Well, she'd broken it, in words of one syllable.

You Do Not Own Me. Go Away. Leave Me Alone.

OK, mostly one syllable. He'd understood, anyway. He'd flounced off, slamming the door of his car and roaring off into the sunset—except it had been some time after sunrise and he hadn't roared anywhere very much in the traffic off the Fulham Road.

She pulled over to the side of the road and checked her map. It was raining, of course, blurring everything and making it harder to read the signs.

'''Pass the turning to High Corner and take the next track on the right. Follow to the end. It's a bit rough in places.'' Hmm.' She peered at the sandy track ahead. Could that be it? It didn't seem to have a sign, and looked like nothing more than a farm

track, but the address was Ferryview Farm, so it was
possible.

With a resigned shrug, she turned onto the track
and followed it. Some of it was sandy, some stony,
some just downright boggy. It *was* a bit rough in
places, she thought, and then lurched into a pothole.

Make that very rough, she corrected herself, and
picked her way carefully through the next few puddles. Of course, without the rain—

There was a lurch, a nasty crunching grinding
noise and her car came to rest on the centre of the
track, its wheels dangling in matched potholes.

She put it in reverse and tried to drive out, but it
was stuck fast, teetering on a high point. Damn.

Damn, damn, damn.

She got out, straight into a puddle that went over
her ankle, and slammed her car door with a wail of
frustration. Just let Dr Ryan wait until she caught up
with him!

Pulling her coat close around her shoulders and
hitching the collar up against the driving rain, she
headed up the track. It couldn't be far, surely?

Not that it mattered if it was miles. She had no
choice, not until she could get a breakdown truck to
come and drag her car off the track.

Always assuming, of course, that she hadn't shattered the sump!

'Look on the bright side, Lucie,' she told herself,
scraping a muddy hand through her rapidly frizzling
hair. 'It could be snowing.'

Ten seconds later a little flurry of sleet plastered
itself against her face. 'I didn't say that!' she wailed,
and hitched the collar higher. The moment she

caught up with Dr William 'it's a bit rough in places' Ryan, she was going to kill him!

She was late. Typical bloody woman, she was late, just when he needed her. He thought again of struggling to his feet and trying to get inside, but after the effort of sitting up and shuffling back into the lee of the barn, he thought it would probably kill him. Besides, the house keys were in his pocket, and he knew getting them out was beyond him.

So he sat, and he waited, and he fumed.

Still, he had Minnie for company—Minnie, the cause of all his grief. He might have known the damn cat was perfectly capable of getting herself down off the roof. If he'd thought about it at all, which, of course, he hadn't, he would have realised she could jump down on the top of the oil storage tank at the back and thence down to the ground. It was probably the way she'd got up in the first place.

He dropped his head back against the side of the barn and closed his eyes. The sun was out now— typical of April, sleet and driving rain one minute, glorious sunshine the next—and where he was sitting in the shelter of the barn, he was facing directly into it.

Good. It might warm him up, stop him shivering uncontrollably. He was in shock, of course, because of the fracture. Fractures? His right arm was certainly distorted, and his left was still swelling around the wrist. His watch was painfully tight, the flesh bulging each side of the broad metal strap. He tried to undo it with his teeth, but it was too firm and, besides, it hurt too much to prod about with it unnecessarily.

Please, God, don't let me have two broken arms,

he thought in despair. His mind ran through a list of things he couldn't do with two broken arms—and there were a lot in there that were very personal!

God again, teaching him compassion for his patients? Giving him a closer understanding of their needs and suffering?

Or just fate playing a nasty practical joke?

Where was Lucie Compton? Richard had waxed so lyrical about her after he'd interviewed her that Will had had great hopes—but if her medical skills were as good as her timekeeping, it didn't bode well for her patients. And he, he realised, was going to be her first one.

Hell.

Bruno was barking in the house, shut inside because Will had just been on his way out when he'd checked the cottage and found the leak. However, the dog had been quiet until now apart from the odd bark, and now he was letting loose with a volley. Someone coming?

Odd. Surely not Lucie? Will couldn't hear a car, but there was something. Footsteps. Fast, cross little footsteps.

A woman came into view, small, bedraggled and evidently as mad as a wet hen. She marched up to him, fixed him with a glare and said crisply, 'A bit rough in places?'

What? He opened his mouth to speak, but she rattled on, clearly divesting herself of some pent-up rage.

'I could have you up under the Trades Descriptions Act!' she stormed. 'A bit rough! Do you know I've grounded my car and probably trashed it on your damn drive?'

Oh, hell. It *was* Lucie Compton, finally. And now he'd get to test her medical skills, if he could just get a word in—

'I expect the sump's broken, knowing my luck,' she ranted on, 'and I'll have to get the engine replaced! And I'm wringing wet and frozen, and my mobile phone doesn't work out here in this God-forsaken bit of wilderness, and all you can do is sit there and smirk!'

She lifted her foot, and for a sickening moment he thought she was going to kick him, but she stamped it crossly and spun on her heel, walking away and then wheeling round and striding back.

'Well, for goodness' sake, aren't you going to say anything? Apologise or something? I mean, the very least you could do is get off your idle backside and let me in! I'm soaked to the skin, I'm freezing to death and you don't give a damn.'

God, she was beautiful, with her hair a wild tangle of damp curls and steam coming out of her ears! Her eyes were spitting green sparks, and her mouth when she finally paused for breath was soft and lush and too wide for conventional beauty, but he could imagine it trailing over his poor wounded body and kissing it better. He stifled a groan and met her furious eyes.

'You're late. Help me up,' he said gruffly, and she stopped in her tracks and her wide, soft, pretty mouth fell open in surprise.

'Excuse me?'

'The ladder slipped. I think my arms are broken. Could you, please, help me up?'

Her jaw flapped for a moment, and her eyes widened, tracking over him and filling with horror.

'Well, why on earth didn't you *say* so, instead of just sitting there?'

'I would have done, but you made it well nigh impossible to get a word in edgeways,' he said drily. To his satisfaction she coloured, the anger going out of her like air out of a punctured balloon.

'Sorry,' she conceded gruffly. 'Um…how do you suggest we do this? What have you broken?'

'Right radius and ulna, and maybe something in my left wrist. Oh, and I'm a bit concussed and my legs hurt like hell, but they move, at least. Otherwise I'm just peachy.'

'Right. Um.'

She crouched down and bent over him, the damp tendrils of her wildly curling hair teasing his face. 'May I see?'

He lowered his legs, wincing as he did so, and revealed his forearms. 'Don't touch anything,' he warned through gritted teeth, and she nodded. Thank God she only looked, and didn't feel the need to prod him.

'OK. You need a couple of slings before I try and move you. Have you got any in the house?'

'Yes, but until I get up you can't get in. The keys are in my pocket.'

'Oh.' She glanced down at his jeans, snug around his hips, and she coloured slightly. 'Um—are you sure? Which pocket?'

'The right.'

'You could shift onto your left hip and I could see if I could wriggle my hand in…'

He shifted, swallowing hard and hoping for a good hefty jolt of pain to take his mind off those slender little fingers. They wormed and wriggled their way

in, while she blushed and apologised. She gave a
little grunt of effort and her breath puffed soft and
minty-fresh over his face. He closed his eyes and
groaned, and wondered how long it would be before
he embarrassed himself with her prodding and probing about so damn close—

'Got them!' she said victoriously, brandishing
them in front of his nose.

He sighed with relief. 'Mind the dog. He's all
right, but he'll come and jump all over me, and I
don't need it just now.'

'I'll keep him in,' she promised. 'Where are the
slings?'

'Kitchen. Cupboard on the left of the sink. The
dog's called Bruno.' He watched her go, and wondered how, in the midst of so much pain, he could
be so aware of her cute little bottom in those tight,
unbelievably sexy jeans...

Lucie let herself in and greeted the dog, a huge
hairy black thing with doleful eyes and jaws that
could have sheared a man's thigh, and hoped the eyes
would win.

'Good doggie, nice Bruno. Sit.'

To her amazement he sat, his tail wiggling furiously, and she reached out a tentative hand and patted him. 'Good boy,' she said, a little more confi-
dently, and he barked again, standing up and going
to the door to scratch hopefully at it.

'Sorry, babes, you've got to stay inside,' she told
him, and looked around. Sink. Good. Cupboard on
left—and slings. Excellent. She squirmed past the
dog, shut the door and ran back down the steps and
over to the barn.

His eyes were shut, and she could see, now she

was less angry, that his face was grey and drawn. She wondered how long he'd been there, and how on earth she'd get him out.

'Dr Ryan?'

'Will,' he mumbled, opening his eyes. 'Lucie, take my watch off, can you? It hurts like hell.'

She carefully unclipped the metal strap, but she couldn't slide it over his hand. The face was cracked, and it had stopped about three hours ago. Had he been there that long? Probably.

'Let's get a support on that right arm first,' she said, and carefully lifted his hand as he shifted his elbow away from his body.

She was as gentle as possible, but he still bit back a groan and braced himself against the barn. She fixed the sling, then put the left arm, which seemed less painful, in a lower sling so it wouldn't interfere with the right.

'OK. Now I need to get you up and out to hospital. Any ideas?'

His eyes flickered open. 'Teleporting?'

Humour, even in all that pain. She felt a flicker of admiration. 'Sorry, not an option. Do you have a car?'

'Yes. It's round the corner in the barn. The keys are with the door keys. Lock the back door again and get the car out and bring it round.'

'What about insurance?' she asked, being practical for once in her life.

'You're covered if you're over twenty-five.' He gave her a sceptical look.

'Well, of course I am!' she said in disgust, and stomped off. 'Idiot. He knows quite well how old I am!' She locked the back door, ignoring Bruno's pleas, and went round the corner.

Oh, lord, it was a massive great Volvo estate! Miles long, and hugely wide. Terrific. She'd never driven anything this big before, and she was going to have to do it smoothly and carefully. With an audience.

Marvellous. She could hardly wait.

She got in, stared at the gear lever and got out again, stomping back round the corner to Will.

'It's automatic,' she said accusingly.

'Yes—that makes it easier.'

'Fiddlesticks.'

'Trust me, I'm a doctor. D is drive, P is park, R is reverse, N is neutral. Leave it in Park, start the engine, put your foot on the brake and put it into Drive. You have to hold down the button on top while you move the lever.'

'Hmm.'

She went back, started it, put it in drive and took her foot cautiously off the brake and screamed when it moved. She hit the brakes, her left foot flailing uselessly, looking for a task. Idiot, she told herself, and eased her foot off the brake again. It rolled gently forwards, and she tried the accelerator, cautiously. OK.

She nosed out of the barn, totally unsure how far she was from anything, and cursed herself for never having driven anything bigger than a supermini. She crept round the end of the barn, stopped as close to Will as she could get and looked at the gear lever in puzzlement.

'Put it in Park,' he told her. 'And put the handbrake on,' he added as an afterthought, as if he didn't quite trust her.

She was about to make a smart-alec retort when she took her foot off the footbrake and the car rolled forwards a fraction.

She gave another little yelp and slammed her foot back down, and he shot her a pitying look.

'It moved!' she said defensively.

'It's fine. It's just taking up the slack. You could have reversed it in so the door was closer.'

'No, I couldn't,' Lucie said tightly, realising with dismay that she was going to have to reverse around the barn to get back to the track. Oh, blast. She got out of the car and slammed the door, and he winced.

'Maybe this wasn't such a good idea,' he muttered.

'You don't have a choice,' she reminded him.

'We could have called an ambulance.'

'We might have to yet. My car's in the way.'

'I've got a tow-rope. We can pull it out.'

'We?' She eyed him up and down, and snorted. 'I don't think so.'

'We'll worry about it later. Just get me in the damn car,' Will said through gritted teeth, and she stood in front of him and grasped him by the shoulders, pulling him forwards and upwards as he got his legs under him and straightened with a groan.

'OK?'

He gave her a dirty look. 'Wonderful. Open the car door.'

She cocked an eyebrow at him. 'Please?'

'Please.'

'Better.'

'Don't push it,' he growled, and she gave up. She stomped round the bonnet, yanked open the front passenger door and came back for him, but he was already on his way, stubborn and self-reliant. Fine. Let him struggle.

Then Will wavered, and she had a sudden vision of him toppling over on those broken arms. Not a good idea, and she needed this post if she was going to finish her training. Stifling her urge to leave him to it, she put her arm around his waist to steady him and helped him round the car, then opened the door and watched as he eased himself in. His jaw was working furiously, his eyes were screwed shut and once he was in he dropped his head back against the headrest and let out a shaky sigh.

'I think we'll pass on the seat belt,' he said through gritted teeth, and she shut the door firmly on him.

Lucie crossed round to the driver's side, wondering how, under these circumstances, she could have been so conscious of the hard, lean feel of his body. Even through the thickness of the soft sweater he was wearing she'd been aware of every rib, every muscle, every breath.

She had a feeling he was, too, and her compassion returned, forcing out her bizarre and untimely thoughts and replacing them with a more appropriate concern for his health. She slid behind the wheel, looked over her shoulder and wondered how on earth she was going to reverse this thing the size of an oil tanker back around the barn...

How could she be so stupid? Will asked himself. How could a woman with apparently enough brain to train and qualify as a doctor be so stupid that she couldn't manage to drive a perfectly normal car?

She panicked, she overreacted, she allowed some-

times too much room, sometimes nothing like
enough, and her judgement on the bumpy drive left
a great deal to be desired.

No wonder she'd got her car stuck.

'Are you trying to do it again, you idiot woman?'
he snapped as she jolted down yet another pothole.

'Don't call me names just because your drive's so
awful! There should be a law against it.'

There should be a law against her smart mouth,
but he didn't suppose he'd get it past all the women
MPs. 'Drive on the centre and the side,' he told her
through gritted teeth, but there were places where
you had to pick your way and, sure as eggs, she'd
pick the wrong one.

And every jolt was agonising. He would have
driven himself, except, of course, he couldn't even
hold the steering-wheel, never mind turn it. Damn.

They lurched through another pothole and he felt
cold sweat spring out on his brow. He needed to lie
down. He needed pain relief. He needed oblivion.

He didn't need to be giving some delinquent female driving lessons!

'There's my car,' she announced defiantly, and he
cracked his eyes open and sighed with relief.

'You can drive round it. Head for the left—the
ground's firm there.'

Well, more or less. They got through it with a bit
of lurching and wheel-spinning, and then the track
improved. Just another few minutes, he told himself.
Just a little longer...

'Yes, it's a lovely clean fracture through the radius
and ulna. Classic Colles'. We'll reduce it here, if you

like. As for the other one, it's just a nasty sprain, you'll be glad to know.'

He was. He was hugely glad to know that he wasn't going to be dependent on anyone for help with his basic functions. It would probably hurt like hell to use it, but at least if it wasn't plastered, he'd have some rotation in the hand, and that would make all the difference.

Will didn't enjoy having the fracture reduced. They bandaged his hand to compress it and drive the blood out of it, which hurt, then stopped the blood supply to his arm and filled the vessels with local anaesthetic.

That bit was fine. Then the doctor grasped his hand and pulled, and the bones slid back into place with an audible crunch.

To his utter disgust, he threw up, and all he could think was thank God Lucie wasn't there watching him with her wide green eyes and sassy mouth. Just for good measure, he retched again, then sagged back against the bed.

'Finished?' the nurse asked him in a kind voice, and he nodded weakly.

The doctor shot him a thoughtful look. 'I think you've got a touch of concussion. Perhaps we need to keep you in overnight.'

'No,' he said firmly, ignoring the pounding in his head and the tingling sensation in his cheek. What concussion? 'I'm fine. I want to go home.'

'Stubborn sod, aren't you?' the doctor said cheerfully, and stood back to survey his handiwork. 'That looks fine. We'll let the anaesthetic out now and see how it feels when it comes round. Oh, and you'll need another X-ray after we put a back-slab on—an open cast, just in case it swells overnight. You'll need to come back tomorrow for a check-up and have a proper cast on if all's well. OK?'

Will nodded.

'I still think you should stay overnight, but so long as you'll have someone with you, that'll have to do. You know what to look out for.'

He did. He'd dished out advice on head injuries for years, but he'd never had to take it. He wasn't thinking too clearly now, and his hand was beginning to tingle as they let the blood back through it.

At least the other one felt safer now, strapped up and supported from his fingers to his elbow in tight Tubigrip with a hole cut for the thumb.

MICE, he was reminded. Mobilisation, ice, compression, elevation. It used to be RICE, but they'd changed the rules and got rid of the resting in favour of mobilisation. That was good, because without his right arm, the left was going to be mobilised a heck of a lot in the next few weeks!

'I'll write you up for some painkillers,' the doctor said. 'You can take up to eight a day, no more than two at a time and no closer together than four hours.'

He had no intention of taking them, except as a last resort, but he accepted them anyway—not that it was exactly difficult to get a prescription. He'd pick one up on Monday morning when he went to work, he thought, and then it hit him.

How on earth was he going to work with one arm in a cast and the other—the wrong one—in a support? Brilliant. And Lucie was just starting a six-month stint as a trainee, and he was the only member of the practice qualified to train her.

He sighed. Well, she'd just have to cover his pa-

tients, and he'd supervise her and tell her what to do
and she could drive him around—always assuming
he could stand it! She'd be staying at the cottage
anyway, he thought, and then remembered the cottage bedroom—the one without a bed, with a stink-
ing, soaked carpet that needed replacing.

He let his breath out on an irritated sigh. She'd
have to stay in the house—which might be as well
for a day or two, but in the long term would drive
him utterly frantic. Still, it wouldn't need to be long
term. He could order a bed and a carpet over the
phone, and have them installed and move her in there
within a couple of days.

He would need to. He guarded his privacy jeal-
ously, and he wasn't sharing his house with anyone
any longer than was absolutely necessary.

Most particularly not a pretty, sassy little thing
with attitude. He'd lose his mind!

Lucie was bored. She'd read all the leaflets, studied
all the posters, walked up and down all the corridors,
tried out the drinks machine and read half the magazines.

How long could it take, she thought, to do a couple
of X-rays and slap on a cast?

A nurse appeared. 'Dr Compton?'

Finally! She bounced to her feet and crossed the
room. 'How is he?'

The nurse smiled understandingly. 'Bit grouchy.
Men don't like losing their independence. He's ready
to go home now.'

Lucie followed her to one of the treatment rooms,
and there was Will sitting in the wheelchair, looking
like something the cat had dragged in. He shot her a

conciliatory look. 'Sorry you've had such a long wait.'

'That's OK. I know more than I ever wanted to know about how to sail the Atlantic, adjust grandfather clocks and make mango chutney. Do you want a wheelchair ride to the car, or shall I bring it to the door?'

'Both,' the nurse said.

'I'll walk,' said Will.

Lucie looked from one to the other, nodded and went out, jingling the car keys in her hand and humming softly, a smile playing around her lips. Stubborn, difficult man. It was going to be an interesting six months.

CHAPTER TWO

'WHAT do you mean, *uninhabitable*?'

Will sighed and shifted his right arm, swore softly and dropped his head back against the wall behind his chair. Lucie had got the distinct impression he'd been about to ram his hand through his hair in irritation. 'There was a missing roof tile. That's what I was doing.'

'You said you were rescuing the cat,' she accused, and he sighed again, even more shortly.

'I was—she'd gone up there because I'd been up there, fixing the roof. Because it was leaking. So the bed was wet. The carpet's ruined. The room is trashed, basically, until I can get a new carpet and bed next week and get the ceiling repainted.'

So not too long to wait, then. Just a few days of each other's company. It might be just as well, the state he was in. Lucie cocked her head on one side and studied Will. He looked awful. She wondered when he was going to relent and have a painkiller. Never, probably.

Stubborn as a mule.

He opened his eyes and looked at her, then looked at the door and dragged in a deep breath. Then he got very slowly and carefully to his feet.

'Can I get you something?'

'I need the loo.'

She went to stand up, and he fixed her with a glare that would have frozen the Atlantic. 'Don't even think about it,' he said tautly, and, suppressing a smile, she fell back in the chair and waited patiently for him to return.

Buttons, Will decided, were the spawn of the devil. Desperation got them undone. Nothing seemed sufficiently urgent to induce him to hurt that much just to do them up. Lord knows why he'd bought buttonfly jeans. He must have been mad. So now what? Flies undone, or change into something more sensible, like tracksuit bottoms?

But they were upstairs, and he was down here, and it was all too much like hard work. His head was spinning, and he felt sick again. Damn. He tried to turn the tap on, but the washer needed changing and he always had to turn it off hard to stop it dripping. The other tap might be better.

Apparently not. It wouldn't budge for the feeble urging of his left hand, and his right was totally out of action.

He leant his head against the wall and winced as he encountered a bruise. If he'd been three, he would have thrown himself down on the floor and wailed, but he wasn't. He was thirty-three, and stubborn and proud, and he wasn't giving Lucie the privilege of seeing him this far down.

'Will? Are you OK?'

'Fine,' he lied through clenched teeth.

'I thought you might want these jogging bottoms—I found them on the chair in your bedroom. They'll be more comfortable to slouch around in, I should think.'

He opened the door—thank the Lord he had levers, not knobs—and took them from her. The damn woman must be psychic. He avoided her eyes. He didn't want to see mockery or, worse still, pity in them. He pushed the door shut with his hip.

Her voice came muffled through the wood. 'Thank you. My pleasure, any time. You're too good to me, Lucie. No, no, not at all.'

'Thank you,' he bit out tightly, and looked at the trousers, then at his feet. All he had to do now was get his shoes off and swap the trousers without falling over.

Will looked awful. Grey and drawn and sick. He'd been ages just changing into the jogging bottoms, and now he was slumped in a chair in his cheerless little sitting room while she struggled to light the fire.

Finally it caught, and Lucie put a log on the kindling and prodded it. It spat at her out of gratitude, so she put another log on to keep it company and put the spark guard in front.

Bruno seemed to approve. He gave a deep grunting sigh as he collapsed in front of it, and proceeded to sleep. It was what Will needed to do, of course, but he was fighting it.

'Why don't you go to bed?' she suggested after an hour of watching him wrestle with his eyelids.

'I need to stay awake—concussion,' he told her in a patronising tone that made her grind her teeth.

'No, you need to be monitored so you don't go into a coma without anyone noticing. I can do that—I am almost qualified to tell if a person's alive or dead, you know.'

He gave her a baleful look and shut his eyes again. 'I'm fine.'

Like hell he was fine, but who was she to argue?

Taking the suitcase with her overnight things, which they'd retrieved from her car, she went upstairs, found a bedroom next to his that was obviously a guest room and made the bed with sheets from the airing cupboard in the bathroom.

Once she'd done that, she went into his room, changed his sheets and turned back the bed. He'd need to sleep, whether he liked it or not, and she'd monitor him, again whether he liked it or not.

She went downstairs and stopped in front of him, studying him. He had dozed off, his head resting awkwardly against the wall, and for a moment she contemplated leaving him.

His eyes were shut, the lashes dark against his ashen cheeks, and his brows arched proudly above them. Most people looked younger and even innocent in sleep. Not Will. He looked hard and craggy and implacable. Tough. Indestructible.

Sexy.

Good grief. *Sexy?* She looked again. Well, maybe. He was probably quite good-looking, really, she conceded absently. Tousled mid-brown hair flopped in disorder over a broad, intelligent brow. Beneath it his nose was lean and aristocratic, despite the kink in it that gave away an old injury. Below the sculpted, full lips were a strong jaw and stubborn chin—no surprise there.

Sexy? Maybe. Certainly interesting in a strictly academic, architectural sense. And he did have beautiful, striking pale grey eyes brought into sharp relief by a darker rim. They weren't comfortable eyes. Too piercing. She wondered if they ever softened, if he ever softened.

Probably not.

They flickered slightly, but didn't open. He was awake now, though. She could tell. 'Will?' she said softly.

He opened them, spearing her with a surprisingly alert gaze. 'What?'

'Your bed's ready. Do you want anything to eat before you go to sleep?'

He sighed heavily. 'No. I feel sick still.'

'Water? You ought to drink plenty to help your kidneys deal with all the rubbish in your bloodstream after your fracture.'

He nodded. 'I know. I'll get some water in a minute.'

'How about painkillers?'

'Don't need them,' he said, a little too quickly.

'I'll get you some water, then I think you should go and lie down. You'll be much more comfortable.'

'Did anyone ever tell you just how damn bossy you are?' he growled.

'Mm-hmm. Lots of times,' she said cheerfully. 'Where does the dog sleep?'

'In here, now you've lit the fire, I should think. Anywhere. Usually outside my bedroom door.'

She went upstairs with the water and his painkillers, and came back for him, only to find him halfway up the stairs with that look on his face that brooked no interference.

She stood back and prayed he didn't fall backwards onto his stubborn behind, and once he was up she followed him to his room.

'I can manage,' he said, and she looked at him.

'Are there buttons on your shirt?'

He gave a short sigh of irritation. 'Yes.'

'Will, just for tonight, why don't you let me help you?' she suggested softly.

The fight went out of Will and he sat on the bed, looking at it in confusion. 'You changed the sheets.' His voice held astonishment and—heavens, gratitude? Surely not!

'I always think fresh sheets make you feel much better,' she said matter-of-factly. 'Right, let's get this sweater off and see if your shirt will come over the cast.'

It did, leaving him naked to the waist and utterly fascinating to her. His body was lean and muscled, healthy—and striped with purpling bruises from the rungs of the ladder. She touched his ribs with a gentle finger.

'You need arnica,' she told him, and he rolled his eyes.

'Not witchcraft,' he groaned.

She smiled. 'Midwives use it. You should open your mind.'

He humphed.

'Pyjamas?'

He shook his head slightly. 'No. I can manage now.'

'Socks?'

He looked at his feet, and his shoulders drooped. 'I can sleep in them.'

'Do you usually?'

'Of course not.'

'Fine.' Lucie crouched down and pulled off his socks.

Nice feet. Strong, straight toes, good firm arches, a scatter of dark hair over the instep.

'Now I really can manage,' he repeated, and she

stood up, putting the shirt and socks out of range so she didn't trip over them in the night.

'Water on the side. Can you hold the glass?'

'I'm sure I'll find a way,' he said drily.

'No doubt. OK, I'll see you later. I'm next door. Shout if you want anything.'

She got ready for bed and lay down, and the silence and darkness was astonishing. She looked out of the bedroom window, and could see nothing. No lights, no sign of any other habitation. Something scuttled in the roof over her head, and she ducked and ran back to bed. Her skin crawled with fear until she realised it was in the roof space and not in the room with her.

'It's probably a tiny little mouse,' she told herself, ignoring the vivid imagination that had always been her worse enemy as well as her greatest friend. That imagination was turning the mouse into a rat of terrifying proportions, and she had to force herself to relax. She buried her head under the pillow and then remembered she was supposed to be listening out for Will.

Damn. She poked her head out and listened.

Nothing. Well, nothing human. There was a snort right outside her window, and fear raced over her skin again. What on *earth* was that? She bit her lip, considering creeping into Will's room and sliding into bed next to him for safety, then dismissed it as ridiculous.

Whatever was out there was *out there*, not in here with her. She'd be fine. Fine. Fine.

She chanted it like a mantra, and eventually she drifted off into a light, uneasy doze...

* * *

He'd thought he'd be all right. He'd really thought the pain wouldn't keep him awake, but the hospital's painkiller had worn off well and truly, and his arm was giving him hell. Well, both of them, really, but especially the right.

Will sat up, swinging his legs over the side of the bed and waiting a moment for the world to steady. He didn't know where Lucie had put his painkillers, but he had a bottle in his medical bag downstairs that he kept for emergencies—other people's, not his, but they'd do.

He went down to the kitchen, creeping past Lucie's open door, and struggled with the combination lock on his bag. Finally he broke into it, pulled out the bottle and stared at it in disbelief.

A safety cap! Marvellous. He didn't know if he could turn it, never mind press and turn simultaneously. He tried holding the bottle in his right hand, but his fingers wouldn't co-operate. He held in it his left, and pressed with the cast to release the safety catch while he turned the bottle.

The cap slipped, of course, and was no further off. However, he still had teeth. He held the bottle to his mouth, clamped the cap in his back teeth and pushed and twisted.

Pain shot through his wrist, and with a gasp he dropped the bottle on the floor.

Damn. He'd never get into the blasted thing.

Bruno came to investigate, giving him a great, wet kiss as he bent to pick up the bottle. 'Hello, you vile hound,' he said affectionately, and could have buried his face in the dog's thick, black ruff and howled with despair.

Then he spotted the hammer on the window sill.

*   *   *

What on earth was Will doing? Lucie tiptoed to the top of the stairs and peered down. She could see his feet in the kitchen, and hear the occasional thump and groan. Then there was an almighty crash, and she ran downstairs and found him slumped over the sink.

'Will?'

He straightened slowly and turned, glaring at her. 'I can't get the bloody lid off,' he bit out through clenched teeth.

'And, of course, it's beyond you to ask for help.'

'I didn't want to wake you.'

'And you think all this crashing around right under my bedroom wouldn't have woken me, even assuming I'd been to sleep? Hell, it's too damn quiet round here to sleep, anyway! I can hear every mouse skittering in the roof, and birds shuffling in their nests, and some—some *thing* snorted outside my window. I nearly died of fright.'

'That would be Henry.'

'Henry?'

'A horse. He lives here.'

A horse? Of course. How obvious. She felt silly. She got back to basics. 'Where's the bottle?'

'Here.' He jerked his head at the worktop, and she picked the bottle up and studied it.

'These aren't the ones.'

'They'll do. I didn't know where the others were.'

'Beside your bed. I put two out.'

He closed his eyes and sighed harshly. 'Right. Fine. Thanks.'

'How's the nausea?'

'Gorgeous. I don't even know if I'll keep them down.'

'Yes, you will,' she said in her best comforting voice. 'Come on, let's get you back upstairs and into bed before you fall over. What was the crash, by the way?'

'The hammer.'

'*Hammer?*' she said in disbelief. 'What, did you think you'd tackle a few outstanding DIY jobs or something?'

He snorted in disgust. 'I was trying to break the bottle. I couldn't even hold the damn thing. It fell in the sink.'

Compassion filled her soft heart. 'Come on,' she said gently, putting an arm around his waist and steering him towards the stairs. 'Bedtime. I'll give you your painkillers and you can get to sleep.'

This time Bruno followed them, and with just the tiniest bit of encouragement he curled up across the foot of her bed and crushed her feet. She didn't care. She felt safe with him there, and she knew he'd hear every move that Will made. Finally able to relax, she went to sleep at last.

Will slept for most of the next day. Lucie took advantage of it to go and rescue her car. The puddles had more or less drained away, and she found some old bricks and put them in the back of Will's Volvo, then drove carefully—on the middle and the side— up to her car. She jacked it up, put bricks under the wheels and leading out of the puddle, then let the jack down and drove out.

No engine damage, or not obviously, and she'd done it herself. She felt disgustingly proud of her achievement, and couldn't wait to see Will's face. Leaving the bricks *in situ* to fill up the pothole a little, she headed back in her car, parked it in the yard beside the cottage and walked back for Will's.

By the time she drove back into the yard the second time, she was hot and sticky and Will was up.

'Where the hell have you been?' he asked crossly as she went into the kitchen.

'Well, pardon me for breathing! I fetched my car.'

He cobbled his eyebrows together. 'You did?'

'Yup. I found some old bricks at the side of the barn—'

'Bricks?'

'Yes—you know, rectangular red things that they build houses out of? Except these are dirty yellow and grey.'

'I know what you're talking about,' he snarled. 'I just wonder if you do! They were floor bricks—carefully cleaned and ready to go down in the kitchen here, once I had a minute. How many did you take?'

She shrugged, feeling a twinge of guilt. 'About forty or so?'

'*Forty!*' He rolled his eyes and gave an exasperated sigh.

Whoops.

'They'll clean up again,' she suggested. 'They only need a wash.'

'Good. You might go and fetch them and do it—and don't put them all covered in mud into the back of my car!'

'Well, what on earth am I supposed to do?' she ranted, finally losing her grip on her temper. 'Lick them clean?'

'At least it would be something useful to do with your tongue,' he shot back, and stalked out of the kitchen, the dog slinking anxiously at his heels.

Lucie thought she was going to scream. At the very least she was going to throw something! She stormed out of the door before she hurled a pan through the window, grabbed a pile of newspapers from the lobby—presumably he wouldn't mind her using them—and headed off in her car to retrieve his precious floor bricks.

How was she supposed to know they were so special? Darn the man, he didn't have to be quite so evil about it! Something useful to do with her tongue, indeed!

Will phoned Richard, his senior partner, and told him about his arms.

'Lord! Are you all right?' he asked, his voice full of concern. 'Let me come round—'

'Richard, I'm fine. I've got Lucie here, don't forget.'

'Lucie?'

'Compton—our new registrar?'

'Ah, yes. Lucie.' Something shifted in his voice. 'How is she? Dear girl.'

Will rolled his eyes. 'She's in fine form. She's a tyrant. My house isn't my own.'

'Excellent. I'm sure she's doing a grand job. Just don't alienate her—she can do your locum work until you recover. You can train her—you *are* still well enough to do that, aren't you?'

'Barely,' he admitted grudgingly. 'I can't write— I can't hold anything in my hand. I've got to go back to the hospital for a check-up and a cast—they've only put a back-slab on.'

'Want me to come and take you?'

He was tempted, but for some perverse reason he

wanted Lucie to do it. To torture him even more by exposure to her endless cheer and mindless chatter? Or was it something to do with the firm press of those taut little buttocks in her jeans, and the pert tilt of her breasts beneath that silky soft sweater?

He dragged his mind back into order. 'I'll be fine. I'll bribe Lucie with a take-away,' he told Richard, and went and watched her from the bedroom window.

He could see her in the distance, struggling with the bricks, hauling them out of the puddles and plopping them into the car. Hers, thankfully, not his. She was going to be furious, of course, and he could have been a bit kinder about it, but his arm hurt and he was frustrated by the pain and the disability.

She came back an hour later, muddy and dishevelled, and hosed the bricks off on the yard. She looked even madder than she had yesterday, and he lurked quietly out of the way, his conscience pricking. Then Amanda came down to ride her horse, and introduced herself to Lucie, and moments later was heading for the kitchen at a lope.

Damn. Lucie must have told her about his accident. Amanda had been fussing round him already, and would, no doubt, seize this opportunity to ingratiate herself with him. She knocked on the door and came in, her eyes anxiously scanning him for signs of damage.

'Are you all right? You poor love! Fancy falling off the ladder! Anything I can do for you?'

He shook his head. 'No, really, I'm fine. Lucie's looking after me.'

Something that could have been jealousy flashed in her eyes. 'There's no need for that—you don't

want strangers doing those sorts of things for you. I
could help—'

'No, really,' Will cut in quickly. The very thought
of Amanda 'helping' him chilled his blood, and he
didn't dare to hazard a guess at what 'those sorts of
things' might be. He suppressed a shudder. 'I'll be
fine. My left hand's good—see?' He held it up and
waggled it, stifling a moan of pain, and grinned con-
vincingly. He hoped.

'Oh. Well, OK, then, but if there's anything I can
do, you will ask, won't you?'

'Of course—and thank you.'

She paused at the door. 'Is she staying in the cottage?'

A hellion in him rose to the surface of the scummy
pond that was his integrity. 'Lucie?' he said innocently. 'Ah—no. She's staying here—with me.' He
winked, just for good measure, and Amanda coloured
and backed away.

'Um. Right. OK. Well, take care.'

He felt guilty. She was a nice enough girl, but she
was so—well, wholesome, really. Earnest and ener-
getic and frightfully jolly.

And he was a rat.

He sighed. He was thirsty, and the orange juice in
the carton was finished. He contemplated the scissors, and got another carton out of the fridge, wincing and juggling it onto the cast to support the
weight. He dropped it on the worktop, picked the
scissors up in his left hand and proceeded to mash
the corner of the carton, not very effectively.

Of course, a decent brand of orange juice would
have a pull tab, but that would probably have been

beyond him, too, he was philosophical enough to realise.

He managed to chew a small hole in it with the scissors, then squeezed it out over a glass. Typically, he ended up with juice soaking down inside the back-slab and drenching the Tubigrip on the other hand. There was damn all in the glass, of course.

Disgusted, he balanced the carton on his cast, tipped it to his mouth and drank it through the mangled hole.

And of course that was how Lucie found him moments later.

She cocked a brow at him, squeezed past and washed her hands and arms in the sink. 'Couldn't you wait?'

'No. I was thirsty. Want some?'

She gave him a withering look, took a glass out of the cupboard and filled it with water, then drained it in a couple of swallows. How did women manage to find their way around kitchens so damned fast?

'Do you want to drink that out of the carton leaking all over your shirt, or would you rather I put some in a glass for you?'

One day, he thought, his pride was going to choke him. He hesitated, then gave up. 'Would you mind?' he said meekly.

She shot him a suspicious look and relieved him of the carton, trimming the opening straight and pouring it neatly into a fresh glass. 'Don't you have to go for a check-up today?' she asked as he drank.

'Mmm.'

'So shouldn't we go?'

'Probably. I've got juice all over these, I could do with some fresh supports.'

'I'm sure they'll oblige.'

She helped him into his sweater, then led the way to her car. He eyed it in dismay.

'Your car? Really?'

She paused in the act of getting in, one hand on the roof, the other on the top of the door. 'Really,' she vowed, refusing to relent. Yesterday had been quite enough. 'You can move the seat back,' she conceded.

She leant across and opened the door, pushing it ajar for him. He folded himself into the seat with much grunting, and slid it back when she lifted the adjustment lever.

'Are you in?'

'Just about,' he muttered ungraciously, and she leant across him to pull the door shut.

Hard, muscled thighs tensed under her weight as she sprawled over him, and she regretted not getting out and going round to close it. She hoisted herself upright, conscious of the heat in her cheeks and the gimlet gaze of Amanda watching them from beside the barn, and fastened his seat belt.

'That woman's got the hots for you,' she said candidly, watching Amanda in the rear-view mirror as they pulled away and hoping Will didn't misconstrue her remark as jealousy.

Apparently not. He rolled his eyes and groaned. 'Tell me about it,' he muttered. 'I'm afraid I rather exaggerated our—er—relationship. She was offering to help me in all sorts of hideously personal ways, so I'm afraid I used you as a way out. No doubt she'll hate you.'

Lucie spluttered with laughter, and Will's lips twitched. Not a smile—quite—but almost.

Maybe working with him wouldn't be so bad after all…

'Right, you met Richard at your interview, and this is Kathy, and Simon's about somewhere, and then there are all the receptionists, the practice manager, the practice and community nurses, the midwives…'

Lucie smiled and nodded and hoped she could remember a tenth of what he was telling her.

It all made sense, of course, and in many ways it was just like her city-centre practice had been, but in other ways it couldn't have been more different.

Take the setting, for example. Her London practice had been in a converted Victorian house, with a rabbit warren of rooms and corridors and odd little corners. This was modern, purpose built and astonishingly unprovincial.

All the equipment and methods in both were right up to date, of course, as they had to be in a training practice, but of the two environments, she had to say this was lighter and more spacious. Whether that was better or not she wasn't sure yet.

She had a pang of nostalgia for the untidy pile of anomalies she'd left behind, and a moment of fear that it wouldn't work out. She would have stayed in the other practice, given a choice, but she hadn't been. The trainer had had a heart attack and had had to take early retirement, and that had left nobody in the practice to take over.

It was only by luck that this vacancy had come up when it had.

She just hoped it was *good* luck.

Will had finished the introductions, and they went into his consulting room and settled down to start her first surgery. 'I'm going to sit in for a few days, make sure you've got all the referrals and so on at your fingertips and that you're up to speed on the way we do things. Then, if we're both happy, I'll leave you to it,' he said.

Great. An audience. And she'd thought driving the car had been bad!

Her first patient was a girl of fifteen, whose mother had brought her in 'because there's nothing wrong with her and I want you to tell her so, Doctor.'

Lucie and Will exchanged glances, and Lucie smiled at the girl. 'Let's see, you're Clare, aren't you?'

'Yes.' She coughed convulsively, and Lucie frowned. She'd already noticed that the teenager had been short of breath when they'd come in, and, unlike her other practice, there were no stairs here to blame!

'Tell me what seems to be wrong,' she coaxed, but the mother butted in again.

'She should have gone back to school today, but she's been flopping about and coughing for the last week, and she's got exams coming up—she's doing her GCSEs and she can't afford to have time off!'

'So what's the matter, Clare?' Lucie asked again. 'Tell me in what way you aren't feeling quite right.'

'My cough,' she began.

'She's not eating. She's starving herself to death— I think she's got anorexia or something. I think the cough is just a big put-on, but if you give her antibiotics she won't have any excuse, she won't be able to swing the lead. I've given her a good talking-to about this eating business. Dr Ryan, you tell her.'

Will shook his head and smiled. 'Dr Compton is

quite capable of making a diagnosis, Mrs Reid. We'll let her see what she comes up with first, shall we?'

Lucie felt like a bug under a microscope. Will had thrown his support behind her, but almost in the form of a challenge, and now she had to find something wrong. She was just warming up to her 'we can't give out antibiotics like sweets' talk, when Clare coughed again.

Listen to her chest, her common sense advised, and, to her huge relief, there was a crackle. Her face broke into a broad smile. 'There's your answer—she's got a chest infection. No anorexia, no skiving, just a genuine sick girl who needs antibiotics.'

'Well, that was easy. I thought you didn't dish them out these days?' Mrs Reid said sceptically, looking to Will for reassurance.

'Only when necessary,' Lucie confirmed, 'and with all those crackles in her chest, trust me, it's necessary. It sounds like someone eating a packet of crisps in there.'

Clare giggled, clearly relieved to have been taken seriously, and Lucie smiled at her. 'You'll soon feel better. You need to rest, drink lots and get back to school as soon as you feel right. When do you do your exams, is it this year or next?'

'Next year, the real thing, but we've got end-of-year ones coming up after half-term, and Dad'll kill me if I don't do well.' She pulled a face. 'He's a teacher.'

Lucie laughed. 'I know the feeling. My father's a teacher, too. He used to look at me over his half-glasses and say, "You don't seem to be doing very much homework these days." It drove me nuts—especially as I was working my socks off!'

'I bet he's pleased with you now, though,' Clare said thoughtfully. 'I want to be a doctor, too, but I don't know if I'm clever enough.'

'You know, there are lots of things you can do apart from medicine in the medical field. Wait and see how it pans out. Your grades might be good enough, and if not, there are lots of other options.'

Will cleared his throat quietly in the background, and Lucie looked at him. He was staring pointedly at the clock on the wall, and she gulped guiltily and brought up the girl's details on the computer, printed off her prescription and sent her and her over-anxious mother away.

Then she sat back and waited for the lecture.

He said nothing.

She looked at him. 'Aren't you going to criticise me?'

He smiled smugly and shook his head. 'Oh, yes— but later. I think your next patient has had to wait quite long enough, don't you?'

She stifled the urge to hit him.

CHAPTER THREE

IT WAS lunchtime. Apart from Clare, her first case, she had seen another fifteen patients that morning—and overrun surgery by an hour.

Now they were going on visits and, because she didn't know the way, Will was having to direct her.

Which meant, of course, that his mouth was busy with 'Turn left, go up there, it's on the right,' instead of 'Why didn't you do such and such?'. That was a huge relief to Lucie, who was coping—just—with his presence, without the added burden of her sins being heaped upon her head.

Actually she thought the surgery had gone quite well, but several times she'd caught Will rolling his eyes in the background or flicking glances at the clock. Had he been able to write, she knew he would have been making copious notes on her abysmal performance.

Tough. Anyway, it wasn't abysmal. Just a tad slow. She told herself it was because she was being thorough.

'Go along that road there to the end,' he instructed. 'It's the white house near the corner.'

There were two white houses near the corner. Of course she pulled up outside the wrong one, and couldn't resist the smirk of satisfaction when he objected.

He heaved a sigh, went to stab his hand through his hair and clonked his head with the cast.

'You should have a sling on,' she reminded him.

'I don't like slings. They mess my neck up.'

'Your hand will swell.'

'That's fine, there's room, it's still got the back-slab on.'

'Only because you won't wear a sling!'

Will turned to her, his eyes flying sparks. 'Lucie, it's my arm. If I don't want to wear a sling, I won't wear a sling. I most particularly won't wear two slings. And I won't be nagged by a junior doctor that I'm training!'

'I am not a junior doctor,' she bit out through clenched teeth. 'I am a registrar. I am not a complete incompetent, whatever you might think, and how you got the job of trainer I can't imagine. You're patronising, unfairly critical and judgmental.'

'I haven't said a word—'

'Yet! No doubt it's coming.'

He sat back and studied her curiously. 'So what did you think you did wrong this morning?' he asked with studied calm.

'Apart from breathe?' Lucie muttered under her breath. 'Overran the surgery time.'

'What else?'

'Nothing,' she said defensively.

'I would have got a sputum sample from Clare to make sure she'd got the right antibiotic.'

Oh, would he? Damn. He was right, and she would have done if he hadn't put her off by clearing his throat pointedly and looking at the clock. She wondered if Clare had taken the first dose yet, or if she should ring—

'I've rung and ordered it. They'll pick the pot up before she takes the first dose,' Will added, as if he'd read her mind. 'They live very close to the surgery. What else?'

She stuffed her irritation into a mental pending tray to deal with later and scanned through her morning list. 'That man with indigestion-like pain—'

'Mr Gregory.'

'Yes. He's obese.'

'Actually, technically he's just overweight. His body mass index is 29.4. He's working on getting it down, but he's aiming for a 10 kg weight loss. That's probably why he's got indigestion. Faddy diets and varied eating habits can cause that.'

'It would have been helpful to know that before the consultation. I was wondering about the choice between angina and *Helicobacter pylori*, and it's probably just too much cucumber!'

A flicker of guilt came and went in his eyes. 'Sorry. It's the painkillers. I'm not really concentrating. You're right.'

Lucie's jaw nearly dropped. An apology? Good grief, wonders will never cease, she thought.

'Since you're on a roll, I don't suppose you want to apologise for that remark about licking the bricks, do you?' she challenged, pushing her luck.

He smiled. It was a dangerous, predatory smile. 'Not really,' he said, and opened the car door with a wince. 'Let's get on or we'll be late.'

'So, are you going to tell me about this patient, or let me go in blind?' she asked his retreating form.

He sat back, letting the door fall shut and looking at her over his shoulder. 'He's fifty-five or so, he's had a heart attack, he's been under a cardiologist but cancelled his follow-up appointment on a flimsy pretext. I reckon he's in line for bypass surgery but he won't stick to a diet or exercise programme and he keeps getting chest pain. This is just a routine check-up. I suggest you take routine obs while I talk.'

'I thought I was taking on your patients?' she objected, but he shook his head.

'Not this one. His wife's too nice—she doesn't deserve all this worry. She needs moral support.'

'And I can't give it?'

'Not like I can. I've known her for years,' he pointed out fairly.

'Not that many, Old Father Time. How old are you?'

He shot her a grin. 'I've been here six years. We've gone through the menopause together, Pam and I. I know her well, trust me.'

She gave a quiet and not very ladylike snort as he got out of the car. Retrieving her bag from the back, she locked the car and followed him across the road.

A woman was standing in the front garden of the other white house, stripping off bright yellow rubber gloves, and he bent and kissed her cheek. 'Hello, Pam,' he said gently. 'How are things?'

She rolled her eyes despairingly, then shot him a keen look. 'Never mind me—is that a cast on your arm? *And* a bandage on the other one—what on earth have you been up to?'

He told her the story, played down the drama and played up the farce, and introduced Lucie as the cavalry. 'Very timely arrival, although, of course, if she hadn't been coming I wouldn't have been mending the roof of the cottage and I wouldn't have been up the ladder, so in a way it's her fault.'

'That's right, blame me,' Lucie said, rolling her

eyes and laughing. 'Although as I remember it, you were rescuing the cat, actually.'

'She's doing all the physical stuff for me, I'm doing the talking,' Will explained, cutting her off with a grin. 'She's our new trainee registrar.'

'Are you? Poor you,' Pam said comfortingly. 'He can be a bit of a slave-driver, I gather. His last one left in a hurry.'

'His last one was useless,' Will pointed out fast. 'Don't slag me off, Pam, she already thinks I've got a broomstick stashed in the barn.'

'Yes—a Swedish one,' Lucie chipped in. 'Estate version.'

He laughed, not unkindly. 'It's a lovely car.'

'It's too big.'

'We're using it tomorrow. That thing of yours gives me backache and cramp.'

'Poor baby.'

Pam eyed them with curiosity. 'I think you'll survive, Lucie,' she said consideringly, and smiled at her. 'Welcome to Bredford.'

'Thank you.' She returned the smile, comforted that at least someone was going to be on her side, and followed them in.

Their patient was sitting in an upright chair, a folded newspaper on the floor at his side and a cup of what looked like very strong coffee on the table next to him.

'Hello, Dick,' Will said easily, perching on the sofa near their patient's chair. 'I won't shake hands, I've mashed myself. This is Lucie Compton, my new registrar.'

Lucie shook hands with him, noticing the pallor of his skin except for the high flush over his nose and cheekbones, and wondered just how bad his heart condition was.

'Lucie, why don't you run the ruler over him while we chat, to save time?' Will suggested, and she opened her bag and took out her stethoscope, listening to the patient's chest first to hear his heart.

It was a little irregular, but without an ECG it was difficult to tell what was wrong about it. His chest was clear, at least. She took his pulse and respiration, while Will propped his arms on his knees and smiled at Dick encouragingly. 'So, tell me, how are you doing?'

'Oh, not so bad.'

'He's been getting chest pain.'

Will looked from Dick to Pam and back again. 'On exertion, or at rest?'

'At night. At least, that's when I know about it,' Pam confirmed.

Will nodded. 'And how about the daytime, Dick? Anything then?'

The man shrugged. 'Off and on.'

'Are you taking the pills?'

'Yes.'

'No.'

Will's eyes flicked to Pam again. 'He's not?'

She shook her head. 'Not always. Not unless I nag him.'

'Which she does all the time, of course,' Dick put in with a rueful, indulgent smile. 'Oh, I don't know, Will, I just feel there's no point. I'm a great believer in Fate. If my number's up, it's up. I'm not going to bugger up the rest of my life taking pills and watching what I eat and drink. It's like the old joke about giving up drinking, women and red meat. It doesn't make you live longer, it just feels that way!'

Will chuckled obediently, and glanced at Pam again. 'I wouldn't suggest you give up women—at least, not this one. She's a star. But the food and drink are real issues, Dick. The next step down the line for you could be bypass surgery, and you really owe it to yourself to be as fit as possible for it.'

'Oh, I know. You're going to tell me to lay off the booze, cut my fat intake and get off my backside and walk two miles a day, aren't you?'

'Something like that. Sounds as if you've heard it before somewhere. And while we're at it, I'll throw in caffeine. Decaff tea and coffee, please.'

Lucie bent down to her bag to remove the blood-pressure cuff, and hid a smile. Dick curled his lip. 'Decaff? Filthy stuff.'

'Rubbish. You can't tell the difference.'

'I can.'

'So drink fruit teas or orange juice.'

Will was treated to another withering look. 'Fruit teas,' Dick said disgustedly.

'Unlaced.'

He shook his head slowly. 'You're a hard man.'

'I'm trying to keep you alive. No point in dying on the waiting list, Dick—always assuming you ever get on it. Have you made another appointment yet?'

Something flickered in Dick's eyes—something that could have been fear.

'Not yet. Keep forgetting.'

Lucie slipped the blood-pressure cuff off his arm and chipped in.

'A patient at my last practice had a by-pass op. He felt like you—what was the point? If it was going to get him, there was no point in worrying. He felt so much better after the op, he realised it had been worth worrying about. I had a letter from him the other day. He's taken early retirement, moved to the country and started playing golf, and he feels great. He's lost two stone, he's fitter than he's been for years and he says there's a twinkle in his wife's eye that's been missing for ages.'

Dick moistened his lips and cleared his throat. 'He feels better?'

'Yes. He felt better straight away. His chest was a bit sore for a while, of course, but he said the hospital were excellent and it was more than worth it. He sent me a photo—he looks terrific. Why don't you give it the benefit of the doubt and find out more?'

He looked thoughtful, and Lucie put the rest of her equipment away and straightened up. 'That all seems OK,' she said to Will. 'Anything else you want me to check?'

He shook his head and stood up. 'Listen to us, Dick. We aren't all telling you the same thing by coincidence, you know. Give it a whirl.'

Dick nodded grudgingly, and Will looked at Pam. 'Your garden's looking good. You must show me round it on the way out—I want to see your osteo-spermums. I can't believe you overwinter them out-side. Mine all die without fail.'

Gardening already, for heaven's sake! Lucie cleared her throat, and glanced pointedly at her watch. Will ignored her.

'I've got some cuttings I've done for you—come down to the greenhouse and I'll give them to you,' Pam was saying.

'You're a marvel.'

Lucie sighed. 'I'll wait here,' she said, and sat down again with Dick. Maybe she could spend the time usefully after all...

For a moment he didn't speak, then he looked at her searchingly. 'Now tell me the truth. How much will it hurt after the op?'

Right for the jugular. 'A lot,' she said honestly, 'but less than another heart attack. The breastbone is the worst bit, and the leg can be quite sore for a few days, apparently, but they give you pain relief intravenously, and you have control over that. If it hurts, you can give yourself a shot, and it really does make it bearable. Everyone who's had it says it's worth it.'

He nodded, and licked his lips nervously. 'I'm scared,' he confessed. 'I can't tell Pam—seems so silly, really, to be afraid of pain, but I've never been good with it. Pam wants me to have it done privately to cut the waiting time, but I don't want to, even though we've got private health insurance as part of my work package. I suppose there's a bit of me that would rather wait longer and maybe die, so I don't have to deal with it. Does that seem strange to you?'

Lucie shook her head and smiled. 'No. Quite normal. Most people aren't afraid of being dead. They're afraid of suffering. I think you're actually very ordinary like that. Nobody likes pain. The thing is, if you have another heart attack, there's no guarantee it will kill you, but it will make you less well for the operation and it will, of course, be very painful in itself. I think at the very least you should see a cardiologist and discuss it.'

'I just—it scares me.'

'I take it you've had an angiogram and aren't suitable for balloon angioplasty?' she said as an after-thought.

He shook his head. 'No. They were talking about it, but I didn't know what it was.'

'So ask.'

'Everyone's always busy.'

Lucie smiled. 'That's life for you. An angiogram is a diagnostic image of the heart with radio-opaque dye injected into the coronary arteries, so they can see just where the arteries are clogging.'

'Oh, I had that. I never got the results, though. I thought you meant the other thing. The pasty thing.'

'Plasty. Angioplasty. If you're a suitable candidate, there's always the possibility that you won't have to have bypass surgery. Lots of people have balloon angioplasty instead. That's where they stick a little inflatable catheter in through a nick in the groin, track it with X-rays until it's in the right place and inflate it. It stretches the arteries and relieves the narrow point, if it's just one small constriction. And, of course, until you get the results of the angiogram, you won't know.'

Dick nodded. 'You're right, of course. I'll go back. I will. Thanks.'

'My pleasure. Have you got a computer? If you have, you could find out more about it on the internet. It's brilliant for things like that.' Lucie stood up. 'You will keep the appointment this time, won't you? It can't hurt to find out, and even if you ended up with surgery, you could have a whole new life ahead of you. Think of all the years you've worked, just to throw it all away before you retire.' She glanced at her watch again. 'I must go—we've got lots of other visits to do yet and I'm already running behind. It's only my first day.'

'And Will with broken arms, eh? Still, he's got such a nice, even temper. Anyone else might be really grumpy.'

Lucie nearly choked, swallowing the retort. Instead she smiled at Dick, exorted him to give the consultant a chance and reached the door just as Will and Pam came in.

'Right, are you all done?' Will asked. He had plant pots balanced on his cast, and Lucie rolled her eyes.

'Scrounging off the patients?' she teased as they went out to the car.

'Absolutely. Cheers, Pam. Thanks. Cheerio, Dick. Mind how you go.'

Lucie stuck her keys in the door of the car and paused. 'It would never happen in the city,' she remarked over the roof in a quiet voice.

'It's a cover. She wanted to talk to me about him. He won't go back to the consultant.'

'Yes, he will,' Lucie said smugly. 'I just talked him into it—at least, I think I did. The only reason he wouldn't do it is because he's afraid of the pain. He's hoping he'll die before he gets to the front of the waiting list. I told him it was possible he'd be suitable for balloon angioplasty, and even if he wasn't, how about his retirement?'

Will stared at her over the top of the car. 'And you've talked him round?'

'Yup.'

Respect dawned in his eyes. 'Good girl, well done,' he said softly. 'It's a shame he can't afford to go privately and get it over with, now he's psyched up. Not that it should be necessary, but I don't want to start on the politics of funding.'

'Pointless, really,' Lucie said with a cheeky grin. 'We'd probably be in agreement, and that would never do, would it? Anyway, he's got private health insurance through his work.'

She opened the car, slid behind the wheel and pushed his door open. He tried to pass the plants to her, but, of course, he dropped one on the seat, and it splattered wet black compost all over her upholstery.

'"Don't you dare put those bricks in my car like that,"' she mimicked, and he groaned and met her eyes, his own apologetic.

'I'm sorry.'

'Don't fret, I don't have to sit on it. Just brush it off for now—you can lick it clean later.'

Shooting her a foul look, he used his sprained wrist to flick the little bits of black aside, leaving dirty streaks on his bandage and the seat.

She stifled a smile. 'On second thoughts, using your car in future might be a good idea, if you're going to take up horticulture as a sideline,' she said sweetly. 'Mind you don't stand on them.'

He clenched his jaw and got into the car, tucking his arm into the seat belt and pulling it through with care and much wincing. She let him struggle for a moment, then took the buckle and clipped it in.

Her hand brushed his thigh, and it tensed again as it had before. She stifled another smile. Interesting.

'When are you going to go back to the hospital? You ought to go to the fracture clinic.'

'I'll go tomorrow,' he said. 'Right, where to next?'

* * *

Lucie was right, of course, he did need a sling on it, but now his pride was going to get in the way and so he surreptitiously propped his right arm up on anything that was handy, just to take the pressure off it.

It was pounding and, of course, with only a back-slab it was marginally unstable, too, and grated nicely every now and again if he was a bit rash. He really should get it seen to, he thought with a sigh.

The day seemed to drag interminably, and Lucie didn't need to be watched every second. She was more than capable of running his afternoon clinic on her own, and in the end he left her to it and called a patient who ran a minicab.

He was an ex-London cabbie, and always good value, and he entertained Will all the way to the hospital. He took himself off for a cup of tea while Will saw the fracture clinic staff and got a lecture about the swelling and resting it in a sling. Then the cabbie took him home, after Will had bribed the man to go down his track.

'Blimey, gov, it's a miracle nobody's got stuck on this,' he said in a broad Cockney accent.

'Mmm,' Will agreed noncommittally, saying nothing about Lucie. He gave the man a hefty tip, crawled into the house and greeted Bruno with guarded enthusiasm.

'Hello, mate. Good dog, get off. Ouch!' He raised his arms out of reach, kneed the dog out of the way and sat down at the table with his arms in front of him, safe. Now all he needed was some pills, and they, of course, were in his pocket. Could he get them out?

He struggled, but came up with them, and even

managed to open the lid. Amazing. He took two, thought about another and put the lid back on. He'd have more later. In the meantime, he was going to stretch out on the sofa with the dog at his feet and have forty winks...

'Hello, Lucie. How are you doing?'

She looked up from her paperwork and smiled at Richard Brayne, the senior partner. 'Oh, hi, there. I'm fine. I don't know where Will is—have you seen him?'

'Gone to the fracture clinic and then home, he said.' Richard settled himself beside her and pushed a mug of tea across the table to her. 'You must be doing well if he'll leave you alone all ready.'

'Or he feels like death warmed up, which is more likely,' Lucie said drily, harbouring no illusions about her brilliance or Will's understanding of it. 'I suppose he wants me to cover his evening surgery—is he on call tonight, by any chance, just to add to the joys?'

Richard shook his head and grinned. 'No. You get lucky. We have night cover—a co-operative. You don't have to do any nights. Will doesn't—he has too much to do on the farm.'

Lucie tipped her head and looked searchingly at Richard, puzzled. 'On the farm?' she asked. 'Such as what?'

'Oh, I don't know, fencing the fields, mending the barn, doing up the house, getting the cottage ready for guests. He's always busy. Just at the moment he's redoing the ground floor of the house, I think—or he was.'

Lucie was relieved. She had wondered, for a moment there, if he had masses of stock all starving to death without him—stock she was about to have to look after. She didn't mind the dog or the cat, and she'd get used to the snorting horse given time, but anything more agricultural was beyond her.

It was a pity, she thought on her way back there later that evening, that Will didn't spend some of that time being busy doing the drive. She picked her way along it with caution, and went in to find him sprawled full length on the sofa.

Bruno had greeted her rapturously, whining and wagging and pushing his great face into her hand, and she'd patted him and done the 'good dog' thing, and had then looked for Will.

And there he was, spark out, looking curiously vulnerable this time. There was a sling round his neck but the arm was out of it, propped beside him on a pillow with a cool pack over the gap in the back of the plaster. He'd obviously been ticked off at the fracture clinic, she thought with wry amusement, and was now doing as he was told.

Or perhaps the pain had finally penetrated his common sense. Whatever, he was now doing what he should have been doing ever since he'd hurt himself.

Finally, she thought, and then wondered what was for supper.

Whatever she cooked, she realised. She went into the kitchen, followed by the clearly hopeful dog, and fed him first. The cat materialised at the sound of Bruno's bowl clunking round the floor, and she fed her, too.

'OK, guys, what about us?' she asked, and Bruno cocked his head on one side for a moment, before going back to his optimistic licking.

She found some steak mince in the freezer, and onions and tinned tomatoes and some ready-made Bolognese sauce, and in the cupboard next to the sink, under the first-aid kit, she found a bag of pasta shells.

Easy—and he could eat it without difficulty. She threw it together, dished up and went and woke him.

'Supper's ready,' she announced, and he propped himself up groggily on his left elbow and peered at her out of dazed eyes.

'Supper?'

'Spag Bol. Well, pasta shells, anyway.'

'Oh, God.' He pulled a face and flopped back down on the cushions. 'Right at the moment, I can't think of anything I want less.'

She stared at him in amazement, then flipped. 'Fine,' she said tightly. 'I'm sure it'll find a more appreciative audience.'

And she stalked into the kitchen, seized his plate and scraped it into the dog's bowl, just as Will came through the doorway.

'What the hell are you doing?' he asked, stunned.

She banged the bowl down defiantly. 'You said you didn't want it.'

'No, I said I couldn't think of anything I wanted less than food. That didn't mean I wouldn't have eaten it! Hells teeth, woman!'

He stared with evident dismay at the dog, who had swallowed the plateful almost whole and was busy doing the dish-licking thing again.

Throwing her one last disbelieving look, he let his breath out on a sharp sigh, turned on his heel and went back into the sitting room, banging the door behind him.

Whoops. OK. So she'd overreacted. Hardly the first time, but he just seemed to set her off. She looked at her own food with regret. She could give it to him...

Or she could eat it, and he could contemplate the wisdom of thinking before he spoke. She was sure he managed it with his patients, so why not her?

No. She was eating it. All of it. Every bite.

It nearly choked her.

Will was starving. Only pride prevented him from going into the kitchen and making himself something to eat—pride and the fact that Lucie was in there with the radio on, singing along to some ghastly noise and chattering to the dog, who was her devoted slave.

'Fickle beast,' he mumbled, flicking through the television channels with the remote control in his reluctant left hand. He found a wildlife programme, and settled down to watch it, disturbed only by the noise from the kitchen.

After five minutes, it had driven him crazy. He stood up, walked over to the door and yanked it open, just stifling the little yelp of pain in time. 'Do you suppose you could turn that bloody awful racket down?' he snarled, and kicked the door shut again, retreating to the sofa to nurse his throbbing wrist.

'Sor-ry,' she carolled through the door, and then started humming and singing, which was worse, because she had a throaty, sexy voice that did unforgivable things to his libido.

He turned the TV up in self-defence, and forced himself to concentrate on the mating habits of some obscure Australian spider. Riveting it wasn't, and finally he went upstairs to bed, propped himself up and read a book until he'd heard Lucie settle for the night.

Then, like a fugitive in his own home, he crept down to the kitchen, raided the bread bin and managed painfully and raggedly to hack the end off the loaf.

He found a chunk of cheese in the fridge, looked in despair at the tub of olive-oil spread and realised that the effort was more than he could be bothered to make. He wrapped the cheese in the wavering doorstep of dry bread, bit the end off and poured a glass of milk. It would have to do. Anything else was beyond him.

He carried the rustic little snack up to bed, wondering as he went where Bruno was, and then saw him through the crack in Lucie's door, curled up across the foot of her bed, one eye open and tail waving gently in apology at his defection.

Lucie was scrunched up at the top, forced out by the dog, and he smiled nastily. Good. Serve her right. If there was any justice Bruno would be sick on her floor and she'd have to clear it up—and lying like that she'd almost inevitably wake up with a crick in her neck.

He sighed and shook his head. Lord, she really brought out the worst in him, but she was so disruptive! He was used to silence, broken only by the sounds of nature or by the television or radio if he chose to have them on, which he often didn't.

It wasn't her fault she was here, of course. The sooner he got the bed ordered, the sooner he could have his peace and quiet back. He vowed to do it the next day.

First thing in the morning…

CHAPTER FOUR

'WHAT do you mean, you can't do it till next week?'

'Sorry, sir, all our carpet-fitters are busy. It's because of the spring, you see.'

Will didn't. All he saw was the next week stretching ahead of him, fighting with Lucie for his personal space.

'But surely you can manage one small room.'

'That's what they all say, sir,' the salesman told him cheerfully. 'Next Wednesday's the earliest we can possibly get to you.'

'But I have to have it!' He heard the rising, frenzied tone and cleared his throat, dropping his voice an octave and striving for authority. 'I really have to have it,' he insisted, and then added coaxingly, 'Can't you manage this Friday? Perhaps for an incentive payment?'

'Not even if you double it, sir,' the man said implacably. 'If you really are in such a hurry, I suggest you buy a piece off the roll and fit it yourself.'

'I might just do that,' he lied. 'Elsewhere.' If he had arms. Hah. He would have hung up with a flourish, but remembered just in time that it would hurt too much. Instead, he replaced the receiver with exaggerated care and swore, just as Lucie came back into the consulting room bearing two cups of coffee and a pile of patient envelopes.

'No joy?' she said sweetly, plonking the mug down in front of him, and if he'd had two hands, he

63

would have strangled her while she was in range. Instead, he withdrew into dignity.

'There are other firms,' he said tautly. 'I shall keep trying. Are those this morning's notes?'

'No, tomorrow's. I thought we could get ahead.'

'Don't get sarky,' he growled, and her lips twitched. Aggravating woman. He dragged his eyes off her lips and tried to stop fantasising about them. He had to concentrate...

Will seemed to be getting a little better, Lucie thought as the day wore on, if his temper was anything to go by. He was crabbier than ever, possibly from pain, but more likely because now he was over the initial shock of his fall, the enforced inactivity was starting to get to him. By all accounts he was usually a busy person, and just now he was having to put up and shut up. It clearly didn't sit well on him.

Nor did not being able to drive, and her refusal to drive his car instead of hers. 'I hate it,' she'd insisted. 'We take mine or we don't go—or you can pay for a taxi.'

It hadn't really been fair, and in truth there was nothing at all wrong with the bigger car. It was easy to drive, but she was used to hers, and anyway, it was the principle.

So he'd folded himself up and threaded himself through the door like a camel through the eye of the needle, and sat in grim-lipped silence most of the time they were out.

And then, after their last call, he climbed out of the car and winced, and she noticed he was limping.

Oh, blast. Guilt washed over her, and she hurried after him.

'Are you OK?' she asked with genuine concern, and he shot her a look like a shard of ice.

'Just peachy. How the hell do you think I am?'

She shrugged. 'Just asking.'

'Well, don't bother,' he snapped. 'Everything hurts like the devil.'

'Did you take your painkillers earlier?' she asked, and got another murderous look for her pains.

No, then. She made him a drink, and they talked through her calls until it was time for her afternoon clinic, and then, because it was a shared antenatal with the midwife and she had plenty of supervision, he took himself off to an empty consulting room.

'To sort this darned carpet out,' he said with determination, and she pitied the salesmen he was about to browbeat into submission.

She enjoyed the antenatal clinic. She'd always liked maternity, mainly because it was the one branch of medicine where everyone, by and large, was well. She felt her first set of triplets, and listened to their heartbeats, and discussed the management of the delivery with the midwife and the mother, Angela Brown.

It had been planned that she would have a hospital delivery by Caesarean section, and was being seen alternately at the hospital and the GP clinic. As the time went on, she would transfer entirely to the hospital, and although she was happy to do that for the sake of the babies, she expressed regret that it couldn't be a more normal birth.

'Are you looking forward to it?' Lucie asked,

wondering how she'd cope with three at once. Apparently she wasn't the only one wondering.

'Actually, I'm dreading it,' the patient confessed. 'I don't know how I'll manage. My mother's said she'll help, and my husband's going to take some time off, but it's going to be hell at first, and we're only in a small house. This wasn't exactly planned, and I was going back to work afterwards, but there's no way I can afford to pay child care for three!'

Good grief, Lucie thought. Accidental triplets on a tight budget? Rather her than me.

They finished their clinic, and she found Will in the office, hunched over a cup of tea. He looked up at her as she approached, and his lip moved a fraction. A smile? Perhaps his face muscles were on a tight budget, like Mrs Brown, she thought, and stifled a chuckle.

'Got your carpet sorted?' she asked, and a frown replaced the sorry excuse for a smile.

'More or less. I've had to pay more, but it comes on Monday. I thought it was worth it.'

She ignored the implied insult. 'So we'll be stuck with each other over the weekend,' she said breezily. 'I dare say we'll survive.'

He muttered something inaudible, and she felt another flicker of irritation and hurt. How silly of her. It wasn't personal, he just liked his space, she told herself. 'How about the bed?'

'From the same place. It'll come later in the day. I've arranged to leave them a key. Security's not a problem—nobody ever goes down my track except for the occasional dog walker who's got mislaid on the footpath from the ferry.'

She settled her chin on her hands and looked

across the table at him, wishing he wasn't quite so prickly with her. 'Tell me about this ferry,' she said, trying to bridge the gulf between them. 'When does it run? I've looked and looked, but I can't see anything.'

'You won't. It doesn't exist. It's just the name of the little jut of land. It used to be a chain ferry that crossed the mouth of the river, but they built a bridge further up. The only thing left is the name.'

'Oh.' And that was the end of that attempt at conversation. She switched to Mrs Brown and her triplets. 'I saw your triplet lady,' she told him. 'She's worried about how she'll cope.'

'She needs to,' he told her bluntly. 'Her husband's quite demanding, and I can't see him tolerating slipping standards. He didn't want her to have one—pressed for a termination before they even discovered it was three.'

Lucie was shocked. 'She didn't tell me that,' she murmured slowly. 'How sad. I wonder if they'll survive?'

'The triplets, or the Browns?'

'I meant the Browns, but all of them, really. The babies seem quite small.'

'Triplets often are, especially at term, and who knows what'll happen to them all? In their financial situation three babies is the last thing they need. Sometimes I'm glad I'm a GP, not a social worker.' He leant back, easing the kinks out of his shoulders and wincing. 'Right, what's next? No surgery tonight—no more calls to make. Do you have paperwork to deal with, or can we go?'

She blinked. 'No surgery?'

'Nope. Not on Tuesdays. Not for me, anyway.'

'Oh. Well, we can go, then. I'm all up to date. How about you? Are you supposed to go back to the fracture clinic?'

He held up his arm, and for the first time she saw the brand-new lightweight cast. 'Oh! You've been!'

'Ten out of ten,' he drawled sarcastically. 'Took you long enough to notice. I went while you were doing the antenatals.'

'That was very quick.'

'I charmed the plaster nurse,' he said, deadpan, and she wondered how on earth he'd done that. There was precious little sign of his charm being exercised around her. She pushed back her chair and stood up.

'Shall we go, then?'

'Sounds like a fine idea.'

He winced again as he threaded himself back into the car, and hit his head on the doorframe as he sat down. She ignored the muttered oath, and let him struggle with the seat belt for a moment before helping him with the clip.

'You really are rather big for this car, aren't you?' she conceded.

'Oh, the penny's dropped,' he said with thinly veiled sarcasm. 'Of course, a less obstructive person…'

He let the rest of the sentence hang, and she snapped her mouth shut and declined to comment. She was damned if she was going to tell him *now* that she'd decided to take his car in future. Let him stew on it for the night.

Talking of which…

'Should we call into a supermarket on the way and pick up some food? There's not a lot in your fridge.'

'Good idea. We can buy some ready meals so you don't have to cook.'

She shot him a sideways glance. Was that guilt after his reaction to her spaghetti dish last night, or a dig at her choice of menu? Whatever, if he chose the food, he couldn't complain that it was the last thing he wanted.

Besides, she didn't like cooking anyway—not your everyday meat and two veg stuff. She liked tinkering about with fancy ingredients and playing with dinner party menus, but that was all. Anything else was just basic nutrition to keep body and soul together, and it bored her senseless. She didn't normally succumb, but she had to admit that just for today an instant meal sounded fine.

Convenience foods, Will decided, were not all they were cracked up to be. He pushed the soggy pasta twirls round in the over-seasoned sauce and sighed. It didn't smell anything like as good as the Bolognese she'd made last night—the Bolognese she'd fed to the dog.

Still, Bruno didn't complain when he put the cardboard dish on the floor and let the dog finish it. Twice running, Will thought. The dog would be huge.

'Don't you like it?' Lucie asked, and his stomach growled.

'I'm not really hungry,' he lied. 'I'll make myself something later.'

She gave him a searching look. 'Do you want me to make you something? A bacon sandwich?'

His stomach growled even more enthusiastically, and he gave a wry, bitter little smile. 'Why would you do that?'

She stood up, dumped her plate on the floor in front of the bemused but receptive dog and headed for the fridge. 'Because I want one and it would seem churlish not to make yours? Because I don't like instant food any more than I imagine you do? Because I need you alive if I'm to finish my training? Take your pick.'

How about, Because I'm sorry I gave your dinner to the dog? Will wanted to suggest, but he thought he'd quit while he was winning. 'A bacon sandwich sounds fine,' he muttered, and then sighed inwardly. Did that sound a bit grudging? Oh, hell. He wasn't used to being dependent, and he didn't like it. 'Please,' he added, too late to be spontaneous, and caught her stifled smile out of the corner of his eye.

'While you do that I think I'll go and change,' he said, and went upstairs and struggled one-handed out of the trousers he'd been wearing for work. They had a hook fastening that was possible even with his reluctant arms, and a little easy-running nylon zip, but the belt was more of a problem. He shut the end in the door, tugged gently until the buckle was free and then slid the end out.

He was getting resourceful, he thought as he squirmed and shuffled his way into his jogging bottoms. Learning to adapt. One thing that was almost impossible, though, was washing. He'd managed so far—more or less—by removing the support on his left wrist and using his left hand, but it wasn't satisfactory and it hurt like hell. And it relied on Lucie to put the support back on.

He thought of the bath longingly. What he wanted more than anything in the world was a long, hot soak, but he didn't think he could manage without help, and he was damned if he was asking Lucie Compton to supervise his ablutions!

Perhaps he should ask Amanda, he thought with a wry twist of humour, and shuddered. The thought was terrifying. She'd probably rub him down with a dandy brush, to get his circulation going.

A wonderful smell of frying bacon drifted up the stairs, and he arrived back in the kitchen just as she set two plates down on the table. 'There you are,' she said cheerfully. 'Wrap yourself around that.'

He did, wondering idly where his five portions of fruit and veg were coming from that day, but there was no point in worrying. He'd eat an apple later. He'd rather have an orange, but he couldn't work out how to peel it.

'Um—about washing,' Lucie said, and he nodded his head towards the washing machine.

'Help yourself. Powder's in the cupboard.'

'Not clothes—you,' she corrected, and he felt a skittering moment of panic and anticipation.

'Me?' Will croaked, almost choking on a bite of sandwich.

'Well, you must be in need of a good long soak, I would have thought. Do you want me to wrap your cast up in plastic bags and run you a bath?'

Was she a mind-reader, or did he smell worse than he realised?

He sniffed experimentally. 'Is it that bad?' he asked, groping for a light note and managing instead to sound defensive.

Lucie gave a pitying smile. 'I just thought, by now, you must be feeling pretty dreadful. Of course,' she added lightly, 'there's always Amanda—perhaps

you'd like me to give her a call and ask her to come
over? I'm sure she'd be more than willing...'

'That won't be necessary,' he growled, not quite
knowing how to take her teasing. 'I think I can manage—and before you offer, I don't need my back
washed.'

Her lips twitched. 'I'm sure I'll live. Still, you can
always yell if you get stuck. I don't suppose you've
got anything that everybody else hasn't got.'

Except a body that even in adversity seemed hell
bent on betraying his baser feelings! He focused on
his sandwich. 'Thanks. Maybe later,' he said, knowing full well that he was going to take her up on it.
He just hoped he didn't get stuck, because the consequences didn't bear thinking about!

Lucie's imagination was running riot. He'd been
ages, and she was hovering in her bedroom, listening
to every splash and groan. The door wasn't locked,
of course. Not even Will Ryan was that bent on self-
destruction.

'Are you OK?' she called.

'Fine,' he yelled, then added a belated, 'thanks.'

She shook her head and smiled. He really, really
hated this. He was so stubborn and fiercely proud,
and it was all so unnecessary. She was quite happy
to help—if he only could bring himself to be at least
civil about it!

While she waited, she thought it might be interesting to have a look at the rest of the house. So far
she'd only seen the rooms they were using, and there
were some intriguing doors...

'Can I look round the house?' she asked, pausing
outside the bathroom, and there was a splash and a

stream of something not quite audible. She decided
she should be probably grateful for that.

'Sure,' he said shortly. 'Be careful upstairs, there's
no light. There's a torch just inside the door. Mind
the holes.'

Holes? Her curiosity well aroused, she opened the
door and went through, flicking on the torch. Its powerful beam pierced the gloom, slicing through the
dusty air and highlighting the cobwebs. She suppressed a shudder and looked around. It was all but
derelict, or it had been. The roof was obviously repaired now—she could see that through the gaps
where the ceiling had fallen down.

Beneath the holes in the ceiling were areas of rot-
ten boards, some taken up, others just gaping and
twisted. Some showed evidence of recent repair, to
her comfort. She looked at the untouched parts, and
rolled her eyes.

'Mind the holes' didn't even begin to scratch the
surface! It was on a par with 'a bit rough in places',
and typical of Will's under-estimation of the awful-
ness of a situation. She had visions of him telling a
dying patient he'd feel 'a little bit dicky for a day or
two'.

Mind the holes, indeed. She picked her way carefully down the long room, sticking to the patched
bits, and peered out of the windows towards the distant river, eerily silvered with moonlight.

It would be a beautiful view in daylight, and the
windows were positioned to take full advantage. She
could see it would be a lovely room once it was
repaired. Rooms, in fact. It would easily make two.

She glanced round again. No wonder he was frustrated with inactivity, if this was waiting for him! She

wondered if he'd done the work himself in the rest of the house, or if he'd had the builders in.

Poor builders, she thought pityingly, and went downstairs. Beyond the hall was the room below the one she'd just investigated, and she opened the door cautiously.

It was a mess. Well, to be exact it was a paint and tool and timber store, and was obviously where he kept everything for the work in progress. Again, it was a lovely room, with a huge inglenook fireplace on one wall and windows on three sides, and at least this one had a light that worked, after a fashion—if you counted a dangling bulb on the end of a bit of flex.

It was heavily timbered, and there was a smell of preservative in the air when she sniffed. Preservative and mice. Lovely.

She shuddered and backed quickly out, bumping into the dog and making herself jump.

'You scared me half to death, you stupid mutt!' she told him with a nervous laugh, conveniently ignoring the fact that it had been her fault in the first place. Conscious of the time, she went back upstairs and listened at the bathroom door, Bruno at her heels.

She could hear nothing. She knocked lightly. 'Will? Are you OK?'

Absolute silence.

'Will?'

Oh, lord, what if he'd slipped and drowned while she'd been downstairs out of earshot? She called his name again, then, when he still didn't reply, she pressed the lever down and inched the door open, her heart in her mouth.

Please, God, don't let him be dead, she prayed

silently, and, pushing the door open, she took a step in.

He was asleep, his plastic-wrapped arm propped up on the side of the bath, his head lolling back against the end of the tub, his lashes dark against his pale cheeks. He was out for the count. Unable to help herself, she let her eyes wander over him—purely professionally, of course, to see how his bruises were progressing.

The water was soapy, but not that soapy. Not so cloudy that she couldn't see every inch of his beautifully made body. Where his chest and knees protruded from the water, wiry curls clung enticingly to the damp, sleek skin, emphasising his maleness.

Not that it needed emphasising, not with the water as clear as it was and none too deep, either. Oh, lord.

She backed away, retreating to safety, and took a long, steadying breath before rapping sharply on the door. 'Will?' she called. 'You all right?'

There was a grunt and a splash, and another oath. His language was taking a battering, she thought with a smile.

'Yes, fine,' he said groggily. 'I'll be out in a minute.'

She hovered, listening to grunts and clonks and the odd cuss, until she heard the creak of a board and a sigh of relief that signalled his safe retreat from the bath.

Heaving a sigh of her own, she retreated with Bruno to the safety of the kitchen, turned on the radio and tried not to think about Will and his delectable naked body while she cleared up after their supper. It didn't work, of course, because she just managed to hit the love-songs happy hour, or that's what it sounded like.

One husky, softly crooned love song after another, all her old favourites, and, of course, she knew the words, so she sang along, misty-eyed and wistful, and for some reason an image of Will kept super-imposing itself on her mental pictures, just to add to the delicious torture.

She wiped down the worktop, humming absently, her mind full of him. He'd looked so—oh, so male, so virile, so incredibly *potent*. A powerful aphrodi-siac. The image was so clear she could have reached out and touched him, felt the smooth silk of his skin, the slight roughness of the hair, the taut, corded mus-cles beneath—

'Oh, hell,' she groaned, throwing the packet of ba-con back into the fridge and trying to put him out of her mind. Not easy. She found herself singing again, the words she knew so well coming naturally to her lips.

Swaying gently to the music, she turned to clear the table, and there he was, standing in the doorway watching her, his face inscrutable.

The song died on her lips. Colour streaming up her cheeks, she turned hastily away, dumping the mugs and plates into the sink and busying herself with the kettle. Lord, she must have looked such a fool! 'Cup of tea?' she suggested briskly, and, stab-bing the 'off' button on the radio she killed the slow, sexy song. In the shocking silence that followed she heard him coming towards her, his bare feet padding softly on the floor.

His voice was deep and husky, right behind her, and made all the little hairs on the nape of her neck stand to attention. 'Please. Could you put this on for me first and take off the plastic bag?'

Reluctantly she turned back to him, avoiding his eyes. Careful not to touch his fingers, she took the support bandage from him and gathered it up to slide it over his left arm. It was still swollen, but less so, the skin discoloured where the bruising had come out. She had an insane urge to kiss it better, and stifled it. She felt enough of an idiot without adding insult to injury.

'How is it?' she asked, easing the support over his fingers and trying still not to touch him.

'Still sore—ouch!'

'Sorry. It would be easier with one of those sleeve things to gather it on.'

'It's fine. Just pull it up. It doesn't hurt that much. I'm just a wimp.'

She gave a soft snort of laughter and eased the bandage into place, smoothing it down with hands that wanted to linger. His arm trembled under her fingertips, and she released it, glad to break the contact that was doing her no good at all.

'Want to do this yourself, or do you want me to do it?' she asked, indicating the shopping bags stuck over the cast to protect it from the water.

'Could you? I tried but I couldn't get the end of the tape.'

'Sure.' She found the end, managed to lift it with her nail and started to peel it off, but he yelped and yanked his arm away.

'Hell, woman! Mind the hairs!' he protested, and she gave him a syrupy smile and took his arm back in an iron grip.

'Now you know how it feels to have your legs

waxed,' she said unsympathetically, and eased off another inch, holding down the hairs with one hand and peeling with the other.

He bore it in grim-lipped silence, and when the bags were off and consigned to the bin, he massaged his sore skin gingerly and gave her a baleful look. 'Next time,' he said clearly, 'we'll use elastic bands.'

She had to turn away to hide the smile. 'How about that cup of tea now?' she said, feeling sorry for him despite herself.

He sighed. 'What I feel like is a damn great Scotch, but I suppose you're going to veto that on medical grounds?'

She arched a brow in surprise. 'Me, with the right of veto? I hardly think so. Since when was I your mother?'

He snorted. 'Doesn't stop you having an opinion on everything else,' he told her bluntly, and she felt a wash of guilty colour sweep her cheeks.

'It's entirely up to you what you do to your body,' she said virtuously. 'Don't hold back on my account.'

'I won't,' he retorted, reaching past her for a glass. He was just lowering it to the worktop when he caught his elbow on the bread crock and the glass slipped from his fingers, shattering on the hard floor.

Bruno rushed forwards to investigate, and as one they turned and yelled, '*No!*' at the poor dog. He stopped in his tracks, and Lucie looked down at Will's bare feet covered in sparkling slivers of glass.

'I should stand right there if I were you,' she told him.

'You don't say,' he murmured drily, and she shot him a look before fetching the dustpan and brush.

She swept carefully around his feet and then went over the whole floor before mopping it to pick up the last tiny shards.

'Right, you can move,' she told him, and with a sigh he sat down at the table and gave a resigned, wry smile.

'I'll settle for tea,' he said, picking a sliver of glass off his foot with his uncooperative right hand. 'God obviously didn't want me to have that Scotch.'

'Apparently not,' Lucie said, returning his smile. She made the tea, put the mugs on the table and they sat together in what could almost have been called companionable silence.

A truce? Wonders will never cease, Lucie thought, but her luck was about to run out. The phone rang, shattering the stillness, and Will answered it.

'For you,' he said, holding out the phone to her.

She took it, puzzled. Who on earth could it be?

'Hello?'

'Lucie? It's me.'

It took her a moment, she was so far away from the reality of London. 'Fergus?' she said, puzzled. 'Hi. How are you?'

Behind her she heard a chair scrape, and Will retreated to the sitting room, the dog following, nails clattering on the bare floor.

The room seemed suddenly empty, and she had to force herself to concentrate on Fergus. He was missing her. He said so, over and over again. He missed her company. He missed her smile. He missed sitting in her flat watching TV. He even missed her temper, he said.

'Do you miss me?' he asked her, and she was shocked to realise that, no, she didn't, not at all. She hadn't given him so much as a passing thought. She made some noncommital reply, and it seemed to satisfy him, probably because his ego was so undentable that he couldn't imagine she wasn't desolate.

'I thought I'd pop down and see you this weekend,' he told her.

'Ah, no. Um. I'm coming to town. I'll see you—I'll ring you from the flat.'

'We'll do lunch.'

'Lovely. I have to go, my tea's getting cold,' she said, and hung up after the briefest of farewells. It was only as she cradled the phone that she realised how cavalier it had sounded.

Poor Fergus. Still, he just wouldn't take the hint.

Her eyes strayed to the sitting-room door, open just a crack. Had Will heard her conversation? And if so, what had he made of it?

And what, in any case, did it matter?

Lucie wasn't sure. She knew one thing, though—it did matter. For some reason that wasn't really clear to her she wanted Will to have a good opinion of her, and it was nothing to do with her professional role and everything to do with a man with a body to die for and the temper of a crotchety rattlesnake.

Oh, dear. She was in big trouble…

CHAPTER FIVE

WILL was annoyed.

Lucie was going back to London for the weekend, and seeing Fergus, whoever the hell Fergus was. It was none of his business, of course, and he kept telling himself that, but it didn't stop it annoying the life out of him all week.

He had a phone call from Pam, to say that Dick had seen the cardiologist and was booked in for angioplasty. The angiogram had shown that he was a suitable candidate, and didn't need the more extensive intervention of open-heart surgery and a bypass operation.

On a professional level Will was pleased for them. On a personal level he was irritated that after all the time he'd spent cajoling Dick, it had been Lucie who'd talked him into taking this final step.

He told himself he was being a child, but she was getting to him. Getting to him in ways he didn't want to think about. Ways that kept him awake at night and then, when he finally slept, coloured his dreams so that even the memory of them made his blood pressure soar.

Crazy, because she drove him mad, but there was just something about her that made him restless and edgy, and made him long for things he couldn't have.

Like her, for instance.

Damn.

He forced himself to concentrate. She was in the

middle of surgery, and he was sitting in, keeping an eye on the time and watching her wheedle and cajole and sympathise and generally make everyone feel better.

Except young Clare Reid, who had come in on Monday with a cough and a disbelieving mother, and was back today with much worse symptoms and a mother who now was berating herself for not listening.

'I knew there was something wrong,' Mrs Reid was saying. 'I can't believe I didn't pay more attention. Whatever is wrong with her?'

Lucie checked through the notes, but the results weren't back. 'I'll check with the lab,' she promised. 'I'll call you back later today, because, I quite agree, it isn't right that she should be feeling so rough.'

Clare coughed again, and Lucie frowned and looked at Will.

'Sounds like whooping cough,' she said thoughtfully, and he frowned. Whooping cough? Although she could have a point...

'Let me ring the lab. If you two could wait outside while Dr Compton sees her next patient, I'll see what I can find out for you, and then we can have you back in and let you know if there's anything to report, OK?'

They nodded, and he went through to another room to make the call.

'Oh, yes, we were just sending that out to you. It's not whooping cough, but it's a related virus. Unfortunately it's not proved susceptible to any of the antivirals. Sorry. Oh, and by the way, it's not notifiable.'

He thanked them and went back to Lucie, and after

she'd finished with her patient, he told her the result.

'So what can we do for her? An anti-viral?'

He shook his head. 'Apparently not. Anyway, I should imagine she's past the acute stage of the illness. Any treatment now will be palliative. I would send her to a good pharmacist for advice on cough remedies, and tell her to sit in a hot, steamy bath and hang wet towels on her radiator at night and sniff Olbas oil.'

'Gorgeous. I wonder if she was still infectious on Monday?' Lucie said drily, and he grinned despite himself.

'Maybe. If so, knowing how my luck's running at the moment, I'll get it. All I need now is a good dose of mumps or chickenpox and my happiness will be complete.'

Lucie chuckled, and he looked at her and thought how incredibly sexy she was with that wide smile and her eyes crinkling with humour. It was just such a hell of a shame they weren't like this with each other all the time, but they weren't. For some reason he couldn't fathom, they seemed to rub each other up the wrong way the entire time.

He stifled a sigh. Probably just as well, really. He didn't need any more complications in his life, particularly not complications that he had to work with, and, like it or not, he and Lucie were stuck with each other for almost six more months.

And, he reminded himself, she was about to go back to London for the weekend to Fergus. Good. He'd have the house to himself again.

Bliss.

* * *

The flat seemed incredibly noisy. Lucie packed up the remainder of her things, and put what she didn't want with her into a cupboard in her room.

Her flatmate's partner was moving in—well, had moved in, more or less, some time ago, and was officially taking over her portion of the rent now, which was a relief. It also meant she could come back and stay for a while until she found another place, and she'd have a bolt-hole if necessary.

And it might well be necessary if Will Ryan was as grumpy for the next six months as he'd been for the last week. She sighed and threw the last few things into a case, clipped it shut and stood it by the wall. She didn't want to put it in her car until she left. Security wasn't London's strong point, and there was no point tempting fate.

She rang Fergus to arrange to meet for lunch, and he was round within minutes. Not quite what she'd had in mind, but he'd insisted on escorting her to their venue.

He spoiled her. He was rich enough to do it, but still, he spoiled her and took her to one of those exclusive places where you had to book weeks in advance. A man of power and influence, she thought with humour, but it didn't influence her at all. All the pomp and ceremony and discreet yet ostentatious service just got on her nerves, and she found herself thinking of eating bacon sandwiches in the kitchen with Will.

Not a good start to their lunch. Lucie forced herself to concentrate on Fergus, and realised that he was talking about himself as usual.

Finally, as they pushed aside the remains of their dark chocolate baskets with summer fruits in Kirch, topped with a delicate trail of cream and chocolate sauce in a puddle of raspberry coulis garnished with a sprig of mint, Fergus asked about her.

'So, how's life in the boonies?' he said, sitting back with an indulgent smile. 'I've missed you, you know.'

'You said—and it's fine,' she lied. 'There's a horse that grazes outside my bedroom window, and a dog called Bruno and a cat called Minnie—and my trainer's fallen off a ladder and broken his arm, so at the moment I'm helping him out a bit in the evenings and doing all the driving to work and back.'

'Poor old boy,' Fergus said kindly, and Lucie thought of Will, dark and irritable and pacing round like a wounded grizzly, and stifled a smile. Poor old boy? Not in this lifetime! Still, she didn't bother to correct Fergus. If he realised that Will was only thirty-three, he'd be down there like a shot, getting possessive and territorial, and Lucie would be forced to kill him.

And that would stuff up her Hippocratic oath and probably interfere more than a little with the progress of her career.

Oh, well. She'd have to keep them apart, which was no hardship. She couldn't see Fergus on Will's farm, picking his way through the puddles and pushing the dog aside when he was muddy and bouncy and over-enthusiastic—and for some reason she didn't care to analyse, she didn't want Fergus there anyway.

'So, how are the patients? Do they all chew straw and say, "Ooh, aa-rr"?' Fergus asked her with a patronising smile.

She thought of Pam and Dick, lovely people—

people she'd been able to help by her presence there. 'Only half of them. The others are mostly inarticulate.'

He laughed as if she'd told the funniest joke in the world, and she sighed. She really couldn't be bothered with this.

'Fergus, it's been a lovely lunch,' she began, but he wasn't one to pick up subtle hints.

'And it's not over,' he announced proudly. 'I thought we could go back to my flat for coffee, and then I thought we could take a stroll through St James's Park, and then tonight I thought we could take in a show—there's that new one that's just opened with rave reviews. I'm sure I can get tickets.'

She was sure he could, too, but she wasn't interested.

'Fergus, I don't really have time,' she told him. 'I have to get back to Suffolk tonight—I'm on duty tomorrow.'

She waited for the lightning bolt to strike her down, but it didn't come. It should. She was starting to tell so many lies. She ought to just say, Look, Fergus, you're a nice man but not for me.

Actually, she had said it! She'd said it over and over again. Most recently last weekend, just before she'd left for Suffolk.

Blast.

'Perhaps next weekend,' he coaxed, and she sighed.

'I can't.'

'Then I'll come to you. I'll fit in round you. I'll buy some wellies and take a stroll while you're busy, and we can find a restaurant and eat out in the evening. I assume they do *have* restaurants?'

'I'm sure we can find a fish-and-chip shop,' she said drily, and he recoiled. Oh, lord, how had she ever let him talk her into this?

She realised with a sense of shock that she was feeling defensive about his attitude—an attitude she'd shared until this last week. How strange.

'I really have to go—I've still got a lot of clearing up to do at the flat before I leave,' she told him, adding another lie to the heap that teetered on the funeral pyre of her conscience.

'Wait for me. I'll pay the bill and take you back.'

'No, don't,' she said, hastily pushing him back into his chair. 'You stay and have coffee, and I'll get on. I've got some shopping to do on the way back.'

She stooped and kissed his cheek, thanked him again and made her escape into the fresh air, or what passed for it in London. She inhaled deeply. It was familiar and comforting, but somehow strange.

She went back to her flat, made coffee and waited till she thought she'd given her glass of wine time to clear her system, then left a note for her flatmate, threw her stuff into the car and headed back to Suffolk and Will.

The house seemed empty. At first Will revelled in the silence, listening to the songs of the birds and the gentle snort of Henry outside the window. Then, after he'd struggled to wash and dress, he went down to the kitchen and looked around for something easy to eat.

Cereal, he thought, and sat at the table with nothing to break the silence but the crunching of corn-flakes and the sigh of the dog. No Lucie humming as she pottered, or chattering brightly about nothing in particular.

It was good, he told himself, but a sliver of loneliness sneaked in and made him restless. He went over to the cottage and let himself in, opening the windows and letting the air circulate. He'd had the old bed and carpet collected and taken away during the week, but the room still smelled musty, and today a man was coming to paint the ceiling.

His incapacity infuriated him. He was perfectly capable of doing all the things he'd just had to pay good money to have done, and much worse than that was having to rely on Lucie for his transport.

He went into the sitting room and looked around. She'd brought some of her things in here last weekend and stacked them in an untidy heap on one side, and he had a burning urge to know what she considered essential. A jumper spilled out of a carrier bag, a belt hung out of the side of a suitcase. And there, in a bag at the back, was a dog-eared teddy bear.

He found himself smiling, and frowned. It wasn't funny. She was hopelessly disorganised, and he had to turn her into a GP. What chance was there? She had to be highly ordered and disciplined to work in a modern practice with all the rules and regulations that applied.

Her cheerful disregard for convention might be all very well in a musician or an artist, but in a doctor it was a recipe for disaster.

Still frowning, he went back to the bedroom and sniffed. Not too bad. The clouds looked a bit threatening, so he closed the windows again, except for the little fanlight, and crossed the yard to his house. Amanda drew up just before he gained the safety of

the back door, and bounded out of the car, waving
cheerfully.

'Hi! How are you?' she asked, bearing down on
him.

He sighed inwardly. 'Better, thanks. My left
hand's almost back to normal,' he told her, waggling
it rather further than it wanted to go and smiling to
cover the wince. 'See? All but fixed.'

'Anything I can do? Shopping, cooking—washing?'

He thought of his back in the bath and nearly
choked. 'No, no, it's fine,' he said hastily. 'I've got
everything I need, and Lucie did my washing before
she went away.'

Amanda's face brightened. 'She's gone?'

'Only for the weekend,' he corrected quickly. 'Just
to sort out her flat.'

Her face fell again. 'Oh, well. If there's anything
I can do, just holler.'

'I will. Thanks.' He retreated inside, closing the
door with indecent haste, and sank down at the
kitchen table. 'She's getting worse, Bruno,' he told
the dog in an undertone. 'What are we going to do?'

Bruno wagged his tail, looking hopeful. 'Come on,
then,' he said, relenting, and with a lot of wiggling
and shoving and swearing he managed to get his
boots on. They headed off down the track to the
woods, turned left and followed the little path down
through the edge of the wood amongst the bluebells.

It was beautiful, peaceful and still and restoring.
He felt the tranquillity easing back into him, and,
tucking his right hand into the pocket of his jacket,
he strolled along, breathing in the cool, fresh air and
listening to the sounds of the countryside while

Bruno fossicked in the undergrowth and chased interesting smells and the odd rabbit.

They reached the edge of the river and he sat down on a stone, ignoring the creeping damp and absorbing the glorious views. The sun was high now, and its warmth caressed his face and seeped through his jacket, driving out the chill.

Bliss. What more could a man possibly want?

Someone to share it with?

'Bruno!' he called, standing abruptly and heading back. He had someone to share it with—someone loyal and devoted and emotionally undemanding.

Well, perhaps not loyal. The mutt had spent the week on Lucie's bed, proving his fickle nature. Just because she was feeding him whole suppers, of course. He'd be her friend for life because of that.

He wondered what Lucie was doing now and who'd slept with her last night.

Fergus?

A writhing knot of something that surely wasn't jealousy wrapped itself around his gut and squeezed. Ridiculous. It was entirely her own business who she slept with!

He went back to the house, hooked his boots off and stomped upstairs. He really ought to be getting on with this room, he thought, and opened the door.

Frustration hit him like a fist in the chest. It would be weeks—months, probably—before he could get back to work in here.

Slamming the door, he went back downstairs and over to the cottage. Pete had arrived and set up his dustsheets, and was priming the ceiling so the damp mark didn't bleed through the new paint.

'Come and have a coffee while that dries,' he suggested, and Pete nodded.

'Will do, mate. Give us a few more minutes.'

'OK.'

Will went back to the kitchen and stared morosely at the washing-up in the sink. Lucie had bought him some huge rubber gloves that he could just about get on over the cast and support bandage, but putting them on was an act that required more patience than he would find in his lifetime, and he gave up. The washing up could wait. She'd be back tomorrow.

Late, probably, and overtired from her activities with Fergus.

'Fergus.' He spat the name, realising he was beginning to hate the man without any justification. Irrational, stupid behavior, he told himself, but the thought of someone—anyone—touching Lucie intimately made him want to kill.

Which was totally ridiculous, because there was no way he wanted her.

Was there?

It had been a lovely day, Lucie realised in surprise. Odd, how insulated from the weather she'd been in London. Much less aware.

Now, driving back down the once-unnerving track towards the house, she wound down the window and breathed in deeply. Something was flowering, and the heady scent wafted through the window. It was gorgeous. Humming to herself, she turned into the farmyard and saw a man in white overalls sitting on the steps by the back door, drinking tea.

Not Will. Her eyes scanned the yard, irrationally disappointed to find him missing, and then he came out of the back door armed with a biscuit tin, and she felt an involuntary smile curve the corners of her mouth.

He lifted one hand in a wave, and she pulled up outside the cottage and got out, strolling over. No London strut, no rush, no hurry, just an amble in the evening sun.

'Hi.'

'You're back early,' Will said, sounding almost accusing. 'I wasn't expecting you till tomorrow.'

Damn. He'd probably planned a quiet evening with a woman, she thought, and felt a soft tide of colour invade her cheeks. 'I'll keep out of the way,' she promised. 'If that's all right. Clearing up the flat didn't take as long as I thought.'

And for some reason she couldn't get away from Fergus quick enough.

'It's fine,' Will said shortly, leaving her with the distinct impression that it was far from fine and it was only good manners that prevented him from telling her where to go.

'Is it all right to put my things straight into the cottage?' she asked, and the man in the white overalls tipped back his baseball cap with one finger and shot her a searching look.

'Mind the bedroom—ceiling's wet and the air might be a bit damp for an hour or two.'

'I'll use the sitting room,' she promised, and since there was no offer of a cup of tea forthcoming, she took herself off and unloaded her car while they sat on the steps and watched her struggle.

Not that Will could do anything, but he could at least have put the kettle on, she thought.

And to think she'd been looking forward to coming back!

By Monday morning Lucie was ready to kill Will. He'd been remote and surly all weekend, and she'd got the distinct impression he was cross with her—but why? He'd said—so firmly that she'd dropped the subject like a hot brick—that she wasn't interfering with his plans.

Perhaps he was just in pain. He'd probably decided he didn't need pills any more, and she was the one to catch the flak. Well, damn him.

By the time they were ready for work he was as crotchety as a bear with a sore head, and when he went outside and sat firmly in the passenger seat of the Volvo, she couldn't be bothered to argue. She got the distinct impression he was spoiling for a fight, and she was damned if she was going to give him one!

Instead she smiled meekly, slid behind the wheel and drove up the track as if she were carrying a nuclear warhead in the back. He shot her a suspicious look, folded his arms across his chest and winced as he bent his left wrist.

Out of the corner of her eye she saw him shuffling his arms uncomfortably, and had to suppress her sympathy. He was being crabby and ungracious, and she had no intention of feeling sorry for him!

Her surgery got off to a flying start with the return of Mr Gregory, her overweight patient who was trying to lose weight and was suffering from indigestion. His pain was worse, and Lucie decided to take the bull by the horns.

'Have you had an ECG recently?' she asked, taking his blood pressure.

'No. Can't say I've ever had one,' he told her.

'Right. Just to eliminate it from our enquiries, then, I'd like you to see the nurse and have an ECG done, and we'll also get her to take some bloods to test for *Helicobacter pylori*.'

'Is that the gastric ulcer bug? A friend of mine had that not so long ago.'

'Really?' Lucie said, thoughtful. 'Is it possible you picked it up in the same place?'

'Maybe. We teach in the same school, and we went on a school trip together. The food was pretty rough.'

'I think it's hygiene rather than quality that matters, but it's possible it came from there. It can give painful symptoms. And while we wait for the results of that we can give you a drug to suppress the symptoms so you don't feel so bad. OK? So if you go and see the nurse, she can get it all under way, and I'll give you a prescription now for the thing to reduce your stomach acid. You should be much more comfortable.'

'So you don't think it's my heart, then?'

She shook her head. 'No, I don't, but I have to be sure. I can't just hope, I have to know, and so do you.'

He stood up. 'Thanks, Doc. When do I see you again?'

She looked at Will. 'How soon do the results come back?'

'Leave it a week,' he advised. 'They should be back then.'

'Next Monday, then,' Lucie suggested, and Mr Gregory nodded.

'Will do. Thanks again.'

She waited, after the door closed, for Will to comment, but he didn't. To her surprise, when she turned round he was slowly writing a comment on a piece of paper. Later, then, she thought, and sighed. Oh, well.

The carpet was down, the bed was in and Lucie was moving out.

Will gave her the bedding out of the little airing cupboard in the cottage, and watched her make the bed. It was a mistake. She ran a slender, capable hand over the sheet, smoothing it flat, and he imagined feeling its texture on his skin.

She plumped the pillows, dropped them in place, straightened and smiled at him, and he felt the heat balloon inside him.

'I'd help you with the quilt but I'm not sure I can be much use,' he said gruffly, and she shrugged and smiled again.

'It's not a problem. I can cope. Shall we christen the kettle?'

And he realised that he would get his kitchen back to himself now. No more cosy chats over tea, no more bickering over the menu or skiving off the washing-up.

No more radio. That was a plus.

No more Lucie singing along to it with that slightly husky voice. That had to be a plus—didn't it?

He went and put the kettle on, as much to distance himself from Lucie and the bed as anything. There wasn't any milk, and there were no teabags or coffee granules, so he went over to his house and brought a selection of bits and pieces to start her off.

By the time the kettle boiled, she was in the kitchen looking hopeful, and he took two mugs down awkwardly with his left hand and looked at her.

'Tea or coffee?'

'Is there a choice?'

'I've even brought you over some hot chocolate.'

Her smile seemed to light up the room, and it touched his heart. 'Oh, thanks. I ought to go shopping. I could do that now, actually, when we've had our tea. You could probably do with some stocking up, as well, couldn't you?'

'Probably. So did you want tea, or was that a figure of speech?'

'Tea. I'll make it, you sit down.'

So he sank gratefully into one of the comfy armchairs and waited, and a moment later she came round the corner from the kitchen area with two mugs and curled herself up in the other chair opposite him, her feet tucked up under her bottom and her nose buried in the mug.

It was so ridiculously homely and cosy that he nearly laughed, but it would have been a cynical, bitter laugh and she didn't deserve it. He wasn't sure why he felt like that, anyway. Frustration? Probably.

And now he was going to have to endure the joys of the supermarket with her. Wonderful. He scowled into his tea.

'Is it all right?' Lucie asked, and he looked up.

'What?'

'The tea. Is it all right? You gave it such a look.'

He laughed self-consciously. 'It's fine. Sorry. I was thinking about something else.'

'Lord, I hope it wasn't me,' she said with her husky chuckle.

'No,' he denied, and realised it was probably true. It wasn't so much Lucie as what she represented that was making him edgy and restless. He drank the tea too hot, and unfolded himself from the chair.

'I'll get ready for the supermarket.'

'Oh, you don't have to go!' she exclaimed. 'You look tired. Why don't you give me a list and stay here and have a rest? I'll get your shopping. You can owe me.'

And then, perversely, he felt disappointed.

Lucie screwed up her eyebrows and peered at his list. What on earth did that say? She should have asked him to translate. She had the distinct feeling that his writing was awful when he had a functioning arm. Now it was atrocious.

Liver? She shuddered gently, but it was on his list. OK, liver, then. She looked in the chiller cabinet, fished out what looked as if it might be the right sort and volume, and dropped it in the trolley. Gross.

She moved on, shaking her head over his list on several more occasions, and finally she reached the end. Oh, well, what she didn't have she—or he—could manage without for another day or two. She was tired, and she wanted to get settled into the cottage.

She was looking forward to being herself, to relaxing and not having to worry about disturbing Will, or doing any of the thousands of things that seemed to make him scowl.

*   *   *

'Liver?'

'It was on your list.'

'Was it, hell. Show me.'

She pulled the list out of her pocket and thrust it under his nose. 'See? Liver.'

'Limes,' he corrected with a short sigh. 'It says limes.'

She looked at him as if he'd grown two heads. 'Limes? Why on earth would you want limes?'

'To squeeze over grilled chicken breasts, with salad. I just fancied some. I *hate* liver.'

A smile lit up her face. 'Hey, we agree on something,' she said cheerfully. 'Never mind, I'm sure Bruno likes liver.'

Will gave the dog a disgusted look. 'I'm sure he does. Are you certain you two aren't in league?'

She took out the rest of his shopping while he watched and commented, and then handed him the bill. 'Charge the dog for the liver,' she advised, and then headed for the door. 'I'm just going to put my shopping away, and I'll be back for my overnight things.'

He nodded and watched her go, and then found himself standing at the window, watching her across the yard. The curtains in the cottage were open, and he could see her moving around, putting her shopping away in the cupboards and the fridge.

Liver, he thought disgustedly, and caught the dog's eye. 'Definitely in cahoots,' he growled, and Bruno wagged his tail cheerfully.

'You're going to have to sleep with me tonight, sport, and don't get any ideas about lying on the bed, either. She's spoiled you.'

The dog woofed softly, and Will relented and

scratched his ears. 'You're a good boy, really,' he murmured, and the dog collapsed on the floor at his feet, quite content. He went back to watching Lucie, and a few moments later he saw her crossing the yard.

She came in with a smile, and ran upstairs, returning a few minutes later with an armful of clothes and her washbag. 'I can get the rest tomorrow. I want to unpack some things tonight.'

He nodded, and then there was an awkward pause.

'Thank you for putting up with me until the cottage was done,' she said softly, and he felt churlish for his resentment.

'It's been a pleasure,' he said, and she laughed.

'Liar.'

He looked down at his hands. 'No, really. You've been very kind while I've been out of action. You've done all sorts of things for me. I'm sorry I haven't been more grateful. I just—I'm usually pretty self-sufficient and it comes a bit hard having to rely on someone else.'

He looked up again, and their eyes locked. 'I'll help you over there—you've got your hands rather full to open the doors.'

'Oh—thanks.'

At the door of the cottage he paused, curiously unwilling to go in. 'I'll leave you to it,' he said gruffly, and she went up on tiptoe and kissed his cheek.

'Thanks,' she murmured.

'Any time,' he said, and then something shifted, tilting the world on its axis. For a moment neither of them moved, and then as if in slow motion he lowered his head and kissed her lips.

For a second they both froze, and then she melted, her mouth soft and yielding, and he could taste her. Heat shot through him, shocking him, and he drew away.

'Goodnight, Lucie,' he said, his voice husky with the desire that was ripping through him, and he backed away, turning on his heel and striding away from her, towards his house and sanity.

He didn't look back.

CHAPTER SIX

LUCIE watched Will go, striding away from her as if she might give him some terrible disease. And yet his kiss had been so tender, so gentle and coaxing—so unlike him.

At first. Then it had taken off, and she'd wanted to hold him, but her arms had still been clutching the clothes in front of her, so that the only point of contact had been their fevered mouths.

The heat had threatened to consume her, but it had been over in seconds, so brief that now she could hardly believe it had happened, and Will had pulled away, his face stunned.

That he hadn't meant the kiss to happen was obvious. What was less obvious to Lucie was why it had been such a beautiful and tender kiss. A cherishing kiss. A needy kiss. Lord, so needy...

Lucie swallowed hard, turned and pushed the door shut behind her, heading for the bedroom. The clothes had to be hung up, her wash things put away in the bathroom, and she could do with sorting out some of her other clothes that had been in a suitcase all week.

Nevertheless, she sank down on the edge of the newly made bed, the clothes still in her arms, and relived the touch of Will's mouth on hers. She could still feel the imprint of his lips, the soft velvet texture so at odds with the slight rasp of his chin.

He'd angled his mouth over hers, taking advantage

of her willing response to deepen the kiss, and it had
grown a little wild then, suddenly. Until he'd pulled
away.

Perhaps it was just as well she'd moved out of the
house and wasn't going to be exposed to him
crossing the landing to the bathroom in nothing more
than a pair of jogging bottoms hanging loosely on
his hips!

Too much sex appeal for comfort, Lucie thought,
and for some reason she had an image of Fergus—
bland, mild-mannered, successful and totally without
that edge that made Will so very tempting. Fergus
was safe—and Lucie realised with some astonishment that she didn't want to be safe. She was sick
of being safe. She'd been safe too long, and now she
wanted more.

She wanted Will.

It was equally clear to her, however, that Will
didn't want her—or, rather, that he didn't *want* to
want her. Because he did want her, that much she
was utterly sure of.

A thread of excitement wove itself along her veins,
and she stood up, humming softly to herself, and put
her clothes away, then started on her boxes. She pottered for ages, quietly working through the strange
collection of things she'd acquired over the years,
and thinking of Will.

Finally the room was clear and she could find a
chair to sit in, so she made a hot drink and curled
up in the chair with the TV on and watched the late
news. She could see Will's house through the window, and after a while she heard him calling Bruno,
then the kitchen light went off and a few moments
later the bedroom light went on.

She wondered how he was coping, and if there was anything he couldn't manage to do for himself. She should have offered to help him still, but she'd got the distinct impression he'd wanted her out as quickly as possible.

No wonder, if all that heat was steaming gently under his collar the entire time! She turned off the television and got ready for bed, enjoying the privacy of a house of her own for the very first time.

Well, sort of enjoying it. It seemed terribly quiet, with not even so much as a passing car to break the silence, and every creak seemed curiously sinister. She wondered what Will was thinking, and if he, too, was remembering their kiss.

She climbed into bed and picked up her diary off the bedside table. She had more than a week's worth to write up, and with all that had happened she was going to be up all night doing it. What on earth had possessed her to pack it?

She wrote furiously, and finally arrived at today's entry. She wrote, 'He kissed me. Don't think he meant to. Don't think he means to do it again—we'll have to see about that! I have a feeling he needs rescuing from himself. It can be my next challenge—RESCUING DR RYAN.'

With a smile on her lips, she put the diary down, turned out the light and snuggled under the quilt, falling asleep almost instantly.

Will had hardly slept a wink. Bruno had insisted on lying across his feet, so he'd woken with two more compromised limbs and a deep and abiding hatred of things canine.

He washed and dressed with difficulty, fed the dog

and cat and pulled on a coat, shoving his feet into his boots. 'Come on, pest,' he said to Bruno, who was still fruitlessly chasing his empty bowl around the floor. 'Let's go and see the river—*if* I can walk that far.'

Bruno, blissfully unaware of his master's sarcasm, shot out of the back door and ran over to the cottage, then sat whining by the door. Will sighed.

'Get in the queue,' he muttered, and turned towards the track. 'Come on, dog. We don't have women in our lives—remember?'

After a last, lingering look at the door, Bruno turned and trotted obediently at his side all the way down to the river and back, cheerfully retrieving dead goodness-knows-whats and presenting them to Will. And gradually the dawning of a beautiful day drove out the blues and restored the peace in his soul, and he wandered back to the house with Bruno in tow. The dog had brought home a souvenir, a festering bit of rabbit leg dangling from his jaws, and he offered it to Will with a grin.

'You're revolting,' he said disparagingly, just as they turned the corner and found Lucie poised at the back door of his house. She looked at the dog and her eyes widened.

'Yuck, Bruno, that's foul! You horrid dog!'

'He's just being a dog. They are foul. Have you got a problem with the cottage?'

She shook her head. 'No. I just thought I ought to pop over and see if there was anything you needed help with—you know, with your arms and everything.'

A genuine offer? Or any feeble excuse to interfere in his life?

How could he tell? He couldn't, so he played safe.

'I'm fine,' he said, possibly a bit shortly, and after a second's startled hesitation she ran down the steps to the yard and gave him a fleeting little smile.

'That's OK, then. Shout if you need anything. I'll be ready to go in twenty minutes.'

And she was gone, all but running round the corner and leaving him nursing a massive guilt trip and a whole truckload of resentment as a result.

Hell. Life had been much simpler before he'd met her!

The rest of the week passed. That was all Lucie could say. The days were sometimes easy, sometimes difficult. The evenings were long and lonely, and the nights—she didn't want to think about the nights. Suffice it to say Will featured extensively in her dreams, and she began to wonder if she'd bitten off more than she could chew with her challenge to rescue him. Certainly she didn't seem to be making any progress.

Nor did her first patient on Friday morning. Mr Gregory's stomach was still proving a problem, pending the result of his blood test, but at least the ECG had proved normal, as she'd expected.

'I think I ought to start him on the treatment,' Lucie said to Will thoughtfully, just before Mr Gregory came in. 'If he's back because it's worse, I have to do something.'

'The treatment's very expensive, and might mask other symptoms,' he warned.

'So what would you do?'

He leant back in his chair, steepled his fingers and pressed them against his lips, peering at her thoughtfully. 'I don't know. Encourage him to wait and give the palliative treatment which was all we had until a short while ago.'

'I've done that. He's coming back. There must be a reason.'

Will shrugged. 'Reassure him. I think he's worried. We'll see.'

Will was right, of course. He was just worried and wanted reassurance that it wasn't, in fact, his heart. Finally satisfied that he was in no danger, Mr Gregory left, and Lucie finished her surgery without any further complications. She was just about to leave on her calls when the receptionist took a call from an anxious mother whose seventeen-year-old daughter was vomiting and looking very peaky.

'We'll call in—we have to go that way,' Will told the receptionist. 'I doubt if it's anything urgent—probably a hangover.'

'Sceptic,' Lucie said with a chuckle, and his mouth cracked into a fleeting smile.

'Absolutely. That's the modern youth for you. No restraint and no stamina.'

Lucie shook her head, stifling the smile. 'Such a sweeping generalisation. I bet you were really wild at university.'

A wry grin tilted his lips. 'I had my moments, I confess—although nothing like they get up to these days.'

'Ah, poor old man,' she teased, and he snorted.

'Can we get on, please? We've got another call to fit in now and, hangover or not, it'll take time.' He scooped up the notes in his right hand, and Lucie noticed that it seemed to be co-operating fairly well.

He'd been using it much more in the last few days, and it was obviously less painful.

Not good enough, though, that he could drive yet, and she could tell that was frustrating him. Will went out to the car park, went round to the driver's side, swore colourfully under his breath and went round to the passenger side instead.

'When can you drive?' she asked him, and he glowered at her over the roof of the car.

'Not until the cast is off. I always advise my patients not to drive until they've had the cast off and their arms are functioning normally without undue pain. It's for insurance reasons, really.'

'So I suppose you ought to take your own advice.'

He snorted. 'Very probably.'

'Mmm,' she agreed, sucking in her cheeks and ducking behind the wheel before he could see the smile that was sure to show in her eyes.

He appeared beside her, shooting her an unreadable look. 'In the meantime,' he continued, 'you're stuck with me, and vice versa, so we might as well both make the best of it.'

He then proceeded to spend the entire journey telling her she was in the wrong lane or had missed a turning.

'For God's sake, didn't you see that cyclist?' he yelled as they neared their destination, and she glowered at him and turned on the radio. Anything was preferable to listening to him ranting!

'Do we have to have that on?'

She pulled over, switched off the engine and turned to face him. 'Will, I am an adult,' she said with exaggerated patience. 'I have a current, valid, clean driving licence. I do not need you giving me a hard time just because you want to be able to drive and can't! I've been driving for ten years and I've never had an accident or been pulled up by the police.'

'That's a miracle!'

'And I don't need you telling me how to do everything all the time!' she finished. 'Now, either we're going to do this in my car, or you're going to shut up, because frankly I've had enough!'

He turned away, letting out a short, harsh sigh and glaring hard enough to melt the glass. 'I'm sorry,' he said gruffly, and she nearly choked. An apology? From Will?

'Thank you,' she replied, struggling for a humble tone. 'Now, where do you want me to go from here—apart from hell?'

He turned and met her eyes, and gave a rueful grin. 'It's not personal,' he confessed. 'I just can't delegate—and I hate being driven. The only accident I've ever been in, someone else was driving. I find it hard not being in control.'

'That's because you're a control freak,' Lucie told him drily. 'If it's any help, I passed first time and I've taken my advanced driving test as well.'

'And passed?' he asked her, picking up on her careful phrasing.

She grinned. 'Not exactly—but I didn't fail drastically.'

He gave a soft snort and shook his head, but the tension was gone, and at least the atmosphere in the car was restored.

'So, where to, boss?' she asked again, and he directed her, and for the rest of the journey he kept his mouth firmly shut.

They arrived at the house of the girl with the 'hangover', and her mother opened the door.

'Mrs Webb? I'm Dr Lucie Compton, and I'm covering for Dr Ryan at the moment. I've come to see Harriet.'

'Oh, I am glad you're here. She's looking awful. Come on up.' She led them to a bedroom where a thin, pale girl lay under a quilt, looking extremely unwell. Her skin was waxy, her eyes were sunken and she looked exhausted. It was certainly more than a simple hangover.

'This is Harriet,' her mother said. 'Harriet, darling, it's the doctor.'

Lucie smiled at her gently and crouched down beside the bed. 'Hello, I'm Lucie Compton, and this is Dr Ryan,' she told the girl. 'I'm covering his patients at the moment. Can you tell me how you're feeling?'

'Sick,' Harriet said weakly. 'So sick. I never feel very hungry, but just now I feel really ill if I eat.'

'Are you being sick?' Lucie asked her.

She nodded. 'A bit. Not enough. I feel I want to do more, but all I can do is retch.'

'Any diarrhoea, or constipation? Any other tummy problems?'

Harriet shook her head. 'Not really.'

'Mind if I have a look at your tummy?' Lucie asked, and at a nod from Harriet she peeled back the quilt.

In contrast to her thin face and arms, her abdomen seemed bloated, and Lucie lifted her nightshirt out of the way and examined the skin. There was no sign of abnormal colouration, no hot spots or rashes, but there was a definite mass in the midline, consistent with an aortic aneurysm or an intestinal obstruction.

'Are you bringing up any blood?' Lucie asked, feeling round the margins of the mass.

'A little—sort of streaks of it.'

'Red, or brown?'

'Oh—I don't know. Maybe both. Brown gritty bits sometimes.'

Lucie shot a look over her shoulder at Will. 'How good are your hands? I'd like a second opinion.'

'I'm sure I can manage,' he murmured, and, bending over Harriet, he worked his way over the mass, his fingers probing gently. A fleeting frown crossed his brow, and he quirked an eyebrow at Lucie.

'It feels like a mass in the stomach,' he said, confirming her fears, and Lucie nodded.

She scanned Harriet's hair, and, yes, it seemed thin and wispy.

'Harriet, have you ever eaten your hair?' she asked gently.

'Oh, no!' her mother said. 'She used to, when she was tiny, so she always had it short. Right up until two years ago, but we thought she'd outgrown it.'

'I have!' Harriet protested feebly. 'I don't do it any more, I swear!'

'You might be doing it in your sleep,' Will suggested. 'It happens, especially during times of stress, and I imagine you're doing the first year of your A-levels?'

Harriet nodded. 'Yes—and I have been worried. Do you think I've got a hairball or something?'

'Very possibly,' Lucie confirmed. 'I think you need to go to hospital for investigation, and if we're right, you'll have to have it removed. They'll know the best way of doing it. I'll contact the hospital now and get you admitted. Is that all right, Mrs Webb?'

Mrs Webb was sitting down on the end of the bed, looking shocked. 'A hairball?'

'The correct term is a trichobezoar,' Will explained. 'It's very rare, but the fact that she used to eat her hair points to it being highly likely in the light of her other symptoms. We do need to get it checked out as a matter of urgency, though.'

'So should I take her in now?'

Will shook his head. 'I would suggest we call an ambulance and admit her direct to the surgical team on take, and they can decide what they want to do. If you take her in yourself, you'll have to queue through Accident and Emergency, which isn't a good idea with Harriet feeling so unwell.'

'Mum,' Harriet said feebly, and Mrs Webb moved up the bed and put her arms round her distressed daughter.

'It's all right, darling. It'll be all right.'

'I thought I'd stopped!' she wept, and then started to retch again.

Will looked at Lucie. 'I think we need to mobilise the ambulance,' he said in an undertone. 'She's very weak, and I don't like the feel of that mass. It's utterly rigid and very large. I think her stomach's within an inch of rupture.'

'Me, too. Can I leave it to you to talk to them? You know who to refer to.'

He nodded. 'Mrs Webb, may I use your phone, please?' he asked, and she looked up.

'Oh. Yes, of course. There's one in the front bedroom, by the bed.'

He went out, and Lucie stayed with them, telling them more about the tests that might be performed and getting a little more history. She made some

notes for the receiving surgical team, and by the time
the ambulance arrived Harriet's bag was packed and
Mrs Webb had contacted her husband and explained
what was going on.

They all left together, Harriet and her mother in
the ambulance, Lucie and Will to their next case, and
as soon as they were out of earshot Lucie let out her
breath in a rush.

'Wow. I've never seen anything like it,' she confessed.

'Nor have I. It's very rare, but there was a tragic
case not all that long ago. I think it's all part and
parcel of the pressure we put kids under. Look at
Clare Reid, worrying because her father will be cross
if she's sick and doesn't do well in her end-of-year
exams. But this, I have to say, is much more serious.
I wonder if she's got psychiatric history. Let me look
in the notes.'

He fumbled through them as Lucie drove, checking through the early correspondence, and then
stabbed the paper with a triumphant finger. 'Yup.
Here it is. Trichotillomania—hair pulling and eating.
Age five. Psychiatric referral, discharged six months
later—presumably after she was ''cured'' with a
haircut. Poor kid.'

'Do you think she'll make it?' Lucie asked, dwell-
ing on the terrified mother's face. She, too, had probably seen the news a couple of years ago about the
teenager who had died with the condition. It must
have struck fear into her heart, and rightly so, given
her daughter's history.

'I hope so,' Will said heavily. 'She looks pretty
grim, though, and she's obviously lost quite a bit of
blood over recent weeks. She's as white as a sheet.

Still, hopefully we were called in time and they'll be able to do something if the inside of her stomach isn't too raw and vulnerable to haemorrhage.'

If.

Their next few calls were much more routine—a case of tonsillitis which could easily have been brought to the surgery, a fall in an elderly lady which had resulted in stiffness and soreness, not surprisingly, a baby with diarrhoea and vomiting who was getting dehydrated but had actually started keeping some boiled water down by the time they arrived. Lucie gave the mother some sachets of electrolyte replacement, and instructions that if the baby didn't pick up by four, they were to be called out again and the baby might have to be admitted to hospital for rehydration.

Then they went back, dealt with the correspondence and notes from the week, had a meeting about practice policy on drug offenders and then while Lucie did the evening surgery, Will called the hospital about Harriet Webb.

He popped his head round the door between patients. 'Harriet's all right—they've removed a massive hairball but they think her stomach will heal. Amazingly it didn't look too bad. She's had a blood transfusion and she's holding well.'

Lucie felt her shoulders drop a few inches, and laughed. 'Excellent. I really wasn't sure she'd make it.'

'Nor was I. How many more have you got?'

'Three—I won't be long.'

'Take your time. I'll have a cup of tea—do you want one?'

'I'll wait,' she said with a shake of her head. 'I'd rather get home.'

He nodded and left her to it, and half an hour later they were on their way.

'Any plans for the weekend?' Will asked her, and she had a sudden chill. Fergus had said he'd come down, but he hadn't contacted her, thank God. Maybe he'd taken the hint from her abrupt departure after lunch on Saturday.

'Not really,' she said evasively. 'How about you?'

He shrugged. 'What can I do? Sit about and fret because I can't get on? Walk the dog till his legs fall off? You tell me.'

'What would you normally have been doing?' she asked.

His laugh was short and wry. 'The house? In case you haven't noticed it's barely habitable. I've done the roof and the dampproofing and started with the kitchen and breakfast room and two bedrooms and some basic plumbing, but nothing's finished, and the rest of it is crying out for some progress. The only rooms that are virtually done are the two bedrooms, and they just need decorating.'

'Why on earth,' she asked, negotiating the track carefully, 'did you take on something so challenging?'

'Because I like a challenge? Because I wanted to live here and it was falling down, so there wasn't a lot of choice. The barn had planning permission for conversion to guest accommodation, so I lived in a caravan and did that first, then lived there while I made the house weathertight and sound and installed the basics.'

'So why don't you still live in the cottage? Or let it?'

'Well, I am letting it. I'm letting it to trainees at the moment.'

'But not for as much as you'd get for holiday lets.'

'No, but it's less hassle, and I'm too busy at the weekends to deal with change-overs and guests and their trivial problems and queries. That's the plan, in the end, but not until I've got the house knocked into shape—and with my arms out of action, DIY's taken a definite back seat.'

Lucie chuckled. 'You amaze me. I would have thought you'd have a go anyway.'

He looked rueful. 'I have to confess I did have a go, during the week. I thought I might be able to tackle some of the simple things upstairs, but I couldn't even hold the electric screwdriver with my right hand, and my left—well, let's just say I'm not ambidextrous. Anyway, it still hurts, so what the hell. I gave up.'

And it didn't agree with him, Lucie realised, because he wasn't a quitter.

And nor, she realised with a sinking heart, was Fergus.

They pulled up on the drive beside his car, and Will arched a brow at her. 'Have you got a visitor?'

'Apparently,' she said tightly, and got out of the car at the same time as Fergus emerged from his, a wide smile on his face.

'Lucie, darling! I thought you'd never get here! The dog's been barking its head off—I stayed in the car just in case it got out.'

'You should have rung,' she told him, unable to

be more welcoming, and dredged up a smile. 'I'm sorry we're late. I had evening surgery.'

She offered a cheek for his kiss, and turned to Will, who was coming round the front of the car with a look in his eye that she didn't want to analyse. 'Will, meet Fergus Daly, a friend of mine from London,' she said smoothly. 'Fergus, this is Will Ryan, my trainer.'

'I won't shake hands,' Will said a little curtly, holding up his cast, and looked at Lucie. 'You're obviously busy. If I can have the keys, I'll leave you to it.'

She dropped them in his outstretched hand, and he turned on his heel and strode away, leaving Fergus staring after him.

'What an odd fellow. Not very welcoming.'

Nor was Lucie, but Fergus hadn't noticed—or wasn't acknowledging it. 'So, is this your little *pied-à-terre*?'

She nodded, unlocking the door and pushing it open. 'Come in. I haven't done anything today, it's a bit of a mess. Tea?'

'Nothing stronger?' he said hopefully.

'No, nothing stronger. You're driving.'

'Am I? Where are we going?'

She gave a short sigh. 'To your hotel?'

He reached for her, his hands cupping her shoulders, drawing her towards him. 'I had rather hoped I might be allowed to stay with you,' he murmured, and bent to kiss her.

She turned her head and moved out of his reach. 'I think not, Fergus. I told you that before I left London, and nothing's changed. It was no then, and it's no now.'

'But I miss you, Lucie.'

'I know you miss me—or you think you do—but I don't miss you, Fergus. I'm sorry, but that's the way it is.'

He stood dumbstruck, staring at her with astonished eyes. 'Lucie?'

'Oh, Fergus, come on, it's not as if it's the first time you've heard me say it! We're friends—nothing more. If you can't accept that, then I don't know how else to tell you to make you understand. There is nothing between us—nothing!'

'Oh.' He suddenly seemed to find the carpet absolutely fascinating, and she felt a pang of guilt.

'Fergus, I'm sorry.'

'I was really looking forward to this weekend,' he murmured.

'Only because you've failed to listen to me for weeks now. If you'd been paying attention, you would have realised it was a waste of time.' She moved closer, putting her hand on his arm. 'Have a cup of tea before you go.'

He pulled his arm away and looked up, his eyes suspiciously moist. 'I won't, thank you. I'll get out of your way.' He moved to the door, then paused, looking back at her. 'It's Will, isn't it?'

She sighed. 'No, it's not Will. This was over before I left London, Fergus. Will has nothing to do with it.'

'He may not have been then, but he is now,' he said with unusual perception. 'I hope you find what you're looking for, Lucie. You deserve to, you're a lovely girl.'

The door closed gently behind him, and Lucie sat down and swallowed hard. Poor Fergus. It wasn't his

fault he was too safe and too boring. Perhaps it was
a failing in her, that she wanted danger and excitement in her relationships?

She looked across at the house, and saw Will
standing at the window, watching Fergus drive away,
and she wondered what he was thinking.

Then he turned his head and looked towards her,
and she felt her heart kick beneath her ribs. Failing
or not, it was the way she was, and perhaps this
weekend would give her an opportunity to get closer
to him. After all, she couldn't rescue him from himself long distance, could she?

A tremor of excitement shivered through her, and
she stood up and went into the kitchen area, clearing
up her breakfast things and tidying, while her mind
plotted her next move.

CHAPTER SEVEN

FERGUS was going off—probably to fetch a take-away or a bottle of fine wine and some candles to romance Lucie. Will was surprised he hadn't brought a hamper with him from Fortnum's. He looked and sounded the type.

The car went up the track away from the house, weaving painstakingly between the potholes, and disappeared from view around the corner of the track. It would probably ground and he'd be back, whimpering about his flashy car that was so tragically unsuited to the rigours of country driving.

He turned away in disgust, and looked at the cottage. Was that Lucie, sitting in the chair on the far side? He couldn't really see, but then she moved, standing up and going into the kitchen, and he wondered what she was doing. Preparing a meal? Setting the scene for the nice romantic dinner Fergus had gone to fetch?

He felt something he didn't really understand and didn't want to analyse, but it burned like a vindaloo. Damn Fergus, with his slick car and polished brogues and slimy manoeuvres. Will didn't know what Fergus had gone to fetch, but he didn't want to hang around and watch the romantic little scene take place.

He called Bruno, put his boots on and stomped down to the river, staying there until it was too cold and too dark for common sense, and then almost had to feel his way back to the house.

There was no sign of Fergus's car, and he thought they'd probably gone out—although he hadn't heard a car. Still, that ostentatious, sexy car wouldn't make a great deal of noise. The engine was the sort that purred rather than growled, and he would certainly take it slowly on the track.

Maybe he *had* grounded it, Will thought, and realised he was gloating. Dammit, that woman was certainly bringing out the worst in him!

He went into the kitchen and put on the kettle, debated lighting the fire and decided he couldn't be bothered. He made some toast, fried a couple of slices of bacon, hacked up a tomato and slapped them together in a sandwich, washing it down with a cup of tea.

He wondered what Lucie and Fergus had had for dinner.

Smoked salmon? Lobster?

Not bacon sandwiches, that was for sure!

There was a knock at the door, and he opened it to find Lucie there, alone.

'Lucie?' he murmured. 'I thought you were out with Fergus.'

She shook her head. 'He's gone,' she said, and he wasn't sure, but he thought she sounded forlorn. Obviously a flying visit that had left her wanting more. Damn.

She looked at the remains of his sandwich clamped in his left hand, then up at his face.

'Is that a bacon sandwich?' she said wistfully, and he gave a crooked smile and opened the door, irrationally pleased to see her and disgustingly glad that Fergus had gone, for whatever reason.

'Want one?'

'I'd kill for one.'

'No need. Just sit patiently at the table and I'll make you one.'

'I'll help.'

So he ended up bumping into her and having her squeeze past him and generally giving his hormones a hard time. She smelt wonderful. He wasn't sure what it was—it might have been shampoo, her hair was still wet from the bath. The thought sent his blood pressure sky-rocketing, and he flipped the bacon onto the toast with an awkward wrist and pushed the plate towards her.

'Here—I'll let you do the tomato, I have to hack it.'

'Forget the tomato, just give me the bacon,' she said with a grin. Picking up the plate, she sat down at the table, one foot hitched up under her bottom, and bit into the sandwich.

Her eyes closed and she groaned with ecstasy, and he had to stifle his own groan of frustration. What *was* it about her?

'This is bliss,' she said with her mouth full. 'I'm starving.'

'Why didn't you eat?'

She shrugged. 'Nothing I fancied in the fridge, and—I don't know, I just didn't feel like it.'

'So you thought you'd come and raid my bacon,' he said, trying hard not to pry and just barely resisting the urge to ask why she hadn't eaten with Fergus.

She laughed self-consciously. 'Actually, I thought I'd see if you were all right. You seemed to be gone for such a long time, and when it got dark I was worried about you.'

'I went down to the river,' he said, a little gruffly

because he was touched at her concern. 'You don't need to worry about me, Lucie, I'm not a kid, you know.'

'I know, but with your arms and everything…'

'Everything?' He smiled. 'You mean my mental disability?'

She grinned. 'You *did* have a head injury.'

He couldn't stop the smile. 'You're crazy,' he said softly, leaning back in the chair and studying her. Her hair was drying in damp tendrils around her face, like a wispy halo, and her mouth was wide and slightly parted and unbelievably sexy. He ached to feel it again under his lips.

'Fancy a coffee?' she suggested. 'It's freezing in here, and I've got the heating on. And Fergus brought me chocolates.'

He'd pass on the chocolates, but only because they'd choke him. Coffee with Lucie in a warm room, though, was too tempting to refuse. He stood up and dumped the plates in the sink. 'Sounds good. What are we waiting for?'

He left Bruno behind, drying off after his frolic in the river, and followed her over to the cottage. She put the kettle on as they went in, then held up a bottle about a third full of something amber and interesting.

'Fancy a malt whisky?' she suggested, and he raised a brow.

'Secret vice?'

She shook her head and smiled. 'My father likes it. He used to pop up to see me from time to time when he was in London on business, and he kept a bottle in my flat. So, do you want some?'

Now he knew it didn't belong to Fergus? 'Just a small one.'

She slopped a hefty measure into a tumbler and handed it to him, and he sat down in one of the wonderfully comfortable armchairs and nursed it while she made the coffee.

It was bliss to sit there with her—not fighting, for once, because he was tired after his walk by the river and the long week and the pain in his arm, and fighting with her would have been too much like hard work.

So he sat, and he sipped his whisky and coffee alternately, and Lucie put some music on softly in the background and curled up opposite him in the other chair, and a great lump of regret formed in his throat that they could never have any more than this.

He sighed softly to himself. What was it about him that made him unable to live with anyone? Every time he'd tried, he'd ended up bitter and resentful. He was just too intolerant, that was the trouble—or maybe nobody had ever been special enough to make the effort for.

Lucie could be special enough, he thought, but they bickered constantly and the irritation he felt was clearly mutual, even if his was largely fueled by sexual frustration.

And anyway, she belonged to Fergus.

'Want a chocolate?' she asked, holding out a box of beautiful hand-made confectionery that must have cost the absent Fergus a small fortune.

He resisted, but Lucie didn't. She tucked in with relish, and he had to watch her sucking and nibbling and fiddling with them—because, of course, being Lucie she couldn't just put one in her mouth and eat it. Oh, no. She had to bite the chocolate off the outside of the hard ones, and curl her tongue inside the soft fondant ones, and generally get totally absorbed in the structure of every single chocolate.

And every bite drove him crazy.

He tried closing his eyes, but that was no better. He imagined her mouth moving over his body, nipping and licking and tormenting the life out of him, and watching her eat the chocolates was probably safer, so he opened them again and found her looking at him, a curious expression on her face.

'What?' he said softly.

'You look as if you're in pain. Is your arm hurting?'

He almost stifled the snort of laughter, but not quite. 'Let's just say I've been more comfortable,' he prevaricated, and crossed one ankle over the other knee to disguise his embarrassment.

She got up to change the CD, and his eyes faithfully tracked the soft curve of her bottom as she bent over the music system. Beautiful. Just lush enough to make the fit of his jeans impossibly tight. Damn. He looked away, into the depths of his malt whisky, and as the slow, sexy music curled round them, he drained the Scotch, stood up and put the glass down with a little smack on the table.

'I have to go.'

'Really?'

She looked wistful, and it occurred to him that she was probably lonely and missing Fergus. He didn't know why the man had left so soon—perhaps it had only ever been meant as a flying visit. Although, thinking about it, she hadn't seemed overjoyed to see him.

'Really,' he said gently. Whatever she was feeling

about Fergus, he didn't want to be used as a substitute.

Liar, his body screamed, but he ignored it until he got to the door, and then he turned to thank her for the coffee and bumped into her, and his hands flew up to cup her shoulders and steady her, and instead of steadying her they drew her closer, just as his head lowered of its own accord and his lips found hers.

She tasted of chocolate and coffee, and her mouth yielded with a tiny sound of surrender that nearly blew his control. Her back was to the bedroom door, and beyond it the bed was only a pace or two away. The knowledge tortured him.

He let go of her shoulders, meaning to ease back, but his arms slid round her of their own volition, drawing her closer, cupping her soft, lush bottom and lifting her into the cradle of his hips.

She gasped softly, and he plundered her mouth, need clawing at him. He wanted her—wanted to hold her and touch her and bury himself deep inside her.

He wanted things he had no business wanting, and she belonged to Fergus.

With a deep groan he released her, stepping back and fumbling behind him for the doorhandle. 'Lucie, I...' He trailed off, lost for words, and she put a finger over his lips.

'Shh. Don't say anything.'

He took her hand, lifting it slightly and pressing a lingering kiss into the palm. 'I have to go.'

'I know. I'll see you tomorrow.'

She came up on tiptoe and kissed his cheek, her soft breasts bumping into his chest and tormenting him again. He pulled the door open and backed through it, almost falling over the cat.

'Damn, she's sneaked in,' he said, but Lucie laughed, a low sexy little laugh that tortured him.

'She always sneaks in. I don't mind. She comes through the bedroom window most nights and sleeps on the bed.'

Lucky cat, he thought enviously, and dredged up a crooked, rather tragic smile. 'See you tomorrow.'

He turned and strode back to his house, refusing to allow himself to look back over his shoulder, and let himself in. Bruno greeted him with a thump of his tail, and he patted the dog absently and went upstairs to bed.

There was no way he would sleep, but his body was tired and he needed to rest.

Correction. He needed Lucie, and he wasn't about to get her.

Not now, not ever.

Lucie went to bed, her lips still tingling from his kiss. Poor Fergus. He was right. Will hadn't been an issue before she'd left London, but he certainly was now, and even if Fergus had been in with a chance before, that would have changed.

Especially after Will's kiss.

Fergus had kissed her before, of course, but only fairly briefly, because it had been all she'd allowed. She would have given Will anything he'd asked for.

Anything.

She reached for her diary, and wrote, 'Progress. We kissed again. He still seemed to regret it, but I don't. Oh, no! Wish he could have stayed the night.'

She put the diary down and switched off the light, then curled up on her side and relived the kiss. It brought an ache that wouldn't go away, an ache that was more than just physical and gave her a lump in her throat, because some time in the course of that kiss, she'd realised that she loved him.

How could she possibly have fallen in love with someone so grumpy and touchy and difficult?

Because that isn't the real him? her alter ego suggested. Because the real him is gentle and tender and loving, and crying out for a partner to share life's trials?

Crying out for peace and quiet and solitude, more like, she corrected herself. She didn't think for a moment that Will was looking for a partner. A more solitary person she didn't think she'd ever met, and even now, wanting her as he very obviously did, he still resented it.

Why?

Maybe Richard would know, but it seemed a little unfair to ask his senior partner to tell her about Will's personal life. She wouldn't want it done to her.

So, then, she'd have to ask him directly.

Or not!

Will rapped on Lucie's door at ten-thirty, just as she finished clearing up after her breakfast. She wiped her hands on her jeans and opened the door, greeting him with a smile that probably said far too much. She'd never been good at keeping her feelings secret.

'Hi, come in,' she said cheerfully. 'Coffee?'

'I get a definite feeling of *déjà vu*,' he murmured, and she swallowed hard. Heavens, he looked sexy today! He was wearing jeans, the same snug-fitting jeans he'd been wearing when he'd fallen, if she remembered correctly, so his fingers must be better with buttons now.

'Is that a yes or a no?' she asked, going to put the kettle on anyway.

'Make it a yes,' he said, following her. 'I've been thinking—about your training.'

Her heart sank. Oh, no, she thought, he's going to say he can't go on doing it because of our personal involvement and I'm going to have to go away.

'The patients are all being too obliging,' he continued. 'Apart from Harriet with her hairball and Mr Gregory with his gastric problems, they're all too cut and dried, and none of them are being awkward. You aren't getting enough experience with the awkward ones.'

She laughed and turned to face him, astonished. 'So what are you asking me to do? Argue with them? Tell them they're boring?'

'Role play,' he said, and her jaw dropped.

'Role play?' she parroted weakly. Of all the things she'd hated about her entire education, role play was top of the list. Oh, she was good at it—but she couldn't seem to take it seriously, and she always wanted to add something trivial to mess it up.

She'd been in constant trouble with the drama teacher at school, and her clinical medicine tutors had thrown up their hands in despair at her attitude.

And now Will, who already thought she was a silly, flighty little piece, wanted her to do role-play exercises *with him*?

'I can't do it,' she said firmly.

'Yes, you can,' he told her, just as firmly. 'You just have to try. You'll feel self-conscious for a while, but then you'll get used to it.'

Self-conscious? Not a chance! She'd probably just shock him so badly she'd fail this part of her training.

Still, he had that implacable look on his face, and she had a feeling he intended to win this argument.

'When?' she said, resigning herself to disaster.

'Now?'

'Now!' She nearly dropped the coffee. 'Now, as in *now*?'

He shrugged. 'Are you busy? We can always do it another time.'

'But it's your weekend,' she said feebly, hunting for excuses.

He raised his hands, one in a cast, the other still swollen and in a support. 'And there's so much else I can do.'

You could make love to me, she thought, and for a moment she wondered if she'd said it out loud. Apparently not, because he calmly took the coffee she passed him and set it down without incident on the table beside him.

'I don't bite,' he said softly, and she stifled a laugh.

'OK,' she agreed, giving in. It might be a bit of fun, and if she didn't overdo it, maybe he wouldn't get too mad with her.

He knocked on the door, and she opened it and drew him in. 'Hello, there,' she said brightly. 'I'm Dr Compton—come in and sit down. What can I do for you?'

Wouldn't you like to know? Will thought, and limped over to the chair. 'I'm having trouble with my bowels, Doctor,' he said, and met her eyes.

They were sparkling with mischief, and he sighed inwardly. She'd make a lousy poker player. 'What sort of trouble?' she asked.

'Oh, you know—either I go or I don't.'

Her lips twitched. 'How long's it been going on?' she said. 'Is it a recent problem, or have you always been like this, or does it come and go?'

'Oh, comes and goes,' he ad libbed. 'Well, it has done recently. Never used to. I used to have it all the time.'

'And what exactly is the trouble?' she probed.

'Well, as I say, either I go, or—I don't.'

'Have you changed your diet?'

'Well, not really. Stopped eating vegetables after my Katie died.'

'Oh, I see. So your wife died recently?'

'Oh, no, not my wife. Katie was the dog.'

Her mouth twitched, and Will had to admit he was having trouble keeping a straight face. However, she carried on. 'So, are you still eating less vegetables?'

'I get meals on wheels. I don't like soggy sprouts. Every day it's soggy sprouts—either that or cabbage, or those awful tinned carrots. You ever had those tinned carrots, Doctor?'

'Not that I recall. So, you're probably not eating enough vegetables. How about fruit?'

'I like tinned peaches,' he said, wondering how long he could keep her going. 'Strawberries, though—they're my favourite, although they usually give me the trouble.'

'You mean, you go?'

'Oh, yes. Well, of course, it depends how many I have. If I have too many, then I do, but if I don't have too many, I—'

'Don't,' she said with him, meeting his eyes in a direct challenge. 'I see. So how about apples, pears, that sort of thing? Breakfast cereal?'

'You're talking about roughage, aren't you, Doctor? Never had no shortage of that in the war. I remember—'

'And you were all probably a lot healthier for it,' she said, cutting him off neatly before he had time to ramble. 'Still, we need to worry about what would help you now, and see what we can do to make things more regular.'

'Oh, yes, regular, that's what I'd like to be,' he said fervently, stifling the smile. Her eyes twinkled. He should have been warned, but he wasn't, and her next remark shocked him.

'I think I need to examine you,' she said blandly. 'If you could slip your trousers down and lie on the couch.' She pointed at the settee, and he raised an eyebrow. 'Please?' she added.

'Is this really necessary?' he asked in his usual voice.

She propped her hands her hips and looked at him with that sassy little smile, all innocent and wicked at once. 'Of course. How will you know if I've been sufficiently thorough if I don't do everything I would normally do?'

'Hmm,' he muttered under his breath. 'We'll imagine the trousers,' he said firmly, and lay down, his legs dangling over the end.

'I'll just undo them,' she said, and before he could protest the button fly was popping open and her little hands were in there, prodding and poking about at his innards and getting perilously close to finding out just how much he was getting out of this whole bit of nonsense.

She tugged up his shirt and peered at the skin of

his abdomen. 'Nice neat scar—is that appendix or a hernia repair?' she asked innocently.

'Appendix,' he said in a strangled voice.

'And have you had trouble ever since it was removed?'

Damn, how did she keep it going? 'Well, off and on. Like I said, sometimes I go, and—'

'Sometimes you don't. Yes. I remember.' She pressed down in the centre of his abdomen and released sharply, and he obligingly grunted, feigning rebound tenderness.

'Oh, dear, was that a bit sore?' she asked sympathetically.

'It was.'

Mischief danced in her eyes. 'What about if I do it here, further down?'

He caught her wrists, just in the nick of time. 'I think we get the picture,' he said, swinging his legs off the settee and struggling to fasten his jeans.

'Here, let me,' she said, and then those little fingers were in there again, brushing against his abdomen and driving him crazy. He sucked in his breath to get out of her way, but she was done, and he tugged the rest of the shirt out of the waistband and let it provide a little modesty.

Had she noticed? Goodness knows, but he wasn't taking any chances. He sat back down in his chair and crossed his leg over his other knee. He seemed to spend a lot of time in this position, he thought, and sighed.

Perhaps role play wasn't such a good idea after all.

*　*　*

Lucie was enjoying herself. They swapped roles, they touched on difficult and serious issues, and other more trivial and silly ones, and she did learn a lot from him.

She also learned a lot about him. She learned that he had a sense of humour—a wonderful sense of humour, every bit as wicked as her own—and that he cared deeply about his patients, and that he was a stickler for exactitude and wouldn't tolerate inconsistencies.

If she was vague he chivvied her up, making her be more specific, and although she threw in the odd bit of nonsense to liven the proceedings, in fact it was astonishingly easy to get into the roles with him and she found herself doing it seriously.

She also learned that she could turn him on just by stroking her fingers over the tender skin of his abdomen, so that his body betrayed his true reactions despite the fact that he stayed in role.

And she learned that as far as he was concerned, that was a no-go area and she wasn't to be allowed to tease him into breaking out of role.

Finally, at about lunchtime, he sat back and blew out his breath in a long stream. 'Well?'

'Thank you,' she said, genuinely meaning it. 'That was very useful. How did I do?'

'When you were being serious? Fine. Very good, mostly. The rest is just experience, but I think you've got what it takes. I think you'll do, Lucie Compton. If you were my GP, I'd be confident I was being looked after properly.'

Her cheeks coloured softly, and she let out a soft laugh. 'Well—thanks, Dr Ryan.'

'My pleasure. I think we deserve lunch. How about going to the pub?'

She wrinkled her nose. 'Typical. I'm driving, of course.'

He grinned. 'That's right, but fair's fair. As you so rightly pointed out, I just gave up my Saturday morning for you, so I deserve a drink more than you.'

There was no answer to that.

CHAPTER EIGHT

WITH her confidence bolstered by Will's praise, Lucie found working with him easier after that, although he continued to make notes and criticise and nit-pick.

Still, his comments were all fair and helpful and, although it annoyed her, she could see the point.

A fortnight after their role-play session, Harriet Webb came to see her for a check-up. She'd been discharged from hospital a week earlier, and before they arranged to go on holiday at the end of May, her mother wanted to be sure she would be well enough. Lucie had to admit Harriet looked considerably better than she had when they'd first seen her.

Her hair was cut short, as well—spiky and fun and a very pretty style that was too short to pull out in her sleep.

'Are you finding it easier to eat now?' Lucie asked her, and Harriet laughed.

'I'm starving. I've never been so hungry in my life. I think it's having room to really eat—I've probably never had that before. They said the hairball has probably been forming all my life. It was amazing—they showed it to me, and it was just the shape of my stomach and so huge! All my clothes are loose now, and my waist is so much smaller. They're putting it in their museum at the hospital, for the nurse training department, so I'll be famous. How cool is that?'

Lucie chuckled. 'Ultra-cool. You look good. I like the hair.'

She patted it experimentally. 'I'm still getting used to it. I used to fiddle with it all the time. It's like having my hands cut off! Still, I don't want another of those things, no way!' She shuddered.

'Are you seeing anyone about why you might have done it?' Lucie asked cautiously, and Harriet pulled a face.

'You mean the therapist? She's useless.'

'Give her a chance,' Lucie urged. 'She might be able to help you find out why you did it, and I know it might not be what you want to do, rummaging around inside all your personal thoughts and feelings, but if it stops it happening again and helps you move forward, that has to be good, doesn't it?'

Harriet nodded. 'I s'pose. It's just all a bit—I don't know. She keeps going back to when I was little and my sister died, and it—you know. It's difficult to talk about. I don't like to remember.'

'I'm sure,' Lucie said with sympathy.

Mrs Webb was sitting quietly in the background, and she met Lucie's eyes and shrugged helplessly. 'She seemed all right at the time, although it was awful, but that's when the hair thing started. Maybe this girl can get to the bottom of her problems. We're hopeful.'

'Well, as far as I'm concerned she's in excellent physical shape now and I can't see any reason why you shouldn't go on holiday. I expect it will do you all good. Are you going anywhere nice?'

'Only France,' Mrs Webb said. 'We go most years, but we thought we'd go earlier this year, to give Harriet a treat.'

'Well, I hope you have a lovely time,' Lucie said with a smile as they left.

'Make a note of that,' Will said from behind her.

'Of the sister?'

'Yes. Sounds as if Harriet was involved in some way in her death—maybe she found her, or feels it was her fault. Whatever, it could be relevant. Just jot it down.'

'I have.' She turned to face him. 'She's looking better, isn't she? Funny hangover, that.'

Will smiled slightly, letting her score the point. 'Who's next?' he asked.

'Mr Gregory. He's had the course of treatment for his *H. pylori*—this is a follow-up. Hopefully he's better.'

He was. He felt better than he had for months, he said, and although the treatment had been awful, it had done the trick and he felt much more like his old self.

'So, how's the diet going now?' Lucie asked. 'Dr Ryan tells me you're trying to cut down and lose a few kilos.'

'Oh, well, I gave all that up when this got out of hand, but I suppose I could start again. Maybe I need a bit less dressing on the salad. That seemed to set me off.'

'You don't have to eat salad just because you're on a diet,' Lucie reminded him. 'You can have normal meals, but cooked with much less fat, and with low-fat gravy and sauces and loads of veg. It doesn't have to be cold and raw to be less fattening!'

He chuckled. 'I know. Somehow it feels more like a diet, though, if it's cold. Still, I'll persevere.'

'Why don't we weigh you now, since you're here,

and we can check you again in a few weeks? Slip off your jacket and shoes, that's right.'

She weighed him, jotted it down on his notes and smiled. 'Well, I'm glad the treatment worked.'

'So am I. I'll go and have some hot tomatoes.'

He went out chuckling, and Will rolled his eyes. 'The nurse can weigh him.'

'He was in here.'

'And your next patient should have been. You're running behind now.'

She turned to face him again. 'Are you sure you aren't well enough to go and do something useful, like run a surgery?'

'With only one hand? Hardly. I've told you, I'm hopeless with my left hand. How could I do internals?'

'You couldn't. You'd have to ask for help.'

'And if there was nobody about? Don't worry, Lucie, I've thought about it. This is working.'

Not for me, she wanted to say, but that wasn't fair. They only crossed swords a few times a day now, instead of a few times an hour.

Progress?

The phone rang, and she picked it up. 'Dr Compton.'

'Doctor, I've got Mrs Brown on the line. She's expecting triplets? She says she's got cramp in her stomach and she's a bit worried. Could you go?'

She covered the receiver and repeated the message to Will. 'I'll talk to her,' he said, and took the phone.

After a brief exchange, he said, 'All right, hang on, we'll come now. You stay where you are.'

'I have a surgery.'

'The patients can either wait or switch to Richard,'

he said firmly. 'Angela Brown is about to lose her triplets, unless I'm very much mistaken, and I want to see her now. She can't wait. They can.' He nodded towards the waiting room.

'OK. I'll get my bag.'

'Come on, Lucie, move. She's in distress.'

They moved. They got there within ten minutes, to find that Angela had started to bleed.

It was only a little trickle, but her blood pressure was low and it was likely that she was haemorrhaging.

'I think you need the obstetric flying squad,' he told her gently. 'I'm sorry, but you need to be in hospital now, and you need a qualified obstetric team with you.'

'What about the babies?' she asked worriedly.

'I don't know about the babies. At the moment I'm worried about you. Lucie, can you call?' He told her the number, and she rang, relayed his instructions and asked for immediate assistance while he checked Angela's blood pressure again and listened to the babies through the foetal stethoscope.

'She needs a line in,' he instructed, and Lucie put an intravenous connector into her hand, ready for the drip, and took some blood for cross-matching, just in case.

'Shouldn't you examine me?' Angela asked them, and Will shook his head.

'No. You don't want to be poked about—it can cause the uterus to contract, and it might settle down. I want you in hospital fast, and I want that specialist team with you, just to be on the safe side. And in the meantime, I want you to lie as still as you can and not worry.'

It seemed to take ages for the obstetric team to arrive, but when it did, they moved smoothly into action and Will and Lucie shut up the house and followed them out.

'I wonder if she'll lose them?' Lucie said thoughtfully. 'She was so worried about having them, and now she's worried about not having them.'

'I don't know. Maybe they'll live, maybe not. Whatever, it'll be hard for her. I have to say my instinct is she'd be better without them, but I doubt if she'd see that in the same way as me.'

Lucie doubted it, too, and was glad she didn't have to make those sorts of choices. Nature would take its course, aided and abetted—or thwarted, depending on how you looked at it—by medical intervention, and Mrs Brown would come out at the end somehow, unless there was a drastic hiccup.

They went back to the surgery to find that Richard had finished her patients for her and everyone was in the office, sipping champagne.

'What are we celebrating?' Will asked, and Gina, one of the receptionists, waved her hand at them.

'Look! He finally did it!'

Will grabbed her flailing hand and peered at the ring, then gave her a hug. 'Congratulations. He took some pinning down.'

'Absolutely. Still, it's all going ahead now, and because I don't trust him not to change his mind, it's on Friday afternoon. Now, I know you can't skive off, all of you, but you can come to a party in the evening, can't you?'

'I'm sure we can all manage that, can't we?' Richard agreed, and fixed Will with a look. 'And since Will's broken his arm and won't be up a ladder, I imagine you'll even get him.'

'And Lucie—if you'd like to,' Gina said with a beaming smile. Lucie guessed that just then she'd have invited all the patients as well if there had been any about, but Lucie agreed, as much as anything because she thought it might be interesting to see Will at a party.

And who knows? she thought. It might even be fun.

'I really, really don't want to go,' Will said with a sigh.

Lucie looked at him across the car. 'You have to, Will. You said you would, and it's her wedding day.'

He sighed again. 'I know. I'm going. I just don't want to.'

'It might be fun,' she said encouragingly, and he shot her a black look.

'That's exactly what I'm afraid of,' he said darkly.

'Oh, pooh. You need to lighten up,' she said with grin. 'You never know, we might get you doing Karaoke by the end of the evening.'

'Hmm. See that pig up there in the sky?'

She chuckled, and opened the door. 'Come on. We have to get ready. We've got to leave in an hour. Do you want me to put your glove on?'

'Please,' he agreed, so she went in with him, waited while he stripped off his shirt and helped him into the long loose glove he'd got off a veterinary friend. A rubber band around the top held it in place, and it covered the entire cast without messing around with tape.

And that, they were both agreed, was a huge improvement.

The only problem was that she had to put it on after he'd taken off his shirt, and so she was treated on an almost daily basis to the delicious sight of Will's muscular and enviable torso, just inches away.

Close enough to touch.

She snapped the elastic band in place, flashed him a grin and all but ran back to her cottage. He could get the glove off, so her time was now her own, and she had to bath, wash her hair and get it into some semblance of order, and put her glad rags on.

The party was in a village hall, and she didn't think it would be dreadfully smart, but it might be quite dressy in a different sort of way, and she sifted through her clothes until she found black trousers and a flirty, floaty top with a camisole under it that dressed the whole thing up.

She put on her make-up, added a bit more jewellery and stood back and looked at herself. Fine. A little brash, but what the hell? She wasn't going out to one of Fergus's posh restaurants, she was going to a wedding party in a village hall, and she intended to have fun.

Lucie didn't know what she was doing to him. She was like a bright little butterfly, flitting about in that gauzy bit of nonsense. Granted, she wore a little top under it, but even so!

And she was in her element, of course. She could talk to anyone, and she did. She talked to everyone, without exception, from the bride's father to the kids in the corner who were throwing peanuts at the guests and giggling.

She threw one at him and it landed in his drink, splashing him. He met her eyes, and she was laughing, her hand over her mouth, looking as guilty as the kids and as full of mischief.

He shook his head in despair and turned back to his conversation with Richard's wife. She, however, seemed quite happy to be distracted by Lucie.

'What a charming girl,' she said, and Will nearly groaned.

'Yes, she is. Well, she can be.'

'And you can be charming, too, of course, if you put your mind to it,' Sylvia said in gentle reprimand.

'Sorry.' He gave her a rueful smile. 'I'm just feeling a bit old.'

'Old?' She laughed. 'You wait until you hit forty-five, if you want to feel old! Did Richard tell you we're going to be grandparents?'

'No, he didn't. Congratulations.'

She pulled a face. 'I'm pleased really, I suppose, but I had hoped they'd wait until they were a bit more secure.'

'What, like you did?'

She laughed and slapped his arm, her hand bouncing harmlessly off the cast. 'You know what I mean.'

'Yes, I do. But there's a danger to that, you know, Sylvia. You can be too measured, too organised, too planned. And then you find that life's gone on without you.'

'Well, this party's certainly going on without you,' she admonished, standing up. 'Come on, you can dance with me.'

'What?'

'Come on, you can't refuse, it's rude.' She pulled him to his feet and dragged him to the dance floor, and he could feel Lucie's eyes on his back all the way across the room.

Sylvia was kind to him and let him shuffle without expecting anything too outrageous.

And then the music changed, and Lucie appeared at their sides.

'I believe this is the ladies' excuse-me,' she said with a smile to Sylvia, and slid neatly into Will's arms before he could protest.

The cast felt awkward against her back, but his fingertips could feel the subtle shift of her spine, and he cradled her right hand in his left against his chest, his thumb idly tracing the back of her fingers. Her breast chafed against the back of his hand, and he could feel the occasional brush of her thighs against his.

It felt good. Too good, really, but he wasn't stopping. It was a genuine reason to hold her, and he was going to make the best of it!

And then the best man commandeered the microphone, and announced that the Karaoke machine was now working and they wanted the bride and groom to kick off.

'I'm out of here,' Will muttered, and Lucie laughed and led him back to their table.

'It'll be a laugh. Just go with the flow.'

So he did, and, in fact, it wasn't as awful as he'd imagined. Lots of the guests had a go, and some of them were quite good, and everyone seemed to enjoy themselves. Then, to his horror and amazement, Lucie was pounced on.

'Come on, you can sing, we've heard you,' the receptionists told her, and Will watched, transfixed, as she was towed, laughing, to the stage and presented with the microphone by the best man.

'So, ladies and gentlemen, here we go. It's Dr Lucie Compton singing Whitney Houston's song from *The Bodyguard*, "And I Will Always Love You". Let's hear it for Lucie!'

The crowd clapped and cheered, and then went quiet for the slow, haunting introduction. Lord, she was wonderful! Will felt his skin shiver, and then as she reached the first repeat of the title, her eyes found his, and he felt a huge lump in his throat.

There was no way she was singing it for him, but he could let himself dream, and then she hit the volume and he went cold all over with the power of her voice.

Lord, she was spectacular! He'd had no idea she was *so* good, and neither, by the look of them, had any of the others. She was really into it now, her voice mellow and yet pure, every note true, every word filled with meaning.

She finished, holding the last note until Will thought she'd die of lack of oxygen, but then she cut it and bowed, laughing, as the guests went wild.

'Encore!' 'Again!' 'More!' they yelled, and she turned to the best man and shrugged.

'OK. What have you got?'

'What can you do?'

She laughed. 'Anything. Try me.'

He did, and she was right. She knew them all, and hardly fluffed a note. Most of the time she didn't even glance at the monitor for the words, and Will was stunned. Finally, though, she surrendered the microphone to thunderous applause, and came back to the table.

'Sorry about that, I got hijacked,' she said with a chuckle, and pointed to his drink. 'Is that just mineral water?'

'Yes.'

'May I?'

He pushed it towards her, and she drained it, then set it down with a grin.

'I enjoyed that. I haven't done it for ages.'

'You were good,' he said gruffly. 'Very good.' Stunning.

She smiled a little shyly. 'Thanks,' she said, as if she really cared what he thought, and he wanted to hug her. Well, he wanted to do more than hug her, but it would be a good start.

'So how come you know them all?' he asked, trying to concentrate on something other than holding her in his arms, and she shrugged.

'I used to sing in a nightclub to earn money when I was at college,' she explained. 'The hours fitted, and the money was good, and I enjoyed it mostly, except for the smoke and the lechers.'

Will was feeling pretty much of a lecher himself just now, but he didn't want to think too much about that.

'I could kill a drink,' Lucie said, and he thought for a moment he was going to have to walk across the room in his state of heightened awareness, but he was saved by the best man descending on them and buying them both drinks to thank Lucie for her contribution to the evening.

The Karaoke had packed up after she'd sung. She was, as they said, a hard act to follow, and so they'd gone back to the disco music and everyone was dancing again.

They had a drink, and this time Will had a whisky. Well, he wasn't driving, and he needed something to act as anaesthetic if he was going to sleep that night!

'Are you ready to go?' he asked her a short while later, and she grinned and stuck her finger under his chin, tickling it.

'Is it past your bedtime, you poor old thing?' she crooned, and he nearly choked.

Way past, he thought, but not in the way she was implying! He glowered at her, and she just laughed and stood up. 'Come on, then, Cinderella, your carriage awaits.'

They said goodbye to their hosts, and twenty minutes later they were pulling up outside the house and she was going to go her way and he was going to have to go his, and he suddenly didn't want the evening to end.

God, however, was on his side. 'Coffee?' she said, and he sent up a silent word of thanks.

'That would be lovely.'

He followed her into the cottage and stood leaning on the old timber-stud wall in the kitchen while she put the kettle on. 'So, did you have fun?' she asked him, turning to face him and standing with one hand on her hip in an unconsciously provocative pose.

His libido leapt to life again. 'Yes, I had fun,' he confessed. 'You were wonderful, Lucie. You've got a beautiful voice.'

'Thanks.'

She met his eyes again, that shy smile playing over her lips, and he suddenly knew he'd die if he didn't kiss her.

He hadn't kissed her for weeks—three weeks, to

be exact, not since Fergus had been down, and it had been far too long.

He held out his arms, and she moved into them without a murmur, pressing her body softly up against him as she turned her face up for his kiss.

A deep groan dragged itself up from the depths of his body, and his mouth found hers and relief poured through him.

Not for long, though. He shifted against her, aching for her, and with a tiny moan she pressed herself harder against him and wrapped her arms around his neck. Her fingers tunnelled through his hair, her body wriggled against him and then finally she lifted her head, undid the top buttons of his shirt and laid her lips against his skin.

Heat exploded in him, and he gave a deep groan. 'Lucie, in the name of God, what are you doing?' he asked in a strangled voice, and she laughed a little unsteadily.

'You need lessons?' she said, and her voice was deep and husky and unbelievably sexy.

'I don't need lessons. I thought I was the trainer.'

'Mmm,' she murmured, nuzzling the base of his throat. 'You are. How am I doing?'

'Just fine,' he croaked, and, putting his fingers under her chin, he tilted her face firmly up to face him. 'Don't tease me, Lucie.'

Her eyes lost their playful look and became intensely serious. 'I'm not teasing,' she vowed. 'I want to make love with you.'

Will closed his eyes and let his breath out in a rush. She wanted to make love with him, and had he thought of this in advance? Was he prepared?

He felt as if he'd won the lottery and lost the ticket.

'We can't,' he said. 'No protection.'

'Yes, we have,' Lucie said, and smiled a smile as old as time.

It had lost nothing of its power over the countless generations. He felt as if his knees were going to buckle, and when she moved away and held out her hand, he took it and followed her through to the bedroom.

She was incredible. She was gentle, teasing, earnest—she was a thousand different women, and he wanted them all. He wanted her, and he could think of nothing else.

It was only afterwards, when he lay spent beside her, his heart pounding and his body exhausted, that he remembered that she belonged to Fergus...

CHAPTER NINE

LUCIE woke to a feeling of utter contentment. She'd never—*never*—been loved like that, and she felt whole as she'd never felt whole in her life before.

She opened her eyes, a smile forming on her lips, but Will was gone. She sat up, throwing off the quilt, not heeding her nakedness. 'Will?'

There was no reply, and the cottage was too quiet. Quiet with the silence of emptiness. She felt ice slide over her and, shivering, she pulled on her dressing-gown and went through to the sitting room. She knew he wasn't in the bathroom, because the door had been open and there was no sign of him.

Nor was he in the sitting room. She felt the kettle, and it was stone cold. When had he left? Just now, or earlier in the night?

She looked across at his house, but it was daylight and there would be no lights on anyway. She went back into the bedroom and felt the other side of the bed but, like the kettle, it was cold. He must have gone back to let the dog out, she realised, and stayed.

He was bound to be up, though, so she showered quickly, threw on her jeans and an old rugby shirt and some thick socks, and went over to the house. The back door was open, as usual, and she went in and found him sitting at the table, staring broodingly into a mug.

'Hi,' she said softly.

Will looked up, and to her surprise his eyes were

unreadable. They certainly hadn't been unreadable last night, but today they were. Distant and remote and expressionless. 'Hi.'

She faltered, suddenly uncertain of her welcome and not knowing why. 'Is something wrong?' she asked with her usual directness, and he shrugged.

'I don't do the morning-after thing very well.'

She stared at him. 'I noticed,' she said wryly, and went over to the kettle. 'Mind if I have a cup of tea?'

'Help yourself. You usually do.'

Oh, lord. All that beautiful intimacy, the tenderness, the whispered endearments—all gone, wiped out with the dawn. She felt sick inside, cold and afraid.

'Have you had breakfast?' she asked, striving for normality, and he shook his head.

'Not yet.'

'Want some toast?'

'If you're making it.'

Well, he wasn't going to make it easy, that was for sure, but she wasn't giving up either.

She cut four slices of bread, stuck them in the toaster and sat down opposite him, so he couldn't avoid looking at her.

He did, though. He stared down into his tea as if his life depended on it, and when she reached out a hand and touched him, he all but recoiled.

'Have I done something wrong?' she asked gently.

He looked up then, his eyes piercing and remote. 'No. Ignore me. I'm always like this.'

'Might explain why you're still single at thirty-three, then,' she said lightly, and went to collect the toast.

They ate in silence, and when he'd finished he

scraped his chair back and stood up. 'I'm taking the dog out.'

'Mind if I come?'

He shrugged. 'Please yourself. You usually do, but I'm going down by the river and your trainers will get ruined.'

'I've got boots. Give me a minute.'

She ran over to the cottage, dug out the wellies that hadn't seen the light of day for years and pulled them on, snagged a jacket off the hook by the door and went back out to find Will standing on the edge of the track, his hands rammed in his pockets, Bruno running in circles round the lawn barking impatiently.

As soon as he saw her, he turned and headed off, not waiting for her to catch up, and feeling sick inside she hurried after him, drawing level just in time to fall behind as the path narrowed.

And he wasn't hanging around for her or making any concessions, of course. Oh, no. That would be out of character. Whoever had made such beautiful love to her last night had been put firmly back in his place and the Will she knew—and loved?—was back with a vengeance.

She struggled down the path after him over the uneven ground, and finally, when she thought she'd die of exhaustion, they arrived at the river. Thank God, she thought, but that wasn't the end of it.

He turned sharply left and carried on along the path, striding out so that she almost had to run to catch up. Well, damn him, she wouldn't run! She slowed down, taking her time to enjoy the walk, looking out over the quiet beauty of the morning light on the water, and she thought she'd never seen anything quite so lovely in her life.

They were near the sea, and gulls were wheeling overhead, their keening cry reminding her of seaside holidays as a child. A wader was standing on one leg, and the water was so still she could see the ripples spreading out in the water around it, perfectly concentric rings interrupted only by the thin stalks of the reeds that broke the surface of the water in places.

It stabbed the mud with its beak, breaking the pattern, and she breathed again and moved on, following Will and wondering how anyone who loved this land as he so obviously did could be so changeable.

Maybe he loved it because it, too, constantly changed, continually affected by external influences.

Or was Will just bad-tempered and grumpy, and was she making too many allowances for him?

Probably, she acknowledged, looking ahead to where he was standing waiting for her, staring out over the river, his body utterly motionless.

Then he turned his head, and she told herself she imagined the pain in his eyes. Over that distance she could hardly make out his features, never mind read an expression!

Lucie hurried towards him, and this time he waited until she reached him.

'It's beautiful,' she said softly, and he nodded.

'I try and come down here every day. It's harder in the winter because it's dark so early, but I still try. Sometimes it freezes, and the birds skid about on the ice at the sides and Bruno tries to chase them. He always falls through, though. It never freezes that hard.'

She smiled, imagining it, and looked up at him.

His eyes tracked over her face, and she reached up and laid her hand on his cheek. 'You haven't kissed me this morning,' she said, and, going up on tiptoe, she brushed his lips with hers.

'Lucie,' he whispered, and then his arms went round her and his mouth found hers again and he kissed with a trembling hesitation that brought tears to her eyes.

Then Will lifted his head and stared out over the river again, and this time she saw the pain quite clearly, for the second it took him to gather his composure around him like a cloak.

'We shouldn't have made love last night,' he said, and his voice sounded rusty, as if he'd left it down by the river at the water's edge for the tide to wash over it and reclaim it.

Her knees threatened to buckle. Why? she wanted to cry, but she couldn't speak. Her throat had closed, clogged with tears, and it was as much as she could do to breathe.

She turned away before he could see the tears in her eyes, and headed back up to the house. She was damned if she'd let him see her cry!

She heard the drumming of hoofbeats, and in the distance she could make out Amanda and Henry, flying along the track that ran along the far side of the field beside her.

She felt a pang of envy. To feel the wind in your face and see the trees rushing past and feel so free—it must be wonderful. She brushed aside the tears and turned her attention back to the path, concentrating on putting one foot in front of the other.

And then she heard the unearthly scream, and the

hideous crash, and, looking up, she saw Henry struggling to his feet, unable to stand properly.

'Oh, my God,' she whispered. 'Oh, Amanda!'

She turned her head to call Will, but he'd seen and heard as well, and he was running up the field towards them, his long legs eating up the ground, Bruno streaking ahead.

She ran after him, her breath tearing in her throat, and adrenaline was surging through her, making her heart pound so hard she thought it would come out of her chest.

Will had reached Amanda now, and he was kneeling down when Lucie ran up, and his face was ashen.

'I think she's dead,' he said, and his voice was hollow and empty.

Lucie dropped to her knees beside him. 'She can't be. Let me feel.'

'She's not breathing, and I can't feel a pulse. I think her neck's broken, but I can't do anything with this bloody stupid hand...'

Lucie slipped her fingers behind the back of Amanda's neck, but she could feel nothing displaced. 'Maybe not. She might just be winded. Run and get my bag, and call an ambulance. You can go faster than me, and I've got hands that work. Take the dog with you.'

He was gone before she'd finished speaking, and she quickly ran her fingers down under Amanda's spine, feeling for any irregularity. If there was one, it was undetectable. So why...?

'Come on, Amanda, you can't do this,' she said. Ripping open her shirt, she laid her head on Amanda's chest. Yes, there was a faint heartbeat, but she wasn't breathing. Her airway, Lucie thought, and, supporting the neck by sliding her hand under it, she lifted Amanda's chin.

Amanda gasped, and as Lucie continued to support her neck, her eyelids fluttered open and she dragged in another breath.

Lucie let hers out in a rush. 'You're all right. Just lie still, you'll be OK.'

'Hurt,' she whispered.

'I know. Lie still, Will's getting the ambulance. Where do you hurt?'

'Everywhere. Legs—back—don't know. Pelvis?'

Lucie nodded. Amanda's legs were lying at a very strange angle, and it was obvious that she was very seriously injured. The first thing she needed was a neck brace, just to be on the safe side.

'You'll be OK,' she told her without any great faith, and prayed for Will to hurry. She wanted to get a line in, so that the ambulance crew could get some fluids into her as soon as possible to counteract the shock, because Lucie could tell that Amanda's blood pressure was going down, and goodness knows what internal injuries she might have sustained.

'Henry,' Amanda whispered a little breathlessly. 'Is he…?'

'He's over there, behind you. He's up.' On three legs, with the fourth dangling at a very strange angle, but Amanda didn't need to know that. 'Do you know what happened?'

'No. He—just seemed to—hit something—in the grass. Don't know what. Is he all right?'

'I don't know anything about horses,' Lucie said with perfect truth. 'Just keep very still, sweetheart. Try not to move.'

Amanda's eyes fluttered shut then, and Lucie had

never felt more alone in her life. Come on, Will, she thought, and then he appeared, her medical bag in his left hand, a bundle of towels and sheets under his right arm.

'Any joy?'

'She's breathing. Her airway was obstructed. I think her tongue had been driven back with the force of the fall. She's just resting.'

He looked down at her, just as Amanda's eyes opened and she looked up at him. 'Will? Look after Henry.'

'I will.'

'Got insurance. Call the vet. Anything...'

'OK. Don't worry about Henry. I've called the vet.'

He shot a glance in the horse's direction, and met Lucie's eyes. So they agreed on that, at least. Henry was in deep trouble. 'They're sending an air ambulance, because of the track. It should be here any minute. It was being scrambled from Wattisham airbase.'

She nodded. 'Good. The sooner the better.'

'I've just got to put out markers.' He ran down the field, opening out the sheets and spreading them in a rough H on the emerging crops. Moments later he was back, and knelt down opposite Lucie. 'Anything I can do? She needs a line in.'

'I know. Can you take over her neck so I can do it?'

'Sure.' His fingers slid around hers, cupping the fragile neck, and she eased her hand away carefully and then busied herself opening her bag and finding what she needed to get an intravenous line in. 'She needs saline.'

'They're bringing plenty of fluids. I told them to expect circulatory collapse.'

'Let's hope they get here soon,' Lucie said, checking Amanda's pulse and finding it weaker. 'Her pressure's dropping. Where the hell are they?'

'God knows, but the horse is going to be spooked by the helicopter.'

She'd got the line into Amanda's hand, and she taped the connector down and looked at Henry doubtfully. 'Can you lead him back to the stable?'

'Are you all right with her?'

'I'll manage. I don't need a terrified horse galloping over me.'

'I don't think he's galloping anywhere,' Will said softly, and she slid her fingers back under his and watched him as he went quietly up to Henry, speaking softly to him and holding out a reassuring hand.

The horse was shivering, clearly in shock himself, and Will led him slowly, hobbling on three legs, up the track and over the field towards the house.

He was back in no time, just as the helicopter came into view over the hill.

'That was quick.'

'I met up with the vet on the track. He's taken him on up,' he yelled, and then his voice was drowned out by the whop-whop-whop of the helicopter, and the grass was flattened all around them and Lucie ducked involuntarily.

Never mind spooking the horse, it didn't do a lot for her, but she was pleased to see it!

Seconds later the paramedic team was there, taking over from her, checking what had been done, getting fluids up and running, giving Amanda gas and air for pain relief and straightening her legs out to splint them, before putting on the spinal boards and lifting her into the ambulance.

Then they were away, and Will and Lucie stood watching the helicopter fade to a dot in the distance. 'I need to ring her mother—they'll have to talk to the vet and make decisions about Henry.'

'What did he hit? She said they hit something on the track.'

They walked back along it, and there, sticking up in the grass, was the end of a steel frame from a piece of redundant farm machinery. It had probably been there for ages, but this wasn't Will's land, and he didn't walk along this track often, he said.

It was just bad luck that Henry had gone so far over to the side, rather than sticking to the centre of the tracks, and it might have cost them both their lives.

Lucie shuddered. To think she'd just been envying them their headlong flight!

They went back to the house and found the vet in the stable with Henry, running his hands over the trembling horse and murmuring soothingly.

'How is he?' Will asked tautly.

'Shattered the cannon-bone of his off fore. It's not a clean break. They might be able to save it, but he'll never work again.'

'She's got insurance.'

The vet straightened up and met their eyes. 'I need to speak to his owners. My instinct is to shoot him now, but sentiment often gets in the way.'

'I'm sure they'd want him saved if possible,' Will said, and the vet nodded.

'I'll call Newmarket. They'll have to come and get

him. They have special transport with slings. He can't travel like this, he'll just fall over.'

He came into the house with them, and after Will had spoken to Amanda's parents and told them that Amanda was on her way to hospital, they confirmed that they wanted Henry saved if possible, and so the vet made several calls to set up the transport arrangements.

It seemed to be hours before Henry was loaded and away, the lorry picking its way infinitely slowly along the uneven track.

'I'm going to have to do something about that track,' Will said heavily, and turned away. 'I'm going to ring the hospital,' he said, and went into the house, leaving the door open as if he expected Lucie to follow. She did, sitting impatiently waiting until he finally got through to the right department. After a short exchange he replaced the receiver.

'She's in Theatre. She's got a pelvic fracture, both lower legs and right femur, and a crack in one of her cervical vertebrae, as well as cerebral contusions. Thank God she had her hat on, or she probably would have died of head injuries, but she'll be in for a long time, I think, judging by the sound of it. Her parents are both there, waiting for her to come round.'

Will glanced at his watch, or where his watch would have been, and swore softly before looking up at the clock. 'The day's nearly gone,' he said, and he sounded exasperated and irritable.

'I need another watch,' he went on. 'I don't suppose you feel like a trip to town, do you? I haven't bothered to get one till now because I couldn't wear it on that wrist, but I think the swelling's down enough now, especially if I get one with an adjust-able strap.'

'Sure,' she agreed. She wasn't sure how far she could walk. Her feet were rubbed raw after her long walk in the badly fitting wellies—not to mention run-ning up the field in them with her socks gathered up round her toes. Still, she'd manage. She wanted to be with him, if only so she could try and get their relationship back on an even keel after last night.

She didn't know what had happened to change his attitude, but something had, and if nothing else she wanted at least to go back to how they had been, instead of this icy and terrifying remoteness.

Will felt sick. Lucie was so sweet and open, almost as if Fergus was nothing. How could she be so fickle? He couldn't bear to think about it, so he closed his mind and tried to get back to how things had been, but it was hard.

Too hard.

He withdrew into an emotional safety zone, and then had to endure Lucie's puzzled looks for the rest of the day. He found a watch, the same as the one that he had smashed in his accident five weeks be-fore, and the saleslady was able to adjust it so it hung loosely on his still tender and swollen wrist.

'It's taking a long time to get back to normal,' Lucie said as they left the shop.

'I've been giving it a hard time,' he said shortly. 'I've had no choice, unless I resigned myself to total dependence, and I didn't have anyone to depend on.'

'You could have depended on me,' she said softly, and he gave a brief snort.

'I could. I would rather not.'

'So you've pushed your wrist too hard and probably damaged it more.'

'It's my wrist,' he said flatly, cutting off that line of conversation, and Lucie fell silent. He felt a heel, but he was having enough trouble with his own emotions, without worrying about hers. Damn Fergus, he thought, and had to consciously relax his hands because they were clenched into fists so tight both arms were rebelling.

'Let's go home,' he said, without bothering to ask her if there was anything she wanted to do in town, and then had a pang of guilt. She'd driven him there, after all. 'Unless you want something?'

She shook her head. 'No. We can go back.'

The journey was accomplished in silence, and when they got back she said she was going to sort a few things out and disappeared into the cottage. He let himself into the house, patted Bruno absently and checked the answering machine automatically.

Nothing. No distractions, nothing to take his mind off last night and Lucie's beautiful, willing body under his.

He slammed his fist down on the worktop and gasped with pain. Damn. He really, *really* had to stop abusing this wrist. He massaged it gingerly with the other hand, and could have cried with frustration.

'You're better off than Amanda,' he told himself, and decided he'd swap places with her in an instant if it gave him a chance with Lucie.

There was nothing, of course, to stop him competing with Fergus—except pride.

Fergus had a car that cost more than he earned in a year, flash clothes that would never have seen the inside of Marks and Spencer, and he'd stake his life that Fergus didn't live in a tumbledown, half-restored excuse for a farmhouse in the middle of nowhere, miles from the nearest habitation and out of range of a mobile phone transmitter!

There was no way he could compete with Fergus for the heart of a city girl, and he didn't intend to try. He'd just take last night as a one-off, the night that shouldn't have happened, and cherish the memory for the rest of his life.

He struggled unaided into the long veterinary glove, had a bath and then lit the fire, opened the Scotch and settled down for a night's indifferent television. Nothing could hold his attention—not drama, not talk shows, certainly not puerile comedy.

He was about to go to bed when the phone rang, and he got up to answer it, to find that it was Fergus.

'Could I speak to Lucie, please?' he said in his carefully modulated voice, and Will grunted and dropped the phone on the worktop in the kitchen, going across to the cottage in bare feet and rapping on the door.

Lucie opened it, looking bleary-eyed and sleepy, and he wanted to take her in his arms and rock her back to sleep. Instead, he glared at her. 'Fergus on the phone,' he snapped, and, turning on his heel, he strode across the yard, ignoring the sharp stones that stabbed into his feet.

Lucie followed him in and picked up the phone. Will didn't want to hear her talk to him. A huge lump of something solid was wedged in his chest, and he shut the door into the sitting room with unnecessary force and turned up the television.

'Fergus?' Lucie said, looking at the firmly shut door with dismay. 'What is it?'

'I miss you.'

'I know. Fergus, we've had this conversation a hundred times now. I can't do anything about it. We aren't right for each other.'

'How's Will?'

Sexy. Amazing. The most incredible lover, better than I could have imagined in my wildest dreams.

'He's all right.' Actually, she didn't know how he was. Short-tempered, but that was no surprise, he was usually short-tempered.

Except just recently, and last night.

Last night…

'Sorry, Fergus, you were saying?'

'I was asking if there's any chance for you with Will, or if there's any point in me coming up to see you tomorrow. I want to see you, Lucie. I want to ask you something.'

Oh, no. But, then again, maybe a little competition might sharpen up Will's act.

'Come for lunch,' she said. 'I'll see you at twelve.'

'OK. I'll bring something, don't cook.'

'OK. See you tomorrow.'

She hung up, contemplated the firmly slammed door and shrugged. Will could find out for himself that she was off the phone. She went back to her cottage, shut the curtains and curled up on the chair and howled.

She'd really thought they were getting somewhere, but this morning he'd been so unapproachable, and then he'd said that they shouldn't have made love last night!

How could he believe that? It had been the most beautiful experience of her life, and she didn't think she'd been alone, but there was more going on here than she understood. There had been pain in Will's eyes, a real pain that hinted at some deep and terrible hurt.

A woman in his past? Had he been terribly hurt by her, and was that why he didn't do the morning-after thing very well? Was it that he couldn't bear to confront his feelings, or had he—please, God, no—pretended she'd been the other woman? Had *that* been why he hadn't been able to look at her in the morning?

Lucie scrubbed at the tears on her cheeks, and stood up. Whatever, she couldn't get any closer to understanding him by thrashing it round and round in her head any more, and she might as well go to bed.

Except that the sheets carried the lingering traces of his aftershave.

She sat up in the midst of the crumpled sheets and took her diary on her lap. 'We made love last night,' she wrote. 'At least, I thought we did. Perhaps it was just amazing sex.'

A tear splashed on the page, and she brushed it angrily away. 'Fergus coming for lunch tomorrow. He wants to ask me something. Hope it isn't what I think it is. Amanda and Henry came to grief on the track by the river. Very dramatic. Thought we were going to lose them both, but apparently not. Oh, Will, I love you, but you drive me crazy. Why can't you just open up with me? I thought we had something really special, but it must have been wishful thinking.'

She put the diary down, lay down in the middle of the crumpled bed and cried herself to sleep.

*   *   *

Fergus turned up at twelve. Will saw the car coming down the track from the end window in the house. He was struggling to strip the window, working with the wrong hand, and he paused and watched the car's slow progress. On second thoughts, maybe he wouldn't do anything about the track, and maybe Fergus would stop coming down.

He threw the stripping tool to the floor with a disgusted sigh, and shut the window, abandoning his hopeless task. He went down to the kitchen, arriving coincidentally as Fergus drew up, and he watched as Lucie came out to greet him with a kiss on the cheek.

Oh, well, at least it wasn't a full-flown no-holds-barred kiss of the sort he'd shared with her on Friday night. He should be thankful for small mercies—or perhaps Fergus was just too well bred to do it in public. He opened the boot of his car—a ridiculously small boot—and lifted out a wicker hamper.

If it hadn't hurt so much, Will would have laughed.

Game, set and match, he thought, and turned his back on them. He'd seen enough.

CHAPTER TEN

THE atmosphere between them remained strained over the next couple of days, but Lucie refused to let Will ruffle her, and by ignoring his moodiness it seemed to defuse it a little. At least, it brought a professional edge to their relationship, and for the first two days of the week it was all business.

Then, on Tuesday afternoon, he found her after her clinic and suggested visiting Dick and Pam. 'Dick's had his balloon angioplasty, and it's sort of on the way home. I thought it might be nice to pop in and see them.'

'And scrounge a couple of plants? You could take her back the pots from the others—they're lying dead by the back door, I noticed.'

'I know. I couldn't get them into the ground, and it's been dry,' he said shortly. 'You could have watered them.'

'I could have painted the outside of your house, but it's not in my job description,' she retorted, and put the cap back on her pen. 'Shall we go?'

'Only if you promise not to tell her they're dead.'

'As if I would.' She tossed the car keys in the air and looked at him expectantly. 'You coming, or walking?'

'Coming.' He stood up and headed for the door, holding it open for her so she had to brush past him. She felt him flinch and wanted to howl with frustration.

Why, when they'd been so close?

She drove to Dick's and Pam's in silence, pulling up outside the right white house this time, and she followed Will up the path and stood a little way behind him, admiring the front garden.

It had been five weeks since she'd first seen it, and now it was May, and everything was getting lush and starting to grow away. The bulbs were out, the daffodils finished but the tulips starting to nod their heads, growing up through the perennials that would soon rush up to swamp them.

So different from the boring, orderly town gardens she saw in London, which more often than not had a motorbike or car parked in them and a tattered fringe of forgotten vegetation round the edge.

She heard the door open, and then Will was hugging Pam, and she was smiling at Lucie and beckoning them in.

'Dick will be so delighted to see you—he's so much better. I'm amazed. He's back to work next week, and he certainly seems ready for it. The difference in him is incredible. He's in the garden, helping me with the daffodil leaves. Come and see him. I'll put the kettle on—can you stop?'

'Just for a short while,' Will agreed, arching a brow at Lucie, and she nodded.

'That's fine. A cup of tea would be lovely.'

They followed her through the house and found Dick bending over, tying off the tops of the daffodils, and as they went out he straightened up and beamed at them.

'Hello, there. Is this a social call?'

'It is, really. I just wanted to see how things were. I gather from Pam you're feeling much better.'

'I am, and it's all thanks to this young lady. My dear, I'm going to kiss you,' he announced, and, putting his hands on her shoulders, he planted a smacking kiss on her cheek. 'There. You're wonderful.'

Will shook his head and laughed. 'What did she say that I didn't?' he asked wryly, and Dick shrugged.

'Probably nothing, except you assumed I was afraid to die. Lucie here pointed out what a waste of my retirement it would be if I wasn't here to enjoy it, and I thought of the years I've paid into a pension just to let Pam sit back and squander it on a cruise, and I thought, Blow it, I'm going to do this! So there. That's all she said—just another angle on the same old theme, but it worked, and I can't tell you how grateful I am.'

Lucie laughed. 'Well, I'm delighted to have been of service. I must say, you do look well.'

'I am. Ah, look, here's Pam with the tea. Let's go and sit down in the conservatory.'

He led them up the garden, a riot of blue and yellow with the aubretia and alyssum foaming over the paths and tumbling down the walls, and they sat in the conservatory in the warm spring sunshine and talked about his operation, and how he'd felt, and they stayed far longer than they'd meant to.

Lucie didn't mind because as long as they were with Dick and Pam Will wasn't cold and remote.

Finally, though, he stood up to go, and on the way home he managed to keep the civilised veneer intact.

They got back as the phone was ringing, and he went in and came out again, calling her across the yard.

'Lucie? Phone—it's Fergus,' he said, and the coldness was back.

How odd. Surely it wasn't Fergus that was causing the problem, was it? Goodness knows. She went in, and as before he went through the door and closed it firmly in her face.

'Fergus?'

'Lucie, hi. How are things?'

She looked at the closed door. 'Just peachy, Fergus—just peachy,' she said heavily. 'How are you?'

Fergus again. Damn the man. Will looked morosely out of the window, staring at Henry's empty field. It seemed so odd without him. Apparently it was touch and go, but they were giving him time. Amanda, however, was making progress, and had recovered fully from her head injury. She would be in a neck brace for the next couple of weeks until her cervical fracture healed, and she had an external fixator on her pelvis to hold it, and her femur had been pinned and so had her lower legs, so that she didn't have heavy casts dragging her down once she started getting up and about.

Knowing how ruthless the physios were, Will thought it quite likely that she'd be up and about sooner than she thought or wanted, but he had it on good authority that she was a pretty tough cookie.

He wished he could drive. He wanted to go and see her, but he didn't want to ask Lucie. He was putting on her a lot, and he didn't want to—especially not now, when he was tortured by that night.

He could hear her voice speaking softly on the other side of the door, and, although he couldn't hear the words, every now and again she laughed, a soft, intimate little laugh that turned a knife in his gut.

He gulped and stared hard out of the window, down towards the river that would never be the same again since she'd been down there with him. Now he could see her there, outlined against the morning sky, her hair like a soft cloud around her head, and every time he went there he could feel her presence.

She hung up. He heard the clatter of the phone, and then her voice talking to Bruno, and then a tap on the door. 'Any news of Amanda?' she asked, coming through without waiting for the gruff invitation that was still locked in his throat.

'She's doing well. Everything's pinned and fixed and propped, and she's probably damned uncomfortable, but she's alive, and so is the horse, by a miracle.'

'That's good. I thought I might go and see her. I wondered if you wanted to come?'

Damn. She'd pre-empted him, and now he couldn't escape from her company, because he *did* want to see Amanda and it was more important than his personal feelings.

'I was thinking of going. I thought I'd get a taxi, to save you having to do all the running around.'

'I don't mind.'

So that was that. No way out, and anyway it would have been churlish. He snorted softly to himself. That didn't normally hold him back, he thought, and hated himself a little more.

They arrived at the hospital at seven, and Amanda, although obviously in pain still and very weary, was pleased to see them.

Lucie gave her some flowers to add to the many she already had, and Will showed her the card and hung it on a string over the bed with the others.

There was a cradle over her hips, keeping the bed-clothes off her fixators, and she was lying flat, of course, because of the neck injury, but she said the worst thing was the boredom.

'And it's only been a couple of days!' she wailed laughingly. 'What will I be like in a month?'

'Longing to lie down,' Will advised her. 'You wait till the physios get hold of you!'

'Oh, don't. There's one girl who's already having a go—she's lovely really, but she makes me do all sorts of things and it hurts! Still, it's my own fault. I shouldn't have been galloping along there on the verge. You don't know what it was he fell over, do you?'

'An iron bar, part of a bit of old farm machinery,' Will said. 'I've had a word with the farmer and he's moving it. He said he's very sorry to hear you had such a bad fall, but he pointed out it isn't an official bridleway.'

'Oops,' Amanda said with a grin. 'Oh, dear. My father was muttering about compensation. I'll have to talk him out of it!'

'Might be wise. Anyway, it's gone. Any news of Henry?'

'He's had an operation—they've splinted it with a bit of bone from a rib, and wired it all together, so goodness knows how he's managing to stand up, but he seems to be all right. They don't know how well he'll heal, but he seems to have settled down there, at least, and he's taking an interest in his surroundings. Of course, that's easier if you haven't got your neck wrapped in a plastic tube!'

They chatted a little longer, but then it was obvious that she was tiring, so they stood up to leave, and she reached out and took Will's hand. 'Thank you so much for helping me. They told me you saved my life, both of you, and I don't know what to say.'

Her eyes filled with tears, and Will bent and brushed his lips against hers. 'You don't have to say anything. I'll put it on your livery bill,' he said with a twisted little smile, and Lucie knew he was touched by her words.

She was, too, but she hardly knew Amanda. Will knew her all too well, and had spent months avoiding her. Odd, how he had now been cast in the role of hero.

Amanda held out her hand to Lucie, and she bent and kissed the girl's cheek. 'You take care, OK? We'll see you soon.'

They left her there, surrounded by her flowers and cards, and passed her parents on the way in. It meant another brief delay and another round of thanks, but then they were out and heading for the car.

'Fancy going to the pub for a meal? Or an Indian?'

She met his eyes, and wondered at his motive. Was this an attempt to mend fences, or would it be a chance to find out what had happened between Friday night and Saturday morning? Or was it simply that he was hungry and wanted to eat tonight?

Whatever, she was starving.

'Sounds fine. We'll do whatever you want—I'm easy.'

They went to an Indian restaurant, and discovered a shared passion for chicken korma in a really thick creamy sauce, with lots of twiddly bits to go with it and heaps of plain boiled rice, not the fancy pilau rice with spices, but just the clean, fresh flavour of basmati.

And Lucie wondered why it was that they could be so close in so many ways and yet she couldn't ask him what had happened and why he didn't want to talk to her after she'd given him her soul.

They didn't fight, though, and they kept the conversation trivial and away from anything that might damage the fragile truce that seemed to have sprung up between them.

And when they arrived back at the house, Lucie looked across at him and took a leap of faith. 'Coffee?' she offered, but to her relief and disappointment he shook his head.

'I won't. Thanks. I've got a couple of letters I ought to write and it takes ages with this stupid cast on. Maybe another night.'

'OK.'

She locked the car, handed him the keys and let herself into the cottage. Minnie was there, curled up on the bed, and she stretched and wandered out to the kitchen, asking for food.

'I don't do catfood, you'll have to speak to Will,' she told Minnie, and opened the door for her. Half an hour later she was back through the bedroom window, licking her lips, and curled up on Lucie's bed again.

Lucie was in bed herself, with her diary on her lap, telling it about Will and their meal.

'It was a really nice evening, but we were both walking on eggshells. What's happened? I must ring

Fergus tomorrow and give him an answer about those
concert tickets for Saturday. Bet I forget.'

She did. She forgot on Wednesday, and so on
Thursday morning, she stuck herself a note on the
front of the fridge.

GIVE FERGUS AN ANSWER! it said, in big red letters, but she still forgot to ring him.

The truce with Will was still holding, and it really
seemed as if they were about to make some progress.
They got back from the surgery shortly before seven
on Thursday evening, and on impulse she turned to
him in the car and invited him in.

'Goodness knows what I've got, but you're welcome to it. I can probably throw something edible
together.'

'OK,' he said cautiously. 'I'll just feed the dog and
cat, and I'll be back.'

It took him a few minutes because he took Bruno
for a run, but by the time he returned she'd thrown
together a scratch supper with eggs and pasta and
bacon, with a grating of cheese over the top.

'Perfect timing,' she said, handing it to him with
a smile. It was gorgeous, and he sat there in the
comfy armchair opposite her and wondered if she
really felt that much about Fergus, or if there might
be a chance for him.

Then Lucie got up to make coffee and he followed
her through to the kitchen with his plate. 'Here, you
can make the coffee, I'll wash up,' she suggested,
and put the dishes in the sink while he started pot-
tering with the mugs.

She'd tied her hair back in a scrunchie and he
could see the nape of her neck, and he bent, unable
to stop himself, and nuzzled it gently. 'I've got a

better idea,' he murmured, and drew her into his arms. His kiss was gentle, nothing too demanding, but his pulse rocketed and his knees felt weak and it was like coming home.

'I tell you what, let's forget the coffee and the washing-up, shall we?' she suggested softly, and he smiled.

'I'll put the milk back,' he said, and then he saw the note. GIVE FERGUS AN ANSWER! With great care he put the milk in the fridge and shut the door, and turned to her, slamming down the pain and refusing to let it take control of him. Fergus again, he thought. And what answer?

'On second thoughts, maybe I'll have an early night,' he said, his voice sounding as if it came from miles away.

'What?'

'I—I can't stay. I'm not feeling all that good—my arm. I need some painkillers.'

'Is it all right if I come over and use the phone in a minute?' she said.

'Sure,' he agreed, and with great reserve he managed not to bolt for the door, hanging onto his control by a thread. Once he was in his kitchen he leant back against the door and banged his head against it firmly.

'Idiot,' he growled. 'How could you be so stupid? You know damn well Fergus is still after her.'

The door pushed behind him, and he moved away from it to let her in.

'Sorry, I was leaning on it, doing up my shoes,' he lied, and kicked them off anyway in favour of his boots. 'I'm walking the dog. Help yourself to the phone.'

'OK.' She dialled while he struggled into his boots, his right arm still too weak to pull hard enough, and then she started to speak before he had time to escape.

'Fergus? Hi, it's Lucie. The answer's yes.'

Will slammed the door behind him, taking the steps in one and veering onto the track at the end of the yard, heading down to the river at a run, Bruno at his heels.

Hell. What answer? *That* answer? Please, no, he thought, and ran faster, his legs pumping, his heart slamming against his ribs. Please, no, please, no, please...

Lucie hung up the phone, looked out of the window at Will heading down the track like a greyhound and shook her head. What the hell had got into him to-night—unless it was her ringing Fergus? He didn't seem to like it but, anyway, it had been before then.

She went back, cleared up her kitchen, watched television and then just before it was pitch dark she saw Will coming back, walking heavily as if he was exhausted.

Idiot. His arm would be playing up if he was treat-ing it like that. She shut her curtains, went into the bedroom and turfed the cat off the pillow then went to bed with her diary.

I GIVE UP! she wrote. 'I can't rescue him, he's unrescuable. I'm going to London for the weekend, I've had enough. I told Fergus yes, so must meet up with him on Friday night. At least he's reliable and won't change his mind every ten seconds about whether he likes me or not.'

And throwing the diary on the floor, she settled

back and glared at the ceiling while it went slowly out of focus and blurred. She blinked and it came back into focus, but only for a second.

Damn. Not again!

She sniffed, pushed the cat out of the way again and turned out the light. To hell with him. To hell with all men. They were more trouble than they were worth.

Except that this one, she knew, was worth ten of any other man, and she couldn't seem to get through to him.

Defeated, she let the tears fall, and in the morning she packed her case, put it in her car ready, turned the cat out and shut the windows. She'd come and pick the car up after work, when she brought Will back.

And then at least she'd have the weekend to cool off before trying again.

If she could bring herself to try any more. Just at the moment, she wasn't sure she could.

'Oh, Minnie, no! You are such a pain, cat. How did you get in there?'

The cat mewed at him through the closed window, and Will went into the house, fetched the spare keys of the cottage and went back to let her out. She must have darted in when Lucie left for London, he thought, and a great heavy lump settled in his chest.

He might as well get used to it, though. He went in through the cottage door, and Minnie ran into the bedroom and jumped on the bed, settling down to wash herself.

'You, little cat, are a nuisance,' he told her, and scooped her up.

A book caught his eye, fallen open on the floor, and he sat on the edge of the bed and bent to pick it up. Then he froze, suddenly realising what it was.

A diary, written in Lucie's neat hand. Three words stood out in bold—RESCUING DR RYAN! Rescuing him? From what—apart from her? Oh, lord.

Slowly he picked it up and scanned the entry, guilt nudging at him, but he ignored it. She was writing about him, and somehow that made it seem less wrong. He read, 'He kissed me. Don't think he meant to. Don't think he means to do it again—we'll have to see about that! I have a feeling he needs rescuing from himself. It can be my next challenge—RESCUING DR RYAN!'

Rescuing me from myself? Am I so tragic? Yes, his honest self replied. Tragic and lonely and an object of pity. Oh, hell.

Will went on, flicking through the pages, scanning the odd entry until he arrived at last Saturday, almost a week ago. 'We made love last night,' she'd written. 'At least, I thought we did. Perhaps it was just amazing sex.'

There was something so poignant about that that he felt tears fill his eyes. He blinked them away. There was a smudge on the page, as if it something wet had splashed on it and been brushed aside. One of Lucie's tears, to match his own? He swallowed hard and read on.

'Fergus coming for lunch tomorrow. He wants to ask me something. Hope it isn't what I think it is. Amanda and Henry came to grief on the track by the river. Very dramatic. Thought we were going to lose them both, but apparently not. Oh, Will, I love you, but you drive me crazy. Why can't you just open up with me? I thought we had something really special, but it must have been wishful thinking.'

I love you? *I love you?*

Oh, lord. He read on, but there was nothing very much. Comments on his temper, on their fragile truce, and then last night, after she'd phoned Fergus, she'd written, 'I GIVE UP! I can't rescue him, he's unrescuable.'

No, Lucie, Will's heart cried. Don't give up! I didn't know! Give me a chance. He read on, and horror filled him. 'I'm going to London for the weekend, I've had enough. I told Fergus yes, so must meet up with him on Friday night. At least he's reliable and won't change his mind every ten seconds about whether he likes me or not.'

Oh, lord. She'd given up on him, and gone to Fergus, and she'd told him yes. Yes to what? To sleeping with him? Living with him? Going back to London?

Marrying him?

'No,' he growled. Flinging the diary aside, he scooped up the startled cat and strode out of the cottage, locking it up and taking Bruno out to the kennel he used sometimes if Will was going to be out for long.

'Sorry, old boy,' he told him, giving him another bowl of food. 'I'll be back in the morning, whatever happens. On guard, eh, mate? Good lad.'

He shut the pen, and locked the house, throwing his light overnight bag in the car. He had to go via the surgery and pick up Lucie's address, but he'd already got Fergus's card which Lucie had pinned up on the board by the phone the other week and left there, so that would give him two places to start.

OK, he shouldn't be driving, but needs must, and he had to get to her before she did something irrevocable.

Like what? Sleep with him?

'We made love last night. At least I think we did. Perhaps it was just amazing sex.'

The very thought of Fergus touching her brought a surge of bile to his throat. 'She's mine,' he growled. 'She loves me, not you. Don't you lay a finger on her, you bastard!'

Will went up the track far faster than even the rugged Volvo was designed for, dodging the potholes whenever possible, and shot out onto the road with unwary haste. He picked her address up from her personnel file in the surgery, and then jumped back into the car and headed for the A12.

He needed a clear run and a following wind, and he got both, amazingly. He was in London in record time, probably picked up on scores of speed cameras, but he'd deal with that if and when it mattered. He cruised up and down, scanning the *A-Z* on his lap, and finally found her little street.

And there, right outside her address, was her car, squeezed into an impossibly tiny space. The nearest space he could find that he could fit the car in was three streets away in a residents' parking zone, but that was tough.

He slotted the car in, grabbed his bag and ran back to Lucie's, staring at the bells in puzzlement. This was her address—or it had been. Had she left it completely? He'd thought she'd handed it over to her flatmate, and still had a room here for emergencies. And maybe she was out with Fergus already—or up there with him.

His patience snapped, and he went for the right flat number, standing with his finger on the bell until he heard her voice on the intercom.

'Hello?' she said softly, and he felt suddenly sick with fear.

'Lucie, it's Will. Let me in.'

'Come on up. Third floor.'

The buzzer sounded, and he pushed the door open and ran up the stairs, his heart pounding, and there she was, standing in the doorway with a wary look on her face.

'Is everything all right?' she asked, and he pushed past her and swept through the flat, throwing the doors open, searching...

'Will?'

'Where is he?'

'Who?'

'Don't play games with me, Lucie. Fergus, of course. You said you were coming up here to see him. You said you'd see him on Friday.'

'No, I didn't.'

'Yes, you did, quite clearly—in your diary—'

'My *what*! You've been reading my *diary*?' She flew at him, her fists flailing, and he grabbed her wrists and held her still, wincing as she struggled.

'Yes, I've been reading your damn diary,' he growled. 'Only tonight, not before, but it was on the floor when I let the cat out, and I saw my name—'

'Where?'

'RESCUING DR RYAN. In capitals. And for your information, it wasn't just amazing sex,' he bellowed. 'We *did* make love.' His voice softened to a whisper. 'We did make love, Lucie—didn't we?'

Lucie looked up into his eyes, and her own filled with tears. 'I thought so.'

'You were right. It was just, with Fergus in the background, somehow it seemed wrong, making love to another man's woman—'

'Hey, hey, stop! I'm not Fergus's woman—'

'Don't go feminist on me, Lucie, you know what I mean.'

'Yes, I do,' she said, 'and I'm not. I'm not Fergus's woman! I've never slept with him—'

'Never?'

'No, never. I never will.'

He stared at her, stunned, unable to believe his ears. 'But...you said yes—didn't you?'

She frowned. 'Yes?'

'I don't know. You had to give him an answer.'

She started to laugh, and he let go of her hands and stalked across to the window, bracing his arm against the bar. His stomach was churning, and all she could do was laugh. 'It's not funny, Lucie,' he warned.

'Oh, Will, it is! He wanted to know if I wanted concert tickets for tonight. I said yes, but not for me, for my flatmate and her partner. That's where they are—they've gone to a rock concert in Hyde Park. He wanted me to go with him, but I wouldn't, so he offered me the tickets anyway. Said maybe I'd like to go with you.'

'He did?'

Will turned to face her, and she smiled and walked towards him. 'Uh-huh. He's on your side, Will. I can't imagine why, he's not into Neanderthal behaviour, but he's very magnanimous.'

'Witch,' Will muttered, and Lucie tutted and put her arms round him.

'Don't. No more fighting. I've had enough of it.'

'Me, too,' he said with feeling, and drew her closer. 'I love you, Lucie Compton,' he said softly. 'I'm sorry I didn't say so, but I really thought you were just toying with me, and Fergus was the love of your life, and I didn't want to make a fool of myself.'

'That stubborn pride of yours again,' she teased, and he groaned and dropped his head onto her shoulder.

'Very likely. Will you forgive me?'

She took his face in her hands and stared up at him, and her eyes were like luminous green pools. 'Oh, yes, Dr Ryan, I'll forgive you—just so long as you promise never to jump to conclusions again, and remember to tell me you love me at least three times a day, just so neither of us can forget.'

'You have to do the same.'

'Of course. I love you, I love you, I love you.' She smiled impishly. 'You're two behind.'

He kissed her, just the lightest brush of his lips. 'I love you,' he murmured, and kissed her again.

Then much later, after she'd agreed to marry him, he lifted his head and said again, 'I love you...'

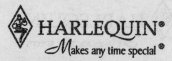

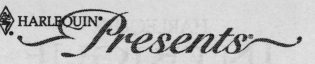

HARLEQUIN Presents

The world's bestselling romance series...
The series that brings you your favorite authors,
month after month:

Helen Bianchin...Emma Darcy
Lynne Graham...Penny Jordan
Miranda Lee...Sandra Marton
Anne Mather...Carole Mortimer
Susan Napier...Michelle Reid

and many more uniquely talented authors!

Wealthy, powerful, gorgeous men...
Women who have feelings just like your own...
The stories you love, set in exotic, glamorous locations...

HARLEQUIN Presents

Seduction and passion guaranteed!

HARLEQUIN®
INTRIGUE

WE'LL LEAVE YOU BREATHLESS!

If you've been looking for thrilling tales of
contemporary passion and sensuous love stories
with taut, edge-of-the-seat suspense—then
you'll love Harlequin Intrigue!

Every month, you'll meet four new heroes
who are guaranteed to make your spine tingle
and your pulse pound. With them you'll enter
into the exciting world of Harlequin Intrigue—
where your life is on the line
and so is your heart!

THAT'S INTRIGUE—
ROMANTIC SUSPENSE
AT ITS BEST!

HARLEQUIN®

Makes any time special ®

Harlequin® Historical

From rugged lawmen and valiant knights to defiant heiresses and spirited frontierswomen, Harlequin Historicals will capture your imagination with their dramatic scope, passion and adventure.

Harlequin Historicals . . . they're too good to miss!

HHDIR1

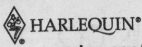

Frommer's®

PORTABLE
Florence

2nd Edition

by Reid Bramblett

Here's what critics say about Frommer's:

"Author Reid Bramblett really knows his subject. . . . He does an excellent job."

—*Times-Picayune*

"Detailed, accurate, and easy-to-read information for all price ranges."

—*Glamour Magazine*

WILEY

Wiley Publishing, Inc.

Published by:

WILEY PUBLISHING, INC.
111 River St.
Hoboken, NJ 07030-5774

ISBN 0-7645-4061-0

Editor: Myka Carroll
Production Editor: M. Faunette Johnston
Photo Editor: Richard Fox
Cartographer: John Decamillis
Production by Wiley Indianapolis Composition Services

For information on our other products and services or to obtain technical support, please contact our Customer Care Department within the U.S. at 800/762-2974, outside the U.S. at 317/572-3993 or fax 317/572-4002.

Wiley also publishes its books in a variety of electronic formats. Some content that appears in print may not be available in electronic formats.

Manufactured in the United States of America

5   4   3   2

Contents

List of Maps

ACKNOWLEDGMENTS

First and foremost, no thanks will ever be enough for **Frances C. Sayers,** without whose diligence, research skills, willingness to put up with my long hours and longer absences, sharp editorial eye, and, um, let's call it "constant gentle prodding," this book would never have gotten finished on time.

Thanks are also in order for all the folks who have helped do some of the grunt work in researching this book, especially my ex-assistants extraordinaire (and good buds) **Jay Sayers** and **Matt Finley.** I also tip my hat to **Myka Carroll,** the able editor who turned this mess of a manuscript into a sleek, useable book.

And, of course, no amount of gratitude will ever be enough for my parents, **Frank and Karen Bramblett,** who in addition to the usual stuff (giving me life, bankrolling the first 20 or so years of my existence), instilled in me from an early age a deep love of the world and its cultures. They taught me to enjoy everything that travel has to offer, on all levels, from camping under the stars to sipping fine wines, admiring the esoterica of fine art and getting good and rowdy with the locals during a festival. They also dragged me off to live in Italy for 2 years when I was 11, which may have had some effect on my later career. Most importantly, they gave me a gift not all kids are lucky enough to receive: They traveled wide, traveled often, and always, but always, took me with them.

ABOUT THE AUTHOR

Reid Bramblett learned Italian on the playground of a Roman parochial school when he was 12, explored Italy with his parents for 2 years in a hippie-orange VW camper, and spent a year studying there during a break from the anthropology department at Cornell. After a stint in Frommer's editorial offices, Reid vaulted over the desk to write Frommer's first guide to Tuscany and Umbria and hasn't stopped exploring, learning, interviewing, taking notes, and reporting it all in guidebooks since. He has also written *Frommer's Northern Italy, Frommer's Memorable Walks in New York,* is a coauthor of *Frommer's Italy from $70 a Day,* and contributes to *Frommer's Europe* and *Frommer's Europe from $70 a Day.* When not on the road, he lives in Maspeth, Queens, New York.

AN INVITATION TO THE READER

In researching this book, we discovered many wonderful places—hotels, restaurants, shops, and more. We're sure you'll find others. Please tell us about them, so we can share the information with your fellow travelers in upcoming editions. If you were disappointed with a recommendation, we'd love to know that, too. Please write to:

Frommer's Portable Florence, 2nd Edition
Wiley Publishing, Inc. • 111 River St. • Hoboken, NJ 07030-5774

AN ADDITIONAL NOTE

Please be advised that travel information is subject to change at any time—and this is especially true of prices. We therefore suggest that you write or call ahead for confirmation when making your travel plans. The authors, editors, and publisher cannot be held responsible for the experiences of readers while traveling. Your safety is important to us, however, so we encourage you to stay alert and be aware of your surroundings. Keep a close eye on cameras, purses, and wallets, all favorite targets of thieves and pickpockets.

FROMMER'S STAR RATINGS, ICONS & ABBREVIATIONS

Every hotel, restaurant, and attraction listing in this guide has been ranked for quality, value, service, amenities, and special features using a **star-rating system.** In country, state, and regional guides, we also rate towns and regions to help you narrow down your choices and budget your time accordingly. Hotels and restaurants are rated on a scale of zero (recommended) to three stars (exceptional). Attractions, shopping, nightlife, towns, and regions are rated according to the following scale: zero stars (recommended), one star (highly recommended), two stars (very highly recommended), and three stars (must-see).

In addition to the star-rating system, we also use **seven feature icons** that point you to the great deals, in-the-know advice, and unique experiences that separate travelers from tourists. Throughout the book, look for:

Finds	Special finds—those places only insiders know about
Fun Fact	Fun facts—details that make travelers more informed and their trips more fun
Kids	Best bets for kids and advice for the whole family
Moments	Special moments—those experiences that memories are made of
Overrated	Places or experiences not worth your time or money
Tips	Insider tips—great ways to save time and money
Value	Great values—where to get the best deals

The following **abbreviations** are used for credit cards:

AE	American Express	DISC	Discover	V	Visa
DC	Diners Club	MC	MasterCard		

FROMMERS.COM

Now that you have the guidebook to a great trip, visit our website at **www.frommers.com** for travel information on more than 3,000 destinations. With features updated regularly, we give you instant access to the most current trip-planning information available. At Frommers.com, you'll also find the best prices on airfares, accommodations, and car rentals—and you can even book travel online through our travel booking partners. At Frommers.com, you'll also find the following:

- Online updates to our most popular guidebooks
- Vacation sweepstakes and contest giveaways
- Newsletter highlighting the hottest travel trends
- Online travel message boards with featured travel discussions

Planning Your Trip to Florence

The capital of Tuscany is **Florence,** one of Italy's most famous cities. It was once the home of the colorful Medici dynasty, which actively encouraged the development of the Renaissance by sponsoring masters such as Donatello, Leonardo, and Michelangelo. Art treasures like those found at the Accademia (Michelangelo's *David*), the Uffizi Galleries (Botticelli's *Birth of Venus*), and the Pitti Palace (Raphael's *La Velata*) draw millions of visitors every year. Throw into the mix fabulous architecture (the Duomo with Brunelleschi's dome, Giotto's campanile, Santa Croce), fine restaurants and earthy trattorie, and leading designer boutiques and bustling outdoor markets, and the city of the Renaissance becomes quite simply one of the world's must-see sights.

Planning a trip doesn't have to be hard work. This chapter will help you smooth out most of your preparations for a trip to Florence.

1 Visitor Information

TOURIST OFFICES

For general information in your home country, try your local branch of the **Italian Government Tourist Board (ENIT)** or www.italiantourism.com. Some Frommer's readers have reported that the office isn't really that helpful.

In the United States: 630 Fifth Ave., Suite 1565, New York, NY 10111 (© **212/245-4822** or 212/245-5618; fax 212/586-9249); 500 N. Michigan Ave., Suite 2240, Chicago, IL 60611 (© **312/644-0996** or 312/644-0990; fax 312/644-3019); and 12400 Wilshire Blvd., Suite 550, Los Angeles, CA 90025 (© **310/820-1898** or 310/820-9807; fax 310/820-6357).

In Canada: 175 Bloor St. E., Suite 907, South Tower, Toronto, Ontario M4W 3R8 (© **416/925-4882;** fax 416/925-4799; enit.canada@on.aibn.com).

   In the United Kingdom: 1 Princes St., London W1B 2AY England (© 020/7399-3562; italy@italiantouristboard.co.uk).

   For more specific details on **Tuscany,** contact the regional tourist office in Florence: APT, Via Manzoni 16, 50121 Firenze (© 055-23-320; fax 055-234-6286; www.firenzeturismo. it). For **Umbria,** contact the Ufficio Promozione Turistica, Corso Vannucci 30, 06100 Perugia (© 075-50-41; fax 075-504-2483).

USEFUL WEBSITES

Websites and e-mail addresses are included throughout this guide for everything from tourist offices, hotels, and restaurants to museums and festivals.

   The official site for Tuscany is **www.turismo.toscana.it**, with links to every provincial tourist office site. The official Florence information site, **www.firenzeturismo.it**, contains a wealth of up-to-date information (events, museums, practical details) on Florence and its province. Included is a searchable "hotels" form allowing you to specify amenities, categories, and the like; it responds by spitting out a list of comparable hotels, and it lists contact info and current room rates.

   Firenze by Net (www.mega.it/florence), **Firenze.Net** (http://english.firenze.net), and **FlorenceOnLine** (www.fol.it) are all Italy-based websites with English translations and good general information on Florence. Also check out **The Heart of Tuscany** (www.nautilus-mp.com/tuscany), and **Chianti Doc Marketplace** (www.chianti-doc.com). And of course there's **Frommer's** (www.frommers.com), where you'll find excerpts from *Florence, Tuscany & Umbria, 4th edition,* occasional updated information, and links to travel packages from Gate 1 Travel.

Integrated City Codes

In 1998, Italy incorporated what were once separate **city codes** (for example, Florence's was 055) into the numbers themselves. Therefore, you must dial the entire number, *including the initial zero,* when calling from *anywhere* outside or inside Italy and even within the same town. For those of you familiar with the old system, this means that now, to call Florence from the States, you must dial **011-39-055-XXX-XXXX.** Increasingly, you'll notice Florence numbers beginning with prefixes other than 055; these are usually cellphone numbers.

Italy

2 Entry Requirements & Customs

ENTRY REQUIREMENTS

U.S., Canadian, U.K., Irish, Australian, and New Zealand citizens with a **valid passport** don't need a visa to enter Italy if they don't expect to stay more than 90 days and don't expect to work there. If after entering Italy you find you want to stay more than 90 days, you can apply for a permit for an extra 90 days, which as a rule is granted immediately. Go to the nearest *questura* (police headquarters) or your home country's consulate.

For passport information and applications in the **U.S.,** call © 202/647-0518 or check http://travel.state.gov; in **Canada,** call © 800/567-6868 or check www.dfait-maeci.gc.ca/passport; in the **U.K.,** call © 0870/521-0410 or visit www.passports.gov.uk; in **Ireland,** call © 01/671-1633 or check www.irlgov.ie/iveagh; in **Australia,** call © 131-232 or visit www.passports.gov.au; and in **New Zealand,** call © 0800/225-050 or check www.passports.govt. nz. Allow plenty of time before your trip to apply for a passport; processing usually takes 3 weeks but can take longer during busy periods (especially spring). When traveling, safeguard your passport and keep a copy of the critical pages with your passport number in a separate place. If you lose your passport, visit the nearest consulate of your native country as soon as possible for a replacement.

CUSTOMS

WHAT YOU CAN BRING INTO ITALY

Foreign visitors can bring along most items for personal use duty-free, including fishing tackle; a sporting gun and 200 cartridges; a pair of skis; two tennis racquets; a baby carriage; two hand cameras with 10 rolls of film; and 200 cigarettes or 50 cigars or pipe tobacco not exceeding 250 grams. There are strict limits on importing alcoholic beverages. However, limits are much more liberal for alcohol bought tax-paid in other countries of the European Union. For more information regarding customs, visit the Italian-language website www.agenziadogane.it and follow links to "carta dogonale del viaggiatore," the travelers' custom charter.

WHAT YOU CAN TAKE HOME

FOR U.S. CITIZENS   A recent change in the personal exemption rule allows returning U.S. citizens who have been away for at least 48 hours to bring back into the States up to $800 worth of goods (per person) without paying a duty once every 30 days. On the first $1,000 worth of goods over $800 you pay a flat 3% duty. Beyond that, it works on an item-by-item basis. There are a few restrictions on amount: 1 liter of alcohol (you must be over 21), 200 cigarettes, and 100 cigars. Antiques more than 100 years old and works of fine art are exempt from the $800 limit, as is anything you mail home. Once per day, you can mail yourself $200 worth of goods duty-free; mark the package FOR PERSONAL USE. You can also mail gifts to other people without paying duty as long as the recipient doesn't receive more than $200 worth of gifts in a single day; label each gift package UNSOLICITED GIFT. Any package must state on the exterior a description of the contents and their values. You can't mail alcohol, perfume (it contains alcohol), or tobacco products worth more than $5.

For more information on regulations, check out the **U.S. Customs and Border Protection** website at www.cbp.gov or write to them at 1300 Pennsylvania Ave., NW, Washington, DC 20229, to request the free *Know Before You Go* pamphlet.

To prevent the spread of diseases, you cannot bring into the States any plants, fruits, vegetables, meats, or most other foodstuffs. This includes even cured meats like salami (no matter what the shopkeeper in Europe says). You may bring in the following: bakery goods, all but the softest cheeses (the rule is vague, but if the cheese is at all spreadable, don't risk confiscation), candies, roasted coffee beans and dried tea, fish, seeds for veggies and flowers (but not for trees), and mushrooms. Check out the **USDA**'s website at www.aphis.usda.gov/oa/travel for more details.

FOR U.K. CITIZENS   You can bring home almost as much as you like of any goods from any EU country as long as the goods are for your own use. You're likely to be questioned by Customs if you bring back more than 90 liters of wine, 3,200 cigarettes, or 200 cigars. If you're returning home from a non-EU country or if you buy your goods in a duty-free shop, you're allowed to bring home 200 cigarettes or 50 cigars, 2 liters of table wine, plus 1 liter of spirits or 2 liters of fortified wine. Get in touch with **Her Majesty's Customs and Excise Office,** New King's Beam House, 22 Upper Ground, London SE1 9PJ (℅ **020/7620-1313;** www.hmce.gov.uk), or call their Advice Service at ℅ **0845/010-9000** for more information.

FOR CANADIAN CITIZENS   For a clear summary of Canadian rules, write for the booklet *I Declare,* issued by **Revenue Canada,** 2265 St. Laurent Blvd., Ottawa K1G 4KE (℅ **613/993-0534** or 800/959-2221; www.ccra-adrc.gc.ca). Canada allows citizens a C$750 exemption if you've been out of the country for at least

7 days. You're allowed to bring back duty-free 200 cigarettes, 2.2 pounds of tobacco, 40 imperial ounces of liquor, 50 cigars, and 1.5 liters of wine. In addition, you're allowed to mail gifts to Canada from abroad at the rate of C$60 a day, provided they're unsolicited and aren't alcohol or tobacco (write on the package "Unsolicited gift, under C$60 value"). All valuables should be declared on the Y-38 form before departure from Canada, including serial numbers of, for example, expensive foreign cameras that you already own. For more information, call the **Automated Customs Service** at ℭ **800/ 461-9999** toll-free within Canada or ℭ 204/983-3500 outside Canada.

FOR AUSTRALIAN CITIZENS   The duty-free allowance in Australia is A$400 or, for those under 18, A$200. Personal property mailed back from Italy should be marked AUSTRALIAN GOODS RETURNED to avoid payment of duty. On returning to Australia, citizens can bring in 250 cigarettes or 250 grams of loose tobacco, and 1,125ml of alcohol. If you're returning with valuable goods you already own, such as foreign-made cameras, you should file form B263. A helpful brochure, available from Australian consulates or Customs offices, is *Know Before You Go*. For more information, contact **Australian Customs Services,** GPO Box 8, Sydney NSW 2001 (ℭ **1300-363-263** within Australia, or 02-6275-6666 from overseas; www.customs.gov.au).

FOR NEW ZEALAND CITIZENS   The duty-free allowance for New Zealand is NZ$700. Citizens over 17 years can bring in 200 cigarettes, or 50 cigars, or 250 grams of tobacco (or a mixture of all three if their combined weight doesn't exceed 250g); plus 4.5 liters of wine or beer, or 1.125 liters of liquor. New Zealand currency doesn't carry import or export restrictions. Fill out a certificate of export, listing the valuables you are taking out of the country; that way, you can bring them back without paying duty. Most questions are answered in a free pamphlet available at New Zealand consulates and Customs offices: *New Zealand Customs Guide for Travellers, Notice no. 4*. For more information, contact **New Zealand Customshouse,** 50 Anzac Ave., Box 29, Auckland, NZ (ℭ **0800/428-786** within New Zealand; 09-359-6655 from overseas; www.customs.govt.nz).

3 Money

In January 2002, Italy retired the lira and joined most of Western Europe in switching to the euro. Coins are issued in denominations of .01€, .02€, .05€, .10€, .20€, and .50€ as well as 1€ and 2€; bills come in denominations of 5€, 10€, 20€, 50€, 100€, 200€, and 500€.

Exchange rates are established daily and listed in most international newspapers (or check www.xe.com). At this writing, 1€ equaled approximately $1.15—a historic high, as the euro and dollar were usually on a par since the euro's inception. To get a transaction as close to the latest rate as possible, pay for as much as possible with credit cards and get cash out of ATMs.

Traveler's checks, while still the safest way to carry money, are going the way of the dinosaur. The aggressive evolution of international computerized banking and consolidated ATM networks has led to the triumph of plastic throughout the Italian peninsula—even if cold cash is still the most trusted currency, especially in smaller towns or cheaper mom-and-pop joints, where credit cards may not be accepted.

You'll get the best rate if you **exchange money** at a bank or one of its ATMs. The rates at "Cambio/change/wechsel" exchange booths are invariably less favorable but still a good deal better than what you'd get exchanging money at a hotel or shop (a last-resort tactic only). The bill-to-bill changers you'll see in some touristy places exist solely to rip you off.

ATMs

The ability to access your personal checking account through the **Cirrus** (© 800/424-7787; www.mastercard.com) or **PLUS** (© 800/843-7587; www.visa.com) network of ATMs—or get a cash advance on an enabled Visa or MasterCard—has grown by leaps and bounds in Italy in the last few years. It works just like at home. All you need do is search out a machine that has your network's symbol displayed, pop in your card, and punch in your PIN (make sure it's four digits; six-digit PINs won't work). It'll spit out local currency drawn directly from your home checking account (and at a more favorable rate than converting traveler's checks or cash). Also keep in mind that many banks impose a fee every time a card is used at a different bank's ATM, and that fee can be higher for international transactions (up to $5 or more) than for domestic ones (where they're rarely more than $1.50). However, banks in Italy do not (at least yet) charge you a second fee to use their ATMs.

An ATM in Italian is a *Bancomat* (though Bancomat is a private company, its name has become the generic word for ATMs).

Increased internationalism has been slowly doing away with the old worry that your card's PIN, be it on a bank card or credit card, need be specially enabled to work abroad, but it always pays to check with the issuing bank to be sure. If at the ATM you get a message saying your card isn't valid for international transactions, it's likely the bank just can't make the phone connection to check it (occasionally this can be a citywide epidemic); try another ATM.

When you withdraw money with your bank card, you technically get the interbank exchange rate—about 4% better than the "street rate" you'd get exchanging cash or traveler's checks. Note, however, that some U.S. banks are now charging a 1% to 3% "exchange fee" to convert the currency. (Ask your bank before you leave.)

Similarly, **Visa** has begun charging a standard 1% conversion fee for cash advances, and many credit card–issuing banks have begun tacking on an additional 1% to 3% (though as we go to press, Visa is currently being taken to court over this practice in a class-action lawsuit, so stay tuned to the news to see what the future holds). Basically, they've gotten into the "commission" game, too. And, unlike with purchases, interest on a credit card cash advance starts accruing *immediately,* not when your statement cycles. Both methods are still a slightly better deal than converting traveler's checks or cash and considerably more convenient (no waiting in bank lines and pulling out your passport as ID). I use credit card advances only as an emergency option and get most of my euros with my bank card.

ATM withdrawals are often limited to 200€ ($230), or sometimes 300€ ($345), per transaction regardless of your cash advance allowance. **American Express** card cash advances are usually available only from the American Express offices in Florence (see "Fast Facts: Florence" in chapter 2 for more information).

CREDIT CARDS

Visa and **MasterCard** are now almost universally accepted at most hotels, restaurants, and shops; the majority also accepts **American Express. Diners Club** is gaining some ground, especially in Florence and in more expensive establishments throughout the region. If you arrange with your card issuer to enable the card's cash advance option (and get a PIN as well), you can also use them at ATMs.

Some credit-card companies recommend that you notify them of any impending trip abroad so that they don't become suspicious when the card is used numerous times in a foreign destination and block your charges. Even if you don't call your credit-card company in advance, you can always call the card's toll-free emergency number if a charge is refused—a good reason to carry the phone number with you.

TRAVELER'S CHECKS

Traveler's checks are something of an anachronism from the days before the ATM made cash accessible at any time. However, keep in mind that you will likely be charged an ATM withdrawal fee if the bank is not your own, so if you're withdrawing money every day, you might be better off with traveler's checks—provided that you don't mind showing identification every time you want to cash one.

Most banks issue checks under the names of **American Express** (© **800/721-9768** in the U.S. and Canada; www.americanexpress. com) and **Thomas Cook** (© **800/223-7373** in the U.S. and Canada, or 44-1733-318-950 collect from anywhere in the world; www.thomascook.com)—both offer versions that can be countersigned by you or your companion—**Visa** (© **800/227-6811** in the U.S. and Canada, or 44-020-7937-8091 collect from anywhere in the world; www.visa.com), or **Citicorp** (© **800/645-6556** in the U.S. and Canada, or 813/623-1709 collect from anywhere in the world). AAA members can obtain Visa checks without a commission fee at most AAA offices or by calling © **866/339-3378.** Note that you'll get the worst possible exchange rate if you pay for a purchase or hotel room directly with a traveler's check; it's better to trade in the traveler's checks for euros at a bank or the American Express office.

To report lost or stolen traveler's checks in Italy, call toll-free: **American Express** (© 800/872-000), **Thomas Cook** (© 800/872-050), **Visa** (© 800/874-155), or **Citicorp** (© 813/623-1709 collect from anywhere).

4 When to Go

The best times to visit Florence are in the **spring** and **fall.** Starting in late May, the **summer** tourist rush really picks up, and from July to mid-September Italy is teeming with visitors. August is the worst month to visit. Not only does it get uncomfortably hot, muggy, and crowded (the lines for the Uffizi and the Accademia can stretch for blocks), but the entire country goes on vacation at least from August 15 until the end of the month, and many Italians take off the entire month. Many hotels, restaurants, and shops are closed—except at the spas, beaches, and islands, which are where 70% of the Italians are headed. In **winter** (late Oct to Easter), most sights go on shorter

Hot Tickets

For major events where tickets should be procured well before arriving on the spot, check out **Box Office** at © **055-210-804** or www.boxoffice.it. They will only deliver tickets to an Italian address, but you can buy ahead of time and have tickets held for you.

winter hours or are closed for restoration and rearrangement, many hotels and restaurants take a month or two off between November and February, spa and beach destinations become padlocked ghost towns, and it can get much colder than most people expect—it may even snow on occasion.

WEATHER

It can get uncomfortably hot at the height of August in Florence, a valley city. The long spring is temperate and very comfortable, with occasional showers. Fall is also fairly mild, with lots of rainfall being the only drawback. Winter, though mild for most months, can get quite cold in late December or January; it can drizzle a great deal, and snowfall isn't impossible.

HOLIDAYS

Official state holidays include January 1, January 6 (Epiphany), Easter Sunday and Monday, April 25 (Liberation Day), May 1 (Labor Day), August 15 (Ferragosto and Assumption Day), November 1 (All Saints Day), December 8 (Day of the Immaculate Conception), December 25, and December 26 (Santo Stefano). Florence also shuts down to honor its patron, St. John the Baptist, on June 24.

5 Travel Insurance

Check your existing insurance policies and credit-card coverage before you buy travel insurance. You may already be covered for lost luggage, canceled tickets or medical expenses. The cost of travel insurance varies widely, depending on the cost and length of your trip, your age, health, and the type of trip you're taking.

TRIP-CANCELLATION INSURANCE   Trip-cancellation insurance helps you get your money back if you have to back out of a trip, if you have to go home early, or if your travel supplier goes bank-rupt. Allowed reasons for cancellation can range from sickness to natural disasters to the State Department declaring your destination unsafe for travel. (Insurers usually won't cover vague fears, though, as many travelers discovered who tried to cancel their trips in Oct 2001 because they were wary of flying.) In this unstable world, trip-cancellation insurance is a good buy if you're getting tickets well in advance—who knows what the state of the world, or of your airline, will be in 9 months? Insurance policy details vary, so read the fine print—and especially make sure that your airline or cruise line is on the list of carriers covered in case of bankruptcy. For informa-tion, contact one of the following insurers: **Access America** (© **800/807-3982;** www.accessamerica.com); **Travel Guard Inter-national** (© 800/826-4919; www.travelguard.com); **Travel Insured International** (© 800/243-3174; www.travelinsured. com); and **Travelex Insurance Services** (© 888/457-4602; www. travelex-insurance.com).

MEDICAL INSURANCE   Most health insurance policies cover you if you get sick away from home—but check, particularly if you're insured by an HMO.

With the exception of certain HMOs and Medicare/Medicaid, your medical insurance should cover medical treatment—even hos-pital care—overseas. However, most out-of-country hospitals make you pay your bills up front, and send you a refund after you've returned home and filed the necessary paperwork. And in a worst-case scenario, there's the high cost of emergency evacuation. If you require additional medical insurance, try **MEDEX International** (© 800/527-0218 or 410/453-6300; www.medexassist.com) or **Travel Assistance International** (© **800/821-2828;** www.travel assistance.com; for general information on services, call the com-pany's Worldwide Assistance Services, Inc., at © **800/777-8710**).

Again, most health insurance plans covering out-of-country ill-nesses and hospital stays require you to pay your local bills up front (your coverage takes the form of a refund after you've returned and filed the paperwork). However, **Blue Cross/Blue Shield members** (© **800/810-BLUE** or www.bluecares.com for a list of participating hospitals) can now use their plans and cards at select hospitals abroad as they would at home, which means much lower out-of-pocket costs. In Florence, the card is honored at the **Villa Donatello,** Piazza Donatello 14 (© **055-323-3373**).

LOST-LUGGAGE INSURANCE   On international flights (including U.S. portions of international trips), checked baggage is automatically covered at approximately $9.07 per pound, up to approximately $635 per checked bag. If you plan to check items more valuable than the standard liability, see if your valuables are covered by your homeowner's policy, get baggage insurance as part of your comprehensive travel-insurance package, or buy Travel Guard's "BagTrak" product. Don't buy insurance at the airport, as it's usually overpriced. Be sure to take any valuables or irreplaceable items with you in your carry-on luggage, as many valuables (including books, money and electronics) aren't covered by airline policies.

If your luggage is lost, immediately file a lost-luggage claim at the airport, detailing the luggage contents. For most airlines, you must report delayed, damaged, or lost baggage within 4 hours of arrival. The airlines are required to deliver luggage, once found, directly to your house or destination free of charge.

6 Health

There are no special health risks you'll encounter in Italy. The tap water is safe, and medical resources are of a high quality. In fact, with Italy's partially socialized medicine, you can usual stop by any hospital emergency room with an ailment, get swift and courteous service, be given a diagnosis and a prescription, and sent on your way with a wave and a smile—and not even a sheet of paperwork to fill out.

In most cases, your existing health plan will provide the coverage you need. But double-check; you may want to buy **travel medical insurance** instead. (See the section on insurance, above.) Bring your insurance ID card with you when you travel.

If you suffer from a chronic illness, consult your doctor before your departure. For conditions like epilepsy, diabetes, or heart problems, wear a **Medic Alert Identification Tag** (© 800/825-3785; www.medicalert.org), which will immediately alert doctors to your condition and give them access to your records through Medic Alert's 24-hour hot line.

Pack **prescription medications** in your carry-on luggage, and carry prescription medications in their original containers, with pharmacy labels—otherwise they won't make it through airport security. Also bring along copies of your prescriptions in case you lose your pills or run out. Don't forget an extra pair of contact lenses or prescription glasses. Carry the generic name of prescription medicines, in case a local pharmacist is unfamiliar with the brand name.

Contact the **International Association for Medical Assistance to Travelers (IAMAT;** ℅ **716/754-4883** or 416/652-0137; www.iamat.org) for tips on travel and health concerns in the countries you're visiting, and lists of local, English-speaking doctors. In **Canada,** contact them at 40 Regal Road, Guelph, Ont., N1K 1B5 (℅ **519/836-0102;** fax 519/836-3412); and in **New Zealand** at P.O. Box 5049, Christchurch 5 (fax 643/352-4630).

The United States **Centers for Disease Control and Prevention** (℅ **800/311-3435;** www.cdc.gov) provides up-to-date information on necessary vaccines and health hazards by region or country. Any foreign consulate can provide a list of area doctors who speak English. If you get sick, consider asking your hotel concierge to recommend a local doctor—even his or her own. You can also try the emergency room at a local hospital; many have walk-in clinics for emergency cases that are not life threatening. You may not get immediate attention, but you won't pay the high price of an emergency room visit.

7 Specialized Travel Resources

FOR TRAVELERS WITH DISABILITIES

Italy certainly doesn't win any medals for being overly accessible, though a few of the top museums and churches are beginning at least to install ramps at the entrances, and a few hotels are converting first-floor rooms into accessible units by widening the doors and bathrooms. Buses and trains can cause problems as well, with high, narrow doors and steep steps at entrances. There are, however, seats reserved on public transportation for travelers with disabilities.

Luckily, there's an endless list of organizations to help you plan your trip and offer specific advice before you go. Many travel agencies offer customized tours and itineraries for travelers with disabilities. **Flying Wheels Travel** (℅ **507/451-5005;** www.flyingwheels travel.com) offers escorted tours and cruises that emphasize sports and private tours in minivans with lifts. **Accessible Journeys** (℅ **800/846-4537** or 610/521-0339; www.disabilitytravel.com) caters specifically to slow walkers and wheelchair travelers and their families and friends.

Other helpful organizations include the **Society for Accessible Travel and Hospitality** (℅ **212/447-7284;** www.sath.org; annual membership fees $45 adults, $30 seniors and students), which offers a wealth of travel resources for all types of disabilities and informed recommendations on destinations, access guides, travel agents, tour operators, vehicle rentals, and companion services; and the **American Foundation for the Blind** (© 800/232-5463; www.afb.org), which provides information on traveling with Seeing Eye dogs.

FOR GAY & LESBIAN TRAVELERS

Italy isn't the most tolerant country regarding same-sex couples, but it has grown to accept homosexuality, especially over the past few decades. Homosexuality is legal, and the age of consent is 16. Luckily, Italians are already more affectionate and physical than Americans in their general friendships, and even straight men regularly walk down the street with their arms around each other—however, kissing anywhere other than on the cheeks at greetings and goodbyes will certainly draw attention. As you might expect, smaller towns tend to be less permissive and accepting than cities. Florence has the largest and most visible homosexual population (not that that's saying much).

Italy's national association and support network for gays and lesbians is **ARCI-Gay/ARCI-Lesbica.** The national website is www.arcigay.it, but they've recently launched a Tuscany-specific one at www.gaytoscana.it, and the new head regional office is in **Siena** at Via Massetana Romana 18, 53100 Siena (© 0577-288-977; fax 0577-271-538; www.gaysiena.it). There are other offices in **Pisa** (Arcigay Pride!; Via San Lorenzo 38; © 050-555-618; fax 050-831-0605; www.gay.it/pride), in **Pistoia** (no address yet; cellphone contact 333-667-6873; www.gaypistoia.it), and **Grosseto** (Via Ravel 7; © 339-440-9049 or 347-078-8972; www.grossetogay.it). Their cousin association in Florence is called **Ireos** (www.ireos.org), in the Oltrarno at Via dei Serragli 3, 50124 Firenze (© and fax **055-216-907**).

The **International Gay & Lesbian Travel Association (IGLTA;** © **800/448-8550** or 954-776-2626; www.iglta.org) is the trade association for the gay and lesbian travel industry, and offers an online directory of gay and lesbian-friendly travel businesses; go to the website and click on "Members."

FOR SENIORS

Italy is a multigenerational culture that doesn't tend to marginalize its seniors, and older people are treated with a great deal of respect and deference throughout Italy. But there are few specific programs, associations, or concessions made for them. The one exception is on admission prices for museums and sights, where those over 60 or 65 will often get in at a reduced rate or even free. As a senior in Italy, you're *un anciano* (*una anciana* if you're a woman) or "ancient one"—consider it a term of respect and let people know you're one if you think a discount may be in the works.

Members of **AARP**, 601 E St. NW, Washington, DC 20049 (© **800/424-3410** or 202/434-2277; www.aarp.org), get discounts on hotels, airfares, and car rentals. AARP offers members a wide range of benefits, including *AARP The Magazine* and a monthly newsletter. Anyone over 50 can join.

Sadly, most major **airlines** have in recent years canceled their discount programs for seniors, but you can always ask when booking. Of the big **car-rental** agencies, only National currently gives an AARP discount, but the many rental dealers that specialize in Europe—Auto Europe, Kemwel, Europe-by-Car—offer seniors 5% off their already low rates. In most European cities, people over 60 or 65 get reduced admission at theaters, museums, and other attractions, and they can often get discount fares or cards on public transportation and national rail systems. Carrying ID with proof of age can pay off in all these situations.

Grand Circle Travel, 347 Congress St., Boston, MA 02210 (© **800/959-0405** or 800/321-2835; www.gct.com), is one of the literally hundreds of travel agencies specializing in vacations for seniors. But beware: Many packages are of the tour-bus variety. Seniors seeking more independent travel should probably consult a regular travel agent. **SAGA Holidays,** 1161 Boylston St., Boston, MA

Tips **A Note for Families & Seniors**

At most state-run museums, children under 18 and seniors get in free *but only if* they hail from one of the countries that has signed a reciprocal international cultural agreement to allow children and seniors this privilege. These countries include England, Canada, Ireland, Australia, New Zealand, and indeed much of the world—but *not* the United States. (However, many museum guards either don't ask for citizenship ID or wave kids and seniors on through anyway.) Children and seniors, no matter what their nationality, also get discounts on trains.

02115 (© **800/343-0273;** www.sagaholidays.com), has 40 years of experience running all-inclusive tours and cruises for those 50 and older. They also sponsor the more substantial "Road Scholar Tours" (© **800/621-2151**), fun-loving tours with an educational bent. **Elderhostel** (© **877/426-8056;** www.elderhostel.org) arranges study programs for those ages 55 and over (and a spouse or companion of any age) in the U.S. and in more than 80 countries around the world. Most courses last 2 to 4 weeks abroad, and many include airfare, accommodations in university dormitories or modest inns, meals, and tuition.

FOR FAMILIES

If you have enough trouble getting your kids out of the house in the morning, dragging them thousands of miles away may seem like an insurmountable challenge. But family travel can be immensely rewarding, giving you new ways of seeing the world through smaller pairs of eyes. As an added plus, little helps mature the kids faster than international travel.

Familyhostel (© **800/733-9753;** www.learn.unh.edu/family hostel) takes the whole family, including kids ages 8 to 15, on moderately priced domestic and international learning vacations. Lectures, field trips, and sightseeing are guided by a team of academics.

You can find good family-oriented vacation advice on the Internet from sites like the **Family Travel Network** (www.familytravel network.com); **Traveling Internationally with Your Kids** (www. travelwithyourkids.com), a comprehensive site offering sound advice for long-distance and international travel with children; and **Family Travel Files** (www.thefamilytravelfiles.com), which offers an online magazine and a directory of off-the-beaten-path tours and tour operators for families.

FOR WOMEN

Women will feel remarkably welcome in Italy—sometimes a bit too welcome, actually. Yes, it sometimes seems every young Italian male is out to prove himself the most irresistible lover on the planet; remember, this is the land of Romeo and Casanova, so they have a lot to live up to.

From parading and preening like peacocks to wooing each passing female with words, whistles, and, if they can get close enough, the entirely inappropriate butt-pinch, these men and their attentiveness can range from charming and flattering to downright annoying and frustrating. The more exotic you look—statuesque blondes, ebony-skinned beauties, or simply an American accent—the more irresistible you become to these suitors. And, as everyone around the world knows from watching Hollywood movies, American women are all uninhibited and passionate sex kittens. That this isn't actually true doesn't make much of a dent in Italian boys' fantasies.

Flirting back at these would-be Romeos, even mildly, only convinces them that you're ready to jump into bed. Heck, mere eye contact encourages them to redouble their efforts. Unless you want all this attention, take your cue from Italian women, who may wear tight skirts and fishnets but, you'll notice, usually ignore the men around them entirely unless it's someone they're already walking with.

If you find yourself moderately molested on a bus or other crowded place—mostly the infamous bottom-pinching and rather inappropriate rubbing—tell him to *"Smetti la!"* (stop it) and proceed to pinch, scratch, elbow, and so on to further discourage him or enlist the aid of the nearest convenient elderly Italian woman to noisily chastise the offender and perhaps whap him with her purse.

Note that much of the attention is kept to verbal flirtation and that occasional inappropriate touching that deserves a slap in the face. These men want to conquer you with their charm, not their muscles; rape is near unheard-of in Italy. Most women report feeling far safer wandering the deserted streets of an Italian city back to their hotels at 2am than they do in their own neighborhoods back home, and that feeling is largely justified. You'll probably get tons of ride offers, though, from would-be chivalrous knights atop their Vespa or Fiat steeds.

FOR STUDENTS

You'd be wise to arm yourself with an **International Student Identity Card (ISIC),** which offers substantial savings on rail passes, plane tickets, and entrance fees; your own school's ID will often suffice to snag you those discount admission at sights and museums across Europe, but the ISIC helps. It also provides you with basic health and life insurance and a 24-hour help line. The card is available for $22 from **STA Travel** (© **800/781-4040,** and if you're not in North America there's probably a local number in your country; www.statravel.com), the biggest student travel agency in the world.

If you're no longer a student but are still under 26, you can get a **International Youth Travel Card (IYTC)** for the same price from the same people, which entitles you to some discounts (but not on museum admissions). (*Note:* STA Travel bought competitors **Council Travel** and **USIT Campus** after they went bankrupt. It's still operating some offices under the Council name, but they're owned by STA.) **Travel CUTS** (© 800/667-2887 or 416/614-2887; www. travelcuts.com) offers similar services for both Canadians and U.S. residents. Irish students should turn to **USIT** (© 01/602-1600; www.usitnow.ie).

8 Getting There

BY PLANE
FROM NORTH AMERICA

No carrier flies directly from the United States or Canada to any airport in Florence; however, with most airlines (and their affiliates) you can connect through a handful of European cities to the small international airports at Pisa or Florence. You may find it most convenient simply to fly to Rome and connect to Florence by plane (a bit over 1 hr.) or by train (close to 3 hr.).

THE MAJOR AIRLINES   Italy's national airline, **Alitalia** (© 800/ 223-5730; www.alitalia.it), offers more flights daily to Italy than any other airline. It flies direct to both Rome and Milan from New York, Newark, Boston, Chicago, Los Angeles, and Miami. You can connect in Rome or Milan to any other Italian destination, including Florence. If you're flying from the New York City area and planning to connect to Florence, note that itineraries that route you through Milan often have a layover that's 3 hours shorter than one that routes you through Rome's airport.

British Airways (© 800/247-9297; www.ba.com) flies direct from dozens of U.S. and Canadian cities to London, where you can get connecting flights to Pisa, Rome, or Milan. **Air Canada** (© 888/ 247-2262 or 800/361-8071 [TTY]; www.aircanada.ca) flies daily from Toronto and Vancouver to Rome. **Continental** (© 800/231- 0856; www.continental.com) doesn't fly to Italy itself, but it's partnered with Alitalia for the Newark-to-Rome and New York JFK- to-Milan flights, so if you're a Continental Frequent Flyer you can reserve through Continental and rack up the miles.

Delta (© 800/241-4141; www.delta.com) flies daily out of New York JFK (you can connect from most major U.S. cities) to Rome and Milan, where it's possible to change to one of Delta's local partner airlines (Lufthansa, Iberia, and so on) for the last leg to Tuscany. From either city you can take a train to Florence, or from Rome you can connect to an Alitalia flight to Florence.

Possibly less convenient alternatives are **American Airlines** (© 800/433-7300; www.aa.com), whose flights from the United States to Milan all go through Chicago; **United** (© 800/528-2929;

www.ual.com), which flies once daily to Milan out of New York, Newark, and Washington, D.C. Dulles; or **US Airways** (© **800/ 622-1015;** www.usairways.com), which offers one flight daily to Rome out of Philadelphia. (You can connect through Philly from most major U.S. cities.)

FROM GREAT BRITAIN & IRELAND

British Airways (© **0845/773-3377;** www.ba.com) flies twice daily from London's Gatwick to Pisa. **Alitalia (020/8745-8200;** www. alitalia.it) has four daily flights from London to both Rome and Milan and three daily from London Gatwick into Florence. **KLM UK** (formerly Air UK; © **08705/074-074;** www.klmuk.com) flies several times per week from London Heathrow to Milan (both airports) and Rome. In each case, there's a layover in Amsterdam. No-frills upstart **Ryanair** (© **0871/246-0000** in the U.K.; www. ryanair.com) will fly you from London to Pisa (as well as Rome, Milan, Bologna, Ancona, and other Italian destinations); its competitor EasyJet (www.easyjet.com) flies from London to Milan and Bologna. Both usually charge less than £25 each way for such service.

The best and cheapest way to get to Italy from Ireland is to make your way first to London and fly from there to Rome or direct to Pisa (see above; to book through **British Airways** in Ireland, dial © **800/626-747**). **Aer Lingus** (© **0818/365-000** in Ireland; www. aerlingus.com) flies direct from Dublin to both Rome and Milan about 5 days a week. **Alitalia** (© **01/677-5171**) puts you on a British Midland to get you to London, where you change to an Alitalia plane for the trip to Rome. For **RyanAir,** call © **0818/ 303-030** in Ireland.

FROM AUSTRALIA & NEW ZEALAND

Alitalia (© **02-9922-1555;** www.alitalia.it) has a flight from Sydney to Rome every Thursday and Saturday. **Qantas** (© **13-13-13** in Australia, or 0649/357-8900 in Auckland, NZ; www.qantas.com) flies three times daily to Rome via Bangkok, leaving Australia from Sydney, Melbourne, Brisbane, or Cairns. Qantas will also book you through one of these Australian cities from Auckland, Wellington, or Christchurch in New Zealand. You can also look into flying first into London and connecting to Italy from there. (There are more flights, and it may work out to be cheaper.)

GETTING TO FLORENCE FROM ROME'S AIRPORTS

Most international flights to Rome will arrive at **Fiumicino Airport** (officially named **Leonardo da Vinci International Airport,** but few, including the airlines themselves, call it that). Some inter-European and transatlantic charter flights may land at the less convenient **Ciampino Airport.** You can connect to a plane at either to take you to Florence's airport, but it's often simpler, almost as fast in the long run, and cheaper to take the train.

Fiumicino (© **06-659-51;** www.adr.it) is 30km (19 miles) from Rome's center. You can take the **express train** (8.80€/$10) from Fiumicino to Rome's central train station, Termini. A taxi to the station costs about 36€ ($41). From Termini, you can grab one of many daily trains to Florence. If you happen to fly into **Ciampino Airport** (© **06-7934-0297**), 15km (9 miles) south of the city, a none-too-frequent COTRAL bus will take you to the Anagnina metro station, where you can take the metro to Termini, the whole trip costing around 3€ ($3.45). A taxi to Rome's center from Ciampino should run about 25€ ($29).

GETTING TO FLORENCE FROM MILAN'S AIRPORT

Your flight may land at either **Linate Airport** (© **02-7485-2200;** www.sea-aeroportimilano.it), about 8km (5 miles) southeast of the city, or **Malpensa Airport** (© **02-2680-0613**), 45km (28 miles) from downtown—closer to Como than to Milan itself.

From **Malpensa,** a 40-minute express train heads half-hourly to Cadorna train station in western Milan rather than the larger or more central Stazione Centrale from which most trains onward to Florence will leave (you'll have to take the Metro to get there). To grab a bus instead, which will take you directly to that central downtown rail station, your choices are **Malpensa Express** (© **02-9619-2301**) which costs 5.05€ ($5.80), or the slightly cheaper **Malpensa Shuttle** (© **02-5858-3185**)—same service, different price: 4.50€ ($5.20)—two or three times per hour for the 50-minute ride to the east side of Milan's Stazione Centrale.

From **Linate,** buses, **STAM buses** (© **02-717-100**) make the 25-minute trip to Milan's Stazione Centrale, every 20 to 30 minutes daily from 7am to 11pm, and cost 2€ ($2.30; buy on bus). The slightly slower city bus no. 73 leaves hourly for the S. Babila metro stop downtown (1€/$1.15 for a regular bus ticket bought from any news agent inside the airport, but not on-board).

From Milan's Stazione Centrale, you can get trains to Florence (see "Arriving" in chapter 2).

GETTING THROUGH THE AIRPORT

With the federalization of airport security, security procedures at U.S. airports are more stable and consistent than ever. Generally,

> **Tips** **The Milan Connection**
>
> Note that if you find yourself flying into Milan, the domestic
> airport (Linate) is separate from the international one
> (Malpensa), and transferring planes to a connecting flight to
> Florence requires switching airports (an 8€/$9.20 bus connects
> the two airports), sometimes changing airlines, and an innate
> trust in the gods of luggage transfer. If you fly into Milan, a
> train to Florence is probably your best bet. This isn't a problem
> for flights on Alitalia, however, which uses Milan's Malpensa
> airport for both international arrivals and domestic depar-
> tures—a blatantly nationalistic protectionist scheme which has
> all other major airlines, European and American, up in arms.

you'll be fine if you arrive at the airport **2 hours** before an international flight; if you show up late, tell an airline employee and she'll
probably whisk you to the front of the line.

Bring your **passport** as photo ID (you need that to get into Italy
anyway!) and if you've got an E-ticket, print out the **official confirmation page;** you might need to show it at the security checkpoint.

Security lines are getting shorter, but some doozies remain. If you
have trouble standing for long periods of time, tell an airline
employee; the airline will provide a wheelchair. Speed up security by
not wearing metal objects such as big belt buckles or clanky earrings. If you've got metallic body parts, a note from your doctor can
prevent a long chat with the security screeners. Keep in mind that
only **ticketed passengers** are allowed past security, except for folks
escorting passengers with disabilities or children.

Federalization has stabilized **what you can carry on** and **what you
can't.** The general rule is that sharp things are out, nail clippers are
okay, and food and beverages must be passed through the X-ray
machine—but that security screeners can't make you drink from
your coffee cup. Bring food in your carry-on rather than checking it,
as explosive-detection machines used on checked luggage have been
known to mistake food (especially chocolate, for some reason) for
bombs. Travelers in the U.S. are allowed one carry-on bag, plus a
"personal item" such as a purse, briefcase, or laptop bag. Carry-on
hoarders can stuff all sorts of things into a laptop bag; as long as it
has a laptop in it, it's still considered a personal item. The Transportation Security Administration (TSA) has issued a list of restricted
items; check its website at **www.tsa.gov** for details.

The TSA has phased out **gate check-in** at all U.S. airports. Passengers with E-tickets and without checked bags can still beat the ticket-counter lines by using **electronic kiosks** or even **online check-in.** Ask your airline which alternatives are available, and if you're using a kiosk, bring the credit card you used to book the ticket. If you're checking bags, you will still be able to use most airlines' kiosks; again call your airline for up-to-date information. **Curbside check-in** is also a good way to avoid lines, although a few airlines still ban curbside check-in entirely; call before you go.

At press time, the TSA is also recommending that you **not lock your checked luggage** so screeners can search it by hand if necessary (and in this author's experience, they often find it necessary), and this often happens after you've abandoned it to the baggage handling system, so you won't be on hand to unlock the thing for them; they'll simply destroy the lock to get to your stuff. The agency says to use plastic "zip ties" instead, which can be bought at hardware stores and can be easily cut off.

BY CAR

You'll get the **best rental rate** if you book your car from home instead of renting direct in Italy—in fact, if you decide to rent once you're over there, it's worth it to call home to have someone arrange it all from there. You must be over 25 to rent from most agencies (although some accept 21).

Though it once was smart shopping to see what rates Italian companies were offering, they're all now allied with the big agents in the States: **Avis** (𝄞 **800/230-4898, or** in Italy toll-free 199-100-133; www.avis.com), **Budget** (𝄞 **800/527-0700;** www.budget.com), **Hertz** (𝄞 **800/654-3131** or 800/654-3001; www.hertz.com), and **National** (𝄞 **800/227-7368;** www.nationalcar.com).

You can usually get a better rate by going through one of the rental companies specializing in Europe: **Auto Europe** (𝄞 **888/223-5555;** www.autoeurope.com), **Europe by Car** (𝄞 **800/223-1516** or 212/581-3040; www.europebycar.com), **Kemwell** (𝄞 **800/678-0678;** www.kemwell.com), and **Maiellano** (𝄞 **800/223-1616** or 718/727-0044). With constant price wars and special packages, it always pays to shop around among all the above.

When offered the choice between a compact car and a larger one, always choose the smaller car (unless you have a large group)—you'll need it for maneuvering the winding, steeply graded Italian roads and the impossibly narrow alleyways of towns and cities. Likewise, if you can drive stick shift, order one; it'll help you better navigate the hilly terrain. It's also a good idea to opt for the **Collision Damage Waiver (CDW)** that for only $10 to $20 a day gives you the peace of mind and nerves of steel that driving in Italy requires; you can pay only $7 per day for this service if you buy it through a third party insurer such as Travel Guard (www.travelguard.com). Although the 19% IVA value-added tax is unavoidable, you can do away with the government airport pick-up tax of 10% by picking up your car at an office in town.

BY TRAIN

Every day, up to 14 **Eurostar** trains (reservations in London ℂ **0875/186-186;** www.eurostar.com) zip from London to Paris's Gare du Nord via the **Chunnel (Eurotunnel)** in a bit over 4 hours. In Paris, you can transfer to the Paris Gare de Lyon station or Paris Bercy for one of three daily direct trains to **Milan** (from which you can transfer to Florence) or two to **Florence.** Some of the Milan runs are high-speed TGV trains, a 6½-hour ride requiring a seat reservation. At least one will be an overnight Euronight (EN) train, with reservable sleeping couchettes; the Euronight leaves Paris around 10pm and gets into Milan around 8:45am. The two Euronight trains going directly from Paris to Florence take 12½ hours.

The definitive 500-page book listing all official European train routes and schedules is the *Thomas Cook European Timetable,* available in the United States for $28 (plus $4.50 shipping and handling) from Forsyth Travel Library, P.O. Box 2975, Shawnee Mission, KS 66201 (ℂ **800/367-7984**) or at travel specialty stores. You can also order the schedule online at **www.thomascooktimetables.com**.

Getting to Know Florence

Mary McCarthy famously described Florence *(Firenze)* as a "City of Stone." This assessment digs deeper than merely the fact that the buildings, streets, doorjambs, sidewalks, windowsills, towers, and bridges are all cobbled together in shades of gray, stern rock hewn by generations of the stonecutters Michelangelo grew up with. Florence's stoniness is evident in both its countenance and its character. Florentines often seem more serious and slower to warm to strangers than the stereotypical Italians. The city's fundamental rhythms are medieval, and it's fiendishly difficult to get beyond the touristy surface and see what really makes Florence tick. Although the historic center is compact, it takes time and effort to get to know it personally, get the hang of its alleys, and understand the deep history of its palace-lined streets.

This chapter will equip you with the basic tools (the hammer and chisel, so to speak) you'll need to get under the stony skin of Florence. It breaks down the city layout and neighborhoods and explains the sorts of facts and services you'll need.

1 Essentials

ARRIVING

BY PLANE For flights into Florence, see "Getting There" in chapter 1. Several European airlines are now servicing Florence's expanded **Amerigo Vespucci Airport** (© **055-30-615** for the switchboard, or 055-373-498 for flight updates; 055-306-1700 for national flight info, 055-306-1702 for international flight info; www.safnet.it or www.aeroporto.firenze.it), also called **Peretola,** just 5km (3 miles) northwest of town. There are no direct flights to or from the United States, but you can make easy connections through London, Paris, Amsterdam, Frankfurt, and other major European cities. The regularly scheduled **city bus 62** connects the airport with Piazza della Stazione downtown, taking about 30 minutes and costing 1€ ($1.15). Rather more expensive (4€/$4.60) but without the

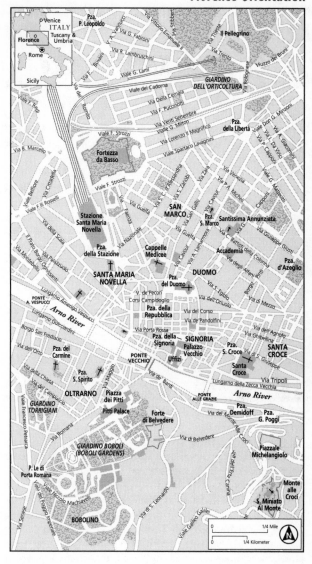

Florence Orientation

Venice
ITALY
Florence
Tuscany &
Umbria
Rome
Sicily

Pza. P. Leopoldo
Via Vittorio Emanuele II
Via G. Fabroni
Via V. A. Vanni
Via F. Bovani
Via R. Lambruschini
Via G. Lami
Il Pellegrino
Via Trento
Viuzzo dei Bruni
Via della Robbia
Via Trieste
Via Stibberti

Viale dei Cadorna
Via Della Cernaia
Via F. Puccinotti
Via Venti Settembre
Viale G. Milton
Via Lorenzo Il Magnifico
Viale Spartaco Lavagnini
GIARDINO DELL'ORTICOLTURA
Pza. della Libertà
Via Don G. Minzoni
Via G. La Pira
Via P. Giacomini
Via G. Matteotti
Viale G. Mazzini

Viale F. Strozzi
Fortezza da Basso
Via S. C. d'Alessandria
Via S. Zanobi
Via Zara
Via Venezia
Via P.A. Micheli
Carponi

Viale F. Strozzi
Via Guelfa
Via S. Gallo
SAN MARCO
Pza. S. Marco
Santissima Annunziata
Via C. Battisti
Via della Colonna
Via Giuseppe Giusti

Stazione Santa Maria Novella
Via Nazionale
Via Guelfa
Via Cavour
Via A. Lamarmora
Accademia
Via degli Alfani
Borgo Pinti
Pza. d'Azeglio

Pza. della Stazione
Cappelle Medicee
DUOMO
Via S. Egidio
Via di Mezzo

SANTA MARIA NOVELLA
Pza. del Duomo
V. de' Pecori
Corsi Campidoglio
Via dell'Oriuolo

Lungarno Amerigo Vespucci
PONTE A. VESPUCCI
Arno River
Lungarno Guicciardini
Borgo San Frediano
Via dell'Orto
Via de' Pecori
Pza. della Repubblica
Via del Corso
Via de Pandolfini
Via Porta Rossa
Pza. della Signoria
SIGNORIA
Palazzo Vecchio
Uffizi
Pza. S. Croce
Via dell'Agnolo
Via Ghibellina
SANTA CROCE
Santa Croce
Via S. Giuseppe
Via Tripoli

Pza. del Carmine
Via della Chiesa
Pza. S. Spirito
PONTE VECCHIO
Via de' Bardi
PONTE ALLE GRAZIE
Lungarno della Zecca Vecchia
Arno River

Via del Campuccio
OLTRARNO
Piazza dei Pitti
Pitti Palace
Forte di Belvedere
Pza. Demidoff
Via del Monte Alle Croci
Pza. G. Poggi

GIARDINO TORRIGIANI
Via Francesco Petrarca
Via Romana
GIARDINO BOBOLI (BOBOLI GARDENS)
Via di Belvedere
Piazzale Michelangiolo

P. Le di Porta Romana
Viale Niccolò Machiavelli
Viale di Poggio Imperiale
Via Senese
BOBOLINO
Via di S. Leonardo
Viale Galileo Galilei
Via dell'Erta Canina
S. Miniato Al Monte
Monte alle Croci

0   1/4 Mile
0   1/4 Kilometer

25

local stops is the half-hourly **SITA bus** to/from downtown's bus station at Via Santa Caterina 15r (© **055-214-721,** 800-424-500, or 800-373-760), behind the train station. Metered **taxis** line up outside the airport's arrival terminal and charge a flat, official rate of 15€ ($17) to the city center.

The closest major international airport is Pisa's **Galileo Galilei Airport** (© **050/500-707;** www.pisa-airport.com), 97km (60 miles) west of Florence. Two to three **trains** per hour leave the airport for Florence (70–100 min., 5.40€/$6.20). If your flight leaves from this airport and you'll be going there by train from Florence, you can check in your baggage and receive your boarding pass at the Air Terminal on Track 5 in Florence's Stazione Santa Maria Novella; show up 30 minutes before your train departure. Early-morning flights might make train connections from Florence to the airport difficult; the solution is the regular train from Florence into downtown Pisa, with a 10-minute taxi 2.60€ ($3) from the Pisa train station to the nearby Pisa airport; the no. 7 bus makes the same hop in twice the time for .77€ (90¢).

BY TRAIN   Florence is Tuscany's rail hub, with connections to all the region's major cities. To get here from Rome, you can take the Pendolino (four daily, 1¾ hr.; make sure it's going to Santa Maria Novella station, not Rifredi; you must reserve tickets ahead), an EC or IC train (24 daily, just under 2 hr.), or an interregionale (seven daily, around 3 hr.). There are also about 16 trains daily from Milan (3 hr.) through Bologna (1 hr.).

Most Florence-bound trains roll into the **Stazione Santa Maria Novella,** Piazza della Stazione (© **800-888-088** toll-free in Italy, or 055-288-765; www.trenitalia.it), which you'll often see abbreviated as **S.M.N.** The station is on the northwestern edge of the city's compact historic center, a 10-minute walk from the Duomo and a 15-minute walk from Piazza della Signoria and the Uffizi. There are loads of budget hotels immediately east of there around Via Faenza and Via Fiume.

With your back to the tracks, toward the station's left exit (across from Track 16) and next to a 24-hour pharmacy you'll find a tiny **tourist info office** open daily from 8:30am to 9pm, with a hotel-booking service (charging 2.30€–8€/$2.65–$9.20). The **train information office** is near the opposite exit to your right, across from Track 5. The yellow posters on the wall inside the anteroom list all train times and routes for this and other major Italian stations. Another copy of the Florence poster is just inside the sliding glass doors of the second, main room. For personalized help, you have to take a number from the color-coded machine (pink is for train information) and wait your turn—often for more than an hour.

Back at the head of the tracks, the **ticketing room** *(Salone Biglietti)* is located through the central doors; at *sportelli* (windows 9–18) you can buy ordinary unreserved train tickets. The automatic ticket machines were installed mainly to taunt us and rarely work. Around the corner from this bank of ticket windows is a smaller room where you can buy **international tickets** (window 7), make **reservations** for high-speed and overnight trains (windows 1–4), or pay for a spot on the **Pendolino/ETR express** to Milan, Bologna, or Rome (window 5).

At the head of Track 16 is a 24-hour luggage depot where you can drop your bags (2.60€/$3 per piece for 12 hr.) while you search for a hotel.

Exit out to the left coming off the tracks and you'll find many bus lines as well as stairs down to the underground **pedestrian underpass** which leads directly to Piazza dell'Unità Italiana and saves you from the traffic of the station's piazza.

Note that some trains stop at the outlying **Stazione Campo di Marte** or **Stazione Rifredi,** both of which are worth avoiding. Although there's 24-hour bus service between these satellite stations and S.M.N., departures aren't always frequent and taxi service is erratic and expensive.

BY BUS Because Florence is such a well-connected train hub, there's little reason to take the longer, less comfortable intercity coaches. Dozens of companies make dozens of runs here daily from all of Tuscany, much of Umbria, and the major cities in Italy (the express bus from Rome's Tiburtina Station takes 4½ hr.). Most bus stations are near the train station.

BY CAR The **A1 autostrada** runs north from Rome past Arezzo to Florence and continues to Bologna. The **A11** connects Florence with Lucca, and **unnumbered superhighways** run to Siena and Pisa.

Driving to Florence is easy; the problems begin once you arrive. Almost all cars are banned from the historic center—only residents or merchants with special permits are allowed in. You'll likely be stopped at some point by the traffic police, who'll assume from your rental plates that you're a visitor heading to your hotel. Have the name and address of the hotel ready and they'll wave you through. You can drop off baggage there (the hotel will give you a sign for your car advising traffic police you're unloading), then you must relocate to a parking lot. Ask your hotel which is most convenient: Special rates are available through most of the hotels and their nearest lot.

Standard rates for parking in private lots near the center are 2€ to 3€ ($2.30–$3.45) per hour; many lots offer a daily rate of 15€ to 30€ ($17–$35). However, it is difficult to find spots, and they often keep weird hours, so your best bet is one of the city-run garages, which are also less pricey. Although the finally finished parking lot under Santa Maria Novella (1.55€/$1.80 per hour) is closer to the city center, the best deal if you're staying the night (better than most hotels' garage rates) is at the **Parterre parking lot** under Piazza Libertà, north of Fortezza del Basso. If you're staying at least 1 night in Florence at a hotel, you can park here, are welcome to a free bike, and (on presentation of your hotel receipt as you leave or the hotel's stamp on your parking receipt) pay only 10€ ($12) per night.

Don't park your car overnight on the streets in Florence; if you're towed and ticketed, it will set you back substantially—and the headaches to retrieve your car are beyond description.

VISITOR INFORMATION

TOURIST OFFICES   The city's **largest tourist office** is at Via Cavour 1r (✆ **055-290-832;** fax 055-276-0383; www.firenze turismo.it), about 3 blocks north of the Duomo. Outrageously, they now charge for basic, useful info: .50€ (60¢) for a city map (though there's still a free one that differs only in lacking relatively inane brief descriptions of the museums and sights), 2€ ($2.30) for a little guide to museums, and 1€ ($1.15) each for pamphlets on the bridges and the piazze of Florence. The monthly *Informacittà* pamphlet on events, exhibits, and concerts is still free. It's open Monday through Saturday from 8:30am to 6:30pm and Sunday from 8:30am to 1:30pm.

At the head of the tracks in Stazione Santa Maria Novella is a **tiny info office** with some maps and a hotel-booking service (see chapter 3), open Monday through Saturday from 9am to 9pm (to 8pm Nov–Mar), but the station's **main tourist office** (✆ **055-212-245**) is outside at Piazza della Stazione 4. With your back to the tracks, take the left exit, cross onto the concrete median, and turn right; it's about 100 feet ahead. The office is usually open Monday through Saturday from 8:30am to 7pm (often to 1:30pm in winter) and Sunday 8:30am to 1:30pm.

Another office sits on an obscure side street south of Piazza Santa Croce, Borgo Santa Croce 29r (✆ **055-234-0444**), open Monday through Saturday from 9am to 7pm and Sunday 9am to 2pm.

PUBLICATIONS At the tourist offices, pick up the free monthly *Informacittà*. The bilingual *Concierge Information* (www.florence-concierge.it) magazine, free from the front desks of top hotels, contains a monthly calendar of events and details on attractions. *Firenze Spettacolo,* a 1.55€ ($1.80) Italian-language monthly sold at most newsstands, is the most detailed and up-to-date listing of nightlife, arts, and entertainment.

WEBSITES The official Florence information, **www.firenze turismo.it**, contains a wealth of up-to-date information on Florence and its province, including a searchable hotels form allowing you to specify amenities, categories, and the like.

Firenze By Net (www.mega.it/florence), **Firenze.Net** (http://english.firenze.net), and **FlorenceOnLine** (www.fol.it) are all Italy-based websites with English translations and good general information on Florence. The site for **Concierge Information** (www.florence-concierge.it) is an excellent little guide to this month's events, exhibits, concerts, and theater. Other sites worth checking out are **Your Way to Florence** www.arca.net/florence.htm), and **Time Out** (www.timeout.com/florence).

CITY LAYOUT

Florence is a smallish city, sitting on the Arno River and petering out to olive-planted hills rather quickly to the north and south but extending farther west and to a lesser extent east along the Arno valley with suburbs and light industry. It is a compact city best negotiated on foot. No two sights are more than a 20- or 25-minute walk apart, and all the hotels and restaurants in this guide are in the relatively small *centro storico* **(historic center),** a compact tangle of medieval streets and *piazze* (squares) where visitors spend most of their time. The bulk of Florence, and most of the tourist sights, lies north of the river, with the Oltrarno, an old artisans' working-class neighborhood, hemmed in between the Arno and the hills on the south side.

MAIN STREETS & PIAZZE The center is encircled by a traffic ring of wide boulevards, the Viale, that were created in the late 1800s by tearing down the city's medieval defensive walls. The descriptions below all refer to the *centro storico* as the visitor's city. From Piazza Santa Maria Novella, south of the train station, Via de' Panzani angles into Via de' Cerretani to Piazza del Duomo and the connected Piazza San Giovanni, the city's religious heart around the cathedral. From Piazza del Duomo, Via dei Calzaiuoli, the wide road popular

The Red & the Black

Florence's address system has a split personality. Private homes, some offices, and hotels are numbered in black (or blue), while businesses, shops, and restaurants are numbered independently in red. This means that 1, 2, 3 (black) addresses march up the block numerically oblivious to their 1r, 2r, 3r (red) neighbors. You might find the doorways on one side of a street numbered: 1r, 2r, 3r, 1, 4r, 2, 3, 5r . . .

Florence keeps proclaiming that it's busily renumbering the whole city without the color system—plain 1, 3, 5 on one side, 2, 4, 6 on the other—and will release the new standard soon, but no one is quite sure when. Conservative Florentines who don't want their addresses to change have been helping to hold up the process. This is all compounded by the fact that the color codes occur only in the *centro storico* and other older sections of town; outlying districts didn't bother with the codes and use the international standard system common in the United States.

during the *passeggiata* (evening stroll), leads south to Piazza della Signoria, Florence's civic heart near the river, home to the Palazzo Vecchio and the Uffizi Galleries. Traffic winds its way from the back of the Duomo to behind the Uffizi along Via del Proconsolo.

Another route south from the Duomo takes you down Via Roma, through cafe-lined Piazza della Repubblica, and continues down Via Calimala and Via Por Santa Maria to the Ponte Vecchio, the most popular and oldest bridge over the Arno, lined with overhanging jewelry shops. Via degli Strozzi leads east of Piazza della Repubblica to intersect Florence's main shopping drag, Via de' Tornabuoni, running north toward Piazza Santa Maria Novella and south to Piazza Santa Trínita on the river. Borgo de' Greci connects Piazza della Signoria with Piazza Santa Croce on the city center's western edge.

North from the Duomo, Via dei Servi leads to Florence's prettiest square, Piazza Santissima Annunziata. Via Riscasoli leads from the Duomo past the Accademia Gallery (with Michelangelo's *David*) to Piazza San Marco, where many city buses stop. Via de' Martelli/Via Cavour is a wide traffic-laden road also connecting the Duomo and Piazza San Marco. From the Duomo, Borgo San Lorenzo leads to

Piazza San Lorenzo, the old neighborhood of the Medici that's these days filled with the stalls of the outdoor leather market.

On the Oltrarno side of the river, shop-lined Via Guicciardini runs toward Piazza dei Pitti and its museum-filled Pitti Palace. From here, Via Mazzetta/Via Sant'Agostino takes you past Piazza Santo Spirito to Piazza della Carmine; these two squares are the Oltrarno's main centers.

STREET MAPS   The tourist offices hand out two versions of a Florence *pianta* (city plan) free: Ask for the one *con un stradario* (with a street index), which shows all the roads and is better for navigation. The white pamphlet-size version they offer you first is okay for basic orientation and Uffizi-finding, but it leaves out many streets and has giant icons of major sights that cover up Florence's complicated back-alley systems.

If you want to buy a more complete city plan, the best selections are at the newsstand in the ticketing area of the train station and at **Feltrinelli International** and **Libreria Il Viaggio** bookstores (see chapter 6 for more information). Falk puts out a good pocket-size version, but my favorite is the palm-size 1:9,000 **Litografica Artistica Cartografia** map with the yellow and blue cover. It covers the city in three overlapping indexed sections that fold out like a pop-up book. If you need to find a tiny street not on your map, ask your hotel concierge to glance at his or her *TuttoCittà,* a very complete magazine of fully indexed streets that you can't buy but residents (and hotels and bars) get along with their phone books.

THE NEIGHBORHOODS IN BRIEF

I've used the designations below to group hotels, restaurants, and sights in Florence. Although the city does contain six "neighborhoods" centered around the major churches (Santa Maria Novella, Il Duomo, Santa Croce, San Lorenzo, and Santo Spirito and San Frediano in the Oltrarno), these are a bit too broad to be useful here. I've divided the city up into more visitor-oriented sections (none much more than a dozen square blocks) focused around major sights and points of reference. The designations and descriptions are drawn to give you a flavor of each area and help you choose a zone in which to base yourself.

The Duomo   The area surrounding Florence's gargantuan cathedral is about as central as you can get. The Duomo is halfway between the two great churches of Santa Maria Novella and Santa Croce as well as at the midpoint between the Uffizi Galleries and the Ponte Vecchio to the south and San Marco and the Accademia Gallery with Michelangelo's *David* to the north. The streets north of the Duomo are long and often traffic-ridden, but those to the south make up a wonderful medieval tangle of alleys and tiny squares heading toward Piazza della Signoria.

This is one of the most historic parts of town, and the streets still vaguely follow the grid laid down when the city began as a Roman colony. Via degli Strozzi/Via dei Speziali/Via del Corso was the *decumanus maximus,* the main east-west axis; Via Roma/Via Calimala was the key north-south *cardo maximus.* The site of the Roman city's forum is today's Piazza della Repubblica. The current incarnation of this square, lined with glitzy cafes, was laid out by demolishing the Jewish ghetto in a rash of nationalism during Italian unification in the late 19th century, and (until the majority of neon signs were removed in the early 1990s) it was by and large the ugliest piazza in town. The area surrounding it, though, is one of Florence's main shopping zones. The Duomo neighborhood is, understandably, one of the most hotel-heavy parts of town, offering a range from luxury inns to student dives and everything in between.

Piazza Della Signoria   This is the city's civic heart and perhaps the best base for museum hounds, because the Uffizi Galleries, Bargello sculpture collection, and Ponte Vecchio leading toward the Pitti Palace are all nearby. It's a well-polished part of the tourist zone but still retains the narrow medieval streets where Dante grew up— back alleys where tour-bus crowds running from the Uffizi to the Accademia rarely set foot. The few blocks just north of the Ponte Vecchio have good shopping, but unappealing modern buildings were planted here to replace the district destroyed during World War II (a Nazi commander with a Romantic soul couldn't bring himself to blow up the Ponte Vecchio during the German army's retreat, as they had every other bridge over the Arno, so he blew up the buildings at either end of it to impede the progress of Allied tanks pushing north). The whole neighborhood can be stiflingly crowded in summer, but in those moments when you catch it off-guard and empty of tour groups, it remains the most romantic heart of pre-Renaissance Florence.

San Lorenzo and the Mercato Centrale   This small wedge of streets between the train station and the Duomo, centered around the Medici's old church of San Lorenzo with its Michelangelo-designed tombs, is market territory. The vast indoor food market is here, and most of the streets are filled daily with hundreds of stalls hawking leather jackets and other wares. It's a colorful neighborhood, though perhaps not the quietest.

Piazza Santa Trinita   This piazza sits just off the river at the end of Florence's shopping mecca, Via de' Tornabuoni, home to

Gucci, Armani, Ferragamo, Versace, and more. Even the ancient narrow streets running out either side of the square are lined with the biggest names in high fashion. It's a very pleasant, well-to-do, but still medieval neighborhood to stay in even if you don't care about haute couture. But if you're a shopping fiend, there's no better place to be.

Santa Maria Novella This neighborhood, bounding the western edge of the *centro storico*, really has two characters: the rundown unpleasant zone around Santa Maria Novella train station and the much nicer area south of it between the church of Santa Maria Novella and the river.

In general, the train station area is the least attractive part of town in which to base yourself. The streets are mostly outside the pedestrian zone and hence heavily trafficked, noisy, and dirty, and you're removed from the major sights and the action. This area does, however, have more budget options than any other quarter. Some streets, like Via Faenza and its tributaries, contain a glut of budget joints, with dozens of choices every block and often two, three, or even six bottom-scraping dives crammed into a single building. It's the best place to go if you can't seem to find a room anywhere else; just walk up the street and try each place you pass. And while many hotels simply pander uninspiredly to tourists, a few (those recommended later) seem to try twice as hard as central inns to cater to their guests and are among the friendliest hotels in town. Just avoid anything on traffic-clogged Via Nazionale.

The situation improves dramatically as you move into the San Lorenzo area and pass Santa Maria Novella church and head toward the river. Piazza Santa Maria Novella and its tributary streets are attracting something of a bohemian nightlife scene (but parts of it can be seedy). Two of Florence's premier inns, the Excelsior and the Grand, are on the Arno at Piazza Ognissanti—just a bit south of the station but miles away in atmosphere.

San Marco and Santissima Annunziata These two churches are fronted by piazze—Piazza San Marco, now a busy traffic center, and Piazza Santissima Annunziata, the most beautiful in the city—that together define the northern limits of the *centro storico*. The neighborhood is home to the University, Michelangelo's *David* at the Accademia, the San Marco monastery, and long, quiet streets with some real hotel gems. The daily walk back from the heart of town up here may tire some, but others welcome its removal from the worst of the high-season tourist crush.

Santa Croce This eastern edge of the *centro storico* runs along the Arno. The bulky Santa Croce church is full of famous Florentine art and famous dead Florentines. The church is also the focal point of one of the most genuine neighborhoods left in the old center. While the area's western edge abuts the medieval district around Piazza della Signoria—Via Bentacordi/Via Torta actually trace the outline of the old Roman amphitheater—much of the district was rebuilt after World War II in long blocks of creamy yellow plaster buildings with residential shops and homes. Few tourists roam off Piazza Santa Croce, so if you want to feel like a city resident, stay here. This neighborhood also boasts some of the best restaurants in the city.

The Oltrarno "Across the Arno" is the artisans' neighborhood, still packed with workshops where craftspeople hand-carve furniture and hand-stitch leather gloves. It began as a working-class neighborhood to catch the overflow from the expanding medieval city on the Arno's opposite bank, but it also became a rather chic area for aristocrats to build palaces on the edge of the countryside. The largest of these, the Pitti Palace, later became the home of the grand dukes and today houses a set of museums second only to the Uffizi. Behind it spreads the landscaped baroque fantasies of the Boboli Gardens, Florence's best park. Masaccio's frescoes in Santa Maria della Carmine here were some of the most influential of the early Renaissance.

Florence tacitly accepted the Oltrarno when the 14th-century circuit of walls was built to include it, but the alleys and squares across the river continued to retain that edge of distinctness. It has always attracted a slightly bohemian crowd—the Brownings lived here from just after their secret marriage in 1847 until Elizabeth died in 1861. The Oltrarno's lively tree-shaded center, Piazza Santo Spirito, is a world unto itself, lined with bars and trendy salad-oriented restaurants (good nightlife, though young druggies have recently been encroaching on it); and, its Brunelleschi-designed church faces pointedly away from the river and the rest of Florence.

In the Hills From just about any vantage point in the center of Florence, you can see the city ends abruptly to the north and south, replaced by green hills spotted with villas, small farms, and the expensive modern homes of the upper-middle class. To the north rises Monte Ceceri, mined for the soft gray *pietra serena* that accented so much of Renaissance architecture and home to the hamlet of Settignango, where Michelangelo was wet-nursed by a stonecutter's wife. The high reaches harbor the Etruscan village of Fiesole, which was here long before the Romans built Florence in the valley below.

Across the Arno, the hills hemming in the Oltrarno—with names like Bellosguardo (Beautiful Glimpse) and Monte Uliveto (Olive Grove Hill)—are blanketed in farmland. With panoramic lookouts like Piazzale Michelangiolo and the Romanesque church of San Miniato al Monte, these hills offer some of the best walks around the city, as Elizabeth Browning, Henry James, and Florence Nightingale could tell you. They're crisscrossed by snaking country roads and bordered by high walls over which wave the silvery-green leaves of olive trees.

Because of the lack of public transportation, first-time visitors who plan a strenuous sightseeing agenda probably will not want to choose accommodations in the hills. But for those who don't need to be in town every day and want a cooler, calmer, and altogether more relaxing vacation, they can be heaven.

2 Getting Around

Florence is a walking city. You can leisurely stroll between the two top sights, the Duomo and the Uffizi, in less than 5 minutes. The hike from the most northerly sights, San Marco with its Fra' Angelico frescoes and the Accademia with Michelangelo's *David,* to the most southerly, the Pitti Palace across the Arno, should take no more than 30 minutes. From Santa Maria Novella across town to Santa Croce is an easy 20- to 30-minute walk.

Most of the streets, however, were designed to handle the moderate pedestrian traffic and occasional horse-drawn cart of a medieval city. Sidewalks, where they exist, are narrow—often less than 2 feet wide. Though much of the *centro storico* is closed to traffic, this doesn't include taxis, residents with parking permits, people without permits who drive there anyway, and the endless swarm of noisy Vespas and *motorini* (scooters).

In high season, especially July and August, the cars and their pollution (catalytic converters aren't yet standard), massive pedestrian

---

Tips **A Walking Warning**

Florentine streets are mainly cobbled or flagstone, as are the sidewalks, and thus can be rough on soles, feet, and joints after awhile. Florence may be one of the world's greatest shoe-shopping cities, but a sensible pair of quality walking shoes or sneakers is highly recommended over loafers or pumps. In dress shoes or heels, forget it.

and tourist traffic, maniac moped drivers, and stifling heat can wear you down. On some days Florence can feel like a minor circle of Dante's Inferno. Evenings tend to be cool year-round, bringing residents and visitors alike out for the traditional before-dinner *passeggiata* stroll up and down Via Calzaiuoli and down Via Roma and its continuations across the Ponte Vecchio.

BY BUS You'll rarely need to use Florence's efficient **ATAF bus system** (© **055-565-0222** or 800-424-500; www.ataf.net) since the city is so wonderfully compact. Many visitors accustomed to big cities like Rome step off their arriving train and onto a city bus out of habit, thinking to reach the center; within 5 minutes they find themselves in the suburbs. The cathedral is a mere 5- to 7-minute walk from the train station.

Bus tickets cost a ridiculous 1€ ($1.15) and are good for an hour. A four-pack *(biglietto multiplo)* is 3.90€ ($4.50), a 24-hour pass 4.50€ ($5.20), a 2-day pass 7.60€ ($8.75), a 3-day pass 9.60€ ($11), and a 7-day pass 16€ ($18). Tickets are sold at *tabacchi* (tobacconists), bars, and most newsstands. Once on board, validate your ticket in the box near the rear door to avoid a steep fine. If you intend to use the bus system, you should pick up a bus map at a tourist office. Since most of the historic center is limited as to traffic, buses make runs on principal streets only, save four tiny electric buses that trundle about the *centro storico.*

BY TAXI Taxis aren't cheap, and with the city so small and the one-way system forcing drivers to take convoluted routes, they aren't an economical way to get about town. Taxis are most useful to get you and your bags between the train station and your hotel in the virtually busless *centro storico.* The standard rate is .80€ (90¢) per kilometer, with a whopping minimum fare of 2.38€ ($2.75) to start the meter (that rises to 4.03€/$4.65 on Sun; 5.16€/$5.90 10pm–6am), plus .57€ (65¢) per bag. There's a taxi stand outside the train station; otherwise, you have to call **Radio Taxi** at © **055-4242,** 055-4798, 055-4390, or 055-4499.

BY BICYCLE & SCOOTER Despite the relatively traffic-free historic center, biking has not really caught on here, but local authorities are trying to change that with free bikes (well, in past years there has been a nominal .50€/60¢ fee). **Firenze Parcheggi,** the public garage authority (© **055-500-0453;** www.firenze parcheggi.it), has set up temporary sites about town (look for stands at the train station, Piazza Strozzi, Via della Nina along the south side of Palazzo Vecchio, and in the large public parking lots) where bikes are furnished free from 8am to 7:30pm; you must return the bike to any of the other sites.

If no bikes are left, you'll have to pay for them at a shop like **Alinari,** Via Guelfa 85r (© **055-280-500;** www.alinarirental.com), renting bikes (2.50€/$2.90 per hour; 12€/$14 per day) and mountain bikes (3€/$3.45 per hour; 18€/$21 per day). It also rents 50cc scooters (8€/$9.20 per hour; 28€/$32 per day) and 100cc mopeds (10€/$12 per hour; 47€/$54 per day). Another renter with the same basic prices is **Florence by Bike,** Via San Zanobi, 120–122r (© **055-488-992;** www.florencebybike.it).

BY CAR   Trying to drive in the *centro storico* is a frustrating, useless exercise. Florence is a maze of one-way streets and pedestrian zones, and it takes an old hand to know which laws to break in order to get where you need to go—plus you need a permit to do anything beyond dropping off and picking up bags at your hotel. Park your vehicle in one of the huge underground lots on the center's periphery and pound the pavement.

BY GUIDED TOUR   **American Express** (see "Fast Facts: Florence" below) teams with venerable **CAF Tours,** Via Roma 4 (© **055-283-200;** www.caftours.com), to offer two half-day bus tours of town (39€/$45), including visits to the Uffizi, the Medici Chapels, and Piazzale Michelangiolo. They also offer several walking tours for 23€ to 33€ ($26–$30); day trips to Pisa, Siena/San Gimignano, the Chianti, Lucca, or Medici villas for 35€ to 69€ ($40–$79); and farther afield to Venice, Rome, or Perugia/Assisi for 82€ to 105€ ($94–$121). You can book similar tours through most other travel agencies around town.

Walking Tours of Florence (© **055-264-5033;** www.artviva. com) offers a basic 3-hour tour daily at 9:45am for 25€ ($29) adults, 20€ ($23) students under 26, or 10€ ($12) children ages 6 to 12. Meet at their office on the mezzanine level of Piazza Santa Stefano 2, a pocket-size piazza hidden off Via Por Santa Maria between Via Lambertesca and the Ponte Vecchio. They provide many other thematic tours as well as private guides.

Call **I Bike Italy** (© **055-234-2371;** www.ibikeitaly.com) to sign up for 1-day rides in the surrounding countryside: Fiesole year-round for $70, or the Chianti April 15 through October for $85. A shuttle bus picks you up at 9am at the Ponte delle Grazie and drives you to the outskirts of town, and an enjoyable lunch in a local trattoria is included. You're back in town by 5pm. It might stretch your budget, but you should get out of this tourist-trodden stone city for a glimpse of the incomparable Tuscan countryside. They also offer a summertime, 2-day trip (Tues–Wed) to Siena for $280.

FAST FACTS: Florence

American Express   Amex, Piazza Cimatori/Via Dante Alghieri 22r, 50122 Firenze (© **055-50-981**), will act as a travel agent (for a commission), accept mail on your behalf (see "Mail" below), and cash traveler's checks at no commission. (They don't have to be Amex checks.) The office is open Monday through Friday from 9am to 5:30pm and Saturday from 9am to 12:30pm (no travel services on Sat).

Business Hours   General open hours for **stores, offices,** and **churches** are from 9:30am to noon or 1pm and again from 3 or 3:30 to 7:30pm. That early afternoon shutdown is the *riposo,* the Italian *siesta.* In Florence, however, many of the larger and more central shops stay open through the midday *riposo* (ORARIO NO-STOP). Most stores close all day Sunday and many also on Monday (morning only or all day). Some shops, especially grocery stores, also close Thursday afternoons. Some services and business offices are open to the public only in the morning. Traditionally, **museums** are closed Mondays, and though some of the biggest stay open all day long, many close for *riposo* or are only open in the morning (9am–2pm is popular). Some churches open earlier in the morning, but the largest often stay open all day. **Banks** tend to be open Monday through Friday from 8:30am to 1:30pm and 2:30 to 3:30pm or 3 to 4pm.

Use the *riposo* as the Italians do—take a long lunch, stroll through a city park, cool off in the Duomo, travel to the next town, or simply go back to your hotel to regroup your energies. The *riposo* is an especially welcome custom during the oppressive afternoon heat of August.

Embassies/Consulates   The **U.S. consulate** in Florence—for passport and consular services but *not* visas—is at Lungarno Amerigo Vespucci 38 (© **055-266-951**; fax 055-284-088), open to drop-ins Monday through Friday from 9am to 12:30pm. Afternoons 2 to 4:30pm, the consulate is open by appointment only; call ahead. The **U.S. Embassy** is in Rome at Via

Vittorio Veneto 119a (℃ **06-46-741;** fax 06-488-2672 or 06-4674-2217; www.usembassy.it). The **U.K. consulate** in Florence is at Lungarno Corsini 2 (℃ **055-284-133;** fax 055-219-112). It's open Monday to Friday 9:30am to 12:30pm and 2:30 to 4:30pm. The **U.K. Embassy** is in Rome at Via XX Settembre 80a (℃ **06-4220-0001;** fax 06-4220-2334; www.UKinitalia.it), open Monday through Friday from 9:15am to 1:30pm.

Of English-speaking countries, only the United States and Great Britain have consulates in Florence. Citizens of other countries must go to their consulates in Rome for help: The **Canadian** consulate in Rome is at Via Zara 30, on the fifth floor (℃ **06-445-981** or 06-44598-2905; www.canada.it), open Monday through Friday from 8:30am to 12:30pm and 1:30 to 4pm. **Australia's** Rome consulate is at Via Alessandria 215 (℃ **06-852-721;** fax 06-8527-2300; www.australian-embassy.it). The consular section is open Monday through Thursday from 8:30am to noon and 1:30 to 4pm. The immigration and visa office is open Monday to Thursday 10am to noon; telephone hours are from 10 to 11:30am. **New Zealand's** Rome consulate is at Via Zara 28 (℃ **06-441-7171;** fax 06-440-2984), open Monday through Friday from 8:30am to 12:45pm and 1:45 to 5pm.

Doctors/Dentists   A **walk-in clinic** (℃ **055-483-363** or 0330-774-731) is run by Dott. Giorgio Scappini. Tuesday and Thursday office hours are brief—5:30 to 6:30pm or by appointment—at Via Bonifacio Lupi 32 (just south of the Tourist Medical Service; see "Hospitals" below); Monday, Wednesday, and Friday, go to Via Guasti 2 from 3 to 4pm (north of the Fortezza del Basso). **Dr. Stephen Kerr** keeps an office at Via Porta Rossa 1 (℃ **0335-836-1682** or 055-288-055 at home), with office hours Monday through Friday from 3 to 5pm without an appointment (home visits or clinic appointments 24 hr.).

For general dentistry, try **Dr. Camis de Fonseca,** Via Nino Bixio 9, northeast of the city center off Viale dei Mille (℃ **055-587-632**), open Monday through Friday from 3 to 7pm; he's also available for emergency weekend calls. The U.S. consulate can provide a list of other English-speaking doctors, dentists, and specialists. See also "Hospitals" below, for medical translator service.

Emergencies   Dial ℃ 113 for an emergency of any kind. You can also call the **Carabinieri** (the national police force; more useful than local branches) at ℃ **112.** Dial an **ambulance** at

© **118,** and report a **fire** at © **115.** All these calls are free from any phone. For **car breakdowns,** call ACI at © **116.**

Hospitals   The **ambulance number** is © **118.** There's a special **Tourist Medical Service,** Via Lorenzo il Magnifico 59, north of the city center between the Fortezza del Basso and Piazza della Libertà (© **055-475-411**), open 24 hours; take bus 8 or 80 to Viale Lavagnini or bus 12 or night bus 91 to Via Poliziano.

Thanks to socialized medicine, you can walk into most any Italian hospital when ill but not an emergency and get taken care of speedily with no insurance questions asked, no forms to fill out, and no fee charged. They'll just give you a prescription and send you on your way. The most central are the **Arcispedale di Santa Maria Nuova,** a block northeast of the Duomo on Piazza Santa Maria Nuova (© **055-27-581**), and the **Misericordia Ambulance Service,** on Piazza del Duomo across from Giotto's bell tower (© **055-212-222** for ambulance).

For a **free translator** to help you describe your symptoms, explain the doctor's instructions, and aid in medical issues in general, call the volunteers at the **Associazione Volontari Ospedalieri (AVO;** © **055-425-0126** or 055-234-4567) Monday, Wednesday, and Friday from 4 to 6pm and Tuesday and Thursday from 10am to noon.

Internet Access   To check or send e-mail, head to the now massive **Internet Train** (www.internettrain.it), with 15 locations in Florence including their very first shop at Via dell'Oriuolo 25r, 3 blocks from the Duomo (© **055-263-8968**); Via Guelfa 24a, near the train station (© **055-214-794**); Borgo San Jacopo 30r, in the Oltrarno (© **055-265-7935**), and in the underground tunnel from the train station towards town (© **055-239-9720**). Actually, there are now 126 offices across Italy (36 in Tuscany, 4 in Umbria—in Perugia and Orvieto), and the magnetic access card you buy is good at all of them, making plugging in throughout your journey that much easier. Access is 4€ ($4.60) per hour, or 1€ ($1.15) for 10 minutes; they also provide printing, scanning, Webcam, and fax services, plus others (bike rental, international shipping, 24-hr. film developing) at some offices. Open hours vary, but run at least daily from 9am to 8:30pm, often later.

The **Netgate,** Via Sant'Egidio 10–20r (© **055-658-0207;** www.thenetgate.it), has similar rates but also offers a Saturday "happy hour" of free access from 10:30 to 11am and from

2 to 2:30pm. It's open daily from 10am to 10:30pm (until 8:30pm in winter).

Laundry/Dry Cleaning Though there are several coin-op shops (mostly of the OndaBlu chain), you can get your wash done for you even more cheaply at a pay-by-weight *lavanderia*—and you don't have to waste a morning sitting there watching it go in circles. The cheapest are around the university (east of San Marco), and one of the best is a nameless joint at **Via Alfani 44r** (✆ **055-247-9313**), where they'll do an entire load for 6€ ($6.90), have it ready by afternoon, and even deliver it free to your hotel. It's closed Saturday afternoon. At other, non-self-service shops, check the price *before* leaving your clothes—some places charge by the item. Dry cleaning *(lavasecco)* is much more costly and available at *lavanderie* throughout the city (ask your hotel for the closest).

Liquor Laws Legal drinking age in Italy is 16, but that's just on paper. Public drunkenness (aside from people getting noisily tipsy and flush at big dinners) is unusual except among some street people—usually among foreign vagabonds, not the Italian homeless.

Mail You can buy *francobolli* (stamps) from any *tabacchi* or from the central post office. Florence's **main post office** (✆ **160** for general info, or 055-211-147) is on Via Pellicceria 3, 50103, Firenze, off the southwest corner of Piazza della Repubblica. You can pick up letters sent *Fermo Posta* (Italian for *poste restante* or held mail) by showing ID; see below. The post office is open Monday through Friday from 8:15am to 7pm and Saturday 8:15am to 12:30pm. All packages heavier than 2kg (4½ lb.) must be properly wrapped and brought around to the parcel office at the back of the building (enter at Via dei Sassetti 4, also known as Piazza Davanzati).

Drop postcards and letters into the boxes outside. To mail larger packages, drop them at *sportello* (window) 9/10, but first head across the room to window 21/22 for stamps. If that window is closed, as it often is, you buy your stamps at the next window, 23/24, which is also the pickup for *Fermo Posta*. You can also send packages via **DHL,** Via della Cupola 243 (✆ **055-308-877,** or 800-345-345 for free pick-up) or **UPS,** Via Pratignone 56a in Calenzano (✆ **055-882-5501**).

To receive mail at the central post office, have it sent to [your name], Fermo Posta Centrale, 50103 Firenze, Italia/ITALY.

They'll charge you .25€ (15¢) per letter when you come to pick it up at window 23/24; bring your passport for ID. For people without an Amex card, this is a much better deal than American Express's similar service, which charges 1.50€ ($1.75) to receive and hold non-cardholder's mail. For Amex members, however, this service is free, so you can have your mail sent to [your name], Client Mail, American Express, Via Dante Alghieri, 22r, 50123 Firenze, Italia/ITALY.

Newspapers & Magazines   You can pick up the *International Herald Tribune* and *USA Today* from almost any newsstand, and you'll find the *Wall Street Journal Europe* and the *London Times*, along with *Time* and *Newsweek* magazines, at most larger kiosks. There's a 24-hour newsstand in the train station. For upcoming events, theater, and shows, see "Visitor Information" earlier in this chapter.

Pharmacies   For pharmacy information, dial ℂ 110. There are 24-hour pharmacies (also open Sun and state holidays) in **Stazione Santa Maria Novella** (ℂ 055-216-761; ring the bell between 1 and 4am); at **Piazza San Giovanni 20r**, just behind the baptistery at the corner of Borgo San Lorenzo (ℂ 055-211-343); and at **Via Cazzaiuoli 7r**, just off Piazza della Signoria (ℂ 055-289-490).

Police   For emergencies, dial ℂ 112 for the Carabinieri police. To report lost property or passport problems, call the *questura* (urban police headquarters) at ℂ 055-49-771.

Restrooms   Public toilets are going out of fashion in northern Italy, but most *bars* will let you use their bathrooms without a scowl or forcing you to buy anything. Ask *"Posso usare il bagno?"* (*poh*-soh oo-*zar*-eh eel *ban*-yo). *Donne/signore* are women and *uomini/signori* men. Train stations usually have a bathroom, for a fee, often of the two-bricks-to-stand-on-and-a-hole-in-the-floor Turkish toilet variety. In many of the public toilets that remain, the little old lady with a basket has been replaced by a coin-op turnstile.

Safety   Central Italy is an exceedingly safe area with practically no random violent crime. There are, as in any city, plenty of pickpockets out to ruin your vacation, and Florence has the added joy of light-fingered gypsy children (especially around the train station), but otherwise you're safe. Do steer clear of the Cascine Park after dark, when it becomes somewhat seedy and you may run the risk of being mugged, and you probably won't want to hang out with the late-night heroin addicts shooting up on the Arno mudflats below the Lungarno embankments on the edges of town.

Telephones/Fax   **Local calls** in Italy cost 0.10€. There are three types of public pay phones: those that take coins only, those that take both coins and phone cards, and those that take only **phone cards** (*carta* or *scheda telefonica*). You can buy these prepaid phone cards at any *tabacchi* (tobacconists), most newsstands, and some bars in several denominations from 1€ to 7.50€. Break off the corner before inserting it; a digital display tracks how much money is left on the card as you talk. Don't forget to take the card with you when you leave!

For **operator-assisted international calls** (in English), dial toll-free ☎ **170**. Note, however, that you'll get better rates by calling a home operator for collect calls, as detailed here: To make **calling card calls,** insert a phone card or 0.10€—it'll be refunded at the end of your call—and dial the local number for your service. For **Americans:** AT&T at ☎ **172-1011,** MCI at ☎ **172-1022,** or Sprint at ☎ **172-1877.** These numbers will raise an American operator for you, and you can use any one of them to place a **collect call** even if you don't carry that phone company's card. **Canadians** can reach Teleglobe at ☎ **172-1001. Brits** can call BT at ☎ **172-0044** or Mercury at ☎ **172-0544.** The **Irish** can get a home operator at ☎ **172-0353. Australians** can use Optus by calling ☎ **172-1161** or Telstra at ☎ **172-1061.** And **New Zealanders** can phone home at ☎ **172-1064.**

To **dial direct internationally from Italy,** dial ☎ **00,** then the country code, the area code, and the number. Country codes are as follows: the United States and Canada 1; the United Kingdom 44; Ireland 353; Australia 61; New Zealand 64. Make international calls from a public phone if possible because hotels charge ridiculously inflated rates for direct dial, but take along plenty of *schede* to feed the phone.

To call free national **telephone information** (in Italian) in Italy, dial ☎ **12.** International information for Europe is available at ☎ **176** but costs 0.60€ (70¢) a shot. For international information beyond Europe, dial ☎ **1790** for 0.50€ (60¢).

Your hotel will most likely be able to send or receive **faxes** for you, sometimes at inflated prices, sometimes at cost. Otherwise, most *cartoleria* (stationery stores), *copista* or *fotocopie* (photocopy shops), and some *tabacchi* (tobacconists) offer fax services.

Time Zone   Italy is 6 hours ahead of Eastern Standard Time in the United States. When it's noon in New York, it's 6pm in Florence.

Tipping   In **hotels,** a service charge is usually included in your bill. In family-run operations, additional tips are unnecessary and sometimes considered rude. In fancier places with a hired staff, however, you may want to leave a 0.50€ daily tip for the maid, pay the bellhop or porter 1€ per bag, and a helpful concierge 2€ for his or her troubles. In **restaurants,** 10% to 15% is almost always included in the bill—to be sure, ask *"è incluso il servizio?"*—but you can leave up to an additional 10%, especially for good service. At **bars and cafes,** leave a 10€ coin per drink on the counter for the barman; if you sit at a table, leave 10% to 15%. **Taxi** drivers expect 10% to 15%.

Where to Stay in Florence

Throughout the 1990s, through the turn of the millennium, and especially at the introduction of the euro in 2002, inflation ran rampant in Italy, and hotel prices more than tripled in cities like Florence. I'm going to say that again because it is pretty astounding and pretty awful: Prices have nearly tripled. It's now fairly difficult to find a double you'd want to stay in for less than 100€ ($115). Because hotel prices actually outpaced inflation, the hoteliers stockpiled some surplus cash, and in the last few years they've been reinvesting in their properties. In many hotels, the amenity levels are now at or above what Americans expect to find at home, and the days of the bathroom-down-the-hall cheap pensione are fading—or at least those properties are now mostly student dives. Almost everyone seems to have put in new bathrooms. Extras like heated towel racks, whirlpool tubs, satellite TVs with CNN and the BBC, and direct-dial phones that once only the top few inns boasted are now in four-fifths of the properties listed here. I've tried to balance the selections to suit all tastes and budgets.

For help finding a room, visit the Santa Maria Novella train station for the **Consorzio Informazioni Turistiche Alberghiere (ITA)** office, near Track 9 (© **055-282-893**), and the tiny tourist office, near Track 16, both of which will find you a room in your price range (for a small commission). Or go to the official tourist office's website subsection on accommodations at **www.toscanaeturismo.net/ dovedormire**.

Many budget hotels are concentrated in the area around the Stazione Santa Maria Novella. You'll find most of the hotels in this convenient and relatively safe (if charmless) area on noisy Via Nazionale and its first two side streets, Via Fiume and Via Faenza; an adjunct is the area surrounding the Mercato San Lorenzo. The area between the Duomo and Piazza della Signoria, particularly along and near Via dei Calzaiuoli, is a good though invariably more expensive place to look.

Peak season is mid-March through mid-July, September through early November, and December 23 through January 6. May and

Where to Stay in Florence

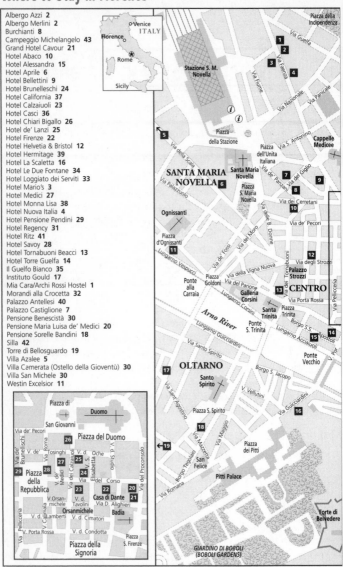

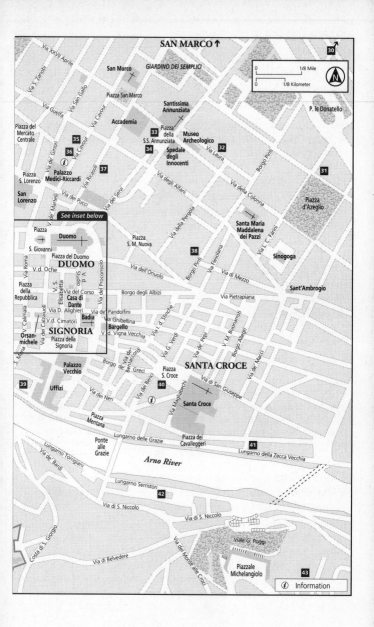

September are particularly popular whether in the city or in the out-lying Tuscan hills.

To help you decide in which area you'd like to base yourself for exploring the city, consult "The Neighborhoods in Brief" section in chapter 2.

1 Near the Duomo

VERY EXPENSIVE

Hotel Savoy *⨂⨂* This 1893 hotel underwent a complete trans-formation in 2000 by Sir Rocco Forte and his sister, who designed the warm, stylishly minimalist modern interiors. Rooms are stan-dardized, with walk-in closets, dark brown marble bathrooms, and mosaics over the tubs. The different room "styles"—classic, execu-tive, and deluxe—really just refer to size. Four suites (two rooms, two TVs, leather easy chairs, white marble bathrooms) are on the back, four on the piazza. Rooms on the fifth floor, added in 1958, just peep over the surrounding buildings for spectacular views, espe-cially those on the Duomo (back) side. You're just a few steps in any direction from all the sights and the best shopping. The building actually belongs to Ferragamo (their decor tip o' the hat is to include shoe images in most public area art).

Piazza della Repubblica 7, 50123 Firenze. ℭ 800/223-6800 in the U.S., or 055-27-351 in Italy. Fax 055-273-5888. www.roccofortehotels.com. 107 units. 495€–627€ ($569–$721) double; 770€ ($886) studio; 1,089€–1,375€ ($1,282–$1,581) suite; 1,870€ ($2,151) Repubblica suite. Breakfast 25.30€ ($29). AE, DC, MC, V. Parking 29€ ($33). Bus: A, 6, 11, 22, 36, or 37. **Amenities:** Restaurant; bar; small gym w/view; concierge; tour desk; car-rental desk; courtesy car; secretarial services; 24-hr. room service; in-room massage; babysitting; laundry service; same-day dry cleaning; nonsmoking rooms. *In room:* A/C, TV w/pay movies, VCR on request, dat-aport, fax on request, minibar, hair dryer, safe.

EXPENSIVE

Hotel Brunelleschi *⨂* The mishmash of historical structures making up this hotel—including a Roman *calidarium* in the foun-dations—was so confusing they installed a small museum in the basement to explain it all. The property rambles through the remains of various medieval houses, a deconsecrated church, and a 6th-century Byzantine tower. Most of the interiors mix curving modern lines with the salvaged vestiges of the medieval buildings. The rooms are spacious and very comfortable, with large bath-rooms, but are disappointingly modern. A few, especially on the upper floors, share with the panoramic roof terrace a view of the Duomo. The location is prime but the price a bit steep for those who don't get a thrill from sleeping near the fossilized remnants of the Middle Ages.

Piazza Sant'Elisabetta 3 (off Via de' Calzioli), 50122 Firenze. ℭ **055-27-370.** Fax 055-219-653. www.hotelbrunelleschi.it. 96 units. 340€ ($391) double; 500€ ($575) suite. Rates include breakfast. AE, DC, MC, V. Valet parking in garage 30€ ($35). Bus: B, 14, 23, or 71. **Amenities:** Intimate restaurant; bar (in the tower); concierge; tour desk; car-rental desk; courtesy car; business center and secretarial services; limited room service; in-room massage; babysitting; laundry service; same-day dry cleaning; nonsmoking rooms. In room: A/C, TV, minibar, hair dryer, safe.

MODERATE

Burchianti 𝒦𝒦 (Finds) In 2002, rising rents forced the kindly owner of this venerable inn (established in the 19th c.) to move up the block into the *piano nobile* of a neighboring 15th-century palazzo. She definitely traded up. Incredible frescoes dating from 17th century and later decorate every ceiling but one tiny single, and many of the walls—actually, virtually all the walls are painted, but the yahoos of a previous age whitewashed over them and the hotel could afford to uncover only a few of them for the time being. When I visited, the workers were painting the trim, wiping off the terra-cotta tile floors, and finishing up installing the inlaid marble baths and period-style furnishings. This promises to become one of the most sought-after little hotels in Florence.

Via del Giglio 8 (off Via Panzani), 50123 Firenze. ℭ **055-212-796.** Fax 055-272-9727. www.hotelburchianti.com. 10 units. 120€–200€ ($138–$230) double; 160€–230€ ($184–$265) suite. Rates include continental breakfast. No credit cards. Parking in garage next door about 23€ ($26). Bus: A, 1, 6, 14, 17, 22, 23, 36, or 37. **Amenities:** Concierge; tour desk; car-rental desk; limited room service (breakfast); babysitting; laundry service; dry cleaning. In room: A/C, TV on request, minibar in suites, hair dryer, safe.

Grand Hotel Cavour 𝒦 The Cavour is an address of some refinement in Dante's old neighborhood, and about as central as you can get. The plush chairs in the large vaulted lobby focus around an antique stone pillar, and the roof terrace has a positively spectacular view of the Duomo, the Palazzo Vecchio, and other Florentine landmarks. The rooms, carpeted and furnished with contemporary good taste, tend to be on the small side, though a few enjoy brick arches and other 10th-century holdovers. The bathrooms are new, and the firm beds are spread with patterned quilts. Accommodations along the front and side get a view of the towers sprouting from the Bargello and the Badia, but be warned: The double-glazed windows are no match for the clamorous buses that grumble down the busy street in front.

Via del Proconsolo 3 (next to the Badia), 50122 Firenze. ⓒ **055-282-461.** Fax 055-218-955. www.hotelcavour.com. 108 units. 198€ ($228) double. Rates include breakfast. AE, DC, MC, V. Valet parking in garage 26€ ($30). Bus: 14, 23, or 71. **Amenities:** Elegant and famous Beatrice restaurant; bike rental; concierge; tour desk; car-rental desk; salon; limited room service; babysitting; laundry service; same-day dry cleaning; nonsmoking rooms. *In room:* A/C, TV, dataport, minibar, hair dryer, safe.

Hotel Calzaiuoli ⓐ

As central as you can get, the Calzaiuoli offers comfortable, well-appointed rooms on the main strolling drag halfway between the Uffizi and the Duomo. The halls' rich runners lead up a *pietra serena* staircase to the midsize and largish rooms decorated with painted friezes and framed etchings. Rooms were refurbished in 2001 with the addition of stylish wood furnishings and mirrored armoires. The firm beds rest on patterned carpets, in the older rooms surrounded by functional furniture beginning to show some wear. The bathrooms range from huge to cramped, but all have fluffy towels (and a few enjoy Jacuzzis). The rooms look over the street, with its pedestrian carnival and some of the associated noise, or out the back—either over the rooftops to the Bargello and Badia towers or up to the Duomo's cupola.

Via Calzaiuoli 6 (near Orsanmichele), 50122 Firenze. ⓒ **055-212-456.** Fax 055-268-310. www.calzaiuoli.it. 45 units. 88€–245€ ($102–$282) double. Rates include breakfast. AE, DC, MC, V. Valet parking 23€–26€ ($26–$30) in garage. Bus: 22, 36, or 37. **Amenities:** Concierge; tour desk; car-rental desk; limited room service; babysitting; laundry service; dry cleaning. *In room:* A/C, TV, minibar, hair dryer, safe.

Hotel Chiari Bigallo ⓐ *Finds*

I was quite cross 2 years ago to find that the owners had decided to renovate this formerly super-cheap standby with *the* single best location (across from the Duomo)—and more than double the prices. Its rooms are modular modern now, but in the location competition, it still wins for being above the Loggia del Bigallo on the corner of Piazza del Duomo. If you get one of the few rooms facing the Duomo, you'll have a view like no other, within poking distance of Giotto's bell tower. The traffic-free zone doesn't mean you won't have significant pedestrian noise that drifts up from the cobbled street below, as this is the city's most tourist-trammeled intersection.

They renovated this place to bring it in line with their other three hotels, including, a few blocks away on Via delle Oche and with side views of this living postcard, the quieter de' Lanzi (below).

Vicolo degli Adimari 2 (off the Via Calzaiuoli near the Piazza Duomo), 50122 Firenze. ⓒ and fax **055-216-086.** www.hotelbigallo.it. 17 units. 186€ ($214) double; 251€ ($289) triple. Rates include continental breakfast. AE, DC, MC, V. Valet parking in garage 21€ ($24). Bus: A, 1, 6, 11, 14, 17, 22, 23, 36, or 37. **Amenities:** Concierge; tour desk; car-rental desk; limited room service; laundry service; dry cleaning; nonsmoking rooms. *In room:* A/C, TV, minibar, hair dryer, safe.

Hotel de' Lanzi ☆☆ A much quieter alternative to the Hotel Chiari Bigallo, its sister hotel around the corner (see above), the Lanzi is just as centrally located and more comfortable; it just doesn't have those drop-dead views of the Duomo and bell tower. The beds have firm mattresses and spreads embroidered in an antique Florentine pattern. The accommodations, in fact, are all done very tastefully for a hotel of this price. (Ask for a Frommer's discount and it may drop into the "Moderate" category.) The rooms come with shiny new bathrooms sporting heated towel racks (in most). Many rooms on the front get a magnificent window-filling side view of the Duomo, but even if you don't get the vista, you can be assured of cozy, relaxing accommodations just steps from the city's major sights and shopping. Breakfast is a full buffet, with fruit and ham.

Via delle Oche 11 (off Via Calzaiuoli around the corner from the Duomo), 50122 Firenze. ✆ and fax 055-288-043. www.florence.ala.it/lanzi. 44 units. 186€ ($214) double, 251€ ($289) triple. Prices can drop up to 80%–100% in low season (the website has details); also ask for Frommer's discounts. Rates include breakfast. AE, DC, MC, V. Valet parking 18€ ($21). Bus: 22, 36, or 37. Amenities: Concierge; tour desk; car-rental desk; limited room service; laundry service; dry cleaning; nonsmoking rooms. In room: A/C, TV, hair dryer, safe.

Hotel Pensione Pendini ☆ Built during the heyday of the 1880s when Florence was briefly the capital of the newly unified Italy, the Pendini rises above the storefronts of Piazza della Repubblica. The Abolaffio brothers, Emmanuele and David, took over this former pensione in 1994 and have since installed double-glazing on all windows so that street noise has virtually disappeared. All bathrooms are also being redone in green tile with large tubs. Many rooms boast an airy country style, with original and reproduction antiques and brass-framed beds. The rather large accommodations on the piazza are best, with views over the bustle of the cafe-lined square. The lounge, offering 24-hour bar service, contains a comfortable mélange of 19th-century furnishings with scattered rugs, plus a computer with free Internet access. The location and price make this hotel a good choice for shoppers who'd rather give their money to Armani and Ferragamo.

Via Strozzi 1 (Piazza della Repubblica), 50123 Firenze. ✆ 055-211-170. Fax 055-281-807. www.florenceitaly.net. 42 units, all with bathroom. 110€–150€ ($127–$173) double; 150€–210€ ($173–$242) triple; 170€–250€ ($196–$288) quad; 170€–330€ ($196–$380) family suite. Rates include continental breakfast. AE, DC,

MC, V. Valet garage parking 21€–31€ ($24–$36). Bus: A, 6, 11, 22, 36, or 37. **Amenities:** Concierge; tour desk; car-rental desk; 24-hr. room service (breakfast and bar). *In room:* A/C, TV, dataport, hair dryer on request.

INEXPENSIVE

Hotel Abaco *Value* Bruno is a bit of a Calabrian dynamo, running his clean, efficient little hotel in a prime location with gusto, and he's one of the more helpful, advice-filled hoteliers in town. The hotel has inherited a few nice touches from its 15th-century palazzo, including high wood ceilings, stone floors (some are parquet), and in tiny room no. 5 a carved *pietra serena* fireplace, and each room is themed after a Renaissance artist, with framed reproductions of the painter's works and a color scheme derived from them. Bruno's slowly replacing the mismatched furnishings with quirky antique-style pieces like gilded frame mirrors and rich half-testers over the beds. It's at a busy intersection, but the double-paned windows help. There's a free Internet point, and he'll do a load of laundry for you for just 7€ ($8.05), wash and dry.

Via dei Banchi 1 (halfway between the station and the Duomo, off Via de' Panzani), 50123 Firenze. ℂ **055-238-1919.** Fax 055-282-2289. www.abaco-hotel.it. 7 units, 3 with shower and sink, 3 with full bathroom. 67€ ($77) double without bathroom; 70€ ($81) double with shower only; 87€ ($100) double with bathroom. Breakfast 5€ ($5.75), free if you pay for the room with cash. AE, MC, V (they prefer cash). Valet parking 25€ ($29) in garage. Bus: 1, 6, 11, 14, 17, 22, 23, 36, or 37. **Amenities:** Bike rental; concierge; tour desk; car-rental desk; coin-op laundry. *In room:* A/C (costs an extra 5€/$5.75 to turn on), TV, dataport, hair dryer.

Hotel Firenze A recent renovation has transformed this former student hangout (still partly used as a study-abroad dorm) into a board-rated two-star hotel. Its location is divine, tucked away on its own little piazza at the heart of the *centro storico*'s pedestrian zone, but it's a bit too institutional to justify the midrange rates. The rooms are brightly tiled but bland. This is a large operation without any of the warmth or ambience of a small, family-run hotel, and the concierge and management are efficient but generally uninvolved.

Piazza Donati 4 (on Via del Corso, off Via dei Calzaiuoli), 50122 Firenze. ℂ **055-268-301** or 055-214-203. Fax 055-212-370. 60 units. 88€ ($102) double; 120€ ($138) triple; 154€ ($177) quad. Breakfast 8€ ($9.20). No credit cards. Parking 26€ ($30) in nearby garage. Bus: A, 14, or 23. **Amenities:** Tour desk. *In room:* TV, hair dryer.

Hotel Medici *Value* In the heart of town with killer views, this place is more than worth it for budgeteers who can secure a room on the fifth or (better yet) sixth floor. All rooms are a good size but plain, with functional furniture, tile floors, tiny bathrooms, and firm beds. But who looks at the room when your window is filled with a vista of Florence's Duomo—facade, campanile, dome, and all? Only the top two levels of rooms get the full effect, but the sixth floor has a wraparound terrace everyone can enjoy. If you're lucky, you might happen in at a moment when one of the many regulars haven't booked one of the sixth-floor rooms with French windows opening directly onto the terrace. The price is excellent for this kind of location and panorama.

Via de' Medici 6 (between Piazza della Repubblica and Via de' Calzaiuoli), 50123 Firenze. ⓒ 055-284-818. Fax 055-216-202. www.hotelmedici.it. 39 units, 26 with bathroom (shower only). 35€–105€ ($40–$121) double without bathroom, 45€–125€ ($52–$144) double with bathroom. MC, V. Rates include breakfast. Valet parking 20€ ($23) in nearby garage. Bus: A, 22, 36, or 37. **Amenities:** Concierge; tour desk; car-rental desk; limited room service (breakfast). *In room:* TV in some units, minibar in 6 units, hair dryer.

Pensione Maria Luisa de' Medici 🅐🅐🅐 *(Kids* *(Finds*   In the 1950s and '60s, Angido Sordi was into Italian design, and the rooms of his hotel—each frescoed with a different Medici portrait by his wife—have lamps, chairs, and tables you'd normally have to go to New York's Museum of Modern Art to see. In the 1970s and '80s, Sordi got into baroque art, so the halls are hung with canvases by the likes of Van Dyck, Vignale, and Sustermans. I can't wait to see what he gets into next. The 1645 palazzo setting goes well with the artistic theme, and while Dr. Sordi convalesces in a back room, his Welsh partner Evelyn Morris runs the place, cooking hearty breakfasts served to you in your room. Most rooms are large enough to accommodate four to five people comfortably. The firm beds are set on carpeted or tiled floors scattered with thick rugs. There are four shared bathrooms, so you usually don't have to wait in the morning. One drawback: You have to walk up three flights. There is a curfew, which varies with the season.

Via del Corso 1 (2nd floor; between Via dei Calzaiuoli and Via del Proconsolo), 50122 Firenze. ⓒ **055-280-048.** 9 units, 2 with bathroom. 67€ ($77) double without bathroom, 80€ ($92) double with bathroom; 93€ ($107) triple without bathroom, 113€ ($130) triple with bathroom; 118€ ($136) quad without bathroom, 140€ ($161) quad with bathroom. Rates include breakfast. No credit cards. Nearby parking about 24€–28€ ($27–$32). Bus: A, 14, or 23. **Amenities:** Concierge; tour desk. *In room:* Hair dryer, no phone.

2 Near Piazza Della Signoria

EXPENSIVE

Hotel Hermitage 🅐   This ever-popular hotel right at the foot of the Ponte Vecchio was renovated in 1998 to give each room wood

Kids Family-Friendly Hotels

Hotel Casci (p. 56)   This inexpensive family favorite near the Palazzo Medici-Ricciardi has a series of extra-large rooms set aside especially for families. The hotel is housed in a 15th-century palazzo, and the family that runs it is very friendly and helpful. A great family value!

Hotel Nuova Italia (p. 61)   The Italian-American couple that runs this hotel near the station are just about the most help-ful hoteliers I've ever run across. The rooms aren't overly large but are immaculate. And here's an added perk: With this Frommer's guidebook in hand, you and your brood can get a discount off the already reasonable prices.

Instituto Gould (p. 70)   The best bet for families on a tight budget is like a hotel masquerading as a hostel. It draws more families than students to its institutionally clean and large accommodations. Almost all rooms have a private bathroom, and you can get a family of four into your own quad with a private bathroom for around 60€ ($69).

Pensione Maria Luisa de' Medici (p. 53)   An amicable pair of proprietors runs this very central hotel just a few blocks from the Duomo. Most rooms are enormous, with multiple beds and dressers and tabletops on which to spread your family's stuff. The home-cooked Welsh breakfast served in your room is included in the low prices. Just be sure to admonish the more curious youngsters from touching the genuine—and valuable—baroque paintings in the hall.

floors or thick rugs, shiny new bathrooms (most with Jacuzzis), and fresh wallpaper. The rooms are of moderate size, occasionally a bit dark, but they're full of 17th- to 19th-century antiques and boast double-glazed windows to cut down on noise. Those that don't face the Ponte Vecchio are on side alleys and quieter. Their famous roof terrace is covered in bright flowers that frame postcard views of the Arno, Duomo, and Palazzo Vecchio. The charming breakfast room full of picture windows gets the full effect of the morning sun. The owners and staff excel in doing the little things that help make your vacation go smoothly—but prices are a bit inflated.

Vicolo Marzio 1/Piazza del Pesce (to the left of the Ponte Vecchio as you're facing it), 50122 Firenze ✆ **055-287-216.** Fax 055-212-208. www.hermitagehotel.com.

28 units. 245€ ($282) double; 260€ ($299) triple; 299€ ($344) family suite. Rates up to 20% lower in winter. Rates include breakfast. MC, V. Parking 21€–34€ ($24–$39) in nearby garage. Bus: 23 or 71. **Amenities:** Concierge; tour desk; limited room service; babysitting; laundry service; dry cleaning. *In room:* A/C, TV, hair dryer, safe.

3 Near San Lorenzo & the Mercato Centrale

MODERATE

Hotel Bellettini *𝒢 Value*   A hotel has existed in this Renaissance palazzo since the 1600s. Gina and Marzia, sisters and third-generation hoteliers, run this gem of terra-cotta tiles, wrought-iron or carved wood beds, antiques, and stained-glass windows. Room no. 44 offers a tiny balcony that, blooming with jasmine and geraniums by late spring, makes it second best only to room no. 45 with its view of the Medici chapels and the Duomo's dome. In 2000, they added a lovely six-room annex with frescoes, marble bathrooms, minibars, and coffeemakers (those are the double rooms that cost 160€/$184). The hotel shares management with the 26-room **Le Vigne,** Piazza Santa Maria Novella 24 (© **055-294-449;** fax 055-230-2263), which absorbs some of the overflow into large but simple renovated rooms. The rates are slightly lower than at the Bellettini, and duplex 119 is great for families. Breakfast is an impressive spread.

Via dei Conti 7 (off Via dei Cerretani), 50123 Firenze. © **055-213-561.** Fax 055-283-551. www.hotelbellettini.com. 28 units. 100€ ($115) double without bathroom, 130€–160€ ($150–$184) double with bathroom; 160€ ($184) triple with bathroom; 200€ ($230) quad with bathroom. Rates include buffet breakfast. AE, DC, MC, V. Nearby parking 18€ ($21). Bus: A, 1, 6, 14, 17, 22, 23, 36, or 37. **Amenities:** Concierge; tour desk; limited room service; laundry service; dry cleaning. *In room:* A/C, TV, hair dryer on request, safe.

INEXPENSIVE

Hotel California *𝒢 Value*   The California is a good budget option on a lightly trafficked street near the Duomo. Rooms were completely overhauled in 2000–01 with stylish modern furnishings, richly colored bedspreads, and spanking new bathrooms—a few with Jacuzzi tubs, and almost all with spacious marble sink counters. There are 18th-century fresco fragments and stuccoes on many of the ceilings, and breakfast is served on a flower-covered terrace in nice weather. A few of the rooms have balconies and views of the Duomo's cupola, and they offer good deals for families.

Via Ricasoli 30 (1½ blocks north of the Duomo), 50122 Firenze. © **055-282-753.** Fax 055-216-268. www.californiaflorence.it. 22 units. 90€–173€ ($104–$199) double; 120€–233€ ($133–$268) triple; 140€–294€ ($161–$338) quad. Ask about special promotions that can lower rates up to 40%. Rates include breakfast.

AE, DC, MC, V. Valet parking around 25€ ($29). Bus: 1, 6, 7, 10, 11, 17, 20, 25, 31, 32, 33, 67, 68, or 91. **Amenities:** Concierge; tour desk; limited room service. *In room:* A/C, TV, dataport, minibar in 10 units, hair dryer, safe.

Hotel Casci *Finds* *Kids*   This clean hotel in a 15th-century palazzo is run by the Lombardis, one of Florence's nicest families. It's patronized by a host of regulars who know a good value when they find it. The Lombardis bicker among themselves Italian style but are amazingly accommodating toward guests—their favorite phrase in English is "No problem!" They even offer a free museum ticket to everyone who stays at least 3 nights (and with admissions running nearly $10 for most major museums, that's saying something). The tiny frescoed bar room was, from 1851 to 1855, part of an apartment inhabited by Giacchino Rossini, legendary composer of *The Barber of Seville* and *The William Tell Overture.* The rooms ramble on toward the back forever, overlooking the gardens and Florentine rooftops, and are mouse-quiet except for the birdsong. A few large family suites in back sleep four to five. The central location means some rooms (with double-paned windows) overlook busy Via Cavour, so for more quiet ask for a room facing the inner courtyard's magnolia tree. They serve an ample breakfast buffet in a frescoed dining room.

Via Cavour 13 (between Via dei Ginori and Via Guelfa), 50129 Firenze. *©* 055-211-686. Fax 055-239-6461. www.hotelcasci.com. 25 units. 90€–140€ ($104–$161) double; 120€–180€ ($138–$207) triple; 180€–220€ ($207–$252) quad. Rates include buffet breakfast. Off-season rates 20%–30% less; check website for special offers, especially Nov–Feb. AE, DC, MC, V. Valet parking 23€–25€ ($26–$29), or in nearby garage (no valet) for 15€ ($17). Bus: 1, 6, 11, or 17. **Amenities:** Bar; concierge; tour desk; babysitting; laundry service; dry cleaning; nonsmoking rooms; free Internet access. *In room:* A/C, TV, dataport, fridge, hair dryer, safe.

Il Guelfo Bianco *Finds* *Value*   Once you enter this refined hotel (completely renovated in 1994 and enlarged in 2001), you'll forget it's on busy Via Cavour. Its windows are triple-paned, blocking out nearly all traffic noise, and many rooms overlook quiet courtyards and gardens out back. It gets a value icon for providing excellent service and luxury rooms at some of the lowest prices for a board-rated three-star hotel in all of Florence—and all that just a few blocks from the Duomo. The room decor is very pretty, with marble-topped desks, antique-style furnishings, modern art, and painted tile work in the large new bathrooms. The ceilings faithfully reproduce the beam and terra cotta look this 15th-century palazzo once had. Some rooms have retained such atmospheric 17th-century features as frescoed or painted wood ceilings, carved wooden doorways, and the occasional parquet floor. Superior rooms are larger than executive ones (and can be made easily into triples), while "de luxe" rooms are larger still with a semi-separate sitting area—think junior suite. The friendly staff is full of advice, and they've installed a new bar and reading room on the ground floor.

Via Cavour 29 (near the corner of Via Guelfa), 50129 Firenze. © 055-288-330. Fax 055-295-203. www.ilguelfobianco.it. 43 units. 105€–135€ ($121–$155) executive double; 144€–180€ ($166–$207) superior double; 170€–210€ ($196–$242) de luxe double; 200€–245€ ($230–$282) superior triple; 225€–265€ ($259–$305) de luxe triple. Rates include breakfast. AE, MC, V. Valet parking 24€–30€ ($27–$35) in garage. Bus: 1, 6, 7, 11, 17, 33, 67, or 68. **Amenities:** Concierge; tour desk; car-rental desk; 24-hr. room service; in-room massage; babysitting; laundry service; same-day dry cleaning. *In room:* A/C, TV, VCR in some units, dataport, minibar, hair dryer, safe.

4 Near Piazza Santa Trínita

VERY EXPENSIVE

Hotel Helvetia & Bristol 🍷🍷   This Belle Epoque hotel is the most central of the top luxury properties in town, host in the past to the Tuscan Macchaioli painters as well as De Chirico, playwright Pirandello, and atom-splitting Enrico Fermi. The attentive staff oversees the rather cushy accommodations outfitted with marble bathrooms; large, firm beds; and heavy curtains. Most rooms have at least one antique work of art on the fabric-covered walls, and all are well insulated from the sounds of the outside world. The large 17th-century canvases add an air of dignity to the plush sofas of the lounge, while the Winter Garden bar/breakfast room is tricked out with trailing ivy and a splashing fountain. Prices, though, are starting to get a little exaggerated.

Via dei Pescioni 2 (near the Palazzo Strozzi), 50123 Firenze. © 888/770-0447 in the U.S., 800-505-050 toll-free in Italy or 055-287-814. Fax 055-288-353. www. hotelhelvetiabristolfirenze.it. 67 units. 330€–470€ ($380–$541) double; 500€–650€ ($575–$748) suite. Breakfast 30€ ($35). AE, DC, MC, V. Valet parking in garage 35€ ($40). Bus: 6, 11, 36, 37, or 68. **Amenities:** Intimate restaurant; bike rental; concierge; tour desk; car-rental desk; 24-hr. room service; in-room massage; babysitting; laundry service; same-day dry cleaning; Internet terminal. *In room:* A/C, TV, VCR in deluxe rooms, minibar.

EXPENSIVE

Hotel Tornabuoni Beacci 🍷   The 80-year-old Beacci continues a 200-year hostelry tradition in this 16th-century Strozzi family palace. The staff greets return guests and new friends alike with genuine warmth. Everything is a bit worn, but there's a concerted effort to furnish the rooms with period pieces. The dining room is sunny, and the lunches and dinners are well prepared. In summer, you can take breakfast on a terrace bursting with flowers and a view of the Bellosguardo hills. Off the terrace is a small bar, and there's an atmospheric reading room with a 17th-century tapestry and a large fireplace that roars to life in winter. They're currently expanding into the floor below with a small conference room and 12 more guest rooms, including a suite overlooking Piazza Santa Trínita and a honeymoon suite covered with beautiful 17th-century frescoes.

Via Tornabuoni 3 (off the north corner of Piazza Santa Trínita), 50123 Firenze. ✆ 055-212-645. Fax 055-283-594. www.tornabuonihotels.com. 28 units. 185€–220€ ($213–$253) double; 240€ ($276) jr. suite; 280€–360€ ($322–$414) suite. Rates include buffet breakfast. AE, DC, MC, V. Parking 23€–25€ ($26–$29) in garage. Bus: 6, 11, 36, 37, or 68. **Amenities:** Restaurant; concierge; tour desk; 24-hr. room service; babysitting; laundry service; dry cleaning. *In room:* A/C, TV, minibar, hair dryer.

MODERATE

Hotel Alessandra ⓡ *Value*   This old-fashioned pensione in a 1507 palazzo just off the river charges little for its simple comfort and kind hospitality. The rooms differ greatly in size and style, and while they won't win any awards from *Architectural Digest,* there are a few antique pieces and parquet floors to add to the charm. Air-conditioning was recently installed in 23 rooms. The bathrooms are outfitted with fluffy white towels, and the shared bathrooms are ample, clean, and numerous enough that you won't have to wait in line in the morning. They also rent out an apartment in a quiet section of the Oltarno (across the bridge from the Santa Croce neighborhood) for 775€ ($891) per week for two people; check it out at www.florenceflat.com.

Borgo SS. Apostoli 17 (between Via dei Tornabuoni and Via Por Santa Maria), 50123 Firenze. ✆ 055-283-438. Fax 055-210-619. www.hotelalessandra.com. 27 units, 19 with bathroom. 108€ ($124) double without bathroom; 145€ ($167) double with bathroom; 160€ ($184) double overlooking river; 145€ ($167) triple without bathroom, 191€ ($220) triple with bathroom; 160€ ($184) quad without bathroom, 212€ ($244) quad with bathroom; 160€ ($184) jr. suite; 200€ ($230) Baccio suite. Rates include breakfast. Ask about low-season rates. AE, MC, V. Parking in nearby garage 20€ ($23). Bus: B, 6, 11, 36, or 37. **Amenities:** Concierge; tour desk; limited room service (breakfast); massage; babysitting; laundry service; same-day dry cleaning; nonsmoking rooms (doubles overlooking river and suites). *In room:* A/C in most units, TV (PlayStation on request), hair dryer, safe in most units.

Hotel Torre Guelfa ⓡⓡⓡ   Giancarlo and Sabina Avuri run one of the most atmospheric hotels in Florence. The first of many reasons to stay here is to drink in the breathtaking 360-degree view from the 13th-century tower, Florence's tallest privately owned tower. Although you're just steps from the Ponte Vecchio, you'll want to put sightseeing on hold and linger in your canopied iron bed. So many people request room no. 15, with a huge private terrace and a view similar to the tower's, they've had to tack 10€ ($12) onto the price. Follow the strains of classical music to the salon, whose vaulted ceilings and lofty proportions hark back to the palazzo's 14th-century origins.

The owners' newest hotel endeavor is the 18th-century **Palazzo Castiglione,** Via del Giglio 8 (© **055-214-886;** fax 055-274-0521; pal.cast@flashnet.it), with four doubles (170€/$196) and two suites (200€/$230). Also ask them about their Tuscan hideaway, the **Villa Rosa di Boscorotondo** outside Panzano.

Borgo SS. Apostoli 8 (between Via dei Tornabuoni and Via Por Santa Maria), 50123 Firenze. © **055-239-6338.** Fax 055-239-8577. www.hoteltorreguelfa.com. 22 units. 155€–210€ ($178–$242) double; 190€–250€ ($219–$288) triple or jr. suite. Rates include continental breakfast. AE, DC, MC, V. Parking in nearby garage 25€ ($29). Bus: B, 6, 11, 36, or 37. **Amenities:** Concierge; tour desk; car-rental desk; courtesy car; limited room service; babysitting; laundry service; dry cleaning. *In room:* A/C, TV (in all but 6 1st-floor doubles), minibar, hair dryer.

5 South of Santa Maria Novella

VERY EXPENSIVE

Westin Excelsior ⚝ This is Florence's prime luxury address; the sumptuousness will bowl you over, if the staggering price tags don't do it first. The old palazzi that make up the hotel, once partly owned by Napóleon's sister Caroline, were unified and decorated in 1927, the rooms decorated in three styles: Florentine 17th-century, Tuscan 18th-century, and Empire. All are done with a liberal use of colored marbles, walnut furniture, *pietra serena* accents, Oriental rugs, and neoclassical frescoes. Try to book a room overlooking the Arno (junior suites do not). The penthouses have terraces with drop-dead views over the city. Second-floor riverside doubles have balconies, and you can sometimes book half a luxurious suite at the price of a regular room. The staff is renowned for its genial attentiveness, offering a full array of amenities and services.

Piazza Ognissanti 3, 50123 Firenze. © **800/937-8461** in the U.S.; 055-264-201 or toll-free 800-3253-5353 in Italy. Fax 055-26-8008. www.starwood.com. 171 units. 599€–756€ ($689–$869) Classic double (no Arno view); 658€–832€ ($757–$957) deluxe double (with Arno view); 3,791€ ($4360) penthouse double; 1,209€ ($1,390) junior suite; 2,290€ ($2,634) suite. Breakfast 45€ ($52). AE, DC, MC, V. Valet parking 17€ ($20) in garage. Bus: B, C, or 9. **Amenities:** Faux 18th-century restaurant; 3-story chic Donatello bar; bike rental; children's program; concierge; tour desk; car-rental desk; courtesy car; business center; secretarial services; 24-hr. room service; in-room massage; babysitting; laundry service; same-day dry cleaning; non-smoking rooms; executive-level rooms (a few outfitted for business work). *In room:* A/C, TV, dataport, fax on request, minibar, hair dryer, safe.

MODERATE

Hotel Aprile The Aprile fills a semi-restored 15th-century palace on this busy hotel-laden street near the station. The corridors are hung with detached fresco fragments, highly ruinous from centuries of exposure on the palazzo's original facade. Portions of 16th- and 17th-century frescoes in much better shape grace many of the accommodations, and those on the ceiling of the breakfast room are beautifully intact (though in summer you can also breakfast in the garden out back). Aside from antique touches, the simple guest rooms are nothing to write home about. The street noise gets through even the double glazing, so light sleepers will want to request a room off the road—besides, some of the back rooms have a breathtaking view of Santa Maria Novella. The frescoes and relative quiet of room no. 16 make it an excellent choice. Historical footnote: Cavernous room no. 3 has had a bathroom attached to it since the 15th century, one of the first "rooms with bathroom" ever!

Via della Scala 6 (1½ blocks from the train station), 50123 Firenze. © 055-216-237. Fax 055-280-947. www.hotelaprile.it. 30 units. 180€ ($207) double; 230€ ($265) triple; 215€ ($247) suite. Rates include breakfast. AE, DC, MC, V. Parking 18€–26€ ($21–$30) in nearby garage. Bus: 1, 2, 12, 16, 17, 22, 29, or 30. **Amenities:** Concierge; tour desk; car-rental desk; babysitting; laundry service; same-day dry cleaning. *In room:* A/C (in all but 1 unit), TV, minibar, hair dryer.

Villa Azalee ★ *Finds* The atmosphere of this 1870 villa on the historic center's edge, with its prizewinning flowers, soundproofed rooms, and comfortable beds, makes you forget the eight lanes of traffic flowing a few dozen feet away along Florence's inner ring road. There's a sunroom in the main villa, tapestries on the walls, and a very friendly staff. The rooms are floral print–oriented—perfect for Laura Ashley buffs, but for others the pink taffeta and gauzy canopies might seem over the top. The old *scuderia* (stables) out back were reconstructed in a hybrid Italian-English style, and many of the rooms in it echo the style of a cozy Cotswalds cottage. The best accommodations are on the *scuderia*'s ground floor, with heavy beamed ceilings, and on the villa's first (upper) floor, with wood floors, sleigh beds, and Empire bathrooms. I'd give it another star if only it weren't so far from the action.

Viale Fratelli Rosselli 44 (at the end of Via della Scala, between the station and Cascine Park), 50123 Firenze. © **055-214-242.** Fax 055-268-264. www.villa-azalee. it. 25 units. 167€ ($192) double; 224€ ($258) triple. Rates include breakfast. AE, DC,

MC, V. Parking 30€ ($35) in nearby garage. Bus: 1, 2, 9, 13, 16, 17, 26, 27, 29, 30, or 35. **Amenities:** Bike rental (3€/$3.45 a day); concierge; tour desk; car-rental desk; 24-hr. room service; laundry service; same-day dry cleaning. *In room:* A/C, TV, minibar, hair dryer.

6 Between Santa Maria Novella & Mercato Centrale

MODERATE

Hotel Mario's ★★ In a traditional Old Florence atmosphere, Mario Noce and his enthusiastic staff run a first-rate ship. Your room might have a wrought-iron headboard and massive reproduction antique armoire and look out onto a peaceful garden; the amenities include fresh flowers and fruit. The beamed ceilings in the common areas date from the 17th century, although the building became a hotel only in 1872. I'd award Mario's three stars if not for its location—it's a bit far from the Duomo nerve center. Hefty discounts during off-season months (as low as the lowest rates listed below) de-splurge this lovely choice.

Via Faenza 89 (1st floor; near Via Cennini), 50123 Firenze. ℂ 055-216-801. Fax 055-212-039. www.hotelmarios.com. 16 units. 80€–165€ ($92–$190) double; 100€–210€ ($115–$242) triple. Rates include continental breakfast. AE, DC, MC, V. Valet parking 20€–25€ ($23–$29). Bus: 7, 10, 11, 12, 25, 31, 32, or 33. **Amenities:** Concierge; tour desk; limited room service (breakfast); babysitting; laundry service; dry cleaning; nonsmoking rooms. *In room:* A/C, TV, hair dryer, safe.

Hotel Nuova Italia ★★ *(Kids)* A Frommer's fairy tale: With her trusty *Frommer's Europe on $5 a Day* in hand, the fair Eileen left the kingdom of Canada on a journey to faraway Florence. At her hotel, Eileen met Luciano, her baggage boy in shining armor. They fell in love, got married, bought a castle (er, hotel) of their own called the Nuova Italia, and their clients live happily ever after. The staff here really puts itself to task for guests, recommending restaurants, shops, day trips—they gave me tips the tourist office didn't know about. The rooms are board-rated two-star standard, medium to small, but the attention to detail makes the Nuova Italia stand out. Every room has a bathroom (with fuzzy towels), orthopedic mattress, and triple-paned windows (though some morning rumble from the San Lorenzo market street carts still gets through). It's also one of a handful of hotels in all of Tuscany with mosquito screens in the windows. Expected soon is new furniture custom-designed by Eileen. The family's love of art is manifested in framed posters and paintings, and Eileen is a great source about local exhibits.

Via Faenza 26 (off Via Nazionale), 50123 Firenze. ℂ 055-268-430 or 055-287-508. Fax 055-210-941. www.hotelnuovaitalia.com. 20 units. *For Frommer's readers:*

125€ ($144) double; 145€ ($167) triple. Rates include continental breakfast. There are frequent discounts, so ask when booking. AE, DC, MC, V. Valet garage parking about 18€–22€ ($21–$25). Bus: 7, 10, 11, 12, 25, 31, 32, or 33. **Amenities:** Concierge; tour desk; car-rental desk; babysitting; laundry service; dry cleaning. *In room:* A/C, TV, hair dryer on request.

INEXPENSIVE

Albergo Azzi Musicians Sandro and Valentino, the new young owners of this ex-pensione (aka the Locanda degli Artisti/Artists' Inn), are creating here a haven for artists, artist manqués, and students. It exudes a relaxed bohemian feel—not all the doors hang straight and not all the bedspreads match, though strides are being made (and they've even recently discovered some old frescoes in room nos. 3 and 4). You'll love the open terrace with a view where breakfast is served in warm weather, as well as the small library of art books and guidebooks so you can enjoy a deeper understanding of Florence's treasures. Four of the rooms without a full bathroom have a shower and sink (but no toilet). In the same building, under the same management and with similar rates, are the **Anna** (eight units, four with bathroom; ✆ **055-239-8322**) and the **Paola** (seven units, four with bathroom and some with frescoes; ✆ **055-213-682**).

Via Faenza 56 (1st floor), 50123 Firenze. ✆ and fax **055-213-806** (fax as of 2004 may be 055-264-8613). hotelazzi@hotmail.com. 12 units, 7 with bathroom. 56€ ($64) double without bathroom; 60€ ($69) double with shower but no toilet; 75€–80€ ($86–$92) double with bathroom; 25€ ($29) bed in shared room. Breakfast 3€ ($3.45). AE, DC, MC, V. Parking in nearby garage 16€ ($18). Bus: 7, 10, 11, 12, 25, 31, 32, or 33. **Amenities:** Concierge; tour desk. *In room:* Hair dryer on request, no phone.

Albergo Merlini ✦ *Value* Run by the Sicilian Gabriella family, this cozy third-floor walk-up boasts rooms appointed with wooden-carved antique headboards and furnishings (and a few modular pieces to fill in the gaps). It's one of only two hotels in all Florence with mosquito screens. The optional breakfast is served on a sunny glassed-in terrace decorated in the 1950s with frescoes by talented American art students and overlooking a leafy large courtyard. Room nos. 1, 4 (with a balcony), and 6 to 8 all have views of the domes topping the Duomo and the Medici Chapels across the city's terra-cotta roofscape. A recent renovation tripled the number of private bathrooms and freshened up everything. This is a notch above your average board-rated one-star place, the best in a building full of tiny pensioni. There's a 1am curfew.

Via Faenza 56 (3rd floor), 50123 Firenze. ✆ **055-212-848.** Fax 055-283-939. www.hotelmerlini.it. 10 units, 6 with bathroom. 45€–65€ ($52–$75) double without bathroom, 50€–79€ ($58–$91) double with bathroom; 60€–90€ ($69–$104) triple without bathroom; 80€–100€ ($92–$115) quad without bathroom. Breakfast 6€ ($6.90). MC, V. Bus: 7, 10, 11, 12, 25, 31, 32, or 33. **Amenities:** Concierge; tour desk. *In room:* Hair dryer on request, no phone.

Mia Cara/Archi Rossi Hostel *(Value)*   The only way you'll pay less than at the Mia Cara is at the Noto family's hostel on the ground floor. At the hotel you'll find double-paned windows, spacious no-frills rooms, renovated plumbing (no shower curtains), and attractive iron headboards. Now if they'd only up the wattage of the light fixtures. The rooms overlooking the small garden out back are more tranquil than those on the street side.

Angela, the English-speaking daughter, can be reached at the numbers below or at ℂ **055-290-804** for information on the downstairs **Archi Rossi Hostel** (www.hostelarchirossi.com), where units sleep four to six, without bathroom for 19€ ($22) per person, and with bathroom for 17€ to 19€ ($20–$22) depending on how many beds in the room (there are also private, bathless singles in the hostel for 29€/$33 including breakfast, and family rooms sleeping three to five for 24€/$27 each including breakfast). The hotel is closed 11am to 2:30pm, with a 1am curfew. Both the hotel and the hostel have their own TV room and public phone. They are planning a renovation that will double the size of both hotel and hostel, and may turn the hotel into a moderate property, but just when this will happen is anybody's guess.

Via Faenza 58 (2nd floor), 50123 Firenze. ℂ 055-216-053. Fax 055-230-2601. 22 units, 9 with bathroom. 50€ ($58) double without bathroom, 60€ ($69) double with bathroom. Extra bed 35% more. Ask about off-season discounts. No credit cards. No breakfast offered in hotel (only in hostel). 4 parking spots, sometimes free, sometimes up to 8€ ($9.20). Bus: 7, 10, 11, 12, 25, 31, 32, or 33. **Amenities:** Concierge; tour desk; nonsmoking rooms. *In room:* No phone.

7 Near San Marco & Santissima Annunziata

VERY EXPENSIVE

Hotel Regency *(★★)*   The Regency, converted from two 19th-century mansions, is set on a wooded piazza at the edge of town that looks remarkably like a giant London residential square. The posh old England feel continues into the salon and bar lounge, furnished with worn antiques and darkly patterned carpets and wall fabrics. This decoration scheme dominates in the comfortable rooms as well, with a liberal use of mirrored wall panels in the smaller rooms (though none are tiny by any stretch). The marble-clad bathrooms feature heated towel racks, and the discreet service includes fresh fruit and candies left in your room and a complimentary *Herald Tribune* each morning.

Piazza Massimo d'Azeglio 3, 50121 Firenze. © **055-245-247.** Fax 055-234-6735. www.regency-hotel.com. 35 units. 297€–363€ ($342–$417) comfort double; 330€–440€ ($380–$506) superior double; 385€–484€ ($443–$557) deluxe double; 473€–605€ ($544–$696) jr. suite; 671€–880€ ($772–$1,012) suite. Rates include breakfast. AE, DC, MC, V. Valet parking 26€ ($30). Bus: 6, 31, or 32. **Amenities:** Justifiably famous Relais le Jardin restaurant; cozy bar; bike rental; concierge; tour desk; car-rental desk; 24-hr. room service; in-room massage; babysitting; laundry service; dry cleaning; nonsmoking rooms. *In room:* A/C, TV, minibar, hair dryer, safe.

EXPENSIVE

Hotel Loggiato dei Serviti 🖈🖈

The Loggiato is installed in the building designed by Antonio da Sangallo the Elder in 1527 to mirror the Ospedale degli Innocenti across the piazza, forming part of one of Italy's most beautiful squares. Twelve years ago, this was a student pensione, but the renovation that converted it into a board-rated three-star hotel has restored the Renaissance aura. High vaulted ceilings in soft creams abound throughout and are particularly lovely supported by the gray columns of the bar/lounge. The wood or brick-tiled floors in the rooms are scattered with rugs, and most of the beds have wood frames and fabric canopies for an antique feel. The rooms along the front can be a bit noisy in the evenings because traffic is routed through the edges of the piazza, but I usually reserve one anyway, just for the magical view. They are in the process of adding 10 rooms to the hotel by expanding into the building next-door.

Piazza Santissima Annunziata 3, 50122 Firenze. © **055-289-592.** Fax 055-289-595. www.loggiatodeiservitihotel.it. 29 units. 205€ ($236) double; 266€ ($306) triple; 230€–380€ ($265–$437) suite. Rates include breakfast. AE, DC, MC, V. Parking 22€ ($25). Bus: 6, 31, or 32. **Amenities:** Concierge; tour desk; car-rental desk; limited room service; babysitting; laundry service; dry cleaning. *In room:* A/C, TV, minibar, hair dryer, safe.

MODERATE

Hotel Le Due Fontane

The only thing this place has over its neighbor the Hotel Loggiato dei Serviti (see above) is that the rooms get a view of all three loggia-blessed sides of the harmonious piazza (in the Loggiato, you look out from one of them). Although installed in a 15th-century palace, both the accommodations and the public areas are done along clean lines of a nondescript modern style. Unless you get a room with the view of the piazza (along with unfortunate traffic noise), it might not be the most memorable place to stay.

Piazza Santissima Annunziata 14, 50122 Firenze. © **055-210-185.** Fax 055-294-461. www.leduefontane.it. 57 units. 160€–181€ ($184–$208) double;

240€–270€ ($276–$311) suite. Rates include breakfast. AE, DC, MC, V. Parking 15€ ($17) in nearby garage. Bus: 6, 31, or 32. **Amenities:** Concierge; tour desk; car-rental desk; courtesy car; limited room service; babysitting; laundry service; dry cleaning; nonsmoking rooms. *In room:* A/C, TV, dataport, minibar, hair dryer.

Morandi alla Crocetta *ff* *(Finds)* This subtly elegant pensione belongs to a different era, when travelers stayed in private homes filled with family heirlooms and well-kept antiques. Though the setting is indeed historic (it was a 1511 Dominican nuns' convent), many of the old-fashioned effects, like the wood beam ceilings, 1500s artwork, and antique furnishings, are the result of a recent redecoration. It has all been done in good taste, however, and there are still plenty of echoes of the original structure, from exposed brick arches to one room's 16th-century fresco fragments. An octogenarian Irishwoman, Katherine Doyle, still oversees the hotel business, but daily operations are mainly handled (with great care and hospitality) by her family and friends. They are currently engaged in a long project to open up a few new rooms on the first floor and transfer the reception there alongside a bar and small library.

Via Laura 50 (a block east of Piazza Santissima Annunziata), 50121 Firenze. *(f)* **055-234-4747.** Fax 055-248-0954. www.hotelmorandi.it. 10 units. 170€ ($196) double; 220€ ($253) triple; 260€ ($299) quad. Breakfast 11€ ($13). AE, DC, MC, V. Parking 16€ ($18) in garage. Bus: 6, 31, or 32. **Amenities:** Concierge; tour desk; car-rental desk; limited room service; babysitting; laundry service; dry cleaning. *In room:* A/C, TV, dataport, minibar, hair dryer, safe.

8 Near Santa Croce

EXPENSIVE

Hotel Monna Lisa *ff* There's a certain old-world elegance to the richly decorated sitting and breakfast rooms and the gravel-strewn garden of this 14th-century palazzo. Among the potted plants and framed oils, the hotel has Giambologna's original rough competition piece for the Rape of the Sabines, along with many pieces by neoclassical sculptor Giovanni Duprè, whose family's descendants own the hotel. They try their best to keep the whole place looking like a private home, and many rooms have the original painted wood ceilings, as well as antique furniture and richly textured wallpaper or fabrics. In 2002, they restructured 15 additional rooms in another, recently acquired building bordering the courtyard and dubbed it "La Limonaia," with rooms overlooking the garden.

Borgo Pinti 27, 50121 Firenze. *(f)* **055-247-9751.** Fax 055-247-9755. www.monnalisa.it. 45 units. 181€–325€ ($208–$374) double; 232€–413€ ($267–$475) triple; 410€–700€ ($472–$805) suite. Rates include breakfast. AE, DC, MC, V. Parking 11€ ($13) in their own garage. Bus: B, 14, 23, or 71. **Amenities:** American bar; small gym; concierge; tour desk; car-rental desk; limited room service; babysitting; massage; laundry service and dry cleaning (not on weekends). *In room:* A/C, TV, minibar, hair dryer, safe.

MODERATE

Hotel Ritz 🍸   One of the more intimate hotels along the Arno, the Ritz was taken over in 1996 and renovated by the Abolaffio brothers—who also own the Hotel Pensione Pendini (p. 51). The walls are hung with reproductions of Italian art from the Renaissance to Modigliani, and the reading room and bar are cozy. The room decor varies—some floors have wood or marble, others are carpeted. The mix-and-match furniture is mostly modern yet tasteful. Two rooms on the front have balconies to better enjoy the Arno view, and two on the back (nos. 37 and 38) have small private terraces, and there's a roof terrace with its view of Fiesole. The rather roomy bathrooms have been completely redone with new tile and heated towel racks.

Lungarno della Zecca Vecchia 24, 50122 Firenze. ℂ **055-234-0650.** Fax 055-240-863. www.florenceitaly.net/ritz. 30 units. 110€–180€ ($127–$207) double; 150€–230€ ($173–$265) triple; 170€–280€ ($196–$322) quad; 170€–330€ ($196–$380) family suite. Rates include breakfast. AE, DC, MC, V. Valet parking in garage 25€ ($29). Bus: B, 13, 14, or 23. **Amenities:** Concierge; tour desk; car-rental desk; 24-hr. room service (breakfast and bar). *In room:* A/C, TV, dataport, minibar, hair dryer, safe.

9 In the Oltrarno

MODERATE

Hotel La Scaletta 🍸 *Kids*   The Barbiere family runs this well-worn old shoe of a place in one of the only remaining palazzi on this block between the Pitti Palace and Ponte Vecchio. The inn's star is the flower-bedecked, sun-kissed terrace offering a 360-degree vista over the Boboli Gardens, the Oltrarno rooftops, and (beyond a sea of antennas) the monumental heart of Florence, plus a shoe-biting turtle they found here when they bought the place 25 years ago. Return visitors book months in advance for the homey rooms that have tiny bathrooms and old tiled floors. Some beds are lumpy to a fault, others fully firm, but street-side accommodations have double-paned windows that really do block the noise, and the worn, dark wood lacquer furniture is pleasantly unassuming. At breakfast, you can ask Manfredo to cook you a superb 11€ ($13) dinner that night.

Via Guicciardini 13 (2nd floor; near Piazza de Pitti), 50125 Firenze. ℂ **055-283-028** or 055-214-255. Fax 055-289-562. www.lascaletta.com. 13 units, 11 with bathroom. 93€ ($107) double without bathroom, 140€ ($161) double with bathroom; 165€ ($190) triple with bathroom; 190€ ($219) quad with bathroom. Rates include continental breakfast. Ask about off-season discounts. MC, V. Nearby parking 10€–28€ ($12–$32). Bus: D, 11, 36, or 37. **Amenities:** Concierge; tour desk; limited room service (breakfast); babysitting; laundry service; dry cleaning. *In room:* A/C in 8 units, TV in 5 units and on request, hair dryer.

Pensione Sorelle Bandini *₲ (Value* This pensione occupies a landmark Renaissance palazzo on one of the city's great squares. You can live like the nobles of yore in rooms with 15-foot ceilings whose 10-foot windows and oversize antique furniture are proportionately appropriate. Room no. 9 sleeps five and offers a Duomo view from its bathroom window; room B is a double with a fantastic cityscape out the window. On closer inspection, you'll see the resident cats have left their mark on common-area sofas, and everything seems a bit ramshackle and musty. But that seems to be the point. The highlight is the monumental roofed veranda where Mimmo, the English-speaking manager, oversees breakfast and encourages brown-bag lunches and the chance to relax and drink in the views. Franco Zeffirelli used the pensione for some scenes in *Tea with Mussolini.* Quite frankly, their fame as a "typical old-fashioned" pensione has gone a bit to their heads—and to the prices, which have slowly crept rather higher than they should be for a budget-class hotel.

Piazza Santo Spirito 9, 50125 Firenze. ⓒ **055-215-308.** Fax 055-282-761. pensione bandini@tiscali.it. 13 units, 5 with bathroom. Single rate on request. 108€ ($124) double without bathroom, 130€ ($150) double with bathroom. Extra person 35% more. Rates include continental breakfast (subtract about 9€/$10 per person if you opt out). No credit cards (but they're expecting to accept them "soon"). Bus: D, 11, 36, or 37. **Amenities:** Concierge; tour desk; car-rental desk; limited room service (breakfast); babysitting. *In room:* No phone.

Silla *₲* On a shaded riverside piazza, this 15th-century palazzo's second-floor patio terrace is one of the city's nicest breakfast settings (in winter, there's a breakfast salon with chandeliers and oil paintings). The Silla's most recent renovation was in 2001, with a few rooms redone in 1997. Many overlook the Arno and, when winter strips the leaves off the front trees, the spire of Santa Croce on the opposite bank. Every room is unique—some with beamed ceilings and parquet floors, others with floral wallpaper and stylish furnishings. The attention to detail and friendly skilled staff should make this hotel better known; word-of-mouth keeps it regularly full in pricey Florence despite its refreshing low profile.

Via dei Renai 5 (on Piazza Demidoff, east of Ponte delle Grazie), 50125 Firenze. ⓒ **055-234-2888.** Fax 055-234-1437. www.hotelsilla.it. 35 units. 170€ ($196) double; 220€ ($253) triple. Rates include buffet breakfast. Ask about off-season discounts. AE, DC, MC, V. Parking in hotel garage 16€ ($18). Often closes late Nov to late Dec. Bus: C, D, 12, 13, or 23. **Amenities:** Concierge; tour desk; limited room service; nonsmoking rooms. *In room:* A/C, TV, minibar, hair dryer, safe.

10 In the Hills

VERY EXPENSIVE

Villa San Michele 𝒜   The peaceful air this place exudes recalls its origins in the 15th century as a Franciscan monastery, but I doubt the good friars had a heated outdoor pool or Jacuzzis in their cells. The facade was reputedly designed by Michelangelo, and everything is in shades of creamy yellow with soft gray *pietra serena* accents. The antique furnishings are the epitome of simple elegance, and some rooms come with canopied beds and linen sheets; others are fitted with wrought-iron headboards and antiques. The regular rooms are all in the main buildings, with modern junior suites dug into the hillside behind it, snuggled into the slopes between the terraces that host the swimming pool and formal gardens (several junior suites enjoy their own mini-gardens or terraces). They've recently converted the tiny hillside chapel into a cozy honeymoon suite with sweeping views, and the limonaia (where potted citrus trees once spent the frosty winters) into a grander suite. The monks never had it this good.

Via Doccia 4 (just below Fiesole off Via Fra Giovanni Angelico), 50014 Fiesole (FI). 𝒞 **800/237-1236** in the U.S., or 055-567-8200 in Italy. Fax 055-567-8250. www. villasanmichele.com. 41 units. 843€–990€ ($969–$1,139) double; 1,351€– 1,601€ ($1,554–$1,841) jr. suite; 2,001€ ($2,301) suite. Rates include breakfast. For half pension add 73€ ($84), full pension add 138€ ($159). AE, DC, MC, V. Free parking. Closed mid-Nov to mid-Mar. Bus: 7 (ask driver for stop, because you get off before Fiesole); free hourly shuttle bus from Piazza del Duomo. **Amenities:** Restaurant; frescoed piano bar; heated outdoor pool; bike rental; concierge; tour desk; car-rental desk; shuttle bus to/from town center; small business center and secretarial services; 24-hr. room service; massage; babysitting; laundry service; same-day dry cleaning; extensive park with nature trails and jogging track. *In room:* A/C, TV/VCR (front desk has free movies), dataport, minibar, hair dryer.

EXPENSIVE

Torre di Bellosguardo 𝒜𝒜𝒜 *Finds*   This castle was built around a 13th-century tower sprouting from a hillside on the southern edge of Florence. Spend a few days here above the city heat and noise, lazing by the pool, hiking the olive orchard roads, or sitting on a garden bench to enjoy the intimate close-range vista of the city. Don't come expecting another climate-controlled and carpeted bastion of luxury. With its echoey halls, airy loggias, and imposing stone staircases, the Bellosguardo feels just a few flickering torches shy of the

Middle Ages—exactly its attraction. It's packed with antiques, and the beds from various eras are particularly gorgeous. Some rooms have intricately carved wood ceilings, others sport fading frescoes, and many have views, including a 360-degree panorama in the romantic tower suite. It's a 15-minute stroll down the hill to Alla Vecchia Bettola (p. 93).

Via Roti Michelozzi 2, 50124 Florence. ✆ 055-229-8145. Fax 055-229-008. www. torrebellosguardo.com. 16 units. 280€ ($322) double; 330€–380€ ($380–$437) suite. Breakfast 20€ ($23). AE, DC, MC, V. Free parking. Bus: 12 or 13 to Piazza Tasso (then taxi up hill). **Amenities:** Outdoor pool (June–Sept), small indoor pool; small exercise room; Jacuzzi; sauna; concierge; tour desk; car-rental desk; 24-hr. room service (bar, no food); massage; babysitting; laundry service; same-day dry cleaning. *In room:* A/C in 3 suites, dataport, hair dryer.

MODERATE

Pensione Benescistà ✹✹ *(Kids*   This comfortable and quiet family-run pensione in a rambling 14th-century villa gets you the same view and escape from the city as the Villa San Michele above it at one-fifth the price. Antiques abound, and the elegantly cluttered salons are straight out of an E.M. Forster novel. Many accommodations have big old chests of drawers, and some open onto the pretty little garden. The dining room has a view of Florence, but in summer take in the vista by breakfasting on the terrace. Although service from the staff is occasionally off-handed, the owners are friendly and truly consider you a guest in their home. They also expect to be treated as hosts and require you to stay for most dinners. (I recommend trading one dinner for a lunch to try the nearby Trattoria le Cave di Maiano; p. 95.)

Via Benedetto da Maiano 4 (just below Fiesole off the main road), 50014 Fiesole (FI). ✆ and fax 055-59-163. 40 units. 176€ ($202) double. Rates include required half pension (full pension available for small supplement). Breakfast included. No credit cards. Free parking. Bus: 7 to Villa San Michele, then backtrack onto side road following signs. **Amenities:** Restaurant; limited room service (breakfast only). *In room:* Hair dryer.

11 Hostels & Camping

Both hostels below are immensely popular, especially in summer. If you aren't able to write or fax to reserve a space—months ahead, if possible—show up when they open. Also check out the private hostel Archi Rossi, listed above (along with its sister hotel Mia Cara) under the Santa Maria Novella/Mercato Central neighborhood.

Campeggio Michelangelo   Back in the good old days of yore when my family was wont to do "Europe on $5 a Day in an Ugly Orange VW Camper-van," this was our Florentine parking spot *de* *choix.* Here we could sleep with a select 1,000 of our fellow campers and have almost the same vista that the tour buses get up above on Piazzale Michelangiolo. (Sadly, a stand of trees blocks the Duomo.) Of course, you're packed in like sardines on this small plateau with very little shade (in Aug, arrive early to fight for a spot along the tree-lined fringe), but you get a bar, a minimart, a laundromat, and that killer view.

Viale Michelangelo 80 (about ⅔ of the way up to Piazzale Michelangiolo), 50125 Firenze. ⓒ **055-681-1977.** Fax 055-689-348. www.ecvacanze.it/michelangelo/info.htm. Open camping (sleeps 1,000). 8€ ($9.20) per person plus 5€ ($5.75) per tent and 4.50€ ($5.20) per car. Rented tents 11€ ($13). No credit cards. Closed Nov to 1 week before Easter. Bus: 12 or 13. **Amenities:** Bar; coin-op laundry. *In room:* No phone.

Instituto Gould (Kids) These are the best hostel-like accommodations in Florence, without a curfew, lockout period, or shower charge but with brand-new furnishings in plain but immaculate rooms—like a college dorm that's never seen a frat party. It's technically not a hostel, though it looks and operates like one. Most rooms are doubles or triples (all with buttonless phones to receive calls), and unless you opt for a five-person room, you're unlikely to bunk with strangers. The institute's real work is caring for orphans, and the proceeds from your room fee go to help needy children. Reception is open Monday through Friday from 9am to 1pm and 3 to 7pm, Saturday from 9am to 1pm (you can stay over and prepay in order to check out during the weekend, but you can't check in).

Via dei Serragli 49 (near Santo Spirito), 50124 Firenze. ⓒ **055-212-576.** Fax 055-280-274. gould.reception@dada.it. 33 units, 27 with bathroom. Depending on how many beds are in room (1–4): 17€–28€ ($20–$32) per person without bathroom; 20€–34€ ($23–$39) per person with bathroom. No credit cards. Bus: 11, 36, or 37. *In room:* No phone.

Villa Camerata (Ostello della Gioventù) Florence's IYH hostel is a ways outside the city center but worth it for the budget-strained. The name doesn't lie—this really is a countryside villa, with an outdoor loggia and is surrounded by greenery. The rooms are regulation hostel bland but livable. You can check in after the lockout (9am–2pm in summer, 9am–3pm in winter), and curfew is midnight. They also offer 180 tent sites for cool camping amid their wooded acres for 5€ ($5.75) per person plus 4€ to 6€ ($4.60–$6.90) per tent.

Viale Augusto Righi 2–4 (3.5km/2 miles northwest of the city center; above Campo di Marte), 50137 Firenze. ⓒ **055-601-451.** Fax 055-610-300. www.ostellionline. org. 322 beds. 16€ ($18) per person; 17€ ($19) per person in 3-person family room; 19€ ($22) per person in 2-person family room. Meals 8€ ($9.20). Rates include breakfast. No credit cards. Bus: 17B (30-min. ride; 17A and 17C take longer). **Amenities:** Coin-op laundry. *In room:* No phone.

12 Long-Term Stays

One of the most reputable specialists in Florence is **Florence and Abroad,** Via San Zanobi 58 (℃ **055-487-004;** fax 055-490-143; www.florenceandabroad.com), which matches different tastes and budgets to a wide range of apartments starting at about $650 per week—though note they take a commission (10% for 1-month rentals, less for longer periods). Another reputable agency for short-term apartment and house rentals (weekly and monthly) is **Windows on Tuscany,** Via Tornabuoni 2 or Via della Vigna Vecchia 2 (℃ **055-268-510;** fax 055-238-1524; www.windowsontuscany.com). To go it alone, check out the classifieds in the biweekly *Le Pulce,* available at newsstands.

Palazzo Antellesi   Here's your chance to set up housekeeping in a chunk of the Renaissance. Many people passing through Piazza Santa Croce notice Giovanni di Ser Giovanni's 1620 graffiti frescoes on the overhanging facade of no. 21, but few realize they can actually stay there. The 16th-century palazzo is owned by the gracious Signora Piccolomini, who rents out truly spacious apartments to anyone who has ever dreamed of lying in bed next to a roaring fire under a 17th-century frescoed ceiling (the Granduca, sleeping two or three) or sipping tea in a living room surrounded by trompe-l'oeil Roman ruins with a 16th-century wood ceiling above (the Donatello, sleeping six to eight). Even in the more standard rooms the furnishings are tasteful, with wicker, wood, or wrought-iron bed frames; potted plants; and the occasional 18th-century inlaid wood dresser to go with the plush couches and chairs. The fourth-floor rooms (the Miravista and Mimi) are booked seasons in advance by those who love the private penthouse terraces overlooking the lively piazza. The kitchens are sizable and fully equipped. Author R.W.B. Lewis wrote extensively about the Antellesi in the final chapter of *The City of Florence.*

Piazza Santa Croce 21–22, 50122 Firenze. ℃ **212/932-3480** in the U.S., or 055-244-456 in Italy. Fax 212/932-9039 in the U.S., or 055-234-5552 in Italy. www.palazzoantellesi.com. 13 apts sleeping 2–6. 1,800€–4,000€ ($2,070–$4,600) per week; 3,960€–8,800€ ($4,244–$10,120) per month. Heating included in some, but most utilities extra. No credit cards. Parking 16€ ($18) in garage. Bus: B, 13, 23, or 71. **Amenities:** Babysitting; nonsmoking rooms. *In room:* A/C, TV, VCR on request, dataport, kitchen, fridge, coffeemaker, hair dryer, safe.

Where to Dine in Florence

Florence is thick with restaurants, though many in the most touristy areas (around the Duomo and Piazza della Signoria) are of low quality, charge high prices, or do both. I'll point out the few that aren't. The highest concentrations of excellent *ristoranti* and *trattorie* are around Santa Croce and across the river in the Oltrarno.

1 Near the Duomo

MODERATE

Da Ganino FLORENTINE   The tiny family-run Ganino has long been a major destination for hungry tourists because it's across from the American Express office as well as halfway between the Duomo and the Uffizi. This has caused the place to jack its prices to eyebrow-raising levels but not sacrifice its friendly service and good food, from the big ol' chunk of mortadella that accompanies your bread basket through the tasty *ribollita* or *gnocchi al pomodoro* (ricotta-and-spinach gnocchi in tomato sauce) to the *filetto all'aceto basalmico* (veal filet cooked in balsamic vinegar) or *coniglio in umido* (rabbit with boiled potatoes on the side) that rounds out your meal.

Piazza de' Cimatori 4r (near the Casa di Dante). ✆ **055-214-125.** Reservations recommended. Primi 6€–12€ ($6.90–$14); secondi 10€–20€ ($12–$23). AE, DC, MC, V. Mon–Sat 12:30–3pm and 7:30–10pm. Closed Aug. Bus: 14.

Paoli TUSCAN   Paoli has one of the most *suggestivo* (oft-used Italian word for "evocative") settings in town, with tables under a 14th-century vaulted ceiling whose ribs and lunettes are covered with fading 18th-century frescoes. It's in the heart of the sightseeing zone, meaning the prices are as high as they can reasonably push them; very few Italians drop by, but the food is actually quite good. The *ravioli verdi alla casalinga* (spinach ravioli in tomato sauce) may not be inspired, but it's freshly made and tasty. In mushroom season you can order *risotto ai funghi,* and year-round the scrumptious secondo *entrecôte di manzo arlecchino* (a thick steak in cognac-spiked cream sauce with peppercorns and sided with mashed potatoes).

Via dei Tavolini 12r. ℭ **055-216-215.** Reservations highly recommended. Primi 6€–12€ ($6.90–$14); secondi 14€–18€ ($16–$21); fixed-price menu with wine 20€ ($23). AE, MC, V. Wed–Mon noon–3pm and 7pm–midnight. Bus: A.

Ristorante Casa di Dante (da Pennello) ℛ TUSCAN/ITAL-IAN   This is one of Florence's oldest restaurants, housed since the late 1400s in a palazzo that once belonged to Renaissance artist Albertinelli (Cellini, Pontormo, and Andrea del Sarto used to dine here). Its claim to fame is the antipasto table, groaning under the day's changing array of two dozen appetizers. Prices vary, but expect to spend 5€ to 8€ ($5.75–$9.20) for a good sampling. The best of the primi are under the handwritten *lo chef consigla* (the chef recommends) and *pasta fresa* (handmade pasta) sections of the menu. They do a perfectly grilled pork chop and, if the antipasti and pasta have done you in, several light omelets for secondo.

Via Dante Alighieri 4r (between Via dei Calzaiuoli and Via del Proconsolo). ℭ **055-294-848.** Reservations suggested. Primi 5.50€–8€ ($6.30–$9.20); secondi 7.50€–13€ ($8.65–$15); menù turistico 20€ ($23) without wine. AE, DC, V. Tues–Sat noon–3pm and 7–10:30pm. Closed Aug.

INEXPENSIVE

Cantinetta del Verrazzano ℛ 𝒱𝒶𝓁𝓊ℯ WINE BAR   Owned by the Castello di Verrazzano, one of Chianti's best-known wine-producing estates, this wood-paneled *cantinetta* with a full-service bar/*pasticceria* and seating area helped spawn a revival of stylish wine bars as convenient spots for fast-food breaks. It promises a delicious self-service lunch or snack of focaccia, plain or studded with peas, rosemary, onions, or olives; buy it hot by the slice or as *farcite* (sandwiches filled with prosciutto, arugula, cheese, or tuna). Try a glass of their full-bodied chianti to make this the perfect respite. Platters of Tuscan cold cuts and aged cheeses are also available.

Via dei Tavolini 18–20r (off Via dei Calzaiuoli). ℭ **055-268-590.** Focaccia sandwiches .95€–2.85€ ($1.10–$3.30); glass of wine 1.30€–8€ ($1.50–$9.20). AE, DC, MC, V. Mon–Sat 8am–9pm.

I Fratellini ℛ SANDWICHES & WINE   Just off the busiest tourist thoroughfare lies one of the last of a dying breed: a *fiaschitteria* (derived from the word for a flask of wine). It's the proverbial hole in the wall, a doorway about 5 feet deep with rows of wine bottles against the back wall and Armando and Michele Perrino busy behind the counter, fixing sandwiches and pouring glasses of vino. You stand munching and sipping on the cobblestones of the narrow street surrounded by Florentines on their lunch break and a few

Where to Dine in Florence

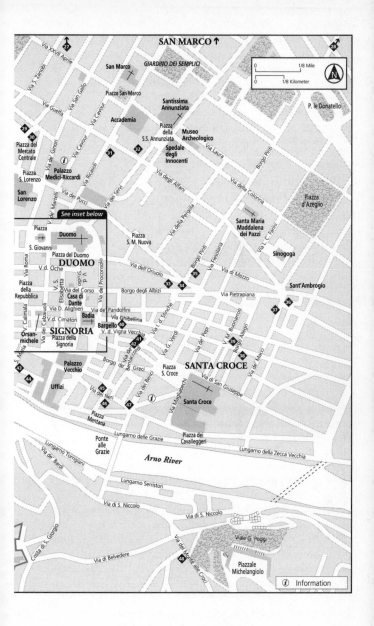

SAN MARCO ↑

GIARDINO DEI SEMPLICI

Via XXVII Aprile

San Marco

P. le Donatello

Piazza San Marco

Accademia

Santissima
Annunziata

Via Guelfa

Via San Gallo

Via Cavour

Via de' Ginori

Piazza
della
S.S. Annunziata

Museo
Archeologico

29

30

Piazza del
Mercato
Centrale

Palazzo
Medici-Riccardi

31

32

Spedale
degli
Innocenti

Via Laura

Borgo Pinti

Piazza
S. Lorenzo

San
Lorenzo

Via de' Servi

Via degli Alfani

Via della Colonna

Piazza
d'Azeglio

Via de' Pucci

Via dei Martelli

See inset below

Piazza
S. M. Nuova

Via della Pergola

Santa Maria
Maddalena
dei Pazzi

Piazza
S. M. Nuova

Via del' Oriuolo

Via Fiesolana

Via di Mezzo

Sinogoga

Sant'Ambrogio

Via de' Ginori

Via Ricasoli

Piazza
Duomo
S. Giovanni
Piazza del Duomo
DUOMO
V.d. Oche

Via del Corso
Casa di
Dante
Badia
Via de' Pandolfini
Via Ghibellina
Bargello
V. d. Vigna Vecchia

33

34

Borgo degli Albizi

Via Pietrapiana

35

36

37

Via de' Pepi

Via M. Buonarroti

Via Verdi

Studio
V. S.
Elisabetta

Piazza
della
Repubblica

V. Calimala

V. del Proconsolo

V. Santa Maria

Via D. Alighieri
V.d. Calzaioli
V.d. Cimatori
Orsan-
michele
SIGNORIA
Piazza della
Signoria

Via L. d. Stinche

Via dei Macci

39

40

Borgo Allegri

SANTA CROCE

38

Via di San Giuseppe

43

44

Palazzo
Vecchio

Borgo de' Greci

Via de' Benci

Piazza
S. Croce

Via Magliabecchi

Santa Croce

Uffizi

45

46

47

Via de' Neri

Piazza
Mentana

Lungarno delle Grazie

Piazza dei
Cavalleggeri

Lungarno della Zecca Vecchia

Ponte
alle
Grazie

Arno River

Lungarno Torrigiani

Via de' Bardi

Lungarno Serristori

Via di S. Niccolo

Via di S. Niccolo

Viale G. Poggi

Costa di S. Giorgio

Via di Belvedere

Via del Monte alle Croci

48

Piazzale
Michelangiolo

ⓘ Information

0   1/8 Mile
0   1/8 Kilometer

28

27

bemused tourists. The *cinghiale piccante con caprino* (spicy raw wild boar sausage with creamy goat cheese) is excellent. Otherwise, choose your poison from among 30 stuffing combinations—the menu posted on the doorjamb has English translations—and accompany it with either a basic *rosso* (red) wine or point to any bottle to try *un bicchiere* (a glass).

Via dei Cimatori 38r (2 blocks from Piazza della Signoria, off Via Calzaiuoli). ✆ **055-239-6096.** Sandwiches 2.10€–2.60€ ($2.40–$3); wine from 1.30€ ($1.50) a glass. No credit cards. Daily 8am–8:30pm (July–Aug closed Sat–Sun). Closed Aug 10–20 and 2 weeks in Mar. Bus: 14, 23, or 71.

Le Mossacce FLORENTINE   Delicious, cheap, abundant, fast home cooking: This tiny *osteria,* filled with lunching businesspeople, farmers in from the hills, locals who've been coming since 1942, and a few knowledgeable tourists, is authentic to the bone. The waiters hate breaking out the printed menu, preferring to rattle off a list of Florentine faves like *ribollita, spaghetti alle vongole, crespelle,* and *lasagne al forno.* Unlike in many cheap joints catering to locals, the secondi are pretty good. You could try the *spezzatino* (goulashy beef stew) or a well-cooked, and for once cheap, *bistecca alla fiorentina,* but I put my money on the excellent *involtini* (thin slices of beef wrapped tightly around a bread stuffing and artichoke hearts, then cooked to juiciness in tomato sauce).

Via del Proconsolo 55r (a block south of the Duomo). ✆ **055-294-361.** Reservations suggested for dinner. Primi 4.20€–4.70€ ($4.80–$5.40); secondi 4.70€–14€ ($5.40–$16). AE, MC, V. Mon–Fri noon–2:30pm and 7–9:30pm.

2 Near Piazza Della Signoria

MODERATE

Acqua al 2 SLIGHTLY ADVENTUROUS ITALIAN   Under a barrel-vaulted ceiling and dim sconce lights, diners sit elbow to elbow at tightly packed tables to sample this innovative restaurant's *assaggi* (tastings) courses. Acqua al 2 is proud of its almost cultish status, attained through the success of its *assaggio di primi,* which offers you a sampling of five flavorful pastas or *risotti.* If you order the *assaggio* for two, you both just may have room left over for a grilled portobello mushroom "steak," one of the many veal dishes, or something more cross-cultural, like *couscous d'agnello* (lamb). They also offer *assaggi* of salads, cheese, and desserts. Tour companies have started bringing in tourists by the busload on occasion, but the crowd still remains a good mix of locals and travelers.

Via della Vigna Vecchia 40r (at Via dell'Acqua). ✆ **055-284-170.** www.acquaal2. com. Reservations required. Primi 7€–8€ ($8.05–$9.20); secondi 7€–17€

($8.05–$20); *assaggio* 8€ ($9.20) for pasta, 5€ ($5.75) for dessert. AE, MC, V. Daily 7:30pm–1am. Closed 1 week in Aug. Bus: 14.

Antico Fattore FLORENTINE   The Antico Fattore was a literary watering hole early in the 20th century and remained a favorite trattoria just a few steps from the city's premier museum until the 1993 Uffizi bomb went off a few feet from its doors. The interior has been rebuilt and the restaurant reopened, but many claim it isn't what it used to be. Although it has indeed put on a few more airs, you can't deny they still make a tantalizing *lombatina all'aceto basalmico* (one of the thickest and most tender veal chops you'll ever find, cooked in balsamic vinegar). You can precede this with a *ribollita* (more souplike than usual) or a traditional Tuscan *pappardelle sul cinghiale* (wide noodles in wild boar sauce). If veal's not your style, try their specialty *piccione* (grilled pigeon).

Via Lambertesca 1–3r (between the Uffizi and the Ponte Vecchio). (C) 055-288-975. www.mega.it/antico.fattore. Reservations recommended. Primi 5.70€–8€ ($6.60–$9.20); secondi 8.80€–14€ ($10–$14). AE, DC, MC, V. Mon–Sat 12:15–3pm and 7:15–10:30pm. Bus: 23 or 71.

Buca dell'Orafo FLORENTINE   A *buca* is a cellar joint with half a dozen crowded tables serving good, basic Florentine fare. Here a few locals hang on every night, but Orafo's years in the guidebooks have made Americans its base of customers—Florentines aren't willing to give this place up yet, though, and you can still find it packed with locals if you reserve a late seating. However, the heavy tourism has jacked its prices above what you'd expect for peasant food. That food is still very well prepared, however, and the location can't be beat. You can't go wrong with the thick *ribollita*. If it's on the menu, go for the *paglia e fieno alla boscaiola* (a "hay and straw" mix of both egg and spinach fettuccine in mushroom-meat sauce). Orafo's best secondo is *arista di maiale con patate* (roast pork loin with potatoes), while candied stewed pears round out the meal nicely.

Volta dei Girolami 28r (under the arched alley left of the Ponte Vecchio). (C) 055-213-619. Reservations strongly recommended (or show up early for a spot at a communal table). Primi 6€–10€ ($6.90–$12); secondi 11€–20€ ($13–$23). No credit cards. Tues–Sat noon–2:30pm and 7:30–9:45pm. Bus: 23 or 71.

I' Cche' c'è c'è ★★ TUSCAN   The name is a dialect variant on "What you see is what you get." What you see is a room with modern art prints and shelves of ancient wine bottles on the walls. What you get is good Tuscan cooking from Gino Noci, who trained in the kitchens of London before returning here to open a traditional

> ### *Kids* **Family-Friendly Restaurants**
>
> It'd be a sin for any family to visit Florence and not drop by one of its premier gelato parlors to sample the rich Italian equivalent of ice cream. See "A Big Step Above Ice Cream: Florentine Gelato" on p. 84. If the kids mutiny and absolutely insist on a hamburger, try the slightly American-style restaurant **Yellow Bar,** Via del Proconsolo 39r (© **055-211-766**). But be warned: The hamburger doesn't come with a bun (a form of blasphemy among certain preteens). They also serve pizzas.
>
> **Il Cantinone** (p. 93)   This noisy old wine cellar is popular with students and has long tables where your family can spread out and bite deep into *crostone* (slabs of peasant bread piled with your choice of toppings like a pizza).
>
> **Il Latini** (p. 83)   This can be one of the most fun places to eat in Florence—you're seated at communal tables under battalions of hanging ham hocks and treated to huge portions of the Tuscan bounty. No food is too fancy or oddball to offend suspicious young palates, the waiters love to ham it up, and a festive atmosphere prevails.
>
> **Il Pizzaiuolo** (p. 90)   When the kids are hankering for a pizza, turn it into a learning experience by visiting the

trattoria. The scrumptious *ravioli rosée* (in creamy tomato sauce) faces serious competition from the *tagliatelle all boscaiola* (same sauce with giant slices of forest mushrooms added). *Topini* are Florentine potato gnocchi, topped with spinach and cream or four cheeses. Follow up with the grilled salmon or one of their specialties, *stracotto al chianti* (beef stuffed with celery and carrot and smothered in a chianti gravy served with fried polenta and an artichoke heart).

Via Magalotti 11r (just east of Via Proconsolo, 2 blocks from the Arno). © **055-216-589**. Reservations recommended (not available for set-price menu at lunch). Primi 4€–9€ ($4.60–$10); secondi 9€–15€ ($10–$17); fixed-price menu without wine 11€ ($13). AE, MC, V. Tues–Sun 12:30–2:30pm and 7:30–10:30pm. Closed Aug 10–17.

Osteria (Vini e Vecchi Sapori) FLORENTINE/TUSCAN
Within a block of the Palazzo Vecchio squats an authentic *osteria*

only pizza parlor in Florence run by a Neapolitan. The "plain pizza," called *pizza margherita* in Italy, was invented about 100 years ago by a Naples chef who wanted to honor Italy's Queen Margherita with a pizza done in patriotic colors. For the newly created Kingdom of Italy, this meant red (tomatoes), white (mozzarella), and green (fresh basil)—the colors of the new flag. If someone at the table prefers pepperoni, order the pizza with *salame piccante* (hot salami slices); *pepperoni* in Italian are bell peppers.

Ristorante Vecchia Firenze (p. 91)   This roomy restaurant has a long menu sure to satisfy everyone's appetites. They love children here, and this was my family's favorite Florentine restaurant when I was 12. The owner, tickled pink one night that a little American boy was struggling to speak Italian, took over our meal, had all the wonders of Tuscan cuisine brought to our table, introduced us to grappa, and kept me up well past my bedtime.

Trattoria da Benvenuto (p. 80)   The dishes here are simple and homey—they're sure to have a plate of plain spaghetti and tomato sauce to please finicky youngsters.

with a wood-beamed ceiling, brick floor, the end of a giant chianti barrel embedded in one wall, and a handwritten menu that starts *Oggi C'è* ("Today we got . . ."). As the sign proudly proclaims, this one-room joint is devoted to "wine and old flavors," which means lunch could consist of anything from a rib-sticking stewlike *ribollita* and a *frittata rustica* (a darkly fried omelet thick with potatoes and vegetables) to an excellent crostini assortment and *scamorza e speck al forno* (smoked mozzarella melted with ham in a bowl, to scoop out and slather onto bread). The paunchy owner will continue pacing back and forth, passing around the lone menu, and welcoming people in off the street until he feels like going home.

Via dei Magazzini 3r (the alley off Piazza della Signoria to the left of the Palazzo Vecchio). © 055-293-045. Primi 6€–8€ ($6.90–$9.20); secondi 10€–14€ ($12–$16). No credit cards. Tues–Sat 9am–11pm; Sun noon–2:30pm. Bus: 14, 23, or 71.

Trattoria da Benvenuto 🍴 *Kids* TUSCAN HOME COOKING
This is a no-nonsense place, simple and good, and Gabriella is a no-nonsense lady who'll get exasperated if you're not ready with your order when she's ready to take it. Da Benvenuto's is basically a neighborhood hangout that somehow found its way into every guidebook over the years. Yet it continues to serve adequate helpings of tasty Florentine home cooking to travelers and locals seated together at long tables in two brightly lit rooms. This is always my first stop on any trip to Florence, where I usually order ravioli or *gnocchi* (potato-dumpling pasta)—both served in tomato sauce—and follow with a *veal scaloppa alla Livornese* or a *frittata* (an omelet filled at the whim of Loriano, Gabriella's husband and cook).

Via Mosca 16r (at the corner of Via dei Neri; walk around the right of the Palazzo Vecchio, under the arch, and it's in front of you after 4 short blocks). ℂ 055-214-833. Primi 4.50€–9.50€ ($5.20–$11); secondi 5.50€–15€ ($6.30–$17). No credit cards. Mon–Tues and Thurs–Sat 12:30–3pm and 7pm–10:30. Bus: 23 or 71.

3 Near San Lorenzo & the Mercato Centrale
MODERATE

Da Mario 🍴 *Value* FLORENTINE   This is down-and-dirty Florentine lunchtime at its best, an *osteria* so basic the little stools don't have backs and a communal spirit so entrenched the waitresses will scold you if you try to take a table all to yourself. Since 1953, their stock in trade has been feeding market workers, and you can watch the kitchen through the glass as they whip out a wipe board menu of simple dishes at lightning speed. Hearty primi include *tortelli di patate al ragù* (ravioli stuffed with potato in ragù), *minestra di farro e riso* (emmer-and-rice soup), and *penne al pomodoro* (pasta quills in fresh tomato sauce). The secondi are basic but good; try the *coniglio arrosto* (roast rabbit) or *girello di vitello ai carciofi* (veal rolled around artichoke hearts, then stewed).

Via Rosina 2r (at the north corner of Piazza Mercato Centrale). ℂ 055-218-550. www.trattoriamario.com. Reservations not accepted. Primi 3.10€–3.40€ ($3.55–$3.90); secondi 4€–10.50€ ($4.60–$12). No credit cards. Mon–Sat noon–3:30pm. Closed Aug. Bus: 10, 12, 25, 31, 32, or 91.

Le Fonticine TUSCAN/BOLOGNESE   Modern paintings carpet the walls like a jigsaw puzzle. Silvano Bruci has taken as much care over the past 40 years selecting the works of art as his Bologna-born wife Bruna Grazia has teaching these Tuscans the finer points of Emilia-Romagna cuisine. Even with the art, this place still feels a bit like a country trattoria. If you can, ask to sit *in dietro* (in the back), if only so you get to walk past the open kitchen and grill. There are so many good primi it's hard to choose, but you can't go wrong with lasagne, *penne al prosciutto punte d'asparagi* (stubby pasta with diced prosciutto and wild asparagus tips), or *ribollita.* Afterward, set to work on the *cinghiale maremmana cipolline* (stewed wild boar with caramelized baby onions) or *baccalà alla livornese* (salt cod covered in tomatoes and served with chickpeas in oil).

Via Nazionale 79r (at Via dell'Ariento, north end of the Mercato San Lorenzo). ℭ 055-282-106. www.lefonticine.com. Reservations recommended. Primi 6€–12€ ($6.90–$14); secondi 8€–16€ ($9.20–$18). AE, DC, MC, V. Tues–Sat noon–2:30pm and 7–10pm. Closed July 25–Aug 25. Bus: 12, 25, 31, or 32.

Trattoria Zà-Zà ☆ TUSCAN CASALINGA (HOME COOK-ING)   This place serves many of the food market workers from across the way—people who appreciate the importance of using simple, fresh ingredients to make filling dishes. Ask to sit downstairs in the brick barrel vault of the old *cantina* if you want some privacy; if you want company (they make even the small wooden tables communal), sit upstairs, where you can gaze at the dozens of photos of the restaurant's more (but mostly less) famous patrons. The *antipasto caldo alla Zà-Zà* has a bit of everything. If you don't want *ravioli strascicati* (in creamy ragù), brace yourself for a *tris di minestre* (three soups: *ribollita, pappa al pomodoro,* and *fagioli con farro*). *Bocconcini di vitella alla casalinga con fagioli all'uccelletto* (veal nuggets with tomato-stewed beans) makes an excellent second course.

Piazza Mercato Centrale 26r. ℭ 055-215-411. www.trattoriazaza.it. Reservations recommended. Primi 5.30€–10€ ($6.10–$12); secondi 10€–18€ ($12–$21); menù turistico without wine 13€ ($15). AE, DC, MC, V. Mon–Sat noon–3pm and 7–11pm. Closed Aug.

INEXPENSIVE

Nerbone ☆ *Moments* FLORENTINE   Nerbone has been stuffing stall owners and market patrons with excellent Florentine *cucina povera* ("poor people's food") since the Mercato Centrale opened in 1874. You can try *trippa alla fiorentina, pappa al pomodoro,* or a plate piled with boiled potatoes and a single fat sausage. But the mainstay here is a *panino con bollito,* a boiled beef sandwich that's *bagnato* (dipped in the meat juices). Eat standing with the crowd of old men at the side counter, sipping glasses of wine or beer, or fight for one of the few tables against the wall.

In the Mercato Centrale, entrance on Via dell'Ariento, stand no. 292 (ground floor). ℭ 055-219-949. All dishes 3.50€–7€ ($4.05–$8.05). No credit cards. Mon–Sat 7am–3pm.

4 Near Piazza Santa Trinita

VERY EXPENSIVE

Cantinetta Antinori FLORENTINE/TUSCAN   The Antinori *marchesi* started their wine empire 26 generations ago, and, taking their cue from an ancient vintner tradition, installed a wine bar in their 15th-century palazzo 30 years ago. Most ingredients come fresh from the Antinori farms, as does all the fine wine. Start with the *fettucini all'anatra* (noodles in duck sauce) or the *ribollita,* and round out the meal with the *trippa alla fiorentina* or the mighty *gran pezzo* (thick slab of oven-roasted Chiana beef). If you choose this worthy splurge as a secondo, skip the first course and instead follow your steak with *formaggi misti,* which may include pecorino and mozzarella made fresh that morning. Their *cantucci* (Tuscan biscotti) come from Prato's premier producer.

Palazzo Antinori, Piazza Antinori 3 (at the top of Via Tornabuoni). © 055-292-234. www.antinori.it. Reservations strongly recommended. Primi 10€–16€ ($12–$18); secondi 14€–24€ ($16–$27). AE, DC, MC, V. Mon–Fri 12:30–3pm and 6:30–10:30pm. Closed Aug, Dec 24–Jan 6. Bus: 6, 11, 36, 37, or 68.

Osteria No. 1 TUSCAN   "Osteria" belies this place's status as a full-fledged restaurant with some of the finer dining in Florence. Well-dressed Italians and Americans sit at well-spaced tables under the vaulted ceilings surrounded by painted coats of arms, musical instruments, and original art. Many opt for a *cocktail di gambereti* (shrimp cocktail) before their first course, which may include *zuppa di fagioli e farro* (bean-and-emmer soup) or the more imaginative *sfogliatine* (giant ravioli stuffed with cheese and carrots in basil-cream sauce). The secondi, all flavorful, range from tasty *sogliola griglia* (grilled sole) and adventurous *cervello* (fried calves' brains with artichokes) to a huge and succulent *bistecca alla fiorentina.* The one major drawback here is that, though service is friendly it's often hurried—fine if you're in a rush, but very un-Italian.

Via del Moro 22 (near the Ponte alla Carraia). © 055-284-897. www.osteria numero1.it. Reservations recommended. Primi 9€–18€ ($10–$21); secondi 8€–35€ ($9.20–$40). AE, DC, MC, V. Tues–Sat noon–2:30pm and 7–11pm; Mon 7pm–12:30am. Closed Aug. Bus: A, C, 6, 9, 11, 36, 37, or 68.

EXPENSIVE

Buca Lapi TUSCAN   The vaulted ceiling is carpeted with travel posters, the cuisine is carefully prepared, and the wine comes from the Antinori vineyards (this was once part of their cellars). This place's prices have recently risen astronomically, and for no apparent reason, but the quality is still spot-on. An interesting start is the *filetto di cinghiale all'olio di rosmarino* (wild boar slices cured like prosciutto and served with rosemary-scented olive oil). One specialty is the *cannelloni gratinati alla Buca Lapi* (pasta canapés stuffed with ricotta and spinach served in a cream sauce of boar and mushrooms). A light secondo could be *coniglio disossato ripieno* (stuffed rabbit), or you can go all out on a masterful *bistecca chianina* (grilled steak, for two only). The desserts are homemade, including a firm and delicate *latte portugese* (a kind of crème caramel) and a richly dense chocolate torte.

Via del Trebbio, 1r (just off Piazza Antinori at the top of Via Tornabuoni). © 055-213-768. Reservations essential. Primi 10€–12€ ($12–$14); secondi 20€–25€ ($23–$29). AE, DC, MC, V. Tues–Sat 12:30–2:30pm; Mon–Sat 7:30–10:30pm. Bus: 6, 11, 14, 17, 22, 36, 37, or 68.

Coco Lezzone FLORENTINE   This tiny trattoria hidden in a tangle of alleys near the Arno consists of long communal tables in a couple of pocket-size rooms wrapped around a cubbyhole of a kitchen whose chef, according to the restaurant's dialect name, is a bit off his rocker. The place is popular with local intellectuals, journalists, and the city soccer team. While enjoying your *ribollita* (known here as a "triumph of humility") or *rigatoni al sugo* (in a chunky ragù), look at where the yellow paint on the lower half of the wall gives way to white: That's how high the Arno flooded the joint in 1966. If you want a *bistecca alla fiorentina,* call ahead first. Friday is *baccalà* (salt cod) day, and every day their *involtini* (thin veal slice wrapped around vegetables) and *crocchette di filetto* (veal-and-basil meatloaf smothered in tomato sauce) are good.

Via del Parioncino 26r (at the corner of Via Purgatorio). © 055-287-178. Reservations recommended. Primi 6.50€–13€ ($7.50–$15); secondi 9.50€–16€ ($11–$18). No credit cards. Mon and Wed–Sat noon–2:30pm and 7–10pm; Tues noon–2:30pm. Closed late July–Aug and Dec 23–Jan 7. Bus: C, 6, 11, 14, or 17.

MODERATE

Il Latini 𝕽𝕽𝕽 *Kids* FLORENTINE   Uncle Narcisso Latini opened this cheap locals' eatin' joint in 1950, though it now gets as many tourists as Florentines. Arrive at 7:30pm to get in the crowd massed at the door, for even with a reservation you'll have to wait as they skillfully fit parties together at the communal tables. In fact, getting thrown together with strangers and sharing a common meal is part of the fun here. Under hundreds of hanging prosciutto ham hocks, the waiters try their hardest to keep a menu away from you and serve instead a filling, traditional set meal with bottomless wine.

A Big Step Above Ice Cream: Florentine Gelato

Gelato is a Florentine institution—a creamy, sweet, flavorful food item on a different level entirely from what Americans call "ice cream." Fine Florentine gelato is a craft taken seriously by all except the tourist-pandering spots around major attractions that serve air-fluffed bland "vanilla" and nuclear-waste pistachio so artificially green it glows.

Here's how to order gelato: First, pay at the register for the size of *coppa* (cup) or *cono* (cone) you want, then take the receipt up to the counter to select your flavors (unlike in America, they'll let you stuff multiple flavors into even the tiniest cup). Prices are fairly standardized, with the smallest serving at around 1.50€ ($1.75) or 2€ ($2.30) and prices going up in .50€ (60¢) increments for six or eight sizes. A warning: Gelato is denser than ice cream and richer than it looks. There's also a concoction called *semifreddo,* somewhere on the far side of the mousse family, in which standard Italian desserts like tiramisù are creamed with milk and then partially frozen.

There are plenty of quality gelaterie besides the ones listed here. A few rules of thumb: Look for a sign that proudly proclaims *produzione propria* (homemade) and take a look at the gelato itself—no matter what kind you plan to order, make sure the banana is gray, the egg-based *crema* (egg-based "vanilla," though there's nary a vanilla bean in it) yellow, and the pistachio a natural, pasty pale olive.

Of all the centrally located gelaterie, **Festival del Gelato,** Via del Corso 75r, just off Via dei Calzaiuoli (✆ **055-239-4386**), has been the only serious contender to the premier Vivoli (below), offering about 50 flavors along with pounding pop music and colorful neon. It's open Tuesday through Sunday: summer 8am to 1am and winter 11am to 1am.

Vivoli, Via Isole delle Stinche 7r, a block west of Piazza Santa Croce (✆ **055-239-2334**), is still the city's institution. Exactly how renowned is this bright gelateria? Taped to the wall is a postcard bearing only "Vivoli, Europa" for the address, yet it was successfully delivered to this world capital of ice cream. It's open Tuesday through Sunday 9am to 1am (closed Aug and Jan to early Feb).

One of the major advantages of the always crowded **Gelateria delle Carrozze,** Piazza del Pesce 3–5r (© **055-23-96-810**), is its location at the foot of the Ponte Vecchio—if you're coming off the bridge and about to head on to the Duomo, this gelateria is immediately off to your right on a small alley that forks off the main street. In summer, it's open daily 11am to 1am; in winter, hours are Thursday through Tuesday 11am to 8pm.

A block south of the Accademia (pick up a cone after you've gazed upon *David's* glory) is what local purists insist is Vivoli's only deserving contender to the throne as gelato king: **Carabé,** Via Ricasoli 60r (© **055-289-476**). It offers genuine homemade Sicilian gelato in the heart of Florence, with ingredients shipped in from Sicily by the hard-working Sicilian owners. Taste for yourself and see if Florentines can hope to ever surpass such scrumptiousness direct from the island that first brought the concept of ice cream to Europe. May 16 through September, it's open daily 10am to midnight; February 15 through May 15 and October through November 15, hours are Tuesday through Sunday 10am to 8pm.

In 1946, the first ice-cream parlor in the city's heart, **Perche No?** ⍟, Via dei Tavolini 19r, off Via del Calzaiuoli (© **055-239-8969**; Bus: 14, 23, or 71), introduced a novelty: the glass display case filled with tubs of flavors that have become standard in ice-cream stores the world over. Wedged into an alley off Via dei Calzaiuoli between Piazza della Signoria and the Duomo, Perche No? has done an admirable job over the years of being many a harried tourist's first introduction to quality Florentine gelato. During World War II when the American army reached Florence after the Nazi withdrawal, they had the power grid specially reconnected so that Perche No?'s gelato production—and G.I. consumption—could continue. Try their *ciocolato bianco* (white chocolate studded with chunks of the main ingredient) or one of the semifreddi, a moussing process they helped invent. It's open Wednesday through Monday from 10am to midnight.

lly kicks off with *ribollita* and *pappa al pomodoro* or *penne* (in a ragù mixed with cream). If everyone agrees on the *arrosto misto,* you can get a table-filling platter heaped high with assorted roast meats. Finish off with a round of *cantucci con vin santo* for everyone.

Via del Palchetti 6r (off Via della Vigna Nuova). ℂ 055-210-916. Reservations strongly recommended. Primi 6€ ($6.90); secondi 8€–16€ ($9.20–$18); unofficial fixed-priced full meal with limitless wine 30€–35€ ($35–$40). AE, DC, MC, V. Tues–Sun 12:30–2:30pm and 7:30–10:30pm. Closed 15 days in Aug and Dec 24–Jan 6. Bus: C, 6, 11, 36, 37, or 68.

Trattoria Belle Donne TUSCAN   Tucked away on a narrow street (whose name refers to the women of the night who once worked this then-shady neighborhood) parallel to exclusive Via dei Tornabuoni, this packed-to-the-gills lunch spot (with no identifying sign) immediately drew the area's chic boutique owners and sales staff. It now tries to accommodate them and countless others in a rather brusque style—no lingering over lunch; dinner isn't as rushed. Tuscan cuisine gets reinterpreted and updated by the talented young chef, who placates the local palate without alienating it: Traditional dishes appear in the company of innovative alternatives like cream of zucchini and chestnut soup or lemon-flavored chicken. The regulars seem inured to the occasional rush job, so don't take it personally.

Via delle Belle Donne 16r (north off Via della Vigna Nuova). ℂ **055-238-2609.** www.osteriabelledonne.com. Reservations not accepted. Primi 5.50€–7.50€ ($6.30–$8.65); secondi 8€–12€ ($9.20–$14). MC, V. Mon–Fri 12:30–2:30pm and 7:15–10:30pm. Closed most of Aug.

5 Near Santa Maria Novella
MODERATE

Trattoria Guelfa FLORENTINE/TUSCAN   Always crowded and always good, the Guelfa has lots of paintings hanging on its walls and a random trattoria decor—pendulous gourds, wine bottles, and an old oxen yoke rule over the tightly packed noisy tables. The kitchen is very traditional, offering *spaghetti alla rustica* (in a cheesy, creamy tomato sauce) and *risotto ai 4 formaggi* (a gooey rice dish made with four cheeses) as proud primi. For a main course, you can go light with the *pinzimonio di verdure crude* (a selection of seasonally fresh raw veggies with oil to dip them in) or indulge your taste buds with the *petti di pollo alla Guelfa* (a chicken breast rolled around a stuffing of prosciutto, cheese, and truffled cream served with a side of olive oil–drenched oven-roasted potatoes).

Via Guelfa 103r (near the Fortezza, beyond Via Nazionale). ℂ **055-213-306.** Reservations strongly recommended. Primi 5€–8€ ($5.75–$9.20); secondi 6€–15€ ($6.90–$17); menù turistico with wine 9€ ($10). AE, MC, V. Thurs–Tues noon–2:30pm and 7–10:30pm. Bus: 4, 10, 13, 14, 23, 25, 28, 31, 32, 33, 67, or 71.

Trattoria Sostanza FLORENTINE   Sostanza is popularly called Il Troia (the trough) because people have been lining up at the long communal tables since 1869 to enjoy huge amounts of some of the best traditional food in the city. The primi are very simple: pasta in sauce, *tortellini in brodo* (meat-stuffed pasta in chicken broth), and *zuppa alla paesana* (peasant soup ribollita). The secondi don't steer far from Florentine traditions either, with *trippa alla fiorentina* or their mighty specialty *petti di pollo al burro* (thick chicken breasts fried in butter). It's an extremely unassuming place, so laid-back you may not realize you're meant to be ordering when the waiter wanders over to chat. They also frown on anybody trying to cheat his or her own taste buds out of a full Tuscan meal.

Via Porcellana 25r (near the Borgo Ognissanti end). ℂ **055-212-691.** Reservations strongly recommended. Primi 6.20€–7.30€ ($7.15–$8.40); secondi 6.80€–180€ ($7.80–$20). No credit cards. Mon–Fri noon–2:15pm and 7:30–9:45pm. Closed Aug.

6 Near San Marco & Santissima Annunziata
MODERATE

Il Vegetariano VEGETARIAN   Come early to Florence's only vegetarian restaurant and use your coat to save a spot at one of the communal wood tables before heading to the back to get your food. You pay at the start of the meal, after choosing from the daily selections penned on the wipe board, and take your dishes self-service style from the workers behind the counter. The menu changes constantly but includes such dishes as risotto with yellow squash and black cabbage; a soupy, spicy Tunisian-style couscous with vegetables; a quichelike pizza rustica of ricotta, olives, tomatoes, and mushrooms; or a plate with *farro* (emmer) and a hot salad of spinach, onions, sprouts, and bean-curd chunks sautéed in soy sauce. You can mix and match your own salad, and they make a good chestnut flour cake stuffed with hazelnut cream for dessert.

Via delle Ruote 30r (off Via Santa Reparata near Piazza Indipendenza). ℂ **055-475-030.** Reservations not accepted. Primi 5€–6€ ($5.75–$6.90); secondi 7.50€–8€ ($8.65–$9.20). No credit cards. Tues–Fri 12:30–2:30pm; Tues–Sun 7:30pm–midnight. Closed 2–3 weeks in Aug and Dec 24–Jan 2. Bus: 12, 91, or anything to San Marco.

La Mescita SANDWICHES & HOME COOKING   This tiny *fiaschetteria* is immensely popular with local businesspeople and students from the nearby university. Lunch can be a crushing affair, and they have signs admonishing you to eat quickly to give others a chance to sit. You'll be eating with Italians, and it's not for the timid because you have to take charge yourself: securing a seat, collecting your own place setting, and getting someone's attention to give your order before going to sit down. They offer mainly sandwiches, though there are always a few simple meat and pasta dishes ready as well. *Melanzana* (eggplant) is overwhelmingly the side dish of choice, and you can look to the cardboard lists behind the counter to select your wine, although the house wine is very good, and a quarter liter of it is cheaper than a can of soda.

Via degli Alfani 70r (near the corner of Via dei Servi). (©) **347-795-1604.** All sandwiches and dishes 4€–7€ ($4.60–$8.05). No credit cards. Mon–Sat 11am–4pm. Closed Aug. Bus: 6, 31, or 32.

Taverna del Bronzino FINE TUSCAN   The 1580 house where Santi di Tito spent the last years of his life painting is now inhabited by polite, efficient, and very accommodating waiters who will show you to a table in the vaulted-ceiling dining room or on the arbor-shaded patio. Among the delectable antipasti are *salmone Scozzese selvatica* (wild Scottish salmon) and *petto d'oca affumicato e carciofi* (thin slices of smoked goose breast on a bed of sliced artichokes drowned in olive oil). The *risotto agli asparagi* is a bit light on the asparagus but still very creamy and tasty. You can also try the excellent *ravioli alla Senese* (ricotta and spinach–stuffed pasta in creamy tomato sauce) or *tagliolini ai pesci* (noodles with fish). To stick with the sea you can order *branzino* (sea bass simmered in white wine) next or select the *paillard di vitella all'ortolana* (a grilled veal steak wrapped around cooked vegetables).

Via delle Ruote 27r (between Piazza Indipendenza and San Marco). (©) **055-495-220.** Reservations strongly recommended. Primi 12€–15€ ($14–$17); secondi 21€–25€ ($24–$29). AE, DC, MC, V. Mon–Sat 12:30–2:30pm and 7:30–10:30pm. Closed 3 weeks in Aug. Bus: 12, 91, or anything to San Marco.

7 Near Santa Croce

VERY EXPENSIVE

Cibrèo ⓖ REFINED TUSCAN   There's no pasta and no grilled meat—can this be Tuscany? Rest assured that while Benedetta Vitale and Fabio Picchi's culinary creations are a bit out of the ordinary, most are based on antique recipes. Cibrèo's actually has a split personality; this is a review not of the trattoria branch (p. 91), but of the fan-cooled main restaurant room, full of intellectual babble, where the elegance is in the substance of the food and the service, not in surface appearances. Waiters pull up a chair to explain the list of daily specials, and those garlands of hot peppers hanging in the kitchen window are a hint at the cook's favorite spice. All the food is spectacular, and dishes change regularly, but if they're available try the yellow pepper soup drizzled with olive oil, the soufflé of potatoes and ricotta spiced and served with pecorino shavings and ragù, or the roasted duck stuffed with minced beef, raisins, and pinoli.

Via Andrea del Verrocchio 8r (at the San Ambrogio Market, off Via de' Macchi). ℂ 055-234-1100. Reservations required. Primi 18€ ($21); secondi 34€ ($39). AE, DC, MC, V. Tues–Sat 12:30–2:30pm and 7:30–11:15pm. Closed July 26–Sept 6. Bus: B or 14.

Ristorante e Vineria alle Murate TUSCAN & CUCINA CRE-ATIVA   Soft illumination, soft jazz, and soft pastels rule in this trendy spot owned by chef Umberto Montano. Alle Murate was one of the first places in the city to experiment with nouvelle cuisine. It tries, however, to balance *cucina creativa* with traditional Tuscan techniques and dishes. You could start with *zuppa di fagioli e gamberi* (soup of creamed white beans with shrimp) or the lasagne. The best fish dish is sea bass on a bed of fried potatoes topped with diced tomatoes, and for a main course you could go in for the *anatra dis-ossata alle erbete e scorze di arancia* (duck à l'orange). The *brasato di Chiana* (steak) in Brunello wine, however, was disappointing. For these prices, the portions could be larger and the presentation better, but the food is good and the antipasti, *contorni* (side dishes), aperitifs, and dessert wines are included in the price of your meal. The *vineria* half—really just a small room off the main one—offers an abbreviated menu at abbreviated prices.

Via Ghibellina 52r (near Borgo Allegri). ℂ 055-240-618. www.caffeitaliano.it. Reservations strongly recommended (specify *vineria* or *ristorante*). Primi 18€ ($21); secondi with side dish 22€–24€ ($25–$27); menu degustazione without wine 52€–60€ ($60–$69). AE, DC, MC, V. Tues–Sun 7:30–11pm. Bus: 14.

EXPENSIVE

Antico Noè SANDWICHES & WINE   A *fiaschitteria* with superior sandwiches masquerading as a regular bar, the Antico Noè is popular with students and shopkeepers for its well-stuffed panini and cheap glasses of quaffable wine—perfect for a light lunch on the go. The place is rather hidden, but you'll know you've found it when you see a small crowd gathered around a door in the shade of a covered alley—though, I should warn you, the alley and tiny piazza off it have of late begun hosting a small community of vagrants and bums. You can order your sandwich from the list, invent your own, or (better yet) let them invent one for you. They surprised me on my last trip with a rather tasty combination of stuffed chicken and sliced porcini mushrooms topped with a slightly spicy creamy tomato spread. The sit-down osteria next door serves simple Tuscan dishes.

Volta di San Piero 6r (the arched alley off Piazza San Pier Maggiore). © 055-234-0838. Sandwiches 2.50€–5€ ($2.90–$5.75); wine .75€–2€ (85¢–$2.30) per glass; primi and secondi 7€–15€ ($8.05–$17). No credit cards. Mon–Sat 8am–midnight (often open Sun, too). Bus: B, 14, 23, or 71.

La Giostra ★★★ ADVENTUROUS TUSCAN   This is one of two restaurants I visit every time I come to town. The chef/owner is Dimitri d'Asburgo Lorena, a Hapsburg prince (with some local Medici blood for good measure) who opened this restaurant merely to indulge his love of cooking. They start you off with a complimentary flute of *spumanti* before you plunge into the tasty *crostini misti* and exquisite primi. Among my favorites are *tortelloni alla Mugellana* (handmade potato-stuffed pasta in ragù), *gnocchetti alla Lord Reinolds* (potato dumplings in a sauce of stilton and Port), homemade *tagliatelle* with tiny wild asparagus spears, and ravioli stuffed with brie in a sauce with thinly sliced, lightly fried artichokes. For an encore, try the *nodino di vitella ai tartufi bianchi* (veal slathered in eggy white truffle sauce with fresh truffle grated on top) or the lighter *spianata alle erbe aromatiche di Maremma* (a huge platter of spiced beef pounded flat and piled with a salad of rosemary sprigs, sage, and other herbs). Don't leave without sampling the sinfully rich Viennese Sachertorte, made from an old Hapsburg family recipe. This place has become (justifiably) popular, and even with a reservation there's often a short wait—laudably, they don't rush anybody to empty up tables—but it's worth it.

Borgo Pinti 10r (off Piazza Salvemini). © 055-241-341. www.ristorantelagiostra. com. Reservations recommended. Primi 10€–14€ ($12–$16); secondi 14€–21€ ($16–$24). AE, DC, MC, V. Daily noon–2:30pm and 7pm–midnight. Bus: A, B, C, 6, 14, 23, 31, 32, or 71.

MODERATE

Il Pizzaiuolo ★ Kids NEAPOLITAN/PIZZA   Despite their considerable skill in the kitchen, Florentines just can't make a decent pizza. It takes a Neapolitan to do that, so business has been booming ever since Naples-born Carmine opened this pizzeria. Even with a reservation, you'll probably have to wait for a spot at a long, crowded, and noisy marble table. Save the pizza for a main dish;

start instead with a Neapolitan first course like *fusilli c'a ricotta* (homemade pasta spirals in creamy tomato-and-ricotta sauce). Of the pizzas, you can't go wrong with a classic *margherita* (mozzarella, tomatoes, and fresh basil), or spice up your evening with a *pizza diavola,* topped with hot salami and olives.

Via de' Macci 113r (at the corner of Via Pietrapiana). ℭ **055-241-171.** Reservations required for dinner. Pizza 4.50€–10€ ($5.20–$12); primi 6.50€–13€ ($7.50–$15); secondi 7.50€–13€ ($8.65–$15). No credit cards. Mon–Sat 12:30–3pm and 7:30pm–midnight. Closed Aug. Bus: B or 14.

Osteria de' Benci INVENTIVE TUSCAN   This popular trattoria serves enormous portions (especially of secondi) on beautiful hand-painted ceramics under high ceiling vaults echoing with the conversation of Florentine trendoids. The menu changes monthly, but you can always be assured of excellent *salumi*—they come from Falorni, the famed butcher of the Chianti. The *eliche del profeta* are fusiloni tossed with ricotta, olive oil, oregano, and fresh tomatoes sprinkled with *parmigiano.* The unique *spaghetti dell'ubriacone* is bright crimson spaghetti that takes its color from being cooked in red wine, sauced with garlic, pepperoncino, and parsley sautéed in olive oil. And the *cibrèo delle regine* is a traditional rich Florentine dish of chopped chicken livers and gizzards served on toast.

Via de' Benci 13r (at the corner of Via de' Neri). ℭ **055-234-4923.** Reservations highly recommended. Primi 6€–9€ ($6.90–$10); secondi 5€–16€ ($5.75–$18). AE, DC, MC, V. Mon–Sat 1–2:45pm and 7:45–10:45pm. Bus: B, 23, or 71.

Ristorante Vecchia Firenze 🅖 🄺🄸🄳🅂 FLORENTINE/TUSCAN   I first dined here with my parents when I was 12, and the place hasn't changed much since. It's set in a 15th-century palazzo, so avoid sitting in the boring front room in favor of the more intimate back rooms or the rowdier stone-lined cantina downstairs full of Florentine students. The *zuppa pavese* is a good vegetable soup, but try the *penne Vecchia Firenze* (pasta quills in a subtle creamy mushroom sauce with tomatoes). By all means order the *bistecca alla fiorentina,* but if your appetite runs more to *coniglio alla griglia* (grilled rabbit) or *branzino alla griglia* (grilled sea bass), you won't be disappointed.

Borgo degli Albizi 76–78r. ℭ **055-234-0361.** Primi 5€–7€ ($5.75–$8.05); secondi 7€–10€ ($8.05–$10); pizza 5€–7€ ($5.75–$8.05); fixed-price menus without wine 13€–15€ ($15–$17). AE, DC, MC, V. Tues–Sun 11am–3pm and 7–10pm. Bus: 14, 23, or 71.

Trattoria Cibrèo FLORENTINE   This is the casual trattoria of celebrated chef-owner Fabio Picchi; its limited menu comes from the same creative kitchen that put on the map his premier and more than twice as expensive *ristorante* next door. The trattoria moved from its back alley location to the main street in 1999, and this higher visibility has only made the lines longer. Picchi takes his inspiration from traditional Tuscan recipes, and the first thing you'll note is the absence of pasta. After you taste the velvety *passata di peperoni gialli* (yellow bell-pepper soup), you won't care much. The stuffed roast rabbit demands the same admiration. My only complaint: They rush you through your meal in an un-Italian fashion in order to free up tables. Enjoy your after-dinner espresso at the Caffè Cibrèo across the way.

Via de' Macci 122r. ☎ 055-234-1100. Primi 6€ ($6.90); secondi 13€ ($15). AE, DC, MC, V. Tues–Sat 1–2:30pm and 7–11:15pm. Closed July 26–Sept 6. Bus: B or 14.

Trattoria Pallottino FLORENTINE   One long room with a few long tables on the cobblestone floor and a second room on the side are all there is to this local favorite, so reserve early or you won't get a seat. The cook makes a mean *bruschetta al pomodoro* (toasted bread topped with tomatoes over which you are invited to drizzle the olive oil liberally). For a first course, I look no further than the *spaghetti alla fiaccheraia,* with a tomato sauce mildly spiked with hot peppers. You might follow it with the *peposo* (beef stew loaded with black pepper). Skip dessert and pop next door for a Vivoli gelato (see the box, "A Big Step Above Ice Cream: Florentine Gelato" on p. 84).

Via Isola delle Stinche 1r. ☎ 055-289-573. Reservations required for dinner. Primi 5€–8€ ($5.75–$9.20); secondi 7€–14€ ($8.05–$16). AE, DC, MC, V. Tues–Sun 12:30–2:30pm and 7:30–10:30pm. Closed Aug 5–21.

8 In the Oltrarno

EXPENSIVE

Osteria Santo Spirito NOUVELLE TUSCAN   Some of the hippest dining in the Oltrarno fills these deep-red rooms with undulating track lighting stacked on top of each other. Funk and dance music pounds from the speakers as they serve up excellent dishes with a modern twist. You can start with a salad like *pollo pinoli e uvetta con dressing* (chicken, pine nut, and raisin), or for pasta try *orecchiette Santo Spirito* (pasta in spicy tomato sauce with ricotta) or *gnocchi di patate gratinati* (oven-baked gnocchi swimming in a bubbling hot mix of soft cheeses flavored with truffle). Afterward, fill up on *filetto di manzo à tartufo* (beef filet with truffles) or the *coscie d'anatre con la panna* (very meaty roasted duck in cream sauce with carrots and bacon).

Piazza Santo Spirito 16r. ⓒ **055-238-2383.** Reservations recommended. Primi 6€–14€ ($6.90–$16); secondi 12€–25€ ($14–$29). AE, DC, MC, V. Daily 12:45–2:30pm and 8pm–midnight. Bus: B, 11, 36, 37, or 68.

MODERATE

Alla Vecchia Bettola FLORENTINE   Founded by the owners of Nerbone in the Mercato Centrale (p. 81), this simple room right on the piazza may not look it, but it's one of the city's premier restaurants in town for ultratraditional Florentine food. It fills up very early with food-loving Florentines, who choose from an always-changing menu that may include *penne alla Bettola* in spicy cream tomato sauce, rigatoni dressed with crushed olives, or *riso sulle testicciole d'agnello* (a "local's" rice dish cooked in a halved sheep's head). Secondi range from *anatra ripiena tartufata* (stuffed duck in truffle sauce) to the superlative *carpaccio con rucola*—pounded disks of beef piled high with arugula and tissue-thin slices of pecorino cheese. As far as wine goes, you simply pay for however much you finish of the light and tangy house wine on the table.

Viale Vasco Pratolini 3/7 (on Piazza Tasso). ⓒ **055-224-158.** Reservations required. Primi 6€–7€ ($6.90–$8.05); secondi 8€–12€ ($9.20–$14). No credit cards. Tues–Sat noon–2:30pm and 7:30–10:30pm. Closed 3 weeks in Aug, Dec 23–Jan 2, and Easter. Bus: 12 or 13.

Il Cantinone 🍴 *Kids* TUSCAN   With tourists and large groups of locals all seated at long tables under the low arc of a brick ceiling, the convivial noise can sometimes get a bit overwhelming. But the feeling of having walked into a party is part of the charm of this place. The specialty is *crostini,* slabs of peasant bread that act as vehicles for toppings like prosciutto, tomatoes, mozzarella, and sausage. The wine list is excellent—due perhaps to this locale's past incarnation as a Chianti cellar—and the best way to sample it is through the menù degustazione. You and your companion get an antipasto, two primi (usually pasta dishes), and a secondo, which might be a tender and tasty wild boar stew. With each course you get a different wine, building from something like a light Orvieto *secco* through a well-chosen chianti to a brawny Brunello for the meat dish.

Via Santo Spirito 6r (off Piazza Santa Trinita). ⓒ **055-218-898** or 055-225-955. Primi and *crostoni* 5.50€–8€ ($6.30–$9.20); secondi 6€–20€ ($6.90–$23). AE, MC, V. Tues–Sun 12:30–2:30pm and 7:30–10:30pm. Bus: D, 8, 11, 36, or 37.

I Raddi 🍴 TUSCAN   Luccio's trattoria hidden in the heart of the Oltrarno is a true find—excellent cooking at reasonable prices in a city rapidly overpricing itself. The beamed ceiling and Tuscan standbys on the menu give it a grounding in tradition while the young staff and light touch in the kitchen lend a fresh bohemian air. The specialty is *tagliolini ardiglione* (with sausage and aromatic herbs), but they also make a mean *crespelle alla fiorentina* (pasta crepes layered with cheese). They do a fine *cibrèo*, a tasty *peposo alla fornacina con spinaci* (beef baked in wine with lots of pepperoncino and served with spinach), and a spicy *fagioli all'uccelleto con salsiccia*.

Via Ardiglione 47r (off Via dei Serragli, near Piazza delle Carmine). ✆ **055-211-072.** www.iraddi.com. Reservations recommended. Primi 7€ ($8.05); secondi 10€–15€ ($12–$17). AE, MC, V. Mon–Sat noon–3pm and 7–11pm. Closed 10 days in Feb and a week in mid-Aug. Bus: D, 11, 36, 37, or 68.

Osteria del Cinghiale Bianco TUSCAN   Massimo Masselli will sooner turn people away at the door than rush you though your meal. The place does a good repeat business of locals (including cooks from other restaurants) and tourists alike who come for the delicious *taglierini* (wide noodles) with pesto or the famous *strozzapreti* ("priest-chokers" made of the spinach-and-ricotta mix normally found inside ravioli, served with melted butter). You can't go wrong ordering anything made of the restaurant's namesake *cinghiale* (wild boar)—from the cold boar slices as an appetizer to *cinghiale alla maremmana con polenta* (wild boar stew cozied up to creamy, firm polenta) as a main course. Set in the base of a 12th-century tower, this place milks its medieval look with exposed stone, odd iron implements hanging everywhere, and lights hidden in suspended cauldrons or the pigeonholed walls. Note that dishes with truffles in them might raise the maximum prices below by about 5€ ($5.75).

Borgo Sant' Jacopo 43r. ✆ **055-215-706.** www.cinghialebianco.it. Reservations required on weekends. Primi 5€–10€ ($5.75–$12); secondi 9.50€–16€ ($11–$18). MC, V. Thurs–Tues 6.30–11pm (Sat–Sun also noon–3pm). Closed July 10–Aug 1. Bus: D, 8, 11, 36, or 37.

INEXPENSIVE

EnotecaBar Fuori Porta ENOTECA/CROSTONI   You can dine out on the sidewalk in nice weather, or sit on the benches at tiny wooden tables inside to taste the excellent pizzalike crostini here. Start with the *pappa al pomodoro* or gnocchi with broccoli rabe and sausage. The *crostoni* are divided by cheese—mozzarella, sharp pecorino, creamy goat-cheese *caprino*—along with a list of the toppings to accompany them. My fave is *caprino con prosciutto arrosto e pomodori secchi* (with goat cheese, roasted prosciutto, and sun-dried tomatoes). The wine is a key part of your meal; the list draws from the more interesting vineyards in Tuscany and beyond. This place is a bit out of the way but worth the trip.

Via del Monte alle Croci 10r (near San Niccolò, through the gate at Via San Miniato). ✆ 055-234-2483. www.fuoriporta.it. Sandwiches and appetizers 2€–7€ ($2.30–$8.05). AE, MC, V. Mon–Sat 12:30–3:30pm and 7pm–1am. Bus: C, D, 12, 13, or 23.

Trattoria La Casalinga FLORENTINE   Their recent expansion sadly removed the last wisps of Renaissance aura from La Casalinga, replacing it with a crowded, almost cafeteria-like feeling—but the home cooking of its name is still some of the most genuine in town. The *ribollita* is thick, the *ravioli al sugo di coniglio* (in a rabbit sauce) rich, and the *pasta della nonna* (short, hollow pasta in a sauce of tomatoes, sausage, and onions) excellent. Don't expect anything fancy in the secondi department either, just solid favorites like *bollito misto* (a mix of boiled meats with green sauce), *trippa alla fiorentina,* and *galletto ruspante al forno* (half a young oven-baked chicken). The starving artists and local artisans have been all but driven out by the tourist hordes, but if you want to stuff yourself on huge portions of Oltrarno workman's food, this is the place to come.

Via Michelozzi 9r (between Via Maggio and Piazza Santo Spirito). ✆ 055-267-9243. Primi 3.50€–4€ ($4.05–$4.60); secondi 5€–10€ ($5.75–$12). Mon–Sat noon–2:30pm and 7–10pm. AE, DC, MC, V. Bus: D, 8, 11, 36, or 37.

9 In the Hills

MODERATE

Trattoria le Cave di Maiano 🐾 TUSCAN   This converted farmhouse is the countryside restaurant of choice for Florentines wishing to escape the city heat on a summer Sunday afternoon. You can enjoy warm-weather lunches on the tree-shaded stone terrace with a bucolic view. In cooler weather, you can dine inside several large rustic rooms with haphazard paintings scattered on the walls. The *antipasto caldo* of varied *crostini* and fried polenta is a good way to kick off a meal, followed by a *misto della casa* (for two only) that gives you a sampling of primi. This may include *penne strascicate* (stubby pasta in cream sauce and tomato ragù), or *riso allo spezza-camino* (rice with beans and black cabbage). The best secondo is the *pollastro al mattone* (chicken roasted under a brick with pepper) or the *lombatina di vitello alla griglia* (grilled veal chop).

Via Cave di Maiano 16 (in Maiano, halfway between Florence and Fiesole east of the main road). ✆ 055-59-133. Reservations required. Primi 7€–10€ ($8.05–$12); secondi 10€–15€ ($12–$17). AE, DC, MC, V. Daily 12:30–3:30pm and 7:30pm–midnight. Bus: 7 (get off at Villa San Michele, then turn around and take the road branching to the left of the winding one your bus took; continue on about ³⁄₄ mile up this side road, past the Pensione Benecistà); a taxi is a better idea.

5

Exploring Florence

Florence is the Renaissance city—home to Michelangelo's *David*, Botticelli's *Birth of Venus*, and Raphael's Madonnas. It's where Fra' Angelico painted delicate *Annunciations* in bright primary colors and Giotto frescoed monks wailing over the *Death of St. Francis*. The city is so dense in art, history, and culture that even a short visit can wear out the best of us. Take a hint from that great pragmatist Mark Twain, who, after acknowledging the genius of Michelangelo, said "I do not want Michelangelo for breakfast—for luncheon—for dinner—for tea—for supper—for between meals. I like a change occasionally."

Don't necessarily pass up the Uffizi or take a rain check on *David* and the Accademia, but do take the time to enjoy the simple pleasures of Florence—wander the medieval streets in Dante's old neighborhood, sip a cappuccino on Piazza della Signoria and people-watch, haggle for a leather jacket at the street market around San Lorenzo, or immerse yourself in the greenery of the Boboli Gardens.

1 On Piazza Del Duomo

The cathedral square is filled with tourists and caricature artists during the day, strolling crowds in the early evening, and knots of students strumming guitars on the Duomo's steps at night. Though it's always crowded, the piazza's vivacity and the glittering facades of the cathedral and the baptistery doors keep it an eternal Florentine sight.

At the corner of the busy pedestrian main drag, Via Calzaiuoli, sits the pretty little **Loggia del Bigallo** (1351–58). Inside is a small museum of 14th-century works, which is unfortunately almost always closed. Call © **055-215-440** if you're interested in trying to make an appointment to get in to see the 1342 *Madonna della Misericordia* by the school of Bernardo Daddi, which features the earliest known cityscape view of Florence.

Note that just south of the Duomo, hidden in the tangle of medieval streets toward Piazza della Signoria, is a 14th-century

---

Tips **The Best Times to Sightsee**

Museums Open on Mondays: Palazzo Vecchio, Museo Bardini, Museo di Firenze Com'Era, Museo di Santa Maria Novella, Casa Buonarroti, Casa di Dante, Opera di Santa Croce, Museo dell'Opera del Duomo, Campanile di Giotto, Duomo's cupola, Opificio Pietre Dure, Museo Stibbert, Instituto e Museo di Storia di Scienza, Palazzo Medici-Riccardi, Museo Horne, Cappella Brancacci, Synagogue, Spedale degli Innocenti, Roman Amphitheater, and Museo Archeologico (Fiesole).

Sights Open During Il Riposo (1–4pm): Uffizi, Accademia, Palazzo Vecchio, Duomo and its cupola, Museo dell'Opera del Duomo, Campanile di Giotto, Baptistery, Palazzo Vecchio, Santa Croce, Galleria Palatina (Pitti Palace), Forte di Belvedere and Boboli Gardens, Cappella Brancacci, Roman Amphitheater, and Museo Archeologico (Fiesole).

Florentine house restored and converted into the **Casa di Dante** (© 055-219-416), a small museum chronicling the life and times of the great poet. But, this isn't likely the poet's actual house. The entrance is up the side alley of Via Santa Margherita, and it's open Monday and Wednesday through Saturday from 10am to 6pm (to 4pm in winter) and Sunday from 10am to 2pm. Admission has nearly tripled this year to a ludicrous 6.50€ ($7.50), so only diehard fans should bother.

Duomo (Cathedral of Santa Maria dei Fiori) For centuries, people have commented that Florence's cathedral is turned inside out, its exterior boasting Brunelleschi's famous dome, Giotto's bell tower, and a festive cladding of white, green, and pink marble, but its interior left spare, almost barren.

By the late 13th century, Florence was feeling peevish: Its archrivals Siena and Pisa sported huge new Duomos filled with art while it was saddled with the tiny 5th- or 6th-century Santa Reparata as a cathedral. So, in 1296, the city hired Arnolfo di Cambio to design a new Duomo, and he began raising the facade and the first few bays before his death in 1302. Work continued under the auspices of the Wool Guild and architects Giotto di Bondone (who concentrated on the bell tower) and Francesco Talenti (who finished up to the drum of the dome and in the process greatly enlarged Arnolfo's original plan). The facade we see today is a neo-Gothic composite

What to See & Do in Florence

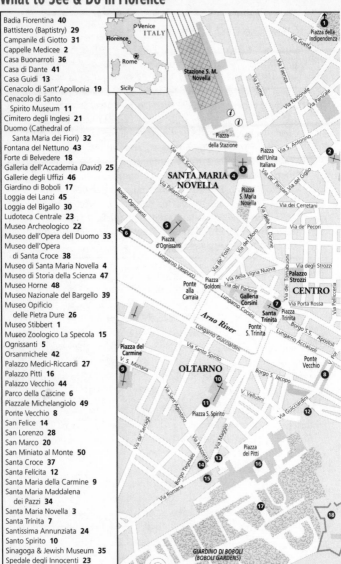

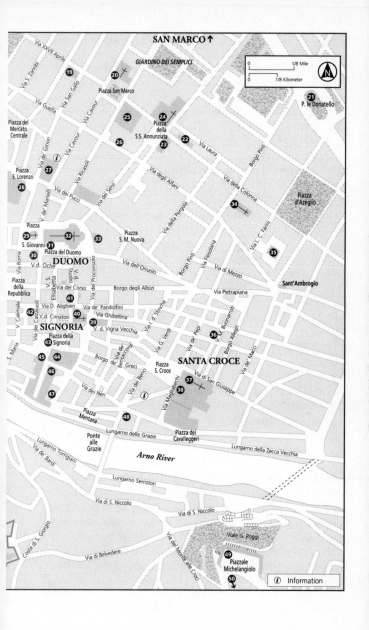

SAN MARCO ↑

GIARDINO DEI SEMPLICI

Piazza San Marco

Piazza del Mercato Centrale

Piazza S. Lorenzo

Piazza S.S. Annunziata

Piazza della S.S. Annunziata

P. le Donatello

Piazza d'Azeglio

Piazza S. M. Nuova

Sant'Ambrogio

Piazza del Duomo

DUOMO

S. Giovanni

Piazza della Repubblica

SIGNORIA

Piazza della Signoria

SANTA CROCE

Piazza S. Croce

Piazza Mentana

Ponte alle Grazie

Piazza dei Cavalleggeri

Arno River

Piazzale Michelangiolo

ⓘ Information

0   1/8 Mile
0   1/8 Kilometer

designed by Emilio de Fabris and built from 1871 to 1887 (for its story, see "Museo dell'Opera del Duomo" below).

The Duomo's most distinctive feature is its enormous **dome** ⚐⚐⚐, which dominates the skyline and is a symbol of Florence itself. The raising of this dome, the largest in the world in its time, was no mean architectural feat, tackled admirably by Filippo Brunelleschi between 1420 and 1436 (see "A Man & His Dome" on p. 102). You can climb up between the two shells of the cupola for one of the classic panoramas across the city. At the base of the dome, just above the drum, Baccio d'Agnolo began adding a balcony in 1507. One of the eight sides was finished by 1515, when someone asked Michelangelo—whose artistic opinion was by this time taken as cardinal law—what he thought of it. The master reportedly scoffed, "It looks like a cricket cage." Work was immediately halted, and to this day the other seven sides remain rough brick.

The Duomo was actually built around **Santa Reparata** so it could remain in business during construction. For more than 70 years, Florentines entered their old church through the freestanding facade of the new one, but in 1370 the original was torn down when the bulk of the Duomo—except the dome—was finished. Ever the fiscal conservatives, Florentines started clamoring to see some art as soon as the new facade's front door was completed in the early 1300s—to be sure their investment would be more beautiful than rival cathedrals. Gaddo Gaddi was commissioned to mosaic an *Enthronement of Mary* in the lunette above the inside of the main door, and the people were satisfied. The stained-glass windows set in the facade were designed by Lorenzo Ghiberti, and Paolo Uccello, a painter obsessed by the newly developed perspective, frescoed the huge *hora italica* clock with its four heads of Prophets in 1443.

At a right-aisle pier are steps leading down to the excavations of the old Santa Reparata. In 1972, a tomb slab inscribed with the name Filippo Brunelleschi was discovered there (visible through a gate). Unless you're interested in the remains of some ancient Roman houses and parts of the paleo-Christian mosaics from Santa Reparata's floor, the 3€ ($3.45) admission isn't worth it.

Against the left-aisle wall are the only frescoes besides the dome in the Duomo. The earlier one to the right is the greenish *Memorial to Sir John Hawkwood* ⚐ (1436), an English *condottiere* (mercenary commander) whose name the Florentines mangled to Giovanni Acuto when they hired him to rough up their enemies. Before he died, or so the story goes, the mercenary asked to have a bronze statue of himself riding his charger to be raised in his honor. Florence solemnly promised to do so, but, in typical tightwad style, after Hawkwood's death the city hired the master of perspective and illusion, Paolo Uccello, to paint an equestrian monument instead— much cheaper than casting a statue in bronze. Andrea Castagno copied this painting-as-equestrian-statue idea 20 years later when he frescoed a *Memorial to Niccolò da Tolentino* next to Uccello's work. Near the end of the left aisle is Domenico di Michelino's *Dante Explaining the Divine Comedy* (1465).

In the back left corner of the sanctuary is the **New Sacristy.** Lorenzo de' Medici was attending Mass in the Duomo one April day in 1478 with his brother Giuliano when they were attacked in the infamous Pazzi Conspiracy. The conspirators, egged on by the pope and led by a member of the Pazzi family, old rivals of the Medici, fell on the brothers at the ringing of the sanctuary bell. Giuliano was murdered on the spot—his body rent with 19 wounds— but Lorenzo vaulted over the altar rail and sprinted for safety into the New Sacristy, slamming the bronze doors behind him. Those doors were cast from 1446 to 1467 by Luca della Robbia, his only significant work in the medium. Earlier, Luca had provided a lunette of the *Resurrection* (1442) in glazed terra cotta over the door, as well as the lunette Ascension over the south sacristy door. The interior of the New Sacristy is filled with beautifully inlaid wood cabinet doors.

The frescoes on the **interior of the dome** were designed by Giorgio Vasari but painted mostly by his less-talented student Frederico Zuccari by 1579. The frescoes were subjected to a thorough cleaning completed in 1996, which many people saw as a waste of restoration lire when so many more important works throughout the city were waiting to be salvaged. The scrubbing did, however, bring out Zuccari's only saving point—his innovative color palette.

Piazza del Duomo. © 055-230-2885. www.operaduomo.firenze.it. Admission to church free; Santa Reparata excavations 3€ ($3.45); cupola 6€ ($6.90), free for children under 6. Church Mon–Wed and Fri 10am–5pm; Thurs 10am–3:30pm; 1st Sat of month 10am–3:30pm, other Sat 10am–4:45pm; Sun 1:30–4:30pm. Free tours every 40 min. daily, 10:30am–noon and 3–4:20pm. Cupola Mon–Fri 8:30am–6:20pm; Sat 8:30am–5pm (1st Sat of month to 3:20pm). Bus: 1, 6, 17, 14, 22, 23, 36, 37, or 71.

Battistero (Baptistery) ★★★   In choosing a date to mark the beginning of the Renaissance, art historians often seize on 1401, the year Florence's powerful wool merchant's guild held a contest to decide who would receive the commission to design the **North**

A Man & His Dome

Filippo Brunelleschi, a diminutive man whose ego was as big as his talent, managed in his arrogant, quixotic, suspicious, and brilliant way to literally invent Renaissance architecture. Having been beaten by Lorenzo Ghiberti in the famous contest to cast the baptistery doors (see below), Brunelleschi resolved he'd rather be the top architect than the second-best sculptor and took off for Rome to study the buildings of the ancients. On returning to Florence, he combined subdued gray *pietra serena* stone with smooth white plaster to create airy arches, vaults, and arcades of classically perfect proportions in his own special variant on the ancient Roman orders of architecture. Apart from designing the serene San Lorenzo, Santo Spirito, and the elegant Ospedale degli Innocenti, his greatest achievement by far was erecting the dome over Florence's cathedral.

The Duomo, then the world's largest church, had already been built, but nobody had been able to figure out how to cover the daunting space over its center without spending a fortune and without filling the church with the necessary scaffolding—plus no one was sure whether they could create a dome that would hold up under its own weight. One of the many ridiculous solutions was making it of pumice (so it would be light) and filling the church with dirt studded with small coins. (After the work was done, the populace would be invited to dig for the money and thus remove the dirt.) Brunelleschi kept insisting he had the answer, but he wouldn't share it, fearful others would use his ideas and get the job over him.

After becoming so heated during several meetings of the Dome Erection Committee that he had to be carried out, he finally came in bearing an egg and issued a challenge (or so Vasari says). He bet he was the only one of the learned

Doors ✿ of the Baptistery to match the Gothic **South Doors** cast 65 years earlier by Andrea Pisano. The era's foremost Tuscan sculptors each designed and cast a bas-relief bronze panel depicting his own vision of The Sacrifice of Isaac. Twenty-two-year-old Lorenzo Ghiberti, competing against the likes of Donatello, Jacopo della

architects and councilmen in the room who could make an egg stand on its end. A marble slab was procured for the balancing act but, try as they might, the others couldn't get the egg to stay vertical. Brunelleschi took the egg in his hand, and with one quick movement slammed it down on the marble, smashing its end—but leaving it standing. The others protested that they, too, could have easily done that, to which Brunelleschi replied they would say the same thing if he showed them his plans for the dome. He was granted the commission and revealed his ingenious plan—which may have been inspired by close study of Rome's Pantheon.

He built the dome in two shells, the inner one thicker than the outer, both shells thinning as they neared the top, thus leaving the center hollow and removing a good deal of the weight. He also planned to construct the dome of giant vaults with ribs crossing over them, with each of the stones making up the actual fabric of the dome being dovetailed. In this way, the walls of the dome would support themselves as they were erected. In the process of building, Brunelleschi found himself as much an engineer as architect, constantly designing remarkable new winches, cranes, and hoists to carry the materials faster and more efficiently up to the level of the workmen. He was even farsighted enough to build in drainage systems for the rain and iron hooks to support interior scaffolding for future cleanings or paint jobs.

His finished work speaks for itself, 45m (150 ft.) wide at the base and 90m (300 ft.) high from drum to lantern—Florentines proudly claim they've lived their whole lives within sight of the dome. For his achievement, Brunelleschi was accorded a singular honor: He's the only person ever buried in Florence's cathedral, under his ingenious and revolutionary dome.

Quercia, and Filippo Brunelleschi, won hands down. He spent the next 21 years casting 28 bronze panels and building his doors. Although limited by his contract to design the scenes within Gothic frames as on Pisano's doors, Ghiberti infused his figures and compositions with an unmatched realism and classical references that helped define Renaissance sculpture. (Ghiberti stuck a self-portrait in the left door, the 4th head from the bottom of the middle strip, wearing a turban.)

The result so impressed the merchant's guild—not to mention the public and Ghiberti's fellow artists—they asked him in 1425 to do the **East Doors** 𝒜𝒜𝒜, facing the Duomo, this time giving him the artistic freedom to realize his Renaissance ambitions. Twenty-seven years later, just before his death, Ghiberti finished 10 dramatic life-like Old Testament scenes in gilded bronze, each a masterpiece of Renaissance sculpture and some of the finest low-relief perspective in Italian art. The panels now mounted here are excellent copies; the originals are displayed in the Museo dell'Opera del Duomo (see below). Years later, Michelangelo was standing before these doors and someone asked his opinion. His response sums up Ghiberti's life accomplishment as no art historian ever could: "They are so beautiful that they would grace the entrance to Paradise." They've been called the Gates of Paradise ever since.

The Baptistery is one of Florence's oldest, most venerated buildings. Florentines long believed it was originally a Roman temple, but it most likely was raised somewhere between the 4th and 7th centuries on the site of a Roman palace. The octagonal drum was rebuilt in the 11th century, and by the 13th century it had been clad in its characteristic green-and-white Romanesque stripes of marble and capped with its odd pyramid-like dome.

The interior is ringed with columns pilfered from ancient Roman buildings and is a spectacle of mosaics above and below. The floor was inlaid in 1209, and the ceiling was covered between 1225 and the early 1300s with glittering **mosaics** 𝒜𝒜. Most were crafted by Venetian or Byzantine-style workshops, which worked off designs drawn by the era's best artists. Coppo di Marcovaldo drew sketches for the over 7.8m (26-ft.) high, ape-toed Christ in Judgment and the Last Judgment that fills over a third of the ceiling.

To the right of the altar is the 1425 wall **tomb of Antipope John XXIII,** designed by Michelozzo and Donatello, who cast the bronze effigy of the deceased, deposed pontiff.

Piazza di San Giovanni. ✆ **055-230-2885.** www.operaduomo.firenze.it. Admission 3€ ($3.45), free for children under 6. Mon–Sat noon–6:30pm; Sun 8:30am–1:30pm. Bus: 1, 6, 17, 14, 22, 23, 36, 37, or 71.

Campanile di Giotto (Giotto's Bell Tower) 𝒜𝒜

In 1334, Giotto started the cathedral bell tower (clad in the same three colors of marble gracing the Duomo) but completed only the first two levels before his death in 1337. He was out of his league with the engineering aspects of architecture, and the tower was saved from falling in on itself by Andrea Pisano, who doubled the thickness of the walls. Andrea, a master sculptor of the Pisan Gothic school, also changed the design to add statue niches—he even carved a few of the statues himself—before quitting the project in 1348. Francesco Talenti finished the job between 1350 and 1359—he exchanged the heavy solidness of the base for a lighter, airier effect.

The **reliefs** and **statues** in the lower levels—by Andrea Pisano, Donatello, and others—are all copies, the weatherworn originals now housed in the Museo dell'Opera del Duomo (see below). You can climb the 414 steps to the top of the tower. What makes the 84m (25-ft.) high view different from what you get out of the more popular climb up the cathedral dome, besides a cityscape vista, are great views of the Baptistery as you ascend and the best close-up shot in the whole city of Brunelleschi's dome.

Piazza del Duomo. ✆ **055-230-2885.** www.operaduomo.firenze.it. Admission 6€ ($6.90). Daily 8:30am–6:50pm. Bus: 1, 6, 17, 14, 22, 23, 36, 37, or 71.

Museo dell'Opera del Duomo (Duomo Works Museum) 𝕽

This museum exists mainly to house the sculptures removed from the niches and doors of the Duomo group for restoration and preservation out of the elements. The dusty old museum was completely rearranged from 1998 to 2000.

The courtyard has now been enclosed so as to show off—under natural daylight, as they should be seen—Lorenzo Ghiberti's original gilded bronze panels from the Baptistery's *Gates of Paradise* 𝕽𝕽𝕽, which are being displayed as they're slowly restored. Ghiberti devoted 27 years to this project (1425–52), and you can now admire up close his masterpiece of *schiacciato* (squished) relief—using the Donatello technique of almost sketching in perspective to create the illusion of depth in low relief.

On the way up the stairs, you pass **Michelangelo's** *Pietà* 𝕽 (1548–55), his second and penultimate take on the subject, which the sculptor probably had in mind for his own tomb. The face of Nicodemus is a self-portrait, and Michelangelo most likely intended to leave much of the statue group only roughly carved, just as we see it. Art historians inform us that the polished figure of Mary Magdalene on the left was finished by one of Michelangelo's students, while storytellers relate that part of the considerable damage to the group was inflicted by the master himself when, in a moment of rage and frustration, he took a hammer to it.

The top floor of the museum houses the **Prophets** carved for the bell tower, the most noted of which are the remarkably expressive figures carved by Donatello: the drooping aged face of the *Beardless Prophet;* the sad fixed gaze of *Jeremiah;* and the misshapen ferocity of the bald ***Habakkuk*** ⚮ (known to Florentines as *Lo Zuccone*— pumpkin head). Mounted on the walls above are two putti-encrusted marble *cantorie* **(choir lofts).** The slightly earlier one (1431) on the entrance wall is by Luca della Robbia. His panels (the originals now displayed at eye level, with plaster casts set in the actual frame above) are in perfect early Renaissance harmony, both within themselves and with each other, and they show della Robbia's mastery of creating great depth within a shallow piece of stone. Across the room, Donatello's ***cantoria*** ⚮ (1433–38) takes off in a new artistic direction as his singing cherubs literally break through the boundaries of the "panels" to leap and race around the entire *cantoria* behind the mosaicked columns.

The room off the right stars one of Donatello's more morbidly fascinating sculptures, a late work in polychrome wood of ***The Magdalene*** ⚮ (1453–55), emaciated and veritably dripping with penitence.

The new exit corridor leading off from the Prophets room houses some of the **machines** used to build the cathedral dome, **Brunelleschi's death mask** as a grisly reminder of its architect, and the **wooden model proposals** for the cupola's drum and for the facade. The original Gothic facade was destroyed in 1587 to make room for one done in High Renaissance style, but the patron behind the work—Grand Duke Francesco de' Medici—died before he could choose from among the submissions by the likes of Giambologna and Bernardo Buontalenti. The Duomo remained faceless until purses of the 18th century, heavy with money and relentless bad taste, gave it the neo-Gothic facade we see today.

Piazza del Duomo 9 (directly behind the dome end of the cathedral). ℂ 055-230-2885. www.operaduomo.firenze.it. Admission 6€ ($6.90), free for children under 6. Mon–Sat 9am–7:30pm; Sun 9am–2pm; last admission 30 min. before close. Bus: 6, 11, 14, 17, or 23.

2 Around Piazza della Signoria

When the medieval Guelf party finally came out on top of the Ghibellines, they razed part of the old city center to build a new palace for civic government. It's said the Guelfs ordered architect Arnolfo di Cambio to build what we now call the Palazzo Vecchio in the corner of this space, but to be careful that not one inch of the building sat on the cursed former Ghibelline land. This odd legend was probably fabricated to explain Arnolfo's quirky off-center architecture.

The space around the palazzo became the new civic center of town, the L-shaped **Piazza della Signoria** 𝄢𝄢, named after the oligarchic ruling body of the medieval city. Today, it's an outdoor sculpture gallery, teeming with tourists, postcard stands, horses and buggies, and outdoor cafes.

The statuary on the piazza is particularly beautiful, starting on the far left (as you're facing the Palazzo Vecchio) with Giambologna's equestrian statue of *Grand Duke Cosimo I* (1594). To its right is one of Florence's favorite sculptures to hate, the *Fontana del Nettuno* (*Neptune Fountain;* 1560–75), created by Bartolomeo Ammannati as a tribute to Cosimo I's naval ambitions but nicknamed by the Florentines *Il Biancone,* "Big Whitey." Michelangelo, to whom many a Renaissance quip is attributed, took one look at it and shook his head, moaning "Ammannato, Ammannato, what a beautiful piece of marble you've ruined." The highly mannerist bronzes surrounding the basin are much better, probably because a young Giambologna had a hand in most of them.

Note the **porphyry plaque** set in the ground in front of the fountain. This marks the site where puritanical monk Savonarola held the Bonfire of the Vanities: With his fiery apocalyptic preaching, he whipped the Florentines into a reformist frenzy, and hundreds filed into this piazza, arms loaded with paintings, clothing, and other effects that represented their "decadence." They consigned it all to the flames of a roaring pile. However, after a few years the pope (not amused by Savonarola's criticisms) excommunicated first the monk and then the entire city for supporting him. On May 23, 1498, the Florentines decided they'd had enough of the rabid-dog monk, dragged him and two followers to the torture chamber, pronounced them heretics, and led them into the piazza for one last day of fire and brimstone. In the very spot where they once burnt their luxurious belongings, they put the torch to Savonarola himself. The event is commemorated by an anonymous painting kept in Savonarola's old cell in San Marco and by the plaque here.

To the right of the Neptune Fountain is a long, raised platform fronting the Palazzo Vecchio known as the *arringheria,* from which soapbox speakers would lecture to crowds before them (we get our word "harangue" from this). On its far left corner is a copy (original in the Bargello) of Donatello's **Marzocco,** symbol of the city, with a Florentine lion resting his raised paw on a shield emblazoned with the city's emblem, the *giglio* (lily). To its right is another Donatello replica, *Judith Beheading Holofernes.* Farther down is a man who needs little introduction, Michelangelo's *David,* a 19th-century copy of the original now in the Accademia. Near enough to David to look truly ugly in comparison is Baccio Bandinelli's *Heracles* (1534). Poor Bandinelli was trying to copy Michelangelo's muscular male form but ended up making his Heracles merely lumpy.

At the piazza's south end, beyond the long U that opens down the Uffizi, is one of the square's earliest and prettiest embellishments, the **Loggia dei Lanzi** ⟨R⟩⟨R⟩ (1376–82), named after the Swiss guard of lancers *(lanzi)* Cosimo de' Medici stationed here. The airy loggia was probably built on a design by Andrea Orcagna—spawning another of its many names, the Loggia di Orcagna (another is the Loggia della Signoria). The three huge arches of its simple, harmonious form were way ahead of the times, an architectural style that really belongs to the Renaissance. This open arcade is filled with statuary, though as we go to press much of it is encased in big wooden boxes as they restore the pieces. At the front left corner stands Benvenuto Cellini's masterpiece in bronze, *Perseus* ⟨R⟩⟨R⟩ (1545), holding out the severed Medusa's head before him, restored from 1996 to 2000. On the far right of the loggia has stood Giambologna's *Rape of the Sabines* ⟨R⟩⟨R⟩, one of the most successful mannerist sculptures in existence, a piece you must walk all the way around to appreciate, catching the action and artistry from different angles. Sadly, once it was boxed up and examined for restoration, authorities determined that the outdoors had wreaked intolerable damage, and the original statue will soon be removed to

---

Tips **Reserving Tickets for the Uffizi & Other Museums**

You can bypass the hours-long ticket line at the **Uffizi Galleries** by reserving a ticket and an entry time in advance by calling **Firenze Musei** at ⟨✆⟩ **055-294-883** (Mon–Fri 8:30am–6:30pm, Sat until 12:30pm) or at www.firenzemusei.it (24/7). By March, entry times can be booked more than a week in advance. You can also reserve for the **Accademia Gallery** (another interminable line, to see *David*), as well as the **Galleria Palatina** in the Pitti Palace, the **Bargello,** and several others. There is a 1.55€ ($1.80) fee (worth every penny), and you can pay by credit card.

the Accademia (to take the place of its plaster model long anchoring the museum's first room) with a marble copy to take its place here.

Across the piazza, on the north end at no. 5, is the **Raccolta della Ragione** (*©* **055-283-078**), a gallery of mainly late-19th- and 20th-century art with some nice second-story views over the piazza. Usually open Wednesday through Saturday from 9am to 4pm and Sunday from 8am to 1pm, the gallery is temporarily closed.

Gallerie degli Uffizi (Uffizi Galleries) 𝕬𝕬𝕬   The Uffizi is one of the world's great museums, and the single best introduction to Renaissance painting, with works by Giotto, Masaccio, Paolo Uccello, Sandro Botticelli, Leonardo da Vinci, Perugino, Michelangelo, Raphael Sanzio, Titian, Caravaggio, and the list goes on. The museum is deceptively small. What looks like a small stretch of gallery space can easily gobble up half a day—many rooms suffer the fate of containing nothing but masterpieces.

Know before you go that the Uffizi regularly shuts down rooms for crowd-control reasons—especially in summer, when the bulk of the annual 1.5 million visitors stampedes the place. Of the more than 3,100 artworks in the museum's archives, only about 1,700 are on exhibit. As they restore the building from the 1993 bombing (see "Rising from the Blast" below), they're also making new exhibition spaces available, but this process has taken years and we've yet to see these new exhibition spaces (just new ticketing and gift shop areas).

The painting gallery is housed in the structure built to serve as the offices (*uffizi* is Florentine dialect for *uffici,* or "offices") of the Medici, commissioned by Cosimo I from Giorgio Vasari in 1560— perhaps his greatest architectural work. The painting gallery was started by Cosimo I as well and is now housed in the second-floor rooms that open off a long hall lined with ancient statues and frescoed with grotesques.

The first room off to your left after you climb Vasari's monumental stairs (**Room 2;** Room 1 is perennially closed) presents you with a crash course in the Renaissance's roots. It houses three huge altarpieces by Tuscany's greatest late-13th-century masters. On the right is Cimabue's *Santa Trínita Maestà* (1280), still very much rooted in the Byzantine traditions that governed painting in the early Middle Ages—gold-leaf crosshatching in the drapery, an Eastern-style inlaid throne, spoonlike depressions above the noses, highly posed figures, and cloned angels with identical faces stacked up along the sides. On the left is Duccio's *Rucellai Maestà* (1285), painted by the master who studied with Cimabue and eventually

The Uffizi

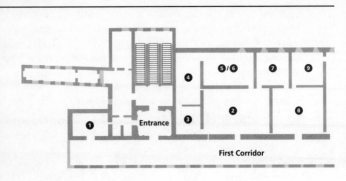

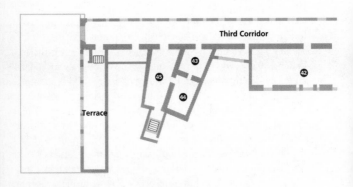

1	Archaeological Room	15	Leonardo da Vinci
2	Giotto & 13th-Century Paintings	16	Geographic Maps
3	Sienese Paintings (14th Century)	17	Ermafrodito
4	Florentine Paintings (14th Century)	18	The Tribune
5/6	International Gothic	19	Perugino & Signorelli
7	Early Renaissance	20	Dürer & German Artists
8	Filippo Lippi	21	Giovanni Bellini & Giorgione
9	Antonio del Pollaiolo	22	Flemish & German Paintings
10/14	Botticelli & Ghirlandaio	23	Mantegna & Correggio

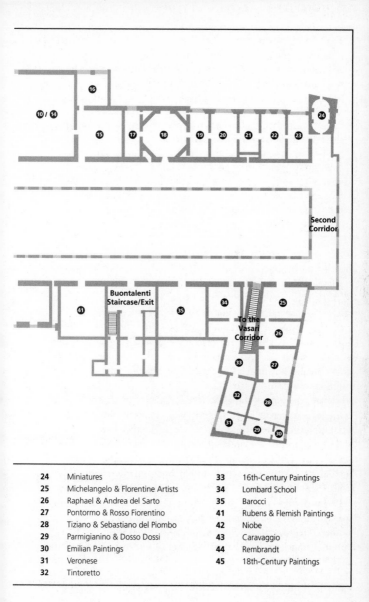

24	Miniatures	33	16th-Century Paintings
25	Michelangelo & Florentine Artists	34	Lombard School
26	Raphael & Andrea del Sarto	35	Barocci
27	Pontormo & Rosso Fiorentino	41	Rubens & Flemish Paintings
28	Tiziano & Sebastiano del Piombo	42	Niobe
29	Parmigianino & Dosso Dossi	43	Caravaggio
30	Emilian Paintings	44	Rembrandt
31	Veronese	45	18th-Century Paintings
32	Tintoretto		

Tips for Seeing the Uffizi

If you have the time, make two trips to the museum. On your first, concentrate on the first dozen or so rooms and pop by the Greatest Hits of the 16th Century, with works by Michelangelo, Caravaggio, Raphael, and Titian. Return later for a brief recap and continue with the rest of the gallery.

Be aware that the **gift shop** at the end of the galleries closes 20 minutes before the museum. You can visit it without reentering the museum at any time; if you plan to stay in the collections until closing, go down to the shop earlier during your visit and get the guards' attention before you pass through the exit turnstile, so they'll know you're just popping out to buy a few postcards and will recognize you when you ask to be let back in.

founded the Sienese school of painting. The style is still thoroughly medieval but introduces innovations into the rigid traditions. There's a little more weight to the Child Madonna holds, and the Madonna's face has a more human, somewhat sad, expression.

In the center of the room is Giotto's incredible *Ognissanti Maestà* ☆☆☆ (1310), by the man who's generally credited as the founding father of Renaissance painting. It's sometimes hard to appreciate just how much Giotto changed when he junked half the traditions of painting to go his own way. It's mainly in the very simple details, the sorts of things we take for granted in art today, such as the force of gravity, the display of basic emotions, the individual facial expressions, and the figures that look like they have an actual bulky body under their clothes. Giotto's Madonna sways slightly to one side, the fabric of her off-white shirt pulling realistically against her breasts as she twists. Instead of floating in mysterious space, Giotto's saints and angels stand on solid ground.

Room 3 pays homage to the 14th-century Sienese school with several delicately crafted works by Simone Martini and the Lorenzetti brothers. Here is Martini's *Annunciation* ☆ (1333). Note that Mary, who in so much art both before and after this period is depicted as meekly accepting her divine duty, looks reluctant, even disgusted, at the news of her imminent Immaculate Conception. Pietro and Ambrogio Lorenzetti helped revolutionize Sienese art and the Sienese school before succumbing to the Black Death in 1348. Of their work here, Ambrogio's 1342 *Presentation at the Temple* is the finest, with a rich use of color and a vast architectural space created to open up the temple in the background.

Room 4 houses the works of the 14th-century Florentine school, where you can clearly see the influence Giotto had on his contemporaries. **Rooms 5 and 6** represent the dying gasps of International Gothic, still grounded in medievalism but admitting a bit of the emergent naturalism and humanist philosophy into their works. Lorenzo Monaco's *Coronation of the Virgin* (1413) is particularly beautiful, antiquated in its styling but with a delicate suffused coloring.

In **Room 7,** the Renaissance proper starts taking shape, driven primarily by the quest of two artists, Paolo Uccello and Masaccio, for perfect perspective. On the left wall is Uccello's *Battle of San Romano* (1456), famously innovative but also rather ugly. This painting depicts one of Florence's great victories over rival Siena, but for Uccello it was more of an excuse to explore perspective—with which this painter was, by all accounts, positively obsessed.

In the far corner is the only example of Masaccio's art here (he died at 27), the *Madonna and Child with St. Anne,* which he helped

Rising from the Blast

On May 27, 1993, a car bomb ripped through the west wing of the Uffizi, seriously damaging it and some 200 works of art and destroying three (thankfully lesser) Renaissance paintings. The bomb killed five people inside, including the museum curator and her family. While everything from a Mafia hit to a government conspiracy was blamed, the motive for the bombing, and the perpetrators, remain unknown to this day.

In December 1998, Italy unveiled what it called the New Uffizi, a $15-million renovation that repaired all damaged rooms, added more than 20,000 square feet of new museum space, and displayed more than 100 works that had never been seen before—part of a larger project to triple exhibit space. Several branches of the book/gift shop were added to the ticketing areas on the ground floor, and the old outdoor cafe at the end of the galleries, atop the Loggia dei Lanzi with a view of the Palazzo Vecchio's tower, was reopened.

his master, Masolino, paint in 1424. Masaccio's earthy realism and sharp light are evident in the figures of Mary and the Child, as well as in the topmost angel peeking down. In the center of the room is Piero della Francesca's ***Portrait of Frederico da Montefeltro and Battista Sforza*** *GG*, painted around 1465 or 1470 and the only work by this remarkable Sansepolcran artist to survive in Florence. The fronts of the panels depict the famous duke of Urbino and his wife, while on the backs are horse-drawn carts symbolic of the pair's respective virtues. Piero's incredibly lucid style and modeling and the detailed Flemish-style backgrounds need no commentary, but do note he purposefully painted the husband and wife in full profile—without diluting the realism of a hooked nose and moles on the duke—and mounted them face to face, so they'll always gaze into each other's eyes.

Room 8 is devoted to Filippo Lippi, with more than half a dozen works by the lecherous monk who turned out rich religious paintings with an earthy quality and a three-dimensionality that make them immediately accessible. His most famous painting here is the *Madonna and Child with Two Angels* (1455–66). Also here are a few works by Filippo's illegitimate son, Filippino. **Room 9** is an interlude of virtuoso paintings by Antonio del Pollaiolo, plus a number of large Virtues by his less-talented brother, Piero. These two masters of anatomical verisimilitude greatly influenced the young Botticelli, three of whose early works reside in the room. This introduction to Botticelli sets us up for the next room, invariably crowded with tour-bus groups.

The walls separating **Rooms 10 to 14** were knocked down in the 20th century to create one large space to accommodate the resurgent popularity of Sandro Filipepi—better known by his nickname, Botticelli (little barrels)—master of willowy women in flowing gowns. Fourteen of his paintings line the walls, along with works by his pupil (and illegitimate son of his former teacher) Filippino Lippi and Domenico Ghirlandaio, Michelangelo's first artistic master. But everybody flocks here for just two paintings, Botticelli's *Birth of Venus* and his *Primavera (Allegory of Spring)*. Though in later life Botticelli was influenced by the puritanical preachings of Savonarola and took to cranking out boring Madonnas, the young painter began in grand pagan style. Both paintings were commissioned between 1477 and 1483 by a Medici cousin for his private villa, and they celebrate not only Renaissance art's love of naturalism but also the humanist philosophy permeating 15th-century Florence, a neo-Platonism that united religious doctrine with ancient ideology and mythological stories.

In the ***Birth of Venus*** 🐿️🐿️, the love goddess is born of the sea on a half shell, blown to shore by the Zephyrs. Ores, a goddess of the seasons, rushes to clothe her. Some say the long-legged goddess was modeled on Simonetta Vespucci, a renowned Florentine beauty, cousin to Amerigo (the naval explorer after whom America is named) and not-so-secret lover of Giuliano de' Medici, Lorenzo the Magnificent's brother). The ***Primavera*** 🐿️🐿️ is harder to evaluate, since contemporary research indicates it may not actually be an allegory of spring influenced by the humanist poetry of Poliziano but rather a celebration of Venus, who stands in the center, surrounded by various complicated references to Virtues through mythological characters. Also check out Botticelli's *Adoration of the Magi,* where the artist painted himself in the far right side, in a great yellow robe and golden curls.

Room 15 boasts Leonardo da Vinci's ***Annunciation*** 🐿️🐿️🐿️, which the young artist painted in 1472 or 1475 while still in the workshop of his master, Andrea del Verrocchio; however, he was already fully developed as an artist. The solid yet light figures and sfumato airiness blurring the distance render remarkably life-like figures somehow suspended in a surreal dreamscape. Leonardo helped Verrocchio on the *Baptism of Christ*—most credit the artist-in-training with the angel on the far left as well as the landscape, and a few art historians think they see his hand in the figure of Jesus as well. The *Adoration of the Magi,* which Leonardo didn't get much beyond the sketching stage, shows how he could retain powerful compositions even when creating a fantasy landscape of ruinous architecture and incongruous horse battles. The room also houses works by Lorenzo di Credi and Piero di Cosimo, fellow 15th-century maestros, and a *Pietà* that shows Perugino's solid plastic style of studied simplicity. (This Umbrian master would later pass it on to his pupil Raphael.) Uffizi officials use **Room 18, the Tribune,** as a crowd-control pressure valve. You may find yourself stuck shuffling around it slowly, staring at the mother-of-pearl discs lining the domed ceiling, studying the antique statues, such as the famous *Medici Venus* (a 1st-c. B.C. Roman copy of a Greek original), and scrutinizing the Medici portraits wallpapering the room. The latter include many by the talented early baroque artist Agnolo Bronzino, whose portrait of ***Eleonora of Toledo*** 🐿️, wife of Cosimo I, with their son Giovanni de' Medici (1545), is particularly well worked. It shows her in a satin dress embroidered and sewn with velvet and pearls. When the Medici tombs were opened in 1857, her body was found buried in this same dress (it's now in the Pitti Palace's costume museum).

Also here are Raphael's late *St. John the Baptist in the Desert* (1518) and mannerist Rosso Fiorentino's 1522 *Angel Musician*, where an insufferably cute little *putto* (cherub) plucks at an oversize lute—it's become quite the Renaissance icon in the recent spate of angel mania.

Room 19 is devoted to both Perugino, who did the luminous *Portrait of Francesco delle Opere* (1494), and Luca Signorelli, whose *Holy Family* (1490–95) was painted as a tondo set in a rectangle, with allegorical figures in the background and a torsion of the figures that were to influence Michelangelo's version (in a later room). **Room 20** is devoted to Dürer, Cranach, and other German artists who worked in Florence, while **Room 21** takes care of 16th-century Venetians Giovanni Bellini, Giorgione, and Carpaccio. In **Room 22** are Flemish and German works by Hans Holbein the Younger, Hans Memling, and others, and **Room 23** contains Andrea Mantegna's triptych of the *Adoration of the Magi, Circumcision, and Ascension* (1463–70), showing his excellent draftsmanship and fascination with classical architecture. Now we move into the west wing, still in the throes of restoration following the bombing (see "Rising from the Blast" above). **Room 25** is overpowered by Michelangelo's **Holy Family** ✸✸✸ (1506–08), one of the few panel paintings by the great master. The glowing colors and shocking nudes in the background seem to pop off the surface, and the torsion of the figures was to be taken up as the banner of the mannerist movement. Michelangelo also designed the elaborate frame.

Room 26 is devoted to Andrea del Sarto and High Renaissance darling Raphael. Of Raphael we have the *Madonna of the Goldfinch* (1505), a work he painted in a Leonardesque style for a friend's wedding, and several important portraits, including *Pope Leo X with Cardinals Giulio de' Medici and Luigi de' Rossi* and *Pope Julius II,* as well as a famous *Self-portrait.* Del Sarto was the most important painter in Florence in the early 16th century, while Michelangelo and Raphael were off in Rome. His consciously developed mannerist style is evident in his masterful *Madonna of the Harpies* (1515–17).

Room 27 is devoted to works by Del Sarto's star mannerist pupils, Rosso Fiorentino and Pontormo, and by Pontormo's adopted son, Bronzino. Fiorentino's **Moses Defends the Daughters of Jethro** ✸ (1523) owes much to Michelangesque nudes but is also wholly original in the use of harsh lighting that reduces the figures to basics shapes of color.

Room 28 is split between honoring the great Venetian Titian, of whose works you'll see a warm full-bodied *Flora* 🌹🌹 and a poetic *Venus of Urbino* 🌹 languishing on her bed; Sienese High Renaissance painter Sebastiano del Piombo (his *Death of Adonis* and *Portrait of a Woman* are both strong works); and a few mediocre works by Palma il Vecchio.

Tiny **Rooms 29-30,** ostensibly honoring works by several Emilian artists, are totally dominated by late mannerist master Il Parmigianino, who carried the mannerist movement to its logical extremes with the almost grotesquely elongated bodies of the *Madonna of the Long Neck* 🌹 (1534). **Room 31** continues to chart the fall of painting into decorative grace with Paolo Veronese's *Martyrdom of St. Justine* (1573), which is less about the saint being stabbed than it is a sartorial study in fashion design.

Room 32 is a nice break provided by the dramatic and visible brushstrokes that boldly swirled rich, somber colors of several lesser works by Venetian master Tintoretto. All the better, as these must see you through the treacle and tripe of **Rooms 33-34,** stuffed with substandard examples of 16th century paintings by the likes of Vasari, Alessandro Allori, and other chaps who grew up in Michelangelo's shadow and desperately wished they could paint like him (note: They couldn't).

Popping back out in the main corridor again, you visit the last several rooms one at a time as each opens off the hall. **Room 35** features the taffeta, cotton candy oeuvre of baroque weirdo Frederico Barocci (whose works are currently coming into vogue—why, I've no idea). Continue right past that exit staircase, because they save a few eye-popping rooms for the very end.

Room 41 is all about Rubens and his famously ample nudes, along with some works by his Flemish cohorts (Van Dyck, Sustermans). **Room 42** is a lovely side hall flooded with sunlight and graced by more than a dozen Roman statues that are copies of Hellenic originals, most of them of the dying Niobids.

And so we come to **Room 43** and the caravaggieschi. Caravaggio was the baroque master of *chiaroscuro*—painting with extreme harsh light and deep shadows. The Uffizi preserves his painting of the severed head of *Medusa,* a *Sacrifice of Isaac,* and his famous *Bacchus* 🌹🌹. Caravaggio's work influenced a generation of artists—the caravaggieschi—including Artemisia Gentileschi, the only female painter to make a name for herself in the late Renaissance/early baroque. Artemisia was eclipsed in fame by her slightly less talented father, Orazio, and she was the victim and central figure in a sensational rape trial brought against Orazio's onetime collaborator. It evidently had an effect on her professional life; among her paintings here is the violent *Judith Slaying Holofernes*.

Duck through the end of this room to pay your respects to Rembrandt in **Room 44,** where he immortalized himself in two *Self-portraits,* one done as a youth and the other as an old man. Hang a right to exit back into the corridor again via **Room 45,** a bit of a letdown after the last two rooms, but still engaging (if you've any art-appreciation energies left after all this) for its Greatest Hits of the 18th Century artists—Giuseppe Maria Crespi, Giovanni Paolo Pannini, Il Canaletto, Francesco Guardi, and Tiepolo—plus a Spanish twist to end it all with two paintings by Francisco Goya.

That's it. The Uffizi is finished. Treat yourself to a cappuccino alfresco in the loggia-top bar just beyond the last room; you've earned it.

Did I say finished? Not quite. Cosimo I de' Medici, after he moved to the Pitti Palace across the river in the Oltrarno, needed a way to get to and from his home and his office without mingling with the peons on the streets. So he had Giorgio Vasari build him the **Corridorio Vasariano (Vasarian Corridor)** in 1565. It took only 5 months to complete this aboveground tunnel running along the Arno, across the tops of the Ponte Vecchio shops, and then zigzagging its way to the Pitti. The corridor, hung with paintings and poked through with lots of windows, has finally reopened to visitors. (Following the 1993 bombing it was closed for restoration and rearrangement.) Tours of the corridor are available on Tuesday and Wednesday and Friday through Sunday. Call © 055-265-4321 for required reservations.

Piazzale degli Uffizi 6 (off Piazza della Signoria). © **055-238-8651,** or © 055-294-883 to reserve tickets. www.uffizi.firenze.it (gallery info), or www.firenzemusei. it (to reserve tickets). Admission 8.50€ ($9.80). Tues–Sun 8:15am–7pm. Ticket window closes 45 min. before museum. Bus: A, B, 23, or 71.

Palazzo Vecchio 🏛 Florence's imposing fortresslike town hall was built from 1299 to 1302 on the designs of Arnolfo di Cambio, Gothic master builder of the city. Arnolfo managed to make it solid and impregnable-looking yet still graceful, with thin-columned Gothic windows and two orders of crenellations—square for the main rampart and swallow-tailed on the 94m (313-ft.) high bell tower.

The palace was once home to the various Florentine republican governments (and today to the municipal government). Cosimo I and his ducal Medici family moved to the palazzo in 1540 and engaged in massive redecoration. Michelozzo's 1453 **courtyard** just through the door was left architecturally intact but frescoed by Vasari with scenes of Austrian cities to celebrate the 1565 marriage of Francesco de' Medici and Joanna of Austria. The grand staircase leads up to the **Sala dei Cinquecento,** named for the 500-man assembly that met here in the pre-Medici days of the Florentine Republic and site of the greatest fresco cycle that ever wasn't. Leonardo da Vinci was commissioned in 1503 to paint one long wall with a battle scene celebrating a famous Florentine victory. He was always trying new methods and materials and decided to mix wax into his pigments. Leonardo had finished painting part of the wall, but it wasn't drying fast enough, so he brought in braziers stoked with hot coals to try to hurry the process. As others watched in horror, the wax in the fresco melted under the intense heat and the colors ran down the walls to puddle on the floor. Michelangelo never even got past making the preparatory drawings for the fresco he was supposed to paint on the opposite wall—Pope Julius II called him to Rome to paint the Sistine Chapel, and the master's sketches were destroyed by eager young artists who came to study them and took away scraps. Eventually, the bare walls were covered by Vasari and assistants from 1563 to 1565 with blatantly subservient frescoes exalting Cosimo I de' Medici and his dynasty.

Off the corner of the room (to the right as you enter) is the **Studiolo di Francesco I,** a claustrophobic study in which Cosimo's eldest son and heir performed his alchemy and science experiments and where baroque paintings hide secret cupboards. Against the wall of the Sala dei Cinquecento, opposite the door you enter, is Michelangelo's statue of *Victory* ✯, carved from 1533 to 1534 for the Julius II tomb but later donated to the Medici. Its extreme torsion—the way the body twists and spirals upward—was to be a great influence on the mannerist movement.

The first series of rooms on the second floor is the **Quartiere degli Elementi,** again frescoed by Vasari. The **Terrazza di Saturno,** in the corner, has a view over the Uffizi to the hills across the Arno. Crossing the balcony overlooking the Sala dei Cinquecento, you enter the **Apartments of Eleonora di Toledo,** decorated for Cosimo's Spanish wife. Her small private chapel is a masterpiece of mid-16th-century painting by Bronzino. Farther on, under the sculpted ceiling of the **Sala dei Gigli,** are Domenico Ghirlandaio's fresco of *St. Zeno-bius Enthroned* with ancient Roman heroes and Donatello's original *Judith and Holofernes* ⚜ bronze (1455), one of his last works.

During the summer evening hours, the following sections, normally closed, are open: the **Loeser Collections,** with paintings by Pietro Lorenzetti and Bronzino and sculptures by Tino di Camaino and Jacopo Sansovino, and, perhaps more fun, the outdoor **Balustrade** running around the roof behind the crenellations—it offers a unique panorama of the city and the piazza below.

Piazza della Signoria. ℰ **055-276-8465.** Admission 6€ ($6.90). Fri–Wed 9am–7pm; Thurs 9am–2pm. Bus: A, B, 23, or 71.

Ponte Vecchio (Old Bridge) ⚜⚜⚜

The oldest and most famous bridge across the Arno, the Ponte Vecchio we know today was built in 1345 by Taddeo Gaddi to replace an earlier version. The characteristic overhanging shops have lined the bridge since at least the 12th century. In the 16th century, it was home to butchers until Cosimo I moved into the Palazzo Pitti across the river. He couldn't stand the stench as he crossed the bridge from on high in the Corridorio Vasariano every day, so he evicted the meat cutters and moved in the classier gold- and silversmiths, tradesmen who occupy the bridge to this day.

A bust of the most famous Florentine goldsmith, the swashbuckling autobiographer and *Perseus* sculptor Benvenuto Cellini, stands off to the side of the bridge's center, in a small piazza overlooking the Arno. From this vantage point Mark Twain, spoiled by the Mighty Mississippi, once wryly commented, "It is popular to admire the Arno. It is a great historical creek, with four feet in the channel and some scows floating about. It would be a very plausible river if they would pump some water into it. They call it a river, and they honestly think it is a river . . . They even help out the delusion by building bridges over it. I do not see why they are too good to wade."

The Ponte Vecchio's fame saved it in 1944 from the Nazis, who had orders to blow up all the bridges before retreating out of Florence as Allied forces advanced. They couldn't bring themselves to reduce this span to rubble—so they blew up the ancient buildings on either end instead to block it off. The Arno flood of 1966 wasn't so discriminating, however, and severely damaged the shops. Apparently, a private night watchman saw the waters rising alarmingly and called many of the goldsmiths at home, who rushed to remove their valuable stock before it was washed away.

Via Por Santa Maria/Via Guicciardini. Bus: B or D.

Museo di Storia della Scienza (Science Museum) 🦋 The mainframe computer and multifunction calculator don't hold a candle to this collection's beautifully engraved intricate mechanical instruments. Galileo and his ilk practiced a science that was an art form of the highest aesthetic order. The cases display such beauties as a mechanical calculator from 1664—a gleaming bronze sandwich of engraved disks and dials—and an architect's compass and plumb disguised as a dagger, complete with sheath.

In the field of astronomy, the museum has the lens with which Galileo discovered four of the moons of Jupiter (which he promptly and prudently named after his Medici patrons) and, alongside telescopes of all sizes and complexity, a tiny "lady's telescope" made of ivory that once came in a box of beauty products. There's also a somewhat grisly room devoted to medicine, with disturbingly realistic wax models of just about everything that can go wrong during childbirth. And what Italian institution would be complete without a holy relic? In this case, it's the middle finger of Galileo's right hand, swiped while he was en route to reinterment in Santa Croce. He was allowed burial in a Christian church only in the 18th century, after he was posthumously vindicated against the Inquisition for supporting a heliocentric view of the universe.

Piazza dei Giudici 1 (next to the Uffizi at the Arno end of Via dei Castellani). 𝄞 055-265-311. www.imss.fi.it. Admission 6.50€ ($7.50) adults, 4.50€ ($5.20) ages 15–25, free for ages 6–14 and over 65. June–Sept Mon and Wed–Fri 9:30am–5pm, Tues and Sat 9:30am–1pm, last Thurs of June and Aug, and 1st Thurs of July and Sept 9–11pm; Oct–May Mon and Wed–Sat 9:30am–5pm, Tues 9:30am–1pm, and 2nd Sun of every month 10am–1pm. Bus: 23.

Orsanmichele 🦋🦋 This tall structure halfway down Via dei Calzaiuoli looks more like a Gothic warehouse than a church—which is exactly what it was, built as a granary/grain market in 1337. After a miraculous image of the Madonna appeared on a column inside, however, the lower level was turned into a chapel. The city's merchant guilds each undertook the task of decorating one of the outside nichelike Gothic tabernacles around the lower level with a statue of their guild's patron saint. Masters such as Ghiberti, Donatello, Verrocchio, and Giambologna all cast or carved masterpieces to set here. Since 1984, these have been removed and are being replaced by casts as the originals are slowly cleaned and exhibited up on the second story.

Unfortunately, the church now keeps erratic hours due to a lack of personnel, so there are no set opening hours; however, you may get lucky and find the doors thrown open when you pass by (or, though this may take even more luck, someone might actually answer the phone number below and give you details on when it will next open). Since it's pretty nifty, and there's a chance you'll be able to pop in, I'll go ahead and describe it all.

In the chapel's dark interior (emerged in 1999 from a long restoration and entered around the "back" side on Via dell'Arte della Lana) are recently restored 14th- to 16th-century paintings by the likes of Lorenzo di Credi and Il Poppi. The elaborate Gothic **Tabernacle** 𝖗 (1349–59) by Andrea Orcagna looks something like a miniature church, covered with statuettes, enamels, inset colored marbles and glass, and reliefs. It protects a luminous 1348 *Madonna and Child* painted by Giotto's student Bernardo Daddi. The prominent statue of the *Madonna, Child, and St. Anne* to its left is by Francesco da Sangallo (1522).

Across Via dell'Arte della Lana from the Orsanmichele's main entrance is the 1308 Palazzo dell'Arte della Lana. This Gothic palace was home to medieval Florence's most powerful body, the guild of wool merchants, which employed about one third of Florence in the 13th and 14th centuries. Up the stairs inside you can cross over the hanging walkway to the first floor (American 2nd floor) of Orsanmichele. These are the old granary rooms, now housing a **museum of the statues** 𝖗 that once surrounded the exterior. A few are still undergoing restoration, but eight of the original sculptures are here, well labeled, including Donatello's marble *St. Mark* (1411–13); Ghiberti's bronze *St. John the Baptist* (1413–16), the first life-size bronze of the Renaissance; and Verrocchio's *Incredulity of St. Thomas* (1473–83). This museum, too, does not always adhere to its posted hours, as those are dependent on someone being around to honor them. Still, it's at least worth a try.

Via Arte della Lana 1/Via de' Calzaiuoli. ℂ **055-284-944.** Free admission. Church open erratic hours (though never open during *riposo*). Museum daily 9–9:45am, 10–10:45am, 11–11:45am (plus Sat–Sun 1–1:45pm); closed the 1st and last Mon of month. Bus: A.

Museo Nazionale del Bargello (Bargello Museum) 𝖗𝖗

Inside this 1255 Gothic palazzo is Florence's premier sculpture museum, with works by Michelangelo, the della Robbias, and Donatello.

In the palazzo's old **armory** are 16th-century works, including some of Michelangelo's earliest sculptures. Carved by a 22-year-old Michelangelo while he was visiting Rome, *Bacchus* 𝖗𝖗 (1497) was obviously inspired by the classical antiquities he studied there but is also imbued with his own irrepressible Renaissance realism—here is a (young) God of Wine who's actually drunk, reeling back on unsteady knees and holding the cup aloft with a distinctly tipsy wobble. Michelangelo polished and finished this marble in the traditional manner, but from 1503 to 1505, soon after finishing his famous *David* with a high polish, he carved the ***Pitti Tondo*** 𝕲 here, a *schiacciato* Madonna and Child scene in which the artist began using the textures of the partially worked marble itself to convey his artistic message. One of his weaker works here is the so-called *Apollo-David* (art historians can't agree on which hero the unfinished work was meant to be), but the master is back in top form with the bust of *Brutus* (ca. 1539). Some people like to see in this sculpture an idealized portrait of Michelangelo himself; a more accurate and less contentious representation sits nearby, the famous and oft-cast bronze bust of *Michelangelo* by his pupil Daniele da Volterra. Also in this room is Giambologna's ***Flying Mercury*** 𝕲 (ca. 1564), looking for all the world as if he's on the verge of taking off from the ground—justifiably one of this mannerist's masterpieces.

The palazzo's inner **courtyard**—one of the few medieval cortile in Florence to survive in more-or-less its original shape—is studded with the coats of arms of various past *podestà* and other notables. The grand stairwell leads up to a second-story loggia filled with a flock of whimsical bronze birds cast by Giambologna for the Medici's gardens. The doorway leads into the old **Salone del Consiglio Generale (General Council Room)** 𝕲𝕲, a vast space with a high ceiling filled with glazed terra-cotta Madonnas by Luca della Robbia and his clan, and some of the most important sculptures of the early Renaissance.

Donatello dominates the room, starting with a mischievously smiling *Cupid* (ca. 1430–40). Nearby is his polychrome bust of *Niccolò da Uzzano,* a bit of hyperrealism next to two much more delicate busts of elfin-featured characters by Desiderio da Settignano. Donatello sculpted the *Marzocco,* lion symbol of the Florentine Republic, out of *pietra serena* between 1418 and 1420. The marble *David* (1408) is an early Donatello, but the bronze ***David*** 𝕲𝕲 (1440–50) beyond it is a much more mature piece, the first freestanding nude since antiquity. The figure is a nubile, almost erotic youth, with a shy, detached air that has little to do with the giant severed head at his feet. Against the far wall is *St. George* 𝕲, carved in 1416 for a niche of Orsanmichele. The relief below it of the saint slaying his dragon is an early example of the sculptor's patented *schiacciato* technique, using thinly etched lines and perspective to create great depth in a very shallow space.

In the back right corner of this room are two bronze relief panels by Brunelleschi and Ghiberti of the *Sacrifice of Isaac,* finalists in the famous 1401 competition for the commission to cast the Baptistery's doors (see "A Man & His Dome" on p. 102). Ghiberti's panel won for the greater dynamism and flowing action in his version.

Out the other end of the room is the **Islamic Collection,** a testament to Florence's wide and profitable trade network. Decorative arts from the Roman era through the 16th century fill the long corridor, at the end of which is the small **Cappella Maddalena,** where condemned prisoners spent their last moments praying for their souls; it was frescoed by Giotto's studio. A perpendicular corridor houses the largest collection of ivories in the world, from the 5th to the 17th centuries.

Upstairs are rooms with glazed terra cottas by Andrea and Giovanni della Robbia and another room devoted to the sculptural production of Leonardo da Vinci's teacher Verrocchio, including yet another *David* (1465), a haughty youth with a tousle of hair inspired by the Donatello version downstairs.

Via del Proconsolo 4. (℅) **055-238-8606**. www.sbas.firenze.it. (Reserve tickets at (℅) 055-294-883 or www.firenzemusei.it.) Admission 4€ ($4.60). Daily 8:30am–1:50pm. Closed 2nd and 4th Mon and 1st, 3rd, and 5th Sun of each month. Bus: A, 14, or 23.

Badia Fiorentina   The slender pointed bell tower of this Benedictine abbey founded in A.D. 978 is one of the landmarks of the Florentine skyline. Sadly, the bells Dante wrote of in his *Paradiso* no longer toll the hours. Serious structural problems have silenced the tower. In the now-baroque interior, some say Dante first laid eyes on his beloved Beatrice, and Boccaccio, of *Decameron* fame, used to lecture on Dante's Divine Comedy here. The church's most arresting sight is a 1485 Filippino Lippi painting of the *Madonna Appearing to St. Bernard.* The box to shed light on it parcels out a measly 10 seconds for each coin, so feed it only the smallest pieces. For a nominal "donation," the sacristan will throw on the lights to the *trompe l'oeil* ceiling.

Via Dante Alighieri and Via del Proconsolo. (℅) **055-287-389**. Free admission. Thurs–Tues 5–7pm (sometimes also in the morning). Bus: A, 14, or 23.

Santa Trínita   Beyond Bernardo Buontalenti's late-16th-century **facade** lies a dark church, rebuilt in the 14th century but founded by the Vallombrosans before 1177. The third chapel on the right has what remains of the detached frescoes by Spinello Aretino (viewable by push-button light), which were found under Lorenzo Monaco's excellent 1422 frescoes covering the next chapel down.

In the right transept, Domenico Ghirlandaio frescoed the **Cappella Sassetti** ✦ in 1483 with a cycle on the *Life of St. Francis* (coin-op lights), but true to form he set all the scenes against Florentine backdrops and peopled them with portraits of the notables of the day. The most famous is *Francis Receiving the Order from Pope Honorius,* which in this version takes place under an arcade on the north side of Piazza della Signoria—the Loggia dei Lanzi is featured in the middle, and on the left is the Palazzo Vecchio. (The Uffizi between them hadn't been built yet.) It's also full of contemporary portraits: In the little group on the far right, the unhandsome man with the light red cloak is Lorenzo the Magnificent.

The chapel to the right of the main altar houses the miraculous **Crucifix** that once hung in San Miniato al Monte. One day the nobleman Giovanni Gualberto was storming up the hillside in a rage, on his way to wreak revenge on his brother's murderer. Gualberto paused at San Miniato and after some reflection decided to pardon the assassin, whereupon this crucifix bowed its head in approval. Gualberto went on to found the Vallombrosan order of monks, who later established this church.

The south end of the piazza leads to the **Ponte Santa Trínita,** one of Italy's most graceful bridges. In 1567, Ammannati built a span here that was set with four 16th-century statues of the seasons in honor of the marriage of Cosimo II. After the Nazis blew up the bridge in 1944, it was rebuilt, and all was set into place again—save the head on the statue of Spring, which remained lost until a team dredging the river in 1961 found it by accident. From the bridge you get a great view upriver of the Ponte Vecchio and downriver of the **Ponte alla Carraia** (another postwar reconstruction), where in 1304 so many people gathered to watch a floating production of Dante's *Inferno* that it collapsed and all were drowned. Florentine wits were quick to point out that all the people who went to see Hell that day found what they were looking for.

Piazza Santa Trínita. ℂ **055-216-912.** Free admission. Mon–Sat 8am–noon and 4–6pm; Sun 4–6pm. Bus: A, B, 6, 11, 36, 37, or 68.

3 Around San Lorenzo & the Mercato Centrale

The church of San Lorenzo is practically lost behind the leather stalls and souvenir carts of Florence's vast **San Lorenzo street market** (see chapter 6). In fact, the hawking of wares and bustle of commerce is what characterizes all the streets of this neighborhood, centered around both the church and the nearby **Mercato Centrale food market.** This is a colorful scene, but one of the most pickpocket-happy in the city, so be wary.

San Lorenzo ⚔ A rough brick anti-facade and the undistin-guished stony bulk of a building surrounded by the stalls of the leather market hide what is most likely the oldest church in Florence, founded in A.D. 393. San Lorenzo was the city's cathedral until the bishop's seat moved to Santa Reparata (later to become the Duomo) in the 7th century. More important, it was the Medici family's parish church, and as those famous bankers began to accumulate their vast fortune, they started a tradition of lavishing it on this church that lasted until the clan died out in the 18th century. Visiting the entire church complex at once is tricky: Though inter-connected, the church proper, the Old Sacristy, and the Laurentian Library have different open hours. The Medici tombs, listed sepa-rately below, have a separate entrance around the back of the church and have still different hours.

The first thing Giovanni di Bicci de' Medici, founder of the fam-ily fortune, did for the church was hire Brunelleschi to tune up the **interior,** rebuilding according to the architect's plans in 1426. At the end of the aisle is a Desiderio da Settignano marble tabernacle that's a mastery of *schiacciato* relief and carefully incised perspective. Across the aisle is one of the two bronze 1460 **pulpits** ⚔⚔—the other is across the nave—that were Donatello's last works. His patron and the first great consolidator of Medici power, which at this early stage still showed great concern for protecting the interests of the people, was Cosimo il Vecchio, Lorenzo the Magnificent's grandfather. Cosimo, whose wise behind-the-scenes rule made him popular with the Florentines, died in 1464 and is buried in front of the high altar. The plaque marking the spot is simply inscribed PATER PATRIAE—father of his homeland.

Off the left transept is the **Sagrestia Vecchia (Old Sacristy)** ⚔, one of Brunelleschi's purest pieces of early Renaissance architecture. In the center of the chapel Cosimo il Vecchio's parents, Giovanni di Bicci de' Medici and his wife, Piccarda Bueri, rest in peace.

On the wall of the left aisle is Bronzino's huge fresco of the *Martyrdom of San Lorenzo* ⚔. The 3rd-century namesake saint of this church, San Lorenzo was a flinty early Christian and the treasurer of the Roman church. When commanded by the Romans to hand over the church's wealth, Lorenzo appeared before Emperor Valerian's prefect with "thousands" of sick, poor, and crippled people saying "Here is all the church's treasure." The Romans weren't amused and decided to martyr him on a gridiron over hot coals. Feisty to the last, at one point while Lorenzo lay there roasting he called out to his tormentors through gritted teeth, "Turn me over, I'm done on this side."

Near this fresco is an entrance to the cloister and just inside it a stairwell to the right leading up to the **Biblioteca Laurenziana (Laurentian Library)** 𝕲𝕲, which can also be entered admission free without going through—and paying for—the church (the separate entrance is just to the left of the church's main doors). Michelangelo designed this library in 1524 to house the Medici's manuscript collection, and it stands as one of the most brilliant works of mannerist architecture. The vestibule is a whacked-out riff on the Renaissance, all *pietra serena* and white plaster walls like a good Brunelleschi piece, but turned inside out. There are phony piers running into each other in the corners, pilaster strips that support nothing, and brackets that exist for no reason. On the whole, however, it manages to remain remarkably coherent. Its star feature is a *pietra serena* flight of curving stairs flowing out from the entrance to the reading room. This actual library part, however—filled with intricately carved wood and handsomely illuminated manuscripts—was closed indefinitely in 1999 until "urgent maintenance" is completed.

Piazza San Lorenzo. ✆ **055-216-634**. Admission 2.50€ ($2.90). Church Mon–Sat 10am–5pm. Old Sacristy (usually) Sept–July Mon, Wed, Fri, and Sat 10–11:45am; Tues and Thurs 4–5:45pm. Laurentian Library Mon–Sat 9am–1pm. Bus: 1, 6, 7, 11, 14, 17, 23, 67, 68, 70, or 71.

Cappelle Medicee (Medici Chapels) 𝕲𝕲

When Michelangelo built the New Sacristy between 1520 and 1533 (finished by Vasari in 1556), it was to be a tasteful monument to Lorenzo the Magnificent and his generation of fairly pleasant Medici. When work got underway on the Chapel of the Princes in 1604, it was to become one of the world's most god-awful and arrogant memorials, dedicated to the grand dukes, some of Florence's most decrepit tyrants. The **Cappella dei Principi (Chapel of the Princes)** 𝕲 is an exercise in bad taste, a mountain of cut marbles and semiprecious stones—jasper, alabaster, mother-of-pearl, agate, and the like—slathered onto the walls and ceiling with no regard for composition and still less for chromatic unity. The pouring of ducal funds into this monstrosity began in 1604 and lasted until the rarely conscious Gian Gastone de' Medici drank himself to death in 1737 without an heir—but teams kept doggedly at the thing, and they were still finishing the floor in 1962. The tombs of the grand dukes in this massive marble mistake were designed by Pietro Tacca in the 17th century, and off to the left and right of the altar are small treasuries full of gruesome holy relics in silver-bedecked cases. The dome of the structure, seen from the outside, is one of Florence's landmarks, a kind of infant version of the Duomo's.

Michelangelo's **Sagrestia Nuova (New Sacristy)** 𝔊𝔊, built to jibe with Brunelleschi's Old Sacristy in San Lorenzo proper, is much calmer. (An architectural tidbit: The windows in the dome taper as they get near the top to fool you into thinking the dome is higher.) Michelangelo was supposed to produce three tombs here (perhaps four) but ironically got only the two less important ones done. So Lorenzo de' Medici the Magnificent—wise ruler of his city, poet of note, grand patron of the arts, and moneybags behind much of the Renaissance—ended up with a mere inscription of his name next to his brother Giuliano's on a plain marble slab against the entrance wall. Admittedly, they did get one genuine Michelangelo sculpture to decorate their slab, a *Madonna and Child* that's perhaps the master's most beautiful version of the theme (the other two statues are later works by less talented sculptors).

On the left wall of the sacristy is Michelangelo's **Tomb of Lorenzo** 𝔊, duke of Urbino (and Lorenzo the Magnificent's grandson), whose seated statue symbolizes the contemplative life. Below him on the elongated curves of the tomb stretch *Dawn* (female) and

The Master's Doodles

On the walls around the small altar in the Medici Chapels are some recently uncovered architectural graffiti that have been attributed to Michelangelo. Even more important are some 50 charcoal drawings and sketches the master left on the walls in the sepulchral chamber below. The drawings include a sketch of the legs of Duke Giuliano, Christ risen, and the Laocoön. Michelangelo found himself hiding out here after the Medici reconquered the city in 1530—he had helped the city keep the dukes out with his San Miniato defenses and, probably rightly, feared a reprisal. You need an appointment to see the sketches; ask at the ticket office.

Dusk (male), a pair of Michelangelo's most famous sculptures, where he uses both high polish and rough cutting to impart strength, texture, and psychological suggestion to the allegorical works. This pair mirrors the similarly fashioned and equally important *Day* (male) and *Night* (female) across the way. One additional point *Dawn* and *Night* bring out is that Michelangelo really wasn't too adept at the female body—he just produced softer, less muscular men with slightly elongated midriffs and breasts sort of tacked on at funny angles.

Piazza Madonna degli Aldobrandini (behind San Lorenzo, where Via Faenza and Via del Giglio meet). (*C*) **055-238-8602;** call Firenze Musei (*C*) 055-294-883 for reservations. Admission 6€ ($6.90). Daily 8:15am–5pm. Closed 1st, 3rd, and 5th Mon and 2nd and 4th Sun of each month. Bus: 1, 6, 7, 11, 14, 17, 23, 67, 68, 70, or 71.

Palazzo Medici-Riccardi ⟡ The Palazzo Medici-Riccardi was built by Michelozzo in 1444 for Cosimo de' Medici il Vecchio; it's the prototype Florentine palazzo, on which the more overbearing Strozzi and Pitti palaces were later modeled. It remained the Medici private home until Cosimo I more officially declared his power as duke by moving to the city's traditional civic brain center, the Palazzo Vecchio. A door off the right of the entrance courtyard leads up a staircase to the **Cappella dei Magi,** the oldest chapel to survive from a private Florentine palace; its walls are covered with gorgeously dense and colorful Benozzo Gozzoli **frescoes** (1459–63). Rich as tapestries, the walls depict an extended *Journey of the Magi* to see the Christ child, who's being adored by Mary in the altarpiece. Gozzoli is at his decorative best here, inheriting an attention to minute detail in plants and animals from his old teacher Fra' Angelico.

Via Cavour 3. (*C*) **055-276-0340.** Admission 4€ ($4.60). Thurs–Tues 9am–7pm. Number of visitors limited; arrive early or call to book a time to visit. Bus: 1, 6, 7, 11, 14, 17, 23, 67, 68, 70, or 71.

4 On or Near Piazza Santa Maria Novella

Piazza Santa Maria Novella boasts patches of grass and a central fountain. The two squat obelisks, resting on the backs of Giambologna tortoises, once served as the turning posts for the "chariot" races held here from the 16th to the mid–19th century. However, these days the piazza sees more action as a roving ground for the few Gypsies picking tourists' pockets in Florence and the hangout for the city's economically depressed small immigrant population and even smaller cache of itinerants. Several bars and pubs have tried to infuse the area with some life, but the night still leans toward the seedy around here.

Santa Maria Novella &&   Of all Florence's major churches, the home of the Dominicans is the only one with an original **facade** & that matches its era of greatest importance. The lower Romanesque half was started in the 14th century by architect Fra' Jacopo Talenti, who had just finished building the church itself (started in 1246). Leon Battista Alberti finished the facade, adding a classically inspired Renaissance top that not only went seamlessly with the lower half but also created a Cartesian plane of perfect geometry.

The church's interior underwent a massive restoration in the late 1990s, returning Gioto's restored *Crucifix* to pride of place, hanging in the nave's center—and becoming the first church in Florence to charge admission. Against the second pillar on the left of the nave is the pulpit from which Galileo was denounced for his heretical theory that Earth revolved around the Sun. Just past the pulpit, on the left wall, is **Masaccio's** *Trinità* &&& (ca. 1428), the first painting in the world to use perfect linear mathematical perspective. Florentine citizens and artists flooded in to see the fresco when it was unveiled, many remarking in awe that the coffered ceiling seemed to punch a hole back into space, creating a chapel out of a flat wall. The **transept** is filled with spectacularly frescoed chapels. The **sanctuary** & behind the main altar was frescoed after 1485 by Domenico Ghirlandaio with the help of his assistants and apprentices, probably including a very young Michelangelo. The left wall is covered with a cycle on *The Life of the Virgin* and the right wall with the *Life of St. John the Baptist.* The works have a highly polished decorative quality and are less biblical stories than snapshots of the era's fashions and personages, full of portraits of the Tornabuoni family who commissioned them.

The **Cappella Gondi** to the left of the high altar contains the *Crucifix* carved by Brunelleschi to show his buddy Donatello how it should be done (see the Santa Croce review on p. 140 for the story). At the end of the left transept is a different **Cappella Strozzi,** covered with restored **frescoes** & (1357) by Nardo di Cione, early medieval casts of thousands where the Saved mill about Paradise on the left and the Damned stew in a Dantean inferno on the right.

Piazza Santa Maria Novella. ⓒ **055-215-918.** 2.50€ ($2.90) adults. 1.50€ ($1.75) ages 12–18. Mon–Thurs and Sat 9:30am–5pm; Fri and Sun 1–5pm. Bus: A, 6, 11, 12, 36, 37, or 68.

Museo di Santa Maria Novella &   The cloisters of Santa Maria Novella's convent are open to the public as a museum. The **Chiostro Verde,** with a cypress-surrounded fountain and chirping birds, is named for the greenish tint in the pigment used by Paolo Uccello in his **frescoes** 🗝🗝. His works line the right wall of the first walkway; the most famous is the confusing, somewhat disturbing first scene you come to, where the *Flood and Recession of the Flood and the Drunkenness and Sacrifice of Noah* (1446) are all squeezed onto one panel as the story lines are piled atop one another and Noah appears several times. The two giant wooden walls on either side are meant to be the Ark, shown both before and after the Flood, seen in extreme, distorting perspective.

The **Cappella degli Spagnoli (Spanish Chapel)** 🗝 got its name when it became the private chapel of Eleonora of Toledo, recently arrived in Florence to be Cosimo de' Medici's bride. The pretty chapel was entirely frescoed by Andrea da Firenze and his assistants in a kind of half Florentine–half Sienese style around 1365.

Piazza Santa Maria Novella (entrance to the left of the church facade). 🕐 **055-282-187.** Admission 1.40€ ($1.60). Sat and Mon–Thurs 9am–2pm; Sun 8am–1pm. Bus: A, 6, 11, 12, 36, 37, or 68.

Ognissanti 🗝 Founded in 1256 by the Umiliati, a wool-weaving sect of the Benedictines whose trade helped establish this area as a textile district, the present Ognissanti was rebuilt by its new Franciscan owners in the 17th century. It has the earliest baroque **facade** in Florence, designed by Matteo Nigetti in 1627 and rebuilt in travertine in 1872.

Ognissanti was the parish church of the Vespucci family, agents of the Medici bank in Seville. A young Domenico Ghirlandaio portrayed several of the family members in his *Madonna della Misericordia* (1470) on the second altar to the right. The lady under the Madonna's left hand may be Simonetta Vespucci, renowned beauty of her age, mistress of Giuliano de' Medici (Lorenzo's brother), and the possible model for Venus in Botticelli's *Birth of Venus*. The young man with black hair to the Madonna's right is said to be Amerigo Vespucci (1454–1512), whose letters about exploring the New World in 1499 and again from 1501 to 1502 would become so popular that a cartographer used a corruption of Amerigo's name on an influential set of maps to describe the newly discovered continent. Sorry, Columbus. The family tombstone (America's namesake rests in peace underneath) is to the left of this altar.

Between the third and fourth altars is Botticelli's fresco of a pensive *St. Augustine in His Study* (1480), a much more intense work than its matching *St. Jerome in His Study* by Ghirlandaio across the nave. Botticelli, whose real name was Sandro Filipepi, is buried

---

Tips **Seeing *David***

The wait to get in to see *David* can be up to an hour if you didn't reserve ahead. Try getting there before the museum opens in the morning or an hour or two before closing time.

---

under a round marker in the second chapel in the right transept. In the left transept's second chapel is the habit St. Francis was wearing when he received the stigmata. You can enter the convent to the left of the church facade at Borgo Ognissanti 42. In the refectory here is Domenico Ghirlandaio's **Last Supper** ✿, painted in 1480 with a background heavy on Christian symbols.

Piazza Ognissanti. ✆ **055-239-8700.** Free admission. Church daily 8am–noon and 4–6:30pm. Convent Mon–Tues and Sat 9am–noon. Bus: B, D, or 12.

5 Near San Marco & Santissima Annunziata

Galleria dell'Accademia (Academy Gallery) ✿✿ Though tour-bus crowds flock here just for Michelangelo's *David,* anyone with more than a day in Florence can take the time to peruse some of the Accademia's paintings as well.

The first long hall is devoted to Michelangelo and, though you pass his *Slaves* and the entrance to the painting gallery, most visitors are immediately drawn down to the far end, a tribune dominated by the most famous sculpture in the world: **Michelangelo's *David*** ✿✿✿. A hot young sculptor fresh from his success with the *Pietà* in Rome, Michelangelo offered in 1501 to take on a slab of marble that had already been worked on by another sculptor (who had taken a chunk out of one side before declaring it too strangely shaped to use). The huge slab had been lying around the Duomo's workyards so long it earned a nickname, *Il Gigante* (the Giant), so it was with a twist of humor that Michelangelo, only 29 years old, finished in 1504 a Goliath-size David for the city.

There was originally a vague idea that the statue would become part of the Duomo, but Florence's republican government soon wheeled it down to stand on Piazza della Signoria in front of the Palazzo Vecchio to symbolize the defeated tyranny of the Medici, who had been ousted a decade before (but would return with a vengeance). During a 1527 anti-Medicean siege on the palazzo, a bench thrown at the attackers from one of the windows hit David's left arm, which reportedly came crashing down on a farmer's toe.

(A young Giorgio Vasari came scurrying out to gather all the pieces for safekeeping, despite the riot going on around him, and the arm was later reconstituted.) Even the sculpture's 1873 removal to the Accademia to save it from the elements (a copy stands in its place) hasn't kept it entirely safe—in 1991, a man threw himself on the statue and began hammering at the right foot, dislodging several toes. The foot was repaired, and *David*'s Plexiglas shield went up.

The hall leading up to *David* is lined with perhaps Michelangelo's most fascinating works, the four famous *nonfiniti* (unfinished) *Slaves,* or *Prisoners* ⓡⓡⓡ. Like no others, these statues symbolize Michelangelo's theory that sculpture is an "art that takes away superfluous material." The great master saw a true sculpture as something that was already inherent in the stone, and all it needed was a skilled chisel to free it from the extraneous rock. That certainly seems to be the case here, as we get a private glimpse into Michelangelo's working technique: how he began by carving the abdomen and torso, going for the gut of the sculpture and bringing that to life first so it could tell him how the rest should start to take form. Whether he intended the statues to look the way they do now or in fact left them only half done has been debated by art historians to exhaustion. The result, no matter what the sculptor's intentions, is remarkable, a symbol of the master's great art and personal views on craft as his Slaves struggle to break free of their chipped stone prisons.

Nearby, in a similar mode, is a statue of *St. Matthew* ⓡⓡ (1504–08), which Michelangelo began carving as part of a series of Apostles he was at one point going to complete for the Duomo. (The *Pietà* at the end of the corridor on the right is by one of Michelangelo's students, not by the master as was once thought.)

Off this hall of *Slaves* is the first wing of the painting gallery, which includes a panel, possibly from a wedding chest, known as the *Cassone Adimari* ⓡ, painted by Lo Scheggia in the 1440s. It shows the happy couple's promenade to the Duomo, with the green-and-white marbles of the Baptistery prominent in the background.

In the wings off *David*'s tribune are large paintings by Michelangelo's contemporaries, mannerists over whom he had a very strong influence—they even say Michelangelo provided the original drawing from which Pontormo painted his amorous *Venus and Cupid.* Off the end of the left wing is a long 19th-century hall crowded wall to wall and stacked floor to ceiling with **plaster casts** of hundreds of sculptures and busts—the Accademia, after all, is what it sounds like: an academy for budding young artists, founded

Michelangelo: The Making of a Renaissance Master

Irascible, moody, and manic-depressive, Michelangelo was quite simply one of the greatest artists of all time. Many feel he represents the pinnacle of the Italian Renaissance, a genius at sculpture, painting, and architecture, and even a master poet.

In 1475, Michelangelo Buonarroti was born near Arezzo in the tiny town of Caprese, where his Florentine father was serving a term as a *podestà* (visiting mayor). He grew up on the family farm at Settignano, outside Florence, and was wet-nursed by the wife of a local stonecutter—he used to joke that he sucked his skill with the hammer and chisel along with the mother's milk. He was apprenticed early to the fresco studio of Domenico Ghirlandaio who, while watching the young apprentice sketching, once remarked in shock, "This boy knows more about it than I do." After just a year at the studio, Michelangelo was recruited by Lorenzo the Magnificent de' Medici to become part of his new school for sculptors.

Michelangelo learned quickly, and soon after his arrival at the school took a chunk of marble and carved it to copy the head of an old faun from an ancient statue in the garden. Lorenzo happened by and saw the skill with which the head was made, but when he saw Michelangelo had departed from his model and carved the mouth open and

in 1784 as an offshoot of the Academy of Art Design that dates from Michelangelo's time (1565).

Via Ricasoli 58–60. ✆ **055-238-8609** or 055-238-8612. www.sbas.firenze.it/accademia. (Reserve tickets at ✆ 055-294-883 or www.firenzemusei.it.) Admission 6.50€ ($7.50) adults, 3.25€ ($3.75) children. Tues–Sun 8:15am–6:50pm; last admission 30 min. before close. Bus: 1, 6, 7, 10, 11, 17, 25, 31, 32, 33, 67, 68, or 70.

San Marco 🕸🕸   In 1437, Cosimo de' Medici il Vecchio, grandfather of Lorenzo the Magnificent, had Michelozzo convert a medieval monastery here into a new home for the Dominicans, in which Cosimo also founded Europe's first public library. From 1491 until he was burned at the stake on Piazza della Signoria in 1498, laughing with teeth and a tongue, he commented only "But you should have known that old people never have all their teeth and there are always some missing." The young artist reflected on this. When Lorenzo returned a while later, he found Michelangelo waiting anxiously, eager to show he had not only chipped out a few teeth but also gouged down into the gums of the statue to make the tooth loss look more realistic. Impressed, Lorenzo decided to take the boy under his wing and virtually adopted him into the Medici household.

After his success at age 19 with the *Pietà* sculpture in Rome, Michelangelo was given the opportunity by the city council to carve the enormous block of marble that became *David.* He worked on it behind shuttered scaffolding so few saw it until the unveiling. Legend has it that when Soderini, the head of the city council, came to see the finished work, he remarked the nose looked a tad too large. Michelangelo, knowing better but wanting to please Soderini, climbed up to the head (out of view), grabbed a handful of leftover plaster dust, and while tapping his hammer lightly against his chisel, let the dust sprinkle down gradually as if he were actually carving. "Much better," remarked Soderini when Michelangelo climbed down again and they stepped back to admire it. "Now you've really brought it to life."

this was the home base of puritanical preacher Girolamo Savonarola. The monastery's most famous friar, though, was early Renaissance painter Fra' Angelico, and he left many of his finest works, devotional images painted with the technical skill and minute detail of a miniaturist or an illuminator but on altarpiece scale. While his works tended to be transcendently spiritual, Angelico was also prone to filling them with earthy details with which any peasant or stonemason could identify.

The museum rooms are entered off a pretty cloister. The old Pilgrim's Hospice has been converted into a **Fra' (Beato) Angelico Gallery** 𝄞𝄞, full of altarpieces and painted panels. Also off the cloister is the **Reffetorio Grande (Great Refectory),** with 16th- and 17th-century paintings, and the **Sala del Capitolo (Chapter House),** frescoed from 1441 to 1442 with a huge *Crucifixion* by Fra' Angelico and his assistants. The door next to this leads past the staircase up to the Dormitory (see below) to the **Sala del Cenacolo (Small Refectory),** with a long fresco of the *Last Supper* by Domenico Ghirlandaio.

The **Dormitorio (Dormitory)** 🟊🟊 of cells where the monks lived is one of Fra' Angelico's masterpieces and perhaps his most famous cycle of frescoes. In addition to the renowned *Annunciation* 🟊🟊 at the top of the stairs to the monks' rooms, Angelico painted the cells themselves with simple works to aid his fellow friars in their meditations. One of these almost anticipates surrealism—a Flagellation where disembodied hands strike at Christ's face and a rod descends on him from the blue-green background. Angelico's assistants carried out the repetitious Crucifixion scenes in many of the cells. At the end of one of the corridors is the suite of cells occupied by Savonarola when he was here prior. In the first are two famous portraits of him by his devout follower and talented painter Fra' Bartolomeo, along with an anonymous 16th-century painting of *Savonarola Burned at the Stake* on Piazza della Signoria. The **Biblioteca (Library)** off the corridor to the right of the stairs was designed by Michelozzo in 1441 and contains beautifully illuminated choir books.

Piazza San Marco 3. 🕐 **055-238-8608.** Admission 4€ ($4.60) adults, 2€ ($2.30) children. Mon–Fri 8:30am–1:50pm; Sat–Sun 8:15am–7pm. Closed 1st, 3rd, and 5th Sun and 2nd and 4th Mon of each month. Bus: 1, 6, 7, 10, 11, 17, 20, 25, 31, 32, 33, 67, 68, or 70.

Cenacolo di Sant'Apollonia 🟊

There are no lines at this former convent and no crowds. Few people even know to ring the bell at the nondescript door. What they're missing is an entire wall covered with the vibrant colors of Andrea del Castagno's masterful *Last Supper* (ca. 1450). Castagno used his paint to create the rich marble panels that checkerboard the *trompe l'oeil* walls and broke up the long white tablecloth with the dark figure of Judas the Betrayer, whose face is painted to resemble a satyr, an ancient symbol of evil.

Via XXVII Aprile 1. 🕐 **055-238-8607.** Free admission. Daily 8:30am–1:50pm. Closed 1st, 3rd, and 5th Sun and 2nd and 4th Mon of each month. Bus: 1, 6, 7, 10, or 11.

Santissima Annunziata

In 1230, seven Florentine nobles had a spiritual crisis, gave away all their possessions, and retired to the forests to contemplate divinity. They returned to what were then the fields outside the city walls and founded a small oratory, proclaiming they were Servants of Mary, or the Servite Order. The oratory was enlarged by Michelozzo (1444–81) and later baroqued. Under the facade's **portico,** you enter the **Chiostro dei Voti (Votice Cloister),** designed by Michelozzo with Corinthian-capitaled columns and decorated with some of the city's finest mannerist frescoes (1465–1515). Rosso Fiorentino provided an *Assumption* (1513) and Pontormo a *Visitation* (1515) just to the right of the door, but the main works are by their master, Andrea del Sarto, whose ***Birth of the Virgin*** ✿ (1513) in the far right corner is one of his finest works. To the right of the door into the church is a damaged but still fascinating *Coming of the Magi* (1514) by del Sarto, who included a self-portrait at the far right, looking out at us from under his blue hat.

The **interior** is excessively baroque. Just to the left as you enter is a huge tabernacle hidden under a mountain of flowers and *ex votos* (votive offerings). It was designed by Michelozzo to house a small painting of the *Annunciation.* Legend holds that this painting was started by a friar who, vexed that he couldn't paint the Madonna's face as beautifully as it should be, gave it up and took a nap. When he awoke, he found an angel had filled in the face for him. Newly-wed brides in Florence don't toss their bouquets—they head here after the ceremony to leave their flowers at the shrine for good luck.

The large circular **tribune** was finished for Michelozzo by Leon Battista Alberti. You enter it from its left side via the left transept, but first pause to pay your respects to Andrea del Sarto, buried under a floor slab at the left-hand base of the great arch.

From the left transept, a door leads into the **Chiostro dei Morti (Cloister of the Dead;** track down a sacristan to open it), where over the entrance door is another of Andrea del Sarto's greatest frescoes, the ***Madonna del Sacco*** ✿, and, a *Rest on the Flight into Egypt* scene that got its name from the sack Joseph is leaning against to do a little light reading. Also off this cloister is the **Cappella di San Luca (Chapel of St. Luke),** evangelist and patron saint of painters. It was decorated by late Renaissance and mannerist painters, including Pontormo, Alessandro Allori, Santi di Tito, and Giorgio Vasari. On the **piazza** ✿✿ outside, flanked by elegant porticos (see "Spedale degli Innocenti" below), is an equestrian statue of *Grand Duke Ferdinando I,* Giambologna's last work; it was cast in 1608 after his death by his student Pietro Tacca, who also did the two little fountains of fantastic mermonkey-monsters. The piazza's beauty is somewhat ruined by the car and bus traffic routed through both ends, but it's kept lively by students from the nearby university, who sit on the loggia steps for lunch and hang out here in the evenings.

Piazza Santissima Annunziata. © 055-266-181. Free admission. Daily 7:30am–12:30pm and 4–6:30pm. Bus: 6, 31, or 32.

Spedale degli Innocenti   Europe's oldest foundling hospital, opened in 1445, is still going strong as a convent orphanage, though times have changed a bit. The lazy Susan set into the wall on the left end of the arcade—where once people left unwanted babies, swiveled it around, rang the bell, and ran—has since been blocked up. The colonnaded **portico** ⚜ (built 1419–26) was designed by Filippo Brunelleschi when he was still an active goldsmith. It was his first great achievement as an architect and helped define the new Renaissance style he was developing. Its repetition by later artists in front of other buildings on the piazza makes it one of the most exquisite squares in all Italy. The spandrels between the arches of Brunelleschi's portico are set with glazed **terra-cotta reliefs** of swaddled babes against rounded blue backgrounds—hands-down the masterpieces of Andrea della Robbia.

Piazza Santissima Annunziata 12. © 055-249-1708. www.istitutodeglinnocenti.it. Admission 2.60€ ($3). Thurs–Tues 8:30am–2pm. Bus: 6, 31, or 32.

Museo Opificio delle Pietre Dure   In the 16th century, Florentine craftsmen perfected the art of *pietre dure,* piecing together cut pieces of precious and semi-precious stones in an inlay process, and the Medici-founded institute devoted to the craft has been in this building since 1796.

Long ago misnamed a "Florentine mosaic" by the tourism industry, this is a highly refined craft in which skilled artisans (artists, really) create scenes and boldly colored intricate designs in everything from cameos and tabletops to never-fade stone "paintings." Masters are adept at selecting, slicing, and polishing stones so that the natural grain or color gradations in the cross sections will, once cut and laid in the design, become the contours, shading, and molding that give good *pietre dure* scenes their depth and illusion of three-dimensionality.

The collection in this museum is small, but the pieces are uniformly excellent. Souvenir shops all over town sell modern *pietre dure* items—much of it mass-produced junk, but some very nice. The best contemporary maestro is Ilio de Filippis, whose workshop is called Pitti Mosaici (see chapter 6).

Via degli Alfani 78. ✆ 055-265-1357, or 055-294-883 for ticket reservations (not necessary). www.opificio.arti.beniculturali.it. Admission 2€ ($2.30), free for children under 6. Mon–Sat 8:15am–2pm (Thurs until 7pm). Bus: 6, 11, 17, 31, or 32.

Museo Archeologico (Archaeological Museum) 🎭🎭   This embarrassingly rich collection is often overlooked by visitors in full-throttle Renaissance mode. It conserves Egyptian artifacts, Roman remains, many Attic vases, and an important Etruscan collection. Parts of it have been undergoing restoration and rearrangement for years and are closed indefinitely, including the garden. The relics to be on the lookout for start in the first ground-floor room with an early 4th-century B.C. bronze **Chimera** 🎭🎭, a mythical beast with a lion's body and head, a goat head sprouting from its back, and a serpent for a tail (the tail was incorrectly restored in 1785). The beast was found near Arezzo in 1553 and probably made in a Chiusi or an Orvieto workshop as a votive offering. The legend that claims Benvenuto Cellini recast the left paws is hogwash; the feet did have to be reattached, but they had the originals to work with. Ground-floor room III contains a **silver amphora** studded with concave medallions, a work from Antioch (ca. A.D. 380).

In room III on the upper floor is an extraordinarily rare **Hittite wood-and-bone chariot** from the 14th century B.C. Room XIV upstairs has a cast bronze *Arringatore,* or orator, found near Perugia. It was made in the 1st century B.C. and helps illustrate how Roman society was having a great influence on the Etruscan world—not only in the workmanship of the statue but also in the fact that the Etruscan orator Aule Meteli is wearing a Roman toga. Room XIII contains the museum's most famous piece, the *Idolino* 🎭. The history of this nude bronze lad with his outstretched hand is long, complicated, and in the end a bit mysterious. The current theory is that he's a Roman statue of the Augustan period (around the time of Christ), with the head perhaps modeled on a lost piece by the Greek master Polycleitus. The rub: *Idolino* was originally probably part of a lamp stand used at Roman banquets. The male torso displayed here was fished out of the sea near Livorno. It was made in Greece around 480 to 470 B.C.—the earliest known Greek bronze cast using the lost wax method. The horse's head also in this room once belonged to the Medici, as did much of this museum's collections, and tradition holds that it was a source of inspiration for Verrocchio and Donatello as they cast their own equestrian monuments. It was probably once part of a Hellenistic sculpture from the 2nd or 1st century B.C.

As we go to press, rooms IX and X, and the garden are under reconstruction.

Via della Colonna 38. ℂ 055-23-575. Admission 4€ ($4.60). Mon 2–7pm; Tues and Thurs 8:30am–7pm; Wed and Fri–Sun 8:30am–2pm. Closed 2nd and 4th Mon of month. Bus: 6, 31, or 32.

Cimitero degli Inglesi (Protestant Cemetery)   When this plot of green was nestled up against the city's medieval walls, it was indeed a quiet, shady, and reflective spot. When those walls were demolished in the late 19th century and the boulevard Viale put in their place, it became a traffic circle instead. We can only hope that frail and gentle Elizabeth Barrett Browning can block out the noise from her tomb off the left of the main path. The **sepulcher** was designed by her husband and fellow poet Robert Browning after her death in Florence in 1861.

Piazzale Donatello 38. ℂ 055-582-608. www.florin.ms/cemetery.html. Free admission, donation suggested (ring at the gate). Easter–Oct Mon 9am–noon, Tues–Fri 3–6pm; Oct–Easter Mon 9am–noon, Tues–Sat 2–5pm. Bus: 6, 8, or 33.

6 Around Piazza Santa Croce

Piazza Santa Croce is pretty much like any in Florence—a nice bit of open space ringed with souvenir and leather shops and thronged with tourists. Its most unique feature (aside from the one time a year it's covered with dirt and violent Renaissance soccer is played on it) is the **Palazzo Antellisi** on the south side. This well-preserved, 16th-century patrician house is owned by a contessa who rents out a bunch of peachy apartments.

Santa Croce The center of the Florentine Franciscan universe was begun in 1294 by Gothic master Arnolfo di Cambio in order to rival the huge church of Santa Maria Novella being raised by the Dominicans across the city. The church wasn't completed and consecrated until 1442, and even then it remained faceless until the neo-Gothic **facade** was added in 1857 (and cleaned in 1998–99). The cloisters are home to Brunelleschi's Cappella de' Pazzi (see "Museo dell'Opera" below), the convent partially given over to a famous leather school (see chapter 6), and the church itself a shrine of 14th-century frescoes and a monument to notable Florentines, whose tombs and memorials litter the place like an Italian Westminster. The best artworks, such as the Giotto frescoes, are guarded by euro-gobbling lightboxes; bring plenty of change.

The Gothic **interior**—for which they now charge a premium admission (it was free until recently)—is wide and gaping, with huge pointed stone arches creating the aisles and an echoing nave trussed with wood beams, in all feeling vaguely barnlike (an analogy the occasional fluttering pigeon only enforces). The floor is paved with worn tombstones—because being buried in this hallowed sanctuary got you one step closer to Heaven, the richest families of the day paid big bucks to stake out small rectangles of the floor. On the right aisle is the first tomb of note, a mad Vasari contraption containing the bones of the most venerated of Renaissance masters, **Michelangelo Buonarroti,** who died of a fever in Rome in 1564 at the ripe age of 89. The pope wanted him buried in the Eternal City, but Florentines managed to sneak his body back to Florence. Past Michelangelo is a pompous 19th-century cenotaph to Florentine **Dante Alighieri,** one of history's greatest poets, whose *Divine Comedy* codified the Italian language. He died in 1321 in Ravenna after a long and bitter life in exile from his hometown (on trumped-up embezzlement charges), and that Adriatic city has never seen fit to return the bones to Florence, the city that would never readmit the poet when he was alive.

Against a nave pillar farther up is an elaborate **pulpit** (1472–76) carved by Benedetto di Maiano with scenes from the life of St. Francis. Next comes a wall monument to **Niccolò Machiavelli,** the 16th-century Florentine statesman and author whose famous book *The Prince* was the perfect practical manual for a powerful Renaissance ruler.

Past the next altar is an *Annunciation* (1433) carved in low relief of *pietra serena* and gilded by Donatello. Nearby is Antonio Rossellino's 1446 tomb of the great humanist scholar and city chancellor **Leonardo Bruni** (d. 1444). Beyond this architectural masterpiece of a tomb is a 19th-century knockoff honoring the remains of **Gioacchino Rossini** (1792–1868), composer of the *Barber of Seville* and the *William Tell Overture.*

Around in the right transept is the **Cappella Castellani** frescoed by Agnolo Gaddi and assistants, with a tabernacle by Mino da Fiesole and a *Crucifix* by Niccolò Gerini. Agnolo's father, Taddo Gaddi, was one of Giotto's closest followers, and the senior Gaddi is the one who undertook painting the **Cappella Baroncelli** ⚔ (1332–38) at the transept's end. The frescoes depict scenes from the Life of the Virgin, and to the left of the window is an *Angel Appearing to the Shepherds* that constitutes the first night scene in Italian fresco. The altarpiece *Coronation of the Virgin* is by Giotto. To the left of this chapel is a doorway, designed by Michelozzo, leading to the *sagrestia* (sacristy) past a huge *Deposition* (1560) by Alessandro Allori that had to be restored after it incurred massive water damage when the church was inundated during the 1966 flood. Past the gift shop is a leather school and store.

In the right transept, Giotto frescoed the two chapels to the right of the high altar. The frescoes were whitewashed over during the 17th century but uncovered from 1841 to 1852 and inexpertly restored. The **Cappella Peruzzi** 🐦🐦 on the right is a late work and not in the best shape. The many references to antiquity in the styling and architecture of the frescoes reflect Giotto's trip to Rome and its ruins. His assistant Taddeo Gaddi did the altarpiece. Even more famous, if only as the setting for a scene in the film *A Room with a View,* is the **Cappella Bardi** 🐦🐦 immediately to the right of the high altar. The key panels here include the *Trial by Fire Before the Sultan of Egypt* on the right wall, full of telling subtlety in the expressions and poses of the figures. One of Giotto's most well-known works is the lower panel on the left wall, the *Death of St. Francis,* where the monks weep and wail with convincing pathos. Alas, big chunks of the scene are missing from when a tomb was stuck on top of it in the 18th century. Most people miss seeing *Francis Receiving the Stigmata,* which Giotto frescoed above the outside of the entrance arch to the chapel.

Agnolo Gaddi designed the stained-glass windows, painted the saints between them, and frescoed a *Legend of the True Cross* cycle on the walls of the rounded **sanctuary** behind the high altar. At the end of the left transept is another Cappella Bardi, this one housing a legendary *Crucifix* 🐦 by Donatello. According to Vasari, Donatello excitedly called his friend Filippo Brunelleschi up to his studio to see this *Crucifix* when he had finished carving it. The famed architect, whose tastes were aligned with the prevailing view of the time that refinement and grace were much more important than realism, criticized the work with the words, "Why Donatello, you've put a peasant on the cross!" Donatello sniffed, "If it was as easy to make something as it is to criticize, my Christ would really look to you like Christ. So you get some wood and try to make one yourself." Secretly, Brunelleschi did just that, and one day he invited Donatello to come over to his studio for lunch. Donatello arrived bearing the food gathered up in his apron. Shocked when he beheld Brunelleschi's elegant *Crucifix,* he let the lunch drop to the floor, smashing the eggs, and after a few moments turned to Brunelleschi and humbly offered, "Your job is making Christs and mine is making peasants." Tastes change, and to modern eyes this "peasant" stands as the stronger work. If you want to see how Brunelleschi fared with his Christ, visit it at Santa Maria Novella.

Past a door as you head back down the left aisle is a 16th-century *Deposition* by Bronzino. A bit farther along, against a pier, is the roped-off floor tomb of Lorenzo Ghiberti, sculptor of the baptistery doors. Against the wall is an altarpiece of the *Incredulity of St. Thomas* by Giorgio Vasari. The last tomb on the right is that of **Galileo Galilei** (1564–1642), the preeminent Pisan scientist who figured out everything from the action of pendulums and the famous law of bodies falling at the same rate (regardless of weight) to discovering the moons of Jupiter and asserting that Earth revolved around the Sun. This last one got him in trouble with the church, which tried him in the Inquisition and—when he wouldn't recant—excommunicated him. At the urging of friends frightened his obstinacy would get him executed as a heretic, Galileo eventually knelt in front of an altar and "admitted" he'd been wrong. He lived out the rest of his days under house arrest near Florence and wasn't allowed a Christian burial until 1737. Giulio Foggini designed this tomb for him, complete with a relief of the solar system—the Sun, you'll notice, is at the center. The pope finally got around to lifting the excommunication in 1992. Italians still bring him fresh flowers.

Piazza Santa Croce. ✆ **055-244-619.** Admission 4€ ($4.60). Mon–Sat 9:30am–5:30pm; Sun 1–5:30pm. Bus: B, 13, 23, or 71.

Museo dell'Opera di Santa Croce 𝑅

Part of Santa Croce's convent has been set up as a museum, mainly to harbor artistic victims of the 1966 Arno flood, which buried the church under tons of mud and water. You enter through a door to the right of the church facade, which spills into an open-air courtyard planted with cypress and filled with birdsong.

At the end of the path is the **Cappella de' Pazzi** 𝑅, one of Filippo Brunelleschi's architectural masterpieces (faithfully finished after his death in 1446). Giuliano di Maiano probably designed the porch that now precedes the chapel, set with glazed terra cottas by Luca della Robbia. The rectangular chapel is one of Brunelleschi's signature pieces and a defining example of (and model for) early Renaissance architecture. Light gray *pietra serena* is used to accent the architectural lines against smooth white plaster walls, and the only decorations are della Robbia roundels of the *Apostles* (1442–52). The chapel was barely finished by 1478, when the infamous Pazzi Conspiracy got the bulk of the family, who were funding this project, either killed or exiled.

From back in the first cloister you can enter the museum proper via the long hall of the **refectory.** On your right as you enter is the painting that became emblematic of all the artworks damaged during the 1966 flood, Cimabue's *Crucifix* ✪, one of the masterpieces of the artist who began bridging the gap between Byzantine tradition and Renaissance innovation, not the least by teaching Giotto to paint.

Piazza Santa Croce 16. ✆ **055-244-619.** Admission included with San Croce; hours same. Bus: B, 13, 23, or 71.

Museo Horne Of the city's several small once-private collections, the one formed by Englishman Herbert Percy Horne and left to Florence in his will has perhaps the best individual pieces, though the bulk of it consists of mediocre paintings by good artists. In a 15th-century palazzo designed by Cronaca (not Sangallo, as had once been believed), the collections are left, unlabeled, as Horne arranged them; the reference numbers on the handout they give you correspond to the stickers on the wall, not the numbers on the frames. The best works are a *St. Stephen* by Giotto and Sienese mannerist Domenico Beccafumi's weirdly colored tondo of the *Holy Family.*

Via dei Benci 6. ✆ **055-244-661.** Admission 5€ ($5.75). Mon–Sat 9am–1pm; in summer also Tues 8:30–11pm. Bus: B, 13, 23, or 71.

Casa Buonarroti Though Michelangelo Buonarroti never actually lived in this modest palazzo, he did own the property and left it to his nephew Lionardo. Lionardo named his own son after his famous uncle, and this younger Michelangelo became very devoted to the memory of his namesake, converting the house into a museum and hiring artists to fill the place with frescoes honoring the genius of his great uncle.

The good stuff is upstairs, starting with a display case regularly rotating pages from the museum's collection of original drawings. In the first room off the landing are Michelangelo's earliest sculptures: the *Madonna of the Steps,* carved before 1492 when he was a 15- or 16-year-old student in the Medici sculpture garden. A few months later, the child prodigy was already finished carving another marble, a confused tangle of bodies known as the *Battle of the Centaurs and Lapiths.* The sculptural ideals that were to mark his entire career are already evident here: a fascination with the male body to the point of ignoring the figures themselves in pursuit of muscular torsion and the use of rough "unfinished" marble to speak sculptural volumes.

Via Ghibellina 70. ✆ **055-241-752.** www.casabuonarroti.it. Admission 6.50€ ($7.50). Wed–Mon 9:30am–2pm. Bus: A, 14, or 23.

Santa Maria Maddalena dei Pazzi The entrance to this church is an unassuming, unnumbered door on Borgo Pinti that opens onto a pretty cloister designed in 1492 by Giuliano da Sangallo, open to the sky and surrounded by large *pietra serena* columns topped with droopy-eared Ionic capitals. The interior of the 13th-century church was remodeled in the 17th and early 18th centuries and represents the high baroque at its restrained best. At the odd hours listed below, you can get into the chapter house to see the church's hidden main prize, a wall-filling fresco of the ***Crucifixion and Saints*** ✿ (1493–96) by Perugino, grand master of the Umbrian school. Typical of Perugino's style, the background is drawn as delicately in blues and greens as the posed figures were fleshed out in full-bodied volumes of bright colors.

Entrance next to Borgo Pinti 58. ✆ **055-247-8420.** Free admission to church and Perugino *Crucifixion* 1€ ($1.15) "donation." Church daily 9am–noon; Mon–Fri 5–5:20pm and 6–6:50pm; Sat 5–6:20pm; Sun 5–6:50pm. Perugino *Crucifixion,* ring bell at no. 58 9–10am or enter through sacristy (knock at the last door on the right inside the church) at 5pm or 6:15pm. Bus: A, 6, 14, 23, 31, 32, or 71.

Sinagoga (Synagogue) and Jewish Museum The center of the 1,000-strong Jewish community in Florence is this imposing Moorish-Byzantine synagogue, built in the 1870s. In an effort to create a neo-Byzantine building, the architects ended up making it look rather like a church, complete with a dome, an apse, a pulpit, and a pipe organ. The intricate polychrome arabesque designs, though, lend it a distinctly Eastern flavor, and the rows of prayer benches facing each other, and the separate areas for women, hint at its Orthodox Jewish nature. Though the synagogue is technically Sephardic, the members of the Florentine Jewish community are Italian Jews, a Hebrew culture that has adapted to its Italian surroundings since the 1st century B.C. when Jewish slaves were first brought to Rome. (The Florentine community dates from the 14th c.)

Via Farina 4. ✆ **055-234-6654.** www.firenzebraica.net. Admission 4€ ($4.60) adults, 3€ ($3.45) students. June–Aug Sun–Thurs 10am–6pm; Apr–May and Sept–Oct Sun–Thurs 10am–5pm; Nov–Mar Sun–Thurs 10am–3pm.; obligatory 45-min. guided tours every 25 min. Bus: 6, 31, 32, or C.

7 In the Oltrarno

Santa Felícita The 2nd-century Greek sailors who lived in this neighborhood brought Christianity to Florence with them, and this little church was probably the second to be established in the city, the first edition of it rising in the late 4th century. The current version was built in the 1730s. The star works are in the first chapel on your right, paintings by mannerist master Pontormo (1525–27). *The Deposition* and frescoed *Annunciation* are rife with his garish color palette of oranges, pinks, golds, lime greens, and sky blues. The four round paintings of the *Evangelists* surrounding the dome are also by Pontormo, except for the *St. Mark* (with the angel), which was probably painted by his pupil Bronzino.

Piazza Santa Felícita (2nd left off Via Guicciardini across the Ponte Vecchio). ℭ 055-213-018. Free admission. Daily 8am–noon and 3:30–6:30pm. Bus: B or D.

Palazzo Pitti & Giardino Boboli (Pitti Palace & Boboli Gardens) 𝔊𝔊𝔊

Though the original, much smaller Pitti Palace was a Renaissance affair probably designed by Filippo Brunelleschi, that palazzo is completely hidden by the enormous mannerist mass we see today. Inside are Florence's most extensive set of museums, including the Galleria Palatina, a huge painting gallery second in town only to the Uffizi, with famous works by Raphael, Andrea del Sarto, Titian, and Rubens. When Luca Pitti died in 1472, Cosimo de' Medici's wife, Eleonora of Toledo, bought this property and unfinished palace to convert into the new Medici home—she hated the dark, cramped spaces of the family apartments in the Palazzo Vecchio. They hired Bartolomeo Ammannati to enlarge the palazzo, which he did starting in 1560 by creating the courtyard out back, extending the wings out either side, and incorporating a Michelangelo architectural invention, "kneeling windows," on the ground floor of the facade. (Rather than being visually centered between the line of the floor and that of the ceiling, kneeling windows' bases extend lower to be level with the ground or, in the case of upper stories, with whatever architectural element delineates the baseline of that story's 1st level.) Later architects finished the building off by the 19th century, probably to Ammannati's original plans, in the end producing the oversize rustication of its outer walls and overall ground plan that make it one of the masterpieces of Florentine mannerist architecture.

The ticket office for the painting gallery—the main, and for many visitors, most interesting of the Pitti museums—is off Ammannati's excellent **interior courtyard** 𝔊 of gold-tinged rusticated rock grafted onto the three classical orders.

GALLERIA PALATINA 𝔊𝔊𝔊 If the Uffizi represents mainly the earlier masterpieces collected by the Medici, the Pitti Palace's painting gallery continues the story with the High Renaissance and later eras, a collection gathered by the Medici, and later the Grand Dukes of Lorraine. The works are still displayed in the old-world fashion, which hung paintings according to aesthetics—how well, say, the Raphael matched the drapes—rather than that boring academic chronological order. In the first long **Galleria delle Statue (Hall of Statues)** are an early Peter Paul Rubens's *Risen Christ,* Caravaggio's ***Tooth-puller*** ✦, and a 19th-century tabletop inlaid in *pietre dure,* an exquisite example of the famous Florentine mosaic craft. The next five rooms made up the Medici's main apartments, frescoed by Pietro da Cortona in the 17th-century baroque style—they're home to the bulk of the paintings.

The **Sala di Venere (Venus Room)** is named after the neoclassical *Venus,* which Napoléon had Canova sculpt in 1810 to replace the *Medici Venus* the Emperor had appropriated for his Paris digs. Four masterpieces by the famed early-16th-century Venetian painter Titian hang on the walls. Art historians still argue whether ***The Concert*** ✦ was wholly painted by Titian in his early 20s or by Giorgione, in whose circle he moved. However, most now attribute at most the fop on the left to Giorgione and give the rest of the canvas to Titian. There are no such doubts about Titian's *Portrait of Julius II,* a copy of the physiologically penetrating work by Raphael in London's National Gallery (the version in the Uffizi is a copy Raphael himself made), or the *Portrait of a Lady (La Bella).* Titian painted the *Portrait of Pietro Aretino* for the writer/thinker himself, but Aretino didn't understand the innovative styling and accused Titian of not having completed the work. The painter, in a huff, gave it to Cosimo I as a gift. The room also contains Rubens's *Return from the Hayfields,* famous for its classically harmonious landscape.

The **Sala di Apollo (Apollo Room)** has another masterful early *Portrait of an Unknown Gentleman* by Titian as well as his sensual, luminously gold ***Mary Magdalene*** ✦, the first in a number of takes on the subject the painter was to make throughout his career. There are several works by Andrea del Sarto, whose late *Holy Family* and especially *Deposition* display the daring chromatic experiments and highly refined spatial compositions that were to influence his students Pontormo and Rosso Fiorentino as they went about mastering Mannerism.

The **Sala di Marte (Mars Room)** is dominated by Rubens, including the enormous ***Consequences of War*** ✦✦, which an aged Rubens painted for his friend Sustermans at a time when both were worried that their Dutch homeland was on the brink of battle. Rubens's ***The Four Philosophers*** ✦ is a much more lighthearted work, in which he painted himself at the far left, next to his seated brother Filippo.

The star of the **Sala di Giove (Jupiter Room)** is Raphael's *La Velata* 🍂🍂, one of the crowning achievements of his short career and a summation of what he had learned about color, light, naturalism, and mood. It's probably a portrait of his Roman mistress called La Fornarina, a baker's daughter who sat for many of his Madonnas.

Raphael is the focus of the **Sala di Saturno (Saturn Room)** 🍂🍂, where the transparent colors of his *Madonna*s and probing portraits show the strong influence of both Leonardo da Vinci (the *Portrait of Maddalena Strozzi Doni* owes much to the *Mona Lisa*) and Raphael's old master Perugino, whose *Deposition* and a *Mary Magdalene* hang here as well. The **Sala dell'Iliade (Illiad Room)** has another Raphael portrait, this time of a *Pregnant Woman* 🍂, along with some more Titian masterpieces. Don't miss *Mary Magdalene* and *Judith* 🍂, two paintings by one of the only female artists of the late Renaissance era, Artemesia Gentileschi, who often turned to themes of strong biblical women.

From here, you enter a series of smaller rooms with smaller paintings. The **Sala dell'Educazione di Giove (Room of Jupiter's Education)** has two famous works: one a 1608 *Sleeping Cupid* 🍂🍂 Caravaggio painted while living in exile from Rome (avoiding murder charges) on the island of Malta; and the other Cristofano Allori's *Judith with the Head of Holofernes* 🍂, a Freudian field day where the artist depicted himself in the severed head, his lover as Judith holding it, and her mother as the maid looking on.

APARTAMENTI REALI 🍂   The other wing of the *piano nobile* is taken up with the Medici's private apartments, which were reopened in 1993 after being restored to their late-19th-century appearance when the kings of the House of Savoy, rulers of the Unified Italy, used the suites as their Florentine home. The over-the-top sumptuous fabrics, decorative arts furnishings, stuccoes, and frescoes reflect the neo-baroque and Victorian tastes of the Savoy kings. Amid the general interior-decorator flamboyance are some thoroughly appropriate baroque canvases, plus some earlier works by Andrea del Sarto and Caravaggio's *Portrait of a Knight of Malta* 🍂. January through May, you can visit the apartments only by guided tour Tuesday and Saturday (and sometimes Thurs) hourly from 9 to 11am and 3 to 5pm (reserve ahead at ✆ **055-238-8614;** inquire about admission fees).

GALLERIA D'ARTE MODERNA 🍂   Modern art isn't what draws most people to the capital of the Renaissance, but the Pitti's collection includes some important works by the 19th-century Tuscan school of art known as the Macchiaioli, who painted a kind of Tuscan Impressionism, concerned with the *macchie* (marks of color on the canvas and the play of light on the eye). Most of the scenes are of the countryside or peasants working, along with the requisite lot of portraits. Some of the movement's greatest talents are here, including Silvestro Lega, Telemaco Signorini, and Giovanni Fattori, the genius of the group. Don't miss his two white oxen pulling a cart in *The Tuscan Maremma* 🐾.

GALLERIA DEL COSTUME & MUSEO DEGLI ARGENTI

These aren't the most popular of the Pitti's museums, and the **Museo degli Argenti** has what seems like miles of the most extravagant and often hideous *objets d'art* and housewares the Medici and Lorraines could put their hands on. If the collections prove anything, it's that as the Medici became richer and more powerful, their taste declined proportionally. Just be thankful their **carriage collection** has been closed for years. The **Costume Gallery** is more interesting. The collections concentrate on the 18th to 20th centuries but also display outfits from back to the 16th century. The dress in which Eleonora of Toledo was buried, made famous by Bronzino's intricate depiction of its velvety embroidered silk and in-sewn pearls on his portrait of her in the Uffizi, is usually on display.

GIARDINO BOBOLI (BOBOLI GARDENS) 🐾🐾

The statue-filled park behind the Pitti Palace is one of the earliest and finest Renaissance gardens, laid out mostly between 1549 and 1656 with box hedges in geometric patterns, groves of ilex, dozens of statues, and rows of cypress. In 1766, it was opened to the Florentine public, who still come here with their families for Sunday-morning strolls. Just above the entrance through the courtyard of the Palazzo Pitti is an oblong **amphitheater** modeled on Roman circuses. Today, we see in the middle a **granite basin** from Rome's Baths of Caracalla and an **Egyptian obelisk** of Ramses II, but in 1589 this was the setting for the wedding reception of Ferdinando de' Medici's marriage to Christine of Lorraine. For the occasion, the Medici commissioned entertainment from Jacopo Peri and Ottavio Rinuccini, who decided to set a classical story entirely to music and called it *Dafne*—the world's first opera. (Later, they wrote a follow-up hit *Erudice*, performed here in 1600; it's the 1st opera whose score has survived.)

Around the park, don't miss the rococo **Kaffehaus,** with bar service in summer, and near the top of the park the **Giardino del Cavaliere,** the Boboli's prettiest hidden corner—a tiny walled garden of box hedges with private views over the wooded hills of Florence's outskirts. At the north end of the park, down around the end of the Pitti Palace, are some fake caverns filled with statuary, attempting to invoke some vaguely classical sacred grotto. The most famous, the **Grotta Grande,** was designed by Giorgio Vasari, Bartolomeo Ammannati, and Bernardo Buontalenti between 1557 and 1593, dripping with phony stalactites and set with replicas of Michelangelo's unfinished *Slave* statues. (The originals were once placed here before being moved to the Accademia.) All the grottoes are being restored, but you can visit them by appointment by calling © **055-218-741.** Near the exit to the park is a Florentine postcard fave, the *Fontana di Bacco* (**Bacchus Fountain;** 1560), a pudgy dwarf sitting atop a tortoise. It's actually a portrait of Pietro Barbino, Cosimo I's potbellied dwarf court jester.

Piazza Pitti. **Galleria Palatina:** © **055-238-8614;** reserve tickets at © **055-294-883** or www.firenzemusei.it; admission 6.50€ ($7.50) adults, 3.25€ ($3.75) children; Easter–Oct Tues–Sat 8:30am–10pm, Sun 8:30am–8pm and winter Tues–Sat 8:30am–6:50pm, Mon 8:30am–1:50pm; last admission 45 min. before close. **Galleria d'Arte Moderna:** © **055-238-8601;** admission 5€ ($5.75) adults, 2.50€ ($2.90) children, cumulative ticket with Galleria del Costume available; daily 8:15am–1:50pm, closed 1st, 3rd, and 5th Mon and 2nd and 4th Sun of each month. **Galleria del Costume:** © **055-238-8713;** admission 5€ ($5.75) adults, 2.50€ ($2.90) children, cumulative ticket with Galleria d'Arte Moderna available; daily 8:15am–1:50pm, closed 1st, 3rd, and 5th Mon and 2nd and 4th Sun of each month. **Museo degli Argenti:** © **055-238-8709;** admission 4€ ($4.60) adults, 2€ ($2.30) children, cumulative ticket with Giardino Boboli available; Nov–Feb daily 8:15am–4:30pm, Mar daily 8:15am–5:30pm, Apr–May and Oct daily 8:15am–6:30pm, and June–Sept daily 8:15am–7:30pm. **Giardino Boboli:** © **055-265-1816;** admission 4€ ($4.60) adults, 2€ ($2.30) children, cumulative ticket with Museo degli Argenti available; Nov–Feb daily 8:15am–4:30pm, Mar daily 8:15am–5:30pm, Apr–May and Oct daily 8:15am–6:30pm, and June–Sept daily 8:15am–7:30pm. Bus: D, 11, 36, 37, or 68.

Santo Spirito & One of Filippo Brunelleschi's masterpieces of architecture, this 15th-century church doesn't look like much from the outside (no true facade was ever built), but the **interior** & is a marvelous High Renaissance space—an expansive landscape of proportion and mathematics worked out in classic Brunelleschi style, with coffered vaulting, tall columns, and the stacked perspective of arched arcading. Good late-Renaissance and baroque paintings are scattered throughout, but the best stuff lies up in the transepts and in the east end, surrounding the extravagant **baroque altar** with a ciborium inlaid in *pietre dure* around 1607.

The **right transept** begins with a *Crucifixion* by Francesco Curradi. Against the back wall of the transept, the first chapel holds an early-15th-century *Madonna del Soccorso* of uncertain authorship. Two chapels down is one of Filippino Lippi's best works, a *Madonna and Child with Saints and Donors.* The background seen through the classical arches was painted with an almost Flemish exacting detail. In the east end of the church, the center two chapels against the back wall contain Alessandro Allori altarpieces: *The Martyred Saints* (1574) on the right has a predella view of what the Palazzo Pitti looked like before its enlargement; and the *Christ and the Adulteress* on the left is extremely advanced in style, already almost a work of the late baroque. In the **left transept,** the first chapel on the right side is a late-15th-century *Madonna Enthroned with Child and Saints.* Next to this is the highly skilled *St. Monica and Augustinian Nuns,* an almost monochrome work of black and pale yellow, faintly disturbing in its eerie monotony and perfection of composition. It's now usually attributed to the enigmatic Andrea del Verrocchio, one-time master of Leonardo da Vinci.

The famed **piazza** outside is one of the focal points of the Oltrarno, shaded by trees and lined with trendy cafes that see some bar action in the evenings. It's not quite the pleasant hangout it once was, however—especially since the heroin set moved in a few years ago, making it a less than desirable place to be after midnight (though early evening is still fine). Stop by Bar Ricci at no. 9r, where more than 300 facade designs for faceless Santo Spirito line the walls, the product of a fun-loving contest the bar held in 1980.

Piazza Santo Spirito. ℂ **055-210-030.** Free admission. Daily 8am–noon; Thurs–Tues 4–6pm. Bus: D, 6, 11, 36, 37, or 68.

Cenacolo di Santo Spirito Museum
The dark and haphazard museum in the church's old refectory (entrance to the left of Santo Spirito's facade) has a gathering of Romanesque and paleo-Christian stone sculptures and reliefs. The main reason to drop by is the end wall frescoed by Andrea Orcagna and his brother Nardo di Cione in 1360 with a *Last Supper* (of which only 1.5 apostles and a halo are left) and above it a beautiful *Crucifixion,* one of 14th-century Florence's masterpieces.

Piazza Santo Spirito 29. ℂ **055-287-043.** Admission 2.20€ ($2.55). Tues–Sat 10:30am–1:30pm (until 2pm Apr–Nov). Bus: D, 6, 11, 36, 37, or 68.

Santa Maria della Carmine ✦✦✦
Following a 1771 fire that destroyed everything but the transept chapels and sacristy, this Carmelite church was almost entirely reconstructed and decorated in high baroque style. Ever since a long and expensive restoration of the famous frescoes of the **Cappella Brancacci** in the right transept,

they've blocked off just that chapel and you have to enter through the cloisters (doorway to the right of the church facade) and pay admission. The frescoes were commissioned by an enemy of the Medici, Felice Brancacci, who in 1424 hired Masolino and his student Masaccio to decorate it with a cycle on the life of St. Peter. Masolino probably worked out the cycle's scheme and painted a few scenes along with his pupil before taking off for 3 years to serve as court painter in Budapest, during which time Masaccio kept painting, quietly creating one of his masterpieces and some of the early Renaissance's greatest frescoes. Masaccio left for Rome in 1428, where he died at age 27. The cycle was completed between 1480 and 1485 by Filippino Lippi, who faithfully imitated Masaccio's technique.

Even before Lippi's intervention, though, the frescoes had been an instant hit. People flocked from all over the city to admire them, and almost every Italian artist of the day came to sketch and study Masaccio's mastery of perspective, bold light and colors, and unheard-of touches of realism. Even later masters like Leonardo da Vinci and Michelangelo came to learn what they could from the young artist's genius. A 1980s restoration cleaned off the dirt and dark mold that had grown in the egg-based pigments used to "touch up" the frescoes in the 18th century and removed additions like the prudish ivy leaves trailing across Adam and Eve's privates.

Masolino was responsible for the *St. Peter Preaching,* the upper panel to the left of the altar, and the two top scenes on the right wall, which shows his fastidiously decorative style in a long panel of *St. Peter Healing the Cripple* and *Raising Tabitha,* and his *Adam and Eve.* Contrast this first man and woman, about to take the bait offered by the snake, with the ***Expulsion from the Garden*** ✯✯ across from it painted by Masaccio. Masolino's figures are highly posed models, expressionless and oblivious to the temptation being offered. Masaccio's Adam and Eve, on the other hand, burst with intense emotion and forceful movement. The top scene on the left wall is also by Masaccio, and it showcases both his classical influences and another of his innovations, perfect linear perspective. On the end wall, Masaccio painted the lower scene to the left of the altar of *St. Peter Healing the Sick with His Shadow,* unique at the time for its realistic portrayal of street beggars and crippled bodies. The two scenes to the right of the altar are Masaccio as well, with the *Baptism of the Neophytes* taking its place among his masterpieces. Most of the rest of the frescoes were painted by Filippino Lippi. The left transept chapel, which isn't blocked off, is one of Florence's most harmonious examples of the baroque (1675–83), with a ceiling painted by Luca Giordano.

Piazza della Carmine. ℭ **055-238-2195.** Free admission to church; Brancacci chapel 4€ ($4.60), cumulative ticket with Palazzo Vecchio available. Daily 10am–5pm; Sun 1–5pm. Bus: D, 6, 11, 36, 37, or 68.

Museo Zoologico La Specola   Italy has very few zoos, but this is the largest zoological collection, rooms full of insects, crustaceans, and stuffed birds and mammals—everything from ostriches and apes to a rhinoceros. The museum was founded here in 1775, and the collections are still displayed in the style of an old-fashioned natural sciences museum, with specimens crowded into beautiful old wood-and-glass cases. The last 10 rooms contain an important collection of human anatomical wax models crafted between 1775 and 1814 by Clemente Susini for medical students. The life-size figures are flayed, dissected, and disemboweled to varying degrees and are truly disgusting, but fascinating.

Via Romana 17. ℭ **055-228-8251.** www.specola.unifi.it. Admission 5€ ($5.75) adults, 2.50€ ($2.90) children 6–18, free for children under 6. Thurs–Tues 9am–1pm. Bus: C, D, 11, 36, or 37.

San Felice   This tiny Gothic church just south of the Pitti Palace sports a High Renaissance facade by Michelozzo (1457) and a *Crucifixion* over the high altar recently attributed to Giotto. Also peek at the remnants of Niccolò Gerini's early-15th-century *Pietà* fresco over the first altar on the right.

At no. 8 on the piazza is the entrance to the **Casa Guidi,** where from 1846 English poet Elizabeth Barrett Browning lived with her husband, Robert, moving in just after their secret marriage. When the unification of Italy became official in Florence, Elizabeth recorded the momentous event in a famous poem, "Casa Guidi Windows": "I heard last night a little child go singing / 'Neath Casa Guidi windows, by the church, / O bella libertà, O bella!" Mrs. Browning died in this house on June 18, 1861.

Piazza di San Felice. No phone. Free admission. Bus: D, 11, 36, 37, or 68.

8 In the Hills

Piazzale Michelangiolo ℛ   This panoramic piazza is a required stop for every tour bus. The balustraded terrace was laid out in 1885 to give a sweeping vista of the entire city, spread out in the valley below and backed by the green hills of Fiesole beyond. The monument to Michelangelo in the center of the piazza is made up of bronze replicas of *David* and his Medici chapel sculptures.

Viale Michelangelo. Bus: 12 or 13.

San Miniato al Monte 🏵🏵   High atop a hill, its gleaming white-and-green facade visible from the valley below, San Miniato is one of the few ancient churches of Florence to survive the centuries virtually intact. San Miniato was an eastern Christian who settled in Florence and was martyred during Emperor Decius's persecutions in A.D. 250. The legend goes that the decapitated saint picked up his head, walked across the river, climbed up the hillside, and didn't lie down to die until he reached this spot. He and other Christians were buried here, and a shrine was raised on the site as early as the 4th century.

The current building began to take shape in 1013, under the auspices of the powerful Arte di Calimala guild, whose symbol, a bronze eagle clutching a bale of wool, perches atop the **facade** 🏵🏵. The Romanesque facade is a particularly gorgeous bit of white Carrara and green Prato marble inlay. Above the central window is a 13th-century mosaic of *Christ Between the Madonna and St. Miniato* (a theme repeated in a slightly later mosaic filling the apse inside).

The **interior** has a few Renaissance additions, but they blend in well with the overall medieval aspect—an airy, stony space with a raised choir at one end, painted wooden trusses on the ceiling, and tombs interspersed with inlaid marble symbols of the zodiac paving the floor.

Below the choir is an 11th-century **crypt** with small frescoes by Taddo Gaddi. Off to the right of the raised choir is the **sacristy,** which Spinello Aretino covered in 1387 with cartoonish yet elegant frescoes depicting the *Life of St. Benedict* 🏵. Off the left aisle of the nave is 15th-century **Cappella del Cardinale del Portogallo** 🏵🏵, a brilliant collaborative effort by Renaissance artists built to honor young Portuguese humanist Cardinal Jacopo di Lusitania, who was sent to study in Perugia but died an untimely death at 25 in Florence. Brunelleschi's student Antonio Manetti started the chapel in 1460 but soon died, and Antonio Rossellino finished the architecture and carving by 1466. Luca della Robbia provided the glazed terra-cotta dome, a cubic landscape set with tondi of the four *Virtues* surrounding the *Holy Spirit* to symbolize the young scholar's devotion to the church and to humanist philosophy. It stands as one of della Robbia's masterpieces of color and classical ideals. The unfinished **bell tower** seen from the outside was designed by Baccio d'Agnolo. In 1530 the combined troops of Charles V and Medici Pope Clement VII, who had recently reconciled with each other, lay siege to the newly declared Republic of Florence in an attempt to reinstate the Medici dukes. San Miniato al Monte was one of the prime fortifications, and an artilleryman named Lapo was stationed up in the tower with two small cannons—he was basically bait, stuck there to draw the fire of the enemy where it would do little harm. The man in charge of the defenses was Michelangelo, who, the authorities figured, was so good at everything else, why not military fortifications? After throwing up dirt ramparts and cobbling together defensible walls out of oak timbers, Michelangelo helped poor Lapo out by devising an ingenious way to protect the tower: He hung mattresses down the sides to absorb the shock of the cannonballs fired at it and left the tower (and, more important, Lapo) still standing.

The siege was eventually successful, however, and the Florentine Republic fell, but while it lasted, Michelangelo spent his day up here and referred to the church of **San Salvatore al Monte** just below as "my pretty country maid." It's a simple 1400 church built by Cronaca, with a Giovanni della Robbia *Deposition* and a Neri di Bicci *Pietà* inside.

Via del Monte alle Croci/Viale Galileo Galilei (behind Piazzale Michelangiolo). © 055-234-2731. Free admission. Easter to early Oct daily 8am–7:30pm; winter Mon–Sat 8am–1pm and 2:30–6pm, Sun 8am–6pm. Bus: 12 or 13.

Museo Stibbert   Half Scotsman, half Italian, Frederick Stibbert was nothing if not eccentric. A sometime artist, intrepid traveler, voracious accumulator, and even hero in Garibaldi's army, he inherited a vast fortune and this villa from his Italian mother. He connected the house to a nearby villa to create an eclectic museum

---

Catching *Calcio* Fever

To Italians, *calcio* (soccer) is something akin to a second religion. You don't know what a "fan" is until you've attended a soccer match in a country like Italy, and an afternoon at the football stadium can offer you as much insight (if not more) into Italian culture as a day in the Uffizi. Catch the local team, the Fiorentina, Sundays September through May at the Stadio Comunale, Via Manfredi Fanti 4 (© 055-262-5537 or 055-50-721; www.acfiorentina.it). Tickets go on sale at the stadium box office 3 hours before each game.

housing his extraordinary collections, including baroque canvases, fine porcelain, Flemish tapestries, Tuscan crucifixes, and Etruscan artifacts. The museum was partially rearranged in past decades to try and make some sense out of 57 rooms stuffed with over 50,000 items. More recently, however, the city has come to appreciate this rare example of a private 19th-century museum and is busily setting it all back the way Stibbert originally intended.

Stibbert's greatest interest and most fascinating assemblage is of **armor** ℛ—Etruscan, Lombard, Asian, Roman, 17th-century Florentine, and 15th-century Turkish. The museum has the largest display of Japanese arms and armor in Europe and a new exhibit of porcelain. The high point of the house is a remarkable grand hall filled with an entire cavalcade of mannequins in 16th-century armor (mostly European, but with half a dozen samurai foot soldiers thrown in for good measure). Stibbert even managed to get some seriously historic Florentine armor, that in which Medici warrior Giovanni delle Bande Nere was buried.

Via Stibbert 26. ℭ **055-475-520.** www.museostibbert.com. Admission 5€ ($5.75) adults, 2€ ($2.30) children. Mon–Wed 10am–4pm; Fri–Sun 10am–6pm. Bus: 4.

Shopping

The cream of the crop of Florentine shopping lines both sides of the elegant **Via de' Tornabuoni,** with an extension along **Via della Vigna Nuova** and other surrounding streets. Here you'll find big names like Gucci, Armani, Ferragamo, and Mila Schön ensconced in old palaces or modern minimalist boutiques.

On the other end of the shopping spectrum is the haggling and general fun of the colorful and noisy **San Lorenzo street market.** Antiques gather dust by the truckload along **Via Maggio** and other

Getting Your VAT Refund

Most purchases have a built-in **value added tax (IVA)** of 17.36%. Non-EU (European Union) citizens are entitled to a refund of this tax if they spend more than 154.94€ (before tax) at any one store. To claim your refund, request an invoice from the cashier at the store and take it to the customs office (dogana) at the airport to have it stamped before you leave. **Note:** If you're going to another EU country before flying home, have it stamped at the airport customs office of the last EU country you'll be visiting (so if flying home via Britain, have your Italian invoices stamped in London).

Once back home, mail the stamped invoice back to the store within 90 days of the purchase, and they'll send you a refund check. Many shops are now part of the "Tax Free for Tourists" network. (Look for the sticker in the window.) Stores participating in this network issue a check along with your invoice at the time of purchase. After you have the invoice stamped at customs, you can redeem the check for cash directly at the tax-free booth in the airport, or mail it back in the envelope provided within 60 days. For more info, check out www.globalrefund.com.

Oltrarno streets. Another main corridor of stores somewhat less glitzy than those on the Via de' Tornabuoni begins at **Via Cerretani** and runs down **Via Roma** through the Piazza della Repubblica area; it keeps going down **Via Por Santa Maria,** across the **Ponte Vecchio** with its gold jewelry, and up **Via Guicciardini** on the other side. Store-laden side tributaries off this main stretch include **Via della Terme, Borgo Santissimi Apostoli,** and **Borgo San Jacopo.**

General Florentine **shopping hours** are daily from 9:30am to noon or 1pm and 3 or 3:30pm to 7:30pm, though increasingly, many shops are staying open through that mid-afternoon *riposo* (especially the larger stores and those around tourist sights).

1 Shopping the Markets

Haggling is accepted, and even expected, at most outdoor markets (but don't try it in stores). The queen of Florentine markets is the **San Lorenzo street market,** filling Piazza San Lorenzo, Via del Canto de' Nelli, Via dell'Ariento, and other side streets. It's a wildly chaotic and colorful array of hundreds of stands hawking T-shirts, silk scarves, marbleized paper, Gucci knockoffs, and lots and lots of leather. Many of the stalls are merely outlets for full-fledged stores hidden behind them. Haggling is tradition here, and though you'll find plenty of leather lemons, there are also great deals on truly high-quality leather and other goods—you just have to commit to half a day of picking through it all and fending off sales pitches. March through October, most stalls are open daily about 8am to 8pm (it varies with how business is doing); November through February, the market is closed Mondays and Sundays, except for the 2 weeks or so around Christmas, when it remains open daily.

Somewhere in the center of this capitalist whirlwind hides the indoor **Mercato Centrale food market** (between Via dell'Ariento and Piazza del Mercato Centrale). Downstairs you'll find meat, cheese, and dry goods. There's one stall devoted to tripe aficionados, a second piled high with *baccalà* (dried salt cod), and a good cheap eatery called **Nerbone** (p. 81). The upstairs is devoted to fruits and veggies—a cornucopia of fat eggplants, long yellow peppers, stacks of artichokes, and pepperoncini bunched into brilliant red bursts. In all, you couldn't ask for better picnic pickings. The market is open Monday through Saturday from 7am to 2pm and Saturday also 4 to 7:30pm.

As if two names weren't enough, the **Mercato Nuovo (Straw Market)** is also known as Mercato del Porcellino or Mercato del

Cinghiale because of the bronze wild boar statue at one end, cast by Pietro Tacca in the 17th century after an antique original now in the Uffizi. Pet the well-polished porcellino's snout to ensure a return trip to Florence. Most of the straw stalls disappeared by the 1960s. These days, the loggia hawks mainly poor-quality leather purses, mediocre bijoux, souvenirs, and other tourist trinkets. Beware of pickpockets. In summer it's open daily around 9am to 8pm, but in winter it closes at 5pm and all day Sunday and Monday.

2 Shopping A to Z

Here's **what to buy in Florence:** leather, high fashion, shoes, marbleized paper, hand-embroidered linens, lace, lingerie, Tuscan wines, gold jewelry, *pietre dure* (aka Florentine mosaic, inlaid semiprecious stones), and Renaissance leftovers and other antiques. Here's where to buy it.

ART & ANTIQUES

The antiques business is clustered where the artisans have always lived and worked: the Oltrarno. Dealers' shops line Via Maggio, but the entire district is packed with venerable chunks of the past. On "this side" of the river, Borgo Ognissanti has the highest concentration of aging furniture and art collectibles.

The large showrooms of **Gallori-Turchi,** Via Maggio 14r (© **055-282-279**), specialize in furnishings, paintings, and weaponry (swords, lances, and pistols) from the 16th to 18th centuries. They also offer majolica and ceramic pieces and scads of excellent desks and writing tables of hand-carved and inlaid wood. Nearby you'll find **Guido Bartolozzi Antichità,** Via Maggio 18r (© **055-215-602**), under family management since 1887. This old-fashioned store concentrates on the 16th to 19th centuries. They might be offering a 17th-century Gobelin tapestry, an inlaid stone tabletop, or wood intarsia dressers from the 1700s. The quality is impeccable: The owner has been president of Italy's antiques association and secretary of Florence's biannual antiques fair. There's another showroom at Via Maggio 11.

For the serious collector who wants his or her own piece of Florence's cultural heritage, the refined showroom at **Gianfranco Luzzetti,** Borgo San Jacopo 28A (© **055-211-232**), offers artwork and furniture from the 1400s to the 1600s. They have a gorgeous collection of 16th-century Deruta ceramics and majolica, canvases by the likes of Vignale and Bilivert, and on last visit even a glazed terra-cotta altarpiece from the hand of Andrea della Robbia. Bring sacks of money.

BOOKS

Even the smaller bookshops in Florence these days have at least a few shelves devoted to English-language books. **Feltrinelli International,** Via Cavour 12–20 (© **055-219-524;** www.lafeltrinelli.it), is one of the few of any size.

For English-only shops, hit **Paperback Exchange,** Via Fiesolana 31r (© **055-247-8154;** www.papex.it); it's not the most central, but it is the best for books in English, specializing in titles relating in some way to Florence and Italy. Much of their stock is used, and you can't beat the prices anywhere in Italy—dog-eared volumes and all Penguin books go for just a few euros. You can also trade in that novel you've already finished for another. **BM Bookshop,** Borgo Ognissanti 4r (© **055-294-575**), is a bit smaller but more central and carries only new volumes. They also have a slightly more well-rounded selection—from novels and art books to cookbooks and travel guides. A special section is devoted to Italian- and Tuscany-oriented volumes.

G. Vitello, Via dei Servi 94–96r (© **055-292-445**), sells coffee table–worthy books on art and all things Italian at up to half off the price you'd pay in a regular bookstore. Other branches are at Via Verdi 40r (© **055-234-6894**) and Via Pietrapiana 1r (© **055-241-063**). **Libreria Il Viaggio,** Borgo degli Albizi 41r (© **055-240-489**), is a cozy niche specializing in specialty travel guides, related literature, and maps, with a sizable selection in English.

DEPARTMENT STORES

Florence's central branch of the national chain **Coin,** Via Calzaiuoli 56r (© **055-280-531;** www.coin.it), is a stylish multifloored display case for upper-middle-class fashions—a chic Macy's. **La Rinascente,** Piazza della Repubblica 2 (© **055-219-113;** www.rinascente.it), is another of Italy's finer department stores. This six-floor store serves as an outlet for top designers (Versace, Zegna, Ferré, and so on). It also has areas set up to sell traditional Tuscan goods (terra cotta, alabaster, olive oils, and wrought iron).

DESIGN, HOUSEWARES & CERAMICS

Viceversa ⟨𝒞⟩, Via dello Stell 3 (© **055-696-392;** www.viceversa shop.com), offers one of the largest selections of the latest Robert Graves–designed teakettle or any other whimsical Alessi kitchen product. The friendly staff will also point out the Pavoni espresso machines, Carl Merkins' totemic bar set, the Princess motorized gadgets, and shelf after shelf of the best of Italian kitchen and houseware designs.

Tiny **La Botteghina,** Via Guelfa 5r (© **055-287-367;** www. labotteghina.it), is about the best and most reasonably priced city outlet for true artisan ceramics I've found in all Italy. Daniele Viegi del Fiume deals in gorgeous hand-painted ceramics from the best traditional artisans working in nearby Montelupo, the famed Umbrian ceramics centers of Deruta and Gubbio, and Castelli, high in the Abruzzi mountains.

If you can't make it to the workshops in the hill towns themselves, La Botteghina's the next best thing. If you like the sample of pieces by **Giuseppe Rampini** you see here and want to invest in a full table setting, Rampini has its own classy showroom at Borgo Ognissanti 32–34 (right at Piazza Ognissanti; © **055-219-720;** www.chiantinet. it/rampiniceramics).

For big-name production-line china and tablewares, visit **Richard Ginori,** Via Giulio Cesare 21 (© **055-420-491;** www. richardginori1735.com). Colorful rims and whimsical designs fill this warehouselike salesroom of the firm that has sold Florence's finest china since 1735. Other houseware bigwigs are represented as well—Alessi coffeepots, Nason and Meretti Murano glass, and Chrisofle flatware.

FASHION & CLOTHING

Although Italian fashion reached its pinnacle in the 1950s and 1960s, the country has remained at the forefront of both high (Armani, Gucci, Pucci, Ferragamo, just to name a few) and popular (as evidenced by the spectacular success of Benetton in the 1980s) fashion. Florence plays second fiddle to Milan in today's Italian fashion scene, but the city has its own cadre of highly respected names, plus, of course, outlet shops of all the hot designers. Also see "Leather, Accessories & Shoes" below.

FOR MEN & WOMEN   Cinzia, Borgo San Jacopo 22r (© **055-298-078**), is a grab bag of hand-knit, usually bulky wool sweaters offered by an elderly couple who've been sending their creations around the world for more than 30 years. **Luisa Via Roma,** Via Roma 19–21r (© **055-217-826;** www.luisaviaroma.com), is a famed gathering place for all the top names in avant-garde fashion, including Jean Paul Gaultier, Dolce & Gabbana, and Issey Miyake. Men can hand over their wallets upstairs, and women can empty their purses on the ground floor. Service can be chilly.

The address may be a hint that this isn't your average fashion shop: **Emilio Pucci,** Palazzo Pucci, Via de' Pucci 6 (© **055-283-061;** www.pucci.com). Marchese Emilio Pucci's ancestors have been a powerful banking and mercantile family since the Renaissance, and in 1950 the marchese suddenly turned designer and shocked the fashion world with his flowing silks in outlandish colors. His women's silk clothing remained the rage into the early 1970s and had a Renaissance of its own in the 1990s club scene. The design team is now headed by daughter Laudomia Pucci. If you don't wish to visit the showroom in the ancient family palace, drop by the shop at Via dei Tornabuoni 20–22r (© **055-265-8082**).

Then there's **Giorgio Armani,** Via Tornabuoni 48r (© **055-219-041;** www.giorgioarmani.com), Florence's outlet for Italy's top fashion guru. The service and store are surprisingly not stratospherically chilly (the Official Armani Attitude at the moment is studied, casual indifference). The **Emporio Armani** branch at Piazza Strozzi 16r (© **055-284-315;** www.emporioarmani.com) is the outlet for the more affordable designs. The merchandise is slightly inferior in workmanship and quality and greatly inferior in price—you can actually dig out shirts for less than $1,000.

But the biggest name to walk out of Florence onto the international catwalk has to be **Gucci,** with the world flagship store at Via de' Tornabuoni 73r (© **055-264-011;** www.gucci.com). This is where this Florentine fashion empire was started by saddlemaker Guccio Gucci in 1904, now run by a gaggle of grandsons. You enter through a phalanx of their trademark purses and bags. Forget the cheesy knockoffs sold on street corners around the world; the stock here is elegant.

Nearby is another homegrown fashion label, **Enrico Coveri,** Via Tornabuoni 81r (© **055-211-263;** www.coveri.com). Enrico started off in the nearby textile town of Prato and has a similar penchant for bright colors as contemporary Emilio Pucci. The major difference is that Enrico Coveri's firm produces downscale fashion that fits the bods and wallets of normal folk—not just leggy models. Some of the men's suits are particularly fine, but the children's collection may be best left alone. There's another tiny branch at Via Tornabuoni 81r.

FOR WOMEN **Loretta Caponi,** Piazza Antinori 4r (© **055-213-668**), is world famous for her high-quality intimates and embroidered linens made the old-fashioned way. Under Belle Epoque ceilings are nightgowns of all types, bed and bath linens of the highest caliber, curtains, and feminine unmentionables. There's also a large section for the little ones in the back. Peek through the pebble-glassed doors to see the workshop.

STOCK HOUSES   To get your high fashion at bargain-basement prices, head to one of the branches of **Guardaroba/Stock House Grandi Firme.** The store at Borgo degli Albizi 78r (© 055-234-0271) carries mainly the past season's models, while the Via dei Castellani 26r branch (© 055-294-853) carries spring/summer remaindered collections, and the Via Verdi 28r (© 055-247-8250) and Via Nazionale 38r (© 055-215-482) offers outfits from the past winter. **Stock House Il Giglio,** Via Borgo Ognissanti 86 (no phone), also carries big name labels at 50% to 60% off.

GIFTS & CRAFTS

Florentine traditional "mosaics" are actually works of inlaid stone called *pietre dure.* The creations of young Ilio de Filippis and his army of apprentices at **Pitti Mosaici,** Piazza Pitti 16r and 23–24r (© 055-282-127; www.pittimosaici.it), reflect traditional techniques and artistry. Ilio's father was a *pietre dure* artist, and his grandfather was a sculptor. (The family workshop was founded in 1900.) Besides the pieces on display down the road toward the Arno at Via Guicciardini 80r and across the river at Lungarno Vespucci 36r, the firm will custom make works to your specifications.

Professore Agostino Dessi presides over the traditional Venetian Carnevale–style maskmaking at **Alice Atelier,** Via Faenza 72r (© 055-287-370). All masks are made using papier-mâché, leather, and ceramics according to 17th-century techniques, hand-painted with tempera, touched up with gold and silver leaf, and polished with French lacquer.

JEWELRY

If you've got the financial solvency of a small country, the place to buy your baubles is the Ponte Vecchio, famous for its gold- and silversmiths since the 16th century. The craftsmanship at the stalls is usually of a very high quality, and so they seem to compete instead over who can charge the highest prices. A more moderately priced boutique is Milan-based **Mario Buccellati,** Via de' Tornabuoni 71r (© 055-239-6579), which since 1919 has been making thick, heavy jewelry of high quality.

Florence is also a good place to root around for interesting costume jewelry. The audacious bijoux at **Angela Caputi,** Borgo San Jacopo 82r (© 055-212-972; www.angelacaputi.com), aren't for the timid. Much of Angela's costume jewelry—from earrings and necklaces to brooches and now even a small clothing line—is at least oversize and bold and often pushes the flamboyance envelope.

LEATHER, ACCESSORIES & SHOES

It has always been a buyers' market for leather in Florence, but these days it's tough to sort out the jackets mass-produced for tourists from the high-quality artisan work. The most fun you'll have leather shopping is without a doubt at the outdoor stalls of the **San Lorenzo** market, even if the market is rife with mediocre goods (see "Shopping the Markets" above). Never accept the first price they throw at you; sometimes you can bargain them down to almost half the original asking price. The shops below should guarantee you at least quality merchandise, but not the bargaining joys of the market. (See also "Fashion & Clothing" above.)

Anna, Piazza Pitti 38–41r (✆ **055-283-787**), is a fine store for handcrafted leather coats and clothing set in the remains of a 14th-century tower. You can also pick up discounted Versace purses and funky colorful Missoni sweaters. For the best of the leather, head down the stairs in the back where you'll find fur-collared coats, suede jackets, and supple pigskin vests. They'll do alterations and even full tailoring in 24 hours. **John F.,** Lungarno Corsini 2 (✆ **055-239-8985;** www.johnf.it), is a purveyor of high-quality leather goods as well as Missoni sweaters, Krizia purses, and Bettina bags.

More fun, but no less expensive, is to watch the artisans at work at the **Scuola del Cuoio (Leather School) of Santa Croce.** You enter through Santa Croce church (right transept), Piazza Santa Croce 16, or on Via San Giuseppe 5r on Sunday morning (✆ **055-244-533** or 055-244-534; www.leatherschool.it). The very-fine-quality soft-leather merchandise isn't cheap.

In the imposing 13th-century Palazzo Spini-Feroni lording over Piazza Santa Trínita are the flagship store, museum, and home of **Ferragamo,** Via de' Tornabuoni 4–14r (✆ **055-292-123;** www. ferragamo.it). Salvatore Ferragamo was the man who shod Hollywood in its most glamorous age and raised footwear to an art form. View some of Ferragamo's funkier shoes in the second-floor museum (call ahead at ✆ **055-336-0456**) or slip on a pair yourself in the show-rooms downstairs—if you think your wallet can take the shock.

If you prefer to buy right from the cobbler, head across the Arno to **Calzature Francesco da Firenze,** Via Santo Spirito 62r (✆ **055-212-428**), where handmade shoes run 80€ to 165€ ($92–$190), and you can hear them tap-tapping away on soles in the back room.

For more made-in-Florence accessorizing, head to **Madova Gloves,** Via Guicciardini 1r (✆ **055-239-6526;** www.madova. com). Gloves are all they do in this tiny shop, and they do them well. The grandchildren of the workshop's founders do a brisk business in brightly colored, supple leather gloves lined with cashmere and silk. Although they display a bit of everything at **Beltrami,** Via de' Tornabuoni 48r (© **055-287-779**), their forte is still beautiful well-built footwear, bags, briefcases, and luggage. Beltrami is based in Florence, so prices are as low here as you're going to find.

MUSIC

Although restrictions are ever tightening, Italy still remains one of the best places in Western Europe to get bootlegs. Quality, obviously, can vary drastically (most places will let you listen before you buy). Some of the more "reputable" pirate labels include Pluto, Great Dane, Bugsy, On Stage, Teddy Bear, Beech Marten, and Red Line. **Data Records,** Via dei Neri 15r (© **055-287-592**), is a hip place with a sassy funk attitude, knowledgeable staff, plenty of cutting-edge music (Italian and international), and scads of good bootlegs. They also run a more mainstream outlet, **Super Records** (© **055-234-9526;** www.superecords.com), in the pedestrian passage leading from Santa Maria Novella train station, with some of the best prices in town on first-run presses from major labels. Both are closed in August.

PAPER & JOURNALS

Giulio Giannini and Figlio, Piazza Pitti 36–37r (© **055-212-621;** www.giuliogiannini.it), offers an expensive but quality selection of leather-bound notebooks, fine stationery, and the shop's specialty, objects garbed in decorative papers. This was one of the first stores to paste marbleized sheets onto desktop items, but its real trademark is objects sheathed in genuine 17th- to 19th-century manuscript and choir-book sheets. **Il Papiro,** Via dei Tavolini 13r (© **055-213-823;** www.madeinfirenze.it/papiro_e.htm), is now a modest Tuscan chain of jewel box–size shops specializing in marbled and patterned paper, as plain gift-wrap sheets or as a covering for everything from pens and journals to letter openers or full desk sets. There are several branches, including the head office at Via Cavour 55r (no phone) and shops at Piazza del Duomo 24r (no phone), Lungarno Acciaiuoli 42r (© **055-215-262**), and Piazza Rucellai 8r (© **055-211-652**).

Scriptorium, Via dei Servi 5–7r (© **055-211-804**), is my own journal supplier, a small shop that's one of the few fine stationery stores in Florence with very little marbleized paper. Come here for hand-sewn notebooks, journals, and photo albums made of thick paper—all bound in soft leather covers. With classical music or Gregorian chant playing in the background, you can also shop for calligraphy and signet wax sealing tools. There's a new branch in the Oltrarno at Piazza de' Pitti 6 (© **055-238-2272;** www.scriptorium firenze.com).

PRINTS

Little Bottega delle Stampe, Borgo San Jacopo 56r (© **055-295-396**), carries prints, historic maps, and engravings from the 1500s through the Liberty-style and Art Deco prints of the 1930s. You can dig out some Dürers here, as well as original Piranesis and plates from Diderot's 1700 Encyclopedia. There are Florence views from the 16th to 19th centuries, plus a fine collection of 18th-century French engravings.

TOYS

Since 1977, Florence's owner-operated branch of national chain **La Città del Sole,** Borgo Ognissanti 37r (© **055-219-345;** www. cittadelsole.it), has sold old-fashioned wooden brain teasers, construction kits, hand puppets, 3-D puzzles, science kits, and books. There's nary a video game in sight.

WINE & LIQUORS

The front room of the **Enoteca Alessi,** Via dell'Oche 27–31r (© **055-214-966;** www.enotecaalessi.it), sells boxed chocolates and other sweets, but in the back and in the large cellars, you can find everything from prime vintages to a simple-quality table wine. This large store, 2 blocks from the Duomo, also offers tastings. The **Enoteca Gambi Romano,** Borgo SS. Apostoli 21–23r (© **055-292-646**), is another central outlet for olive oil, vin santo, grappa, and (upstairs) lots of wine.

Florence After Dark

Florence doesn't have the musical cachet or grand opera houses of Milan, Venice, or Rome, but there are two symphony orchestras and a fine music school in Fiesole. The city's public theaters are certainly respectable, and most major touring companies stop in town on their way through Italy. Get tickets to all cultural and musical events at the city's main clearinghouse, **Box Office,** Via Alamanni 39 (© 055-210-804; www.boxoffice.it). In addition to tickets for year-round events of all genres, they handle the summertime Calcio in Costume folkloric festival and the Maggio Musicale.

1 The Performing Arts

Many concerts and recitals staged in major halls and private spaces across town are sponsored by the **Amici della Musica** (© 055-607-440 or 055-608-420; www.amicimusica.fi.it), so contact them to see what "hidden" concert might be on while you're in town.

CHURCH CONCERTS

Many Florentine churches fill the autumn with organ, choir, and chamber orchestra concerts, mainly of classical music. The tiny **Santa Maria de' Ricci** (© 055-215-044) on Via del Corso seems always to have music wafting out of it; slipping inside to occupy a pew is occasionally free, but sometimes there's a small charge. Around the corner at Santa Margherita 7, the **Chiesa di Dante** (© 055-289-367) puts on quality concerts of music for, and often played by, youths and children (tickets required). **The Florentine Chamber Orchestra,** Via E. Poggi 6 (© 055-783-374), also runs an autumn season in the Orsanmichele; tickets are available at Box Office (see above) or at the door an hour before the 9pm shows.

CONCERT HALLS & OPERA

One of Italy's busiest stages, Florence's contemporary **Teatro Comunale,** Corso Italia 12 (© 055-213-535 or 055-211-158; www.maggiofiorentino.com), offers everything from symphonies to ballet to plays, opera, and concerts. The large main theater seats 2,000, with orchestra rows topped by horseshoe-shaped first and second galleries. Its smaller Piccolo Teatro seating 500 is rectangular, offering good sightlines from most any seat. The Teatro Comunale is the seat of the annual prestigious Maggio Musicale.

The Teatro Verdi, Via Ghibellina 99–101 (© **055-212-320** or 055-263-877; www.teatroverdi.com), is Florence's opera and ballet house, with the nice habit of staging Sunday-afternoon shows during the January-through-April season. **The Orchestra della Toscana** (© **055-280-670;** www.orchestradellatoscana.it) plays classical concerts here December through May. Like the Teatro Comunale, they do a bit of theater, but not of the caliber of La Pergola (see below).

THEATER

The biggest national and international touring companies stop in Florence's major playhouse, the **Teatro della Pergola,** Via della Pergola 12 (© **055-226-4335;** www.pergola.firenze.it). La Pergola is the city's chief purveyor of classical and classic plays from the Greeks and Shakespeare through Pirandello, Samuel Beckett, and Italian modern playwrights. Performances are professional and of high quality, if not always terribly innovative (and, of course, all in Italian).

2 The Club & Live Music Scene

Italian clubs are rather cliquey—people usually go in groups to hang out and dance only with one another. There's plenty of flesh showing, but no meat market. Singles hoping to find random dance partners will often be disappointed.

LIVE MUSIC

For live bands you can dance to in the center, head to **Dolce Zucchero,** Via dei Pandolfini 36–38r (© **055-247-7894**). "Sweet Sugar" is one of the better recent efforts to spice up Florence's nightlife and is popular with all ages. Under high ceilings are a long bar and a small dance floor with a stage for the nightly live musicians, usually a fairly talented cover act cranking out American and Italian dance songs for the packed crowd.

DANCE CLUBS & NIGHTCLUBS

Florence's clubs have a "minimum consumption" charge of 10€ to 16€ ($12–$18). The big hit of 2002 was **Universale,** Via Pisana 77r (© **055-221-122;** www.universalefirenze.it), housed in a converted 1940s cinema and successfully managing to draw everyone from folks in their early 20s to those pushing 50 (how they manage to keep collegians cutting loose from running into their young-at-heart

Cafe Culture

Florence no longer has a glitterati or intellectuals' cafe scene, and when it did—from the late-19th-century Italian *Risorgimento* era through the *dolce vita* of the 1950s—it was basically copying the idea from Paris. Although they're often overpriced tourist spots today, Florence's high-toned cafes are fine if you want designer pastries and hot cappuccino served to you while you sit on a piazza and people-watch.

At the refined, wood-paneled, stucco-ceilinged, and very expensive 1733 cafe **Gilli,** Piazza della Repubblica 36–39r/Via Roma 1r (© **055-213-896**), tourists gather to sit with the ghosts of Italy's *Risorgimento,* when the cafe became an important meeting place of the heroes and thinkers of the unification movement from the 1850s to the 1870s. The red-jacketed waiters at **Giubbe Rosse,** Piazza della Repubblica 13–14r (© **055-212-280**), must have been popular during the 19th-century glory days of Garibaldi's red-shirt soldiers. This was once a meeting place of the Florentine futurists, but aside from organized literary encounters on Wednesdays, today, it too is mainly a tourists' cafe with ridiculous prices.

Once full of history and now mainly full of tourists, **Rivoire,** Piazza della Signoria/Via Vacchereccia 5r (© **055-214-412**), has a chunk of prime real estate on Piazza della Signoria. Smartly dressed waiters serve smartly priced sandwiches to cappuccino-sipping patrons. **Giacosa,** Via de' Tornabuoni 83r (© **055-239-6226**), was a 19th-century hangout for literati and intellectual clutches as elegant as any of the others, but today it's really more of a high-class bar, with no outside tables. It makes a good shopping break, though, with panini, pastries, cold salads, and hot pasta dishes.

parents here is a miracle). From 8pm it's a popular restaurant in the balcony and a pizzeria on the main floor. Around 11pm a live band takes the main floor stage for an hour or so, after which a DJ comes on board to conduct the disco until 3am.

In the city center near Santa Croce, **Full-Up,** Via della Vigna Vecchia 25r (© **055-293-006**), is a long-enduring disco/piano bar that's one of the top (and more restrained) dance spaces in Florence for the postcollegiate set. There are plenty of theme evenings (revival, samba, punk), so call to find out what's on.

Forever known as Yab Yum but recently reincarnated with a new attitude is **Yab,** Via Sassetti 5r ((*Ⓒ* **055-215-160**), just behind the main post office on Piazza della Repubblica. This dance club for 20-somethings is a perennial favorite, a relic of a 1980s disco complete with rope line and surly bouncers.

A balanced combination of visitors and Italians—teenagers, students, and an under-30 crowd—fill the two-floor **Space Electronic,** Via Palazzuolo 37 ((*Ⓒ* **055-293-082**). On the first floor are a video karaoke bar, a pub, an American-style bar, and a conversation area. Head upstairs for the dance floor with laser lights and a flying space capsule hovering above.

3 Pubs & Bars

PUBS & BARS

There's an unsurprising degree of similarity among Florence's half dozen **Irish-style pubs,** dark, woody interiors usually with several back rooms and plenty of smoke; and a crowd (stuffed to the gills on weekends) of students and 20- and 30-something Americans and Brits along with their Italian counterparts. The better ones are the Florence branch of the successful Italian chain **Fiddler's Elbow,** Piazza Santa Maria Novella 7r ((*Ⓒ* **055-215-056**); **The Old Stove,** Via Pellicceria 4r ((*Ⓒ* **055-284-640**), just down from Piazza della Repubblica; and, under the same management, **The Lion's Fountain,** Borgo Albizi 34r ((*Ⓒ* **055-234-4412**), on the tiny but lively Piazza San Pier Maggiore near Santa Croce. You'll find plenty of others around town—they pop up like mushrooms these days, but often disappear just as quickly.

Red Garter, Via de' Benci 33r ((*Ⓒ* **055-234-4904**), is a speakeasy attracting a 20s-to-30s crowd of Italians and some Americans, Australians, and English. There's a small bi-level theater room in the back with live music some nights—once when I stopped in, it was a one-man band with a synth kit playing American and Italian rock hits with some blues mixed in.

WINE BARS

The most traditional wine bars are called *fiaschetterie,* after the word for a flask of chianti. They tend to be hole-in-the-wall joints serving sandwiches or simple food along with glasses filled to the brim—usually with a house wine, though finer vintages are often available. The best are listed in chapter 4, including **I Fratellini,** Via dei Cimatori 38r (℃ **055-239-6096**); **Antico Noè,** off Piazza S. Pier Maggiore (℃ **055-234-0838**); and **La Mescita,** Via degli Alfani 70r (℃ **347-795-1604**). There's also a traditional wine shop in the Oltrarno called simply **La Fiaschetteria,** Via de' Serragli 47r (℃ **055-287-420**), which, like many, doubles as a small locals' wine bar.

A more high-toned spot is the **Cantinetta Antinori,** Piazza Antinori 3 (℃ **055-292-234**), also listed in chapter 4. It's housed in the palace headquarters of the Antinori wine empire at the top of Florence's main fashion drag, Via Tornabuoni. For a trendier wine bar focusing on handpicked labels offered with plates of cheese and other snacks, head to the Oltrarno and a real oenophile's hangout, **Il Volpe e L'Uva,** Piazza de' Rossi, behind Piazza Santa Felícita off Via Guicciardini (℃ **055-239-8132**). The Avuris, who run the Hotel Torre Guelfa (p. 58), have recently opened a great little wine bar right across from the Pitti Palace called **Pitti Gola e Cantina,** Piazza Pitti 16 (℃ **055-212-704**), with glasses of wine from 4€ to 9€ ($4.60–$10) to help unwind from a day of museums. They also have light dishes, meat and cheese platters, and cakes for 7€ to 15€ ($8.05–$17).

4 The Gay & Lesbian Scene

The gay nightlife scene in Florence isn't much, and for lesbians it's pretty much just the Thursday through Saturday nights mixed gay-and-lesbian party at the **Flamingo Bar,** Via Pandolfini 26r (℃ **055-243-356**), whereas the rest of the week it's men only. The main bar is downstairs, where an international gay crowd shows up in everything from jeans and tees to full leather. Upstairs are a lounge and a theater showing videos and the occasional show. September through June, the ground floor becomes a dance floor Friday and Saturday nights pumping out commercial pop and lots of disco. The bar is open Sunday through Thursday from 10pm to 4am (until 6am Fri–Sat).

Florence's dark room is the **Crisco Bar,** Via Sant'Egidio 43r east of the Duomo (℃ **055-248-0580;** www.crisco.it), for men only. Its 18th-century building contains a bar and a dance floor open Wednesday through Monday from 9pm to 3am (until 5am weekends). They also have male strippers and drag shows some weekends.

The only real gay dance floor of note is at the **Tabasco Bar,** Piazza Santa Cecilia 3r (℃ **055-213-000;** www.tabascogay.it). Italy's first gay disco attracts crowds of men (mostly in their 20s and 30s) from all over the country. The music is techno, disco, and retro rock, but entertainment offerings also include cabaret, art shows, and the occasional transvestite comedy. In summer, foreigners arrive in droves. It's open Sunday through Thursday from 10pm to 3 or 4am (until 6am Fri–Sat). Tuesday, Friday, and Saturday it's all disco; Wednesday is leather night. They've also recently opened up a gay cruising bar called **Silver Stud,** Via della Fornace 9 (© **055-688-466**).

Cover charges vary, but it's generally 10€ ($12) or less and often includes the first drink.

Index

See also Accommodations, and Restaurant indexes below.

ACCOMMODATIONS

RESTAURANTS

FROMMER'S® COMPLETE TRAVEL GUIDES

Alaska
Alaska Cruises & Ports of Call
Amsterdam
Argentina & Chile
Arizona
Atlanta
Australia
Austria
Bahamas
Barcelona, Madrid & Seville
Beijing
Belgium, Holland & Luxembourg
Bermuda
Boston
Brazil
British Columbia & the Canadian
  Rockies
Brussels & Bruges
Budapest & the Best of Hungary
California
Cancún, Cozumel & the Yucatán
Cape Cod, Nantucket & Martha's
  Vineyard
Caribbean
Caribbean Cruises & Ports of Call
Caribbean Ports of Call
Carolinas & Georgia
Chicago
China
Colorado
Costa Rica
Cuba
Denmark
Denver, Boulder & Colorado Springs
England
Europe
European Cruises & Ports of Call

Florida
France
Germany
Great Britain
Greece
Greek Islands
Hawaii
Hong Kong
Honolulu, Waikiki & Oahu
Ireland
Israel
Italy
Jamaica
Japan
Las Vegas
London
Los Angeles
Maryland & Delaware
Maui
Mexico
Montana & Wyoming
Montréal & Québec City
Munich & the Bavarian Alps
Nashville & Memphis
New England
New Mexico
New Orleans
New York City
New Zealand
Northern Italy
Norway
Nova Scotia, New Brunswick &
  Prince Edward Island
Oregon
Paris
Peru
Philadelphia & the Amish Country
Portugal

Prague & the Best of the Czech
  Republic
Provence & the Riviera
Puerto Rico
Rome
San Antonio & Austin
San Diego
San Francisco
Santa Fe, Taos & Albuquerque
Scandinavia
Scotland
Seattle & Portland
Shanghai
Sicily
Singapore & Malaysia
South Africa
South America
South Florida
South Pacific
Southeast Asia
Spain
Sweden
Switzerland
Texas
Thailand
Tokyo
Toronto
Tuscany & Umbria
USA
Utah
Vancouver & Victoria
Vermont, New Hampshire & Maine
Vienna & the Danube Valley
Virgin Islands
Virginia
Walt Disney World® & Orlando
Washington, D.C.
Washington State

FROMMER'S® DOLLAR-A-DAY GUIDES

Australia from $50 a Day
California from $70 a Day
England from $75 a Day
Europe from $70 a Day
Florida from $70 a Day
Hawaii from $80 a Day

Ireland from $60 a Day
Italy from $70 a Day
London from $85 a Day
New York from $90 a Day
Paris from $80 a Day

San Francisco from $70 a Day
Washington, D.C. from $80 a Day
Portable London from $85 a Day
Portable New York City from $90
  a Day

FROMMER'S® PORTABLE GUIDES

Acapulco, Ixtapa & Zihuatanejo
Amsterdam
Aruba
Australia's Great Barrier Reef
Bahamas
Berlin
Big Island of Hawaii
Boston
California Wine Country
Cancún
Cayman Islands
Charleston
Chicago
Disneyland®
Dublin
Florence

Frankfurt
Hong Kong
Houston
Las Vegas
Las Vegas for Non-Gamblers
London
Los Angeles
Los Cabos & Baja
Maine Coast
Maui
Miami
Nantucket & Martha's Vineyard
New Orleans
New York City
Paris
Phoenix & Scottsdale

Portland
Puerto Rico
Puerto Vallarta, Manzanillo &
  Guadalajara
Rio de Janeiro
San Diego
San Francisco
Savannah
Seattle
Sydney
Tampa & St. Petersburg
Vancouver
Venice
Virgin Islands
Washington, D.C.

FROMMER'S® NATIONAL PARK GUIDES

Banff & Jasper
Family Vacations in the National
  Parks

Grand Canyon
National Parks of the American West
Rocky Mountain

Yellowstone & Grand Teton
Yosemite & Sequoia/Kings Canyon
Zion & Bryce Canyon

FROMMER'S® MEMORABLE WALKS

Chicago	New York	San Francisco
London	Paris	

FROMMER'S® WITH KIDS GUIDES

Chicago	Ottawa	Vancouver
Las Vegas	San Francisco	Washington, D.C.
New York City	Toronto	

SUZY GERSHMAN'S BORN TO SHOP GUIDES

Born to Shop: France	Born to Shop: Italy	Born to Shop: New York
Born to Shop: Hong Kong, Shanghai & Beijing	Born to Shop: London	Born to Shop: Paris

FROMMER'S® IRREVERENT GUIDES

Amsterdam	Los Angeles	San Francisco
Boston	Manhattan	Seattle & Portland
Chicago	New Orleans	Vancouver
Las Vegas	Paris	Walt Disney World®
London	Rome	Washington, D.C.

FROMMER'S® BEST-LOVED DRIVING TOURS

Britain	Germany	Northern Italy
California	Ireland	Scotland
Florida	Italy	Spain
France	New England	Tuscany & Umbria

HANGING OUT™ GUIDES

Hanging Out in England	Hanging Out in France	Hanging Out in Italy
Hanging Out in Europe	Hanging Out in Ireland	Hanging Out in Spain

THE UNOFFICIAL GUIDES®

Bed & Breakfasts and Country Inns in:	Southwest & South Central Plains	Mexio's Best Beach Resorts
California	U.S.A.	Mid-Atlantic with Kids
Great Lakes States	Beyond Disney	Mini Las Vegas
Mid-Atlantic	Branson, Missouri	Mini-Mickey
New England	California with Kids	New England & New York with Kids
Northwest	Central Italy	New Orleans
Rockies	Chicago	New York City
Southeast	Cruises	Paris
Southwest	Disneyland®	San Francisco
Best RV & Tent Campgrounds in:	Florida with Kids	Skiing & Snowboarding in the West
California & the West	Golf Vacations in the Eastern U.S.	Southeast with Kids
Florida & the Southeast	Great Smoky & Blue Ridge Region	Walt Disney World®
Great Lakes States	Inside Disney	Walt Disney World® for Grown-ups
Mid-Atlantic	Hawaii	Walt Disney World® with Kids
Northeast	Las Vegas	Washington, D.C.
Northwest & Central Plains	London	World's Best Diving Vacations
	Maui	

SPECIAL-INTEREST TITLES

Frommer's Adventure Guide to Australia & New Zealand
Frommer's Adventure Guide to Central America
Frommer's Adventure Guide to India & Pakistan
Frommer's Adventure Guide to South America
Frommer's Adventure Guide to Southeast Asia
Frommer's Adventure Guide to Southern Africa
Frommer's Britain's Best Bed & Breakfasts and Country Inns
Frommer's Caribbean Hideaways
Frommer's Exploring America by RV
Frommer's Fly Safe, Fly Smart

Frommer's France's Best Bed & Breakfasts and Country Inns
Frommer's Gay & Lesbian Europe
Frommer's Italy's Best Bed & Breakfasts and Country Inns
Frommer's Road Atlas Britain
Frommer's Road Atlas Europe
Frommer's Road Atlas France
The New York Times' Guide to Unforgettable Weekends
Places Rated Almanac
Retirement Places Rated
Rome Past & Present

Booked aisle seat.

Reserved room with a view.

With a queen – no, make that a king-size bed.

With Travelocity, you can book your flights and hotels together, so you can get even better deals than if you booked them separately. You'll save time and money without compromising the quality of your trip. Choose your airline seat, search for alternate airports, pick your hotel room type, even choose the neighborhood you'd like to stay in.

Travelocity

Visit **www.travelocity.com** or call **1-888-TRAVELOCITY**

Fly.
Sleep.
Save.

Now you can book your flights and
hotels together, so you can get even better deals
than if you booked them separately.

Travelocity

**Visit www.travelocity.com
or call 1-888-TRAVELOCITY**